Dear competition entrant: In an effort to document and analyze the design process, we'd like you to respond to the 21 questions below. Your candid answers will be tallied and charted in the upcoming edition of **365**, scheduled to be published in the spring of 2002. If you prefer, your answers may be kept anonymous. Multiple entry winners may answer the questions once based on a chosen example.

Thanks in advance for your participation.

In which category
was this project
a winner in?
Advertising/promotional
Branding applications
Branding strategies
Editorial design
Environmental design
Experience design
Illustration
Information design
Motion graphics
Soundblast
Typography and design
50 books/50 covers

What is the project's
title? (optional)

Question
A

B

C

D

E

F

Describe the client for
this project:
an individual decision-
maker
a powerless individual
a committee led by
a leader
a rudderless
committee
other (describe)

Where do you do your
best creative thinking?
at the computer
in the shower
while driving
while exercising
when falling asleep
in a small, private
place
at home
other (describe)

Which of these terms
best describes your
creative process?
methodical
intuitive
arduous
meditative
transporting
other (describe)

Briefly describe the
research methods used
for preliminary design
on this project.

AIGA

# CONTENTS

Were any of the
following useful in
developing preliminary
design for this project?
reading
looking at other work
your own previous
work
life experiences
art or music
other (describe)

While researching,
what – if anything – did
you do differently from
your normal design
process?

On a scale of 0 to 10,
how close did the final
product come to
your initial vision?
0 = not at all
10 = exactly

On a scale of 0 to 10,
how much control
did you feel you
had over the final
product's outcome?
0 = no control
10 = total control

How many
rounds of revision
were involved for
this project?

G

H

I

J

K

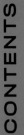

SURVEY RESULTS 8 ABOUT AIGA STAFF, NTS LISTS 26 AIGA MEDALISTS 28 PAULA AM ANTUPIT 48 COMPETITION FINALISTS RATEGIES 66 BRANDING APPLICATIONS AND PROMOTIONAL 112 ILLUSTRATION IGN 148 EDITORIAL DESIGN 50 BOOKS/ FORMATION DESIGN ENVIRONMENTA ENCE DESIGN 360 MOTION GRAPHICS 344 OUNDBLAST CHECKLIS OR BIOS INDEX

SPONSOR PAGES JURORS 386

**148 · 66 · 48 · 26 · 8 · 20 · 28 · 428 · 326 · 360 · 112 · 298 · 160 · 386 · 430 · 433 · 136**

On a scale of 0 to 10, how difficult was it to convince the client of your design direction?
0 = not difficult
10 = very difficult

**A note to the reader** The charts included on the following pages are based on an analysis of responses to a survey (reprinted on pages 1–7) submitted by this year's winners. These charts are a way of conveying the conditions under which these projects were created and, as such, capture something of the emotional and intellectual circuitry propelling each one.

The charts, along with the diversity of thoughtful projects illustrated here, provide some small measure of insight into the process of design – that wild ride from idea (which apparently strikes many designers as they are falling asleep at night) to execution (ideally, of the project and not the client or the designer). They are included in the book to remind us that endless curiosity and shared ideas are integral to the creative process. The results also show that creativity is really not as scientific as the word "process" implies.

On a scale of 0 to 10, how much did budget affect this project's design?
0 = no effect
10 = total effect

On a scale of 0 to 10, how much did the project's deadline affect the final product?
0 = no effect
10 = total effect

How much time did this project require, relative to an average job?
less than average
average
more than average

Was the project's design the result of a sudden epiphany or a slow build of small alterations?
a sudden epiphany
slow build

M

N

O

P

On a scale of
0 to 10, how well
do you deal
with criticism of
your work?
0 = not well
10 = extremely well

Have you ever had
a useful idea
while lying in bed or
in a dream?
yes
no

On a scale of 0 to 10,
please rate the
level of pleasure you
experienced:
at the outset of the
project
in the thick of working
or the project
at the completion of
the project
0 = no pleasure
10 = total pleasure

On a scale of 0 to 10,
please rate the
level of anxiety you
experienced:
at the outset of the
project
in the thick of
working on the
project
at the completion of
the project
0 = no anxiety
10 = total anxiety

On a scale of 0 to 10,
please rate the
level of frustration
you experienced:
at the outset of the
project
in the thick of working
on the project
at the completion of
the project
0 = no frustration
10 = total frustratio

**DESIG**

**D**

**CREA**

instantaneous
sporadic
therapeutic
persistence
fun
enigmatic
collaborative
competitive
simultaneous

day one: arduous;
last day: intuitive;
every day in between:
methodical
jittery, caffeinated,
harried

perpetually braced
for "revisions"
arduous at the
beginning, transporting
at the end

Other responses
included:

methodical +
intuitive

Question E
Which of these
terms best
describes your
creative process?
methodical
intuitive
arduous
meditative
transporting
other

65% OF THE OWNERS SURVEYED DESCRIBED THEIR DRIVE PROCESS AS INTUITIVE

2  3  17  18  19  22  25  30  31  32  41  55  70  71  72  79  81  83  84  88  94  95  96  97  102

**Question S-1**
On a scale of 0–10, please rate the level of pleasure experienced at the outset of the project.

**Question T-1**
On a scale of 0–10, please rate the level of anxiety experienced at the outset of the project.

0 = no anxiety/pleasure
10 = total anxiety/pleasure

Yellow numbers indicate pleasure
Magenta numbers indicate anxiety

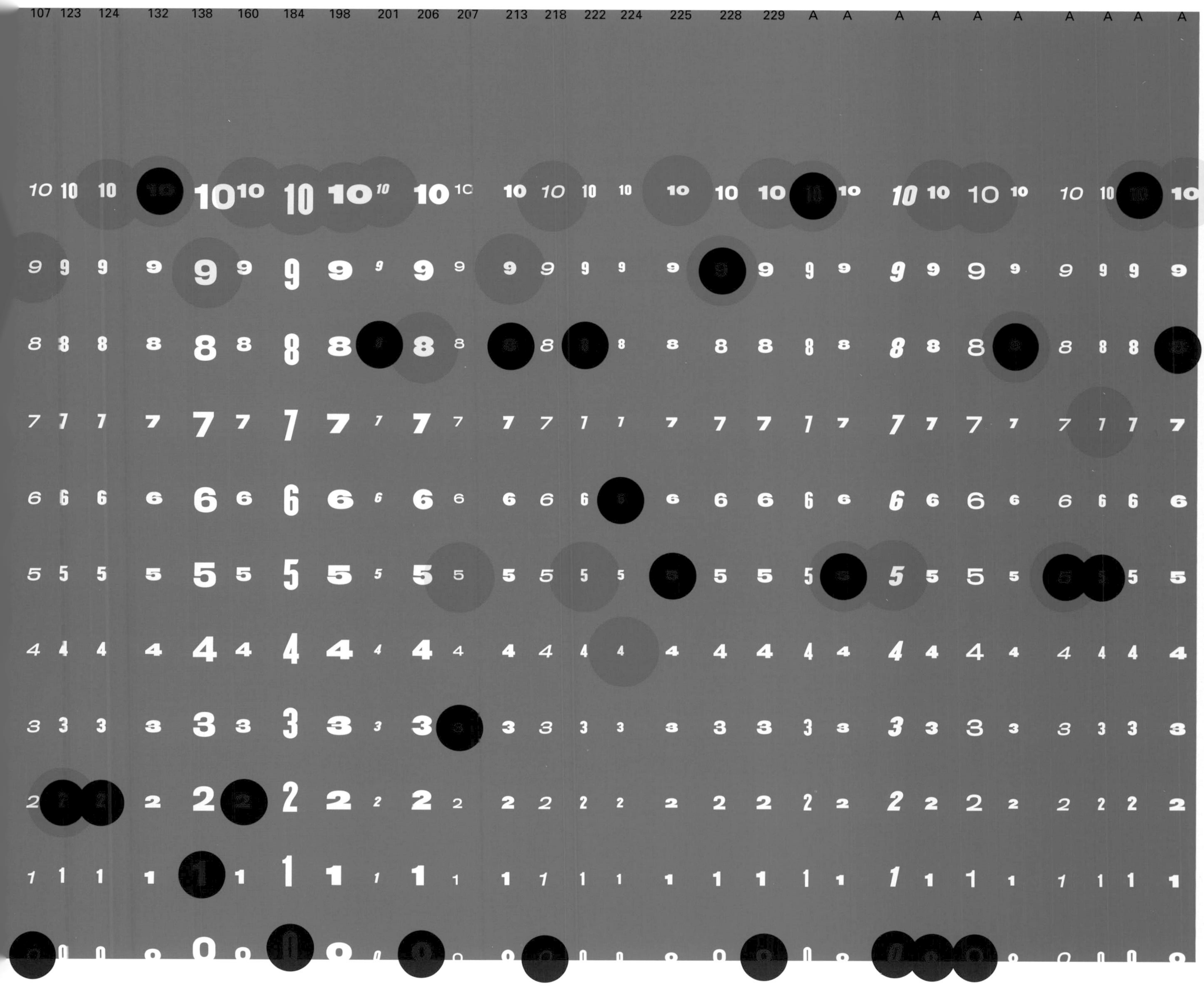

107 123
124
132
138
160
184
198
201
206
207
213
218
222
224
225
228
229
A
A
A
A
A
A
A
A

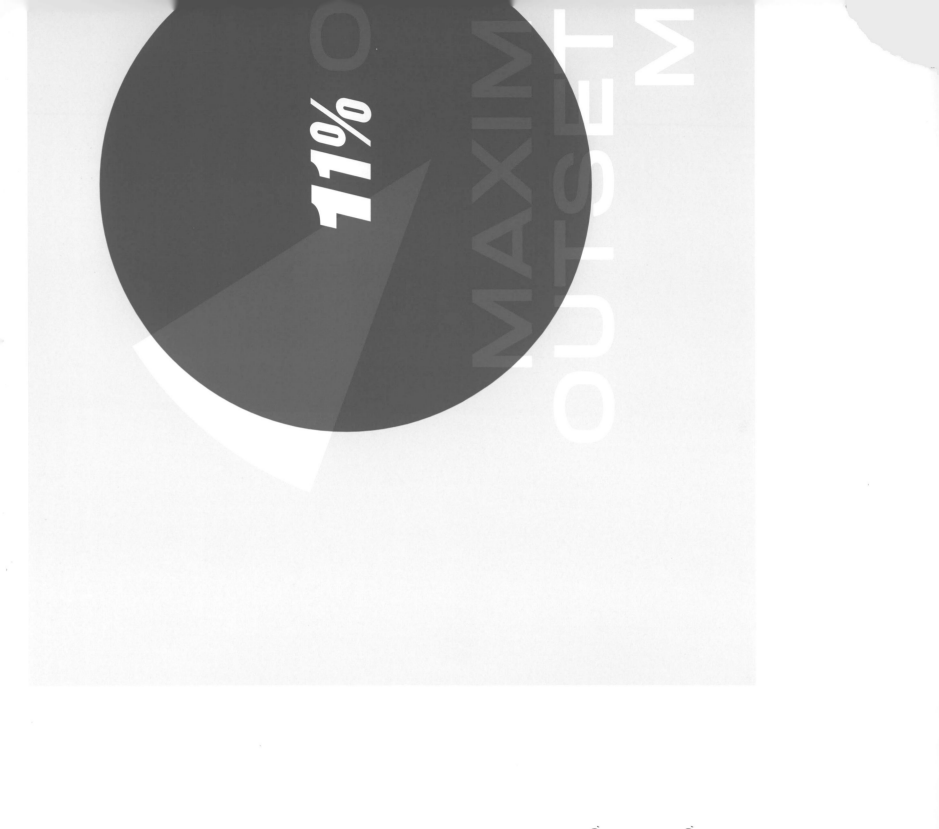

**11%**

MAXIM
OUTSET M

Question S-1
On a scale of 0–10,
please rate the
level of pleasure
experienced at
the outset of the
project.

Question T-1
On a scale of 0–10,
please rate the
level of anxiety
experienced at
the outset of the
project.

RESPONDENTS WHO REPORTED UMPLEASUREAU
ALSO REPORTED MAXIMUM
AXIMUM ANXIETY

AN INDIVIDUAL DECISION

A COMMITTEE LED BY A LE

TWO INDIVIDUAL DECISI

EDITORS, MARKETING, ETC

INDIVIDUALS IN THE PUBLIC

2% SEVERAL INDIVID

TWO EQUAL PLAYERS AND

LOU REED AND HIS PUBL

LEADER AND A RUDDERLES

OLDER BROTHER OWNED TH

IN NEW OR AVANT-GA

2% INDIVIDUAL DECISIONMA

MYSELF 2% PUBLISHE

2%

2%

2%

Question C
Describe the client
for this project:
an individual decisionmaker
a powerless individual
a committee led by a leader
a rudderless committee
other

37% A POWERLESS INDIVIDUAL 4%
ADER 20% A RUDDERLESS COMMITTEE 4%
MAKERS 4% GROUP OF ART DIRECTORS
(DEPARTMENT HEADS) 2% ALL CULTURED
2% PUBLISHER 2% ENLIGHTENED COUPLE
AL LEADERS 2%
A THIRD STRONG VOICE 2% A COUPLE OF PEOPLE 2%
SHER 2% RECORDING ARTISTS 2% OURSELVES
COMMITTEE 2% DECISIONMAKER WHOSE
COMPANY 2% BAND WHO IS INTERESTED
RDE DESIGN AND WAYS OF SEEING THINGS
KER AND "TWO CENTS" PEOPLE
OF PHOTOGRAPHY BOOKS 2% FORMERLY
TENURED UNIVERSITY PROFESSOR
2% AIGA 2%
2% FAN 2%
2%

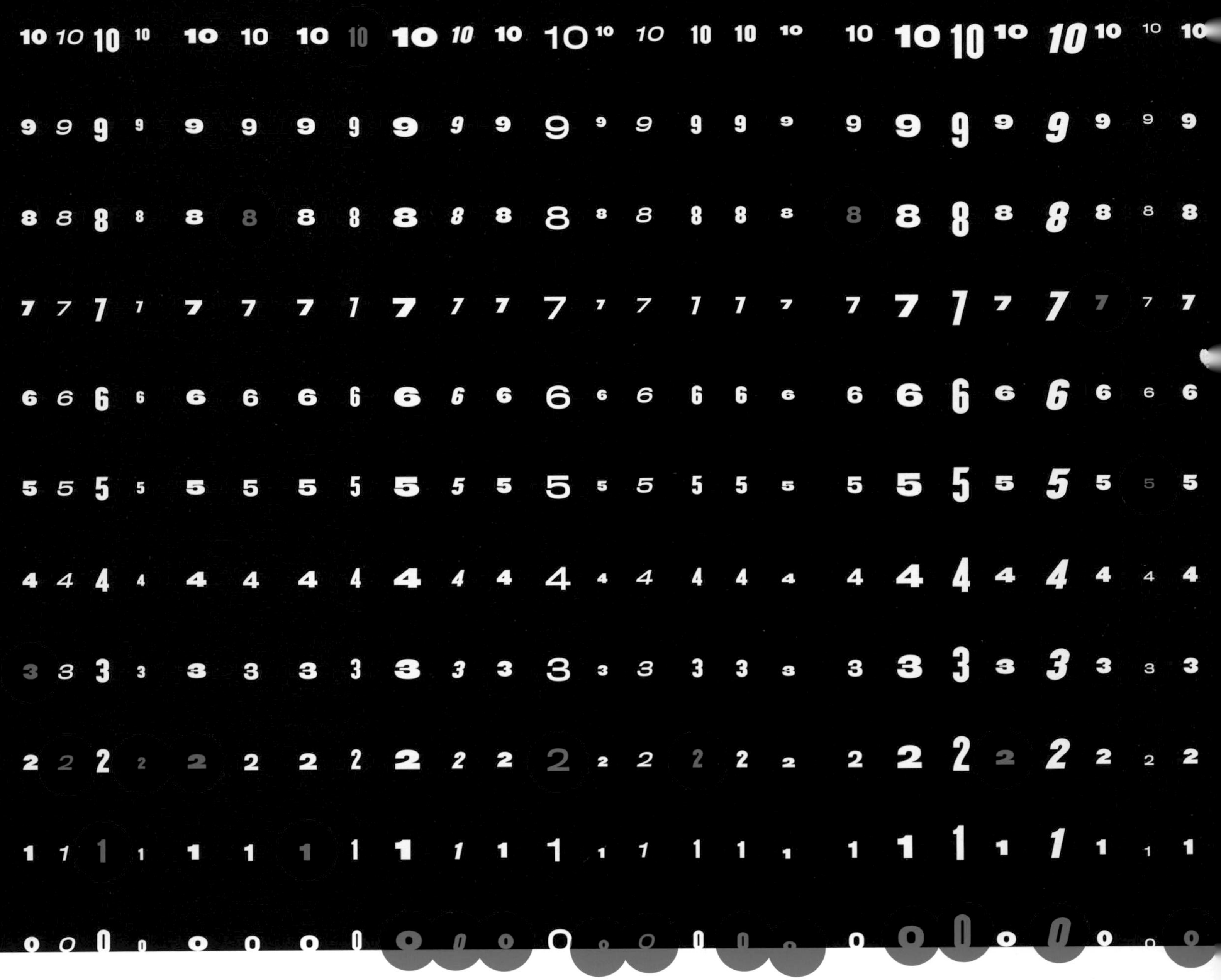

0 = not difficult
10 = very difficult

Question I
On a scale of 0–10,
how close did the
final product come
to your initial vision?
0 = not at all similar
to initial vision
10 = exactly like
initial vision

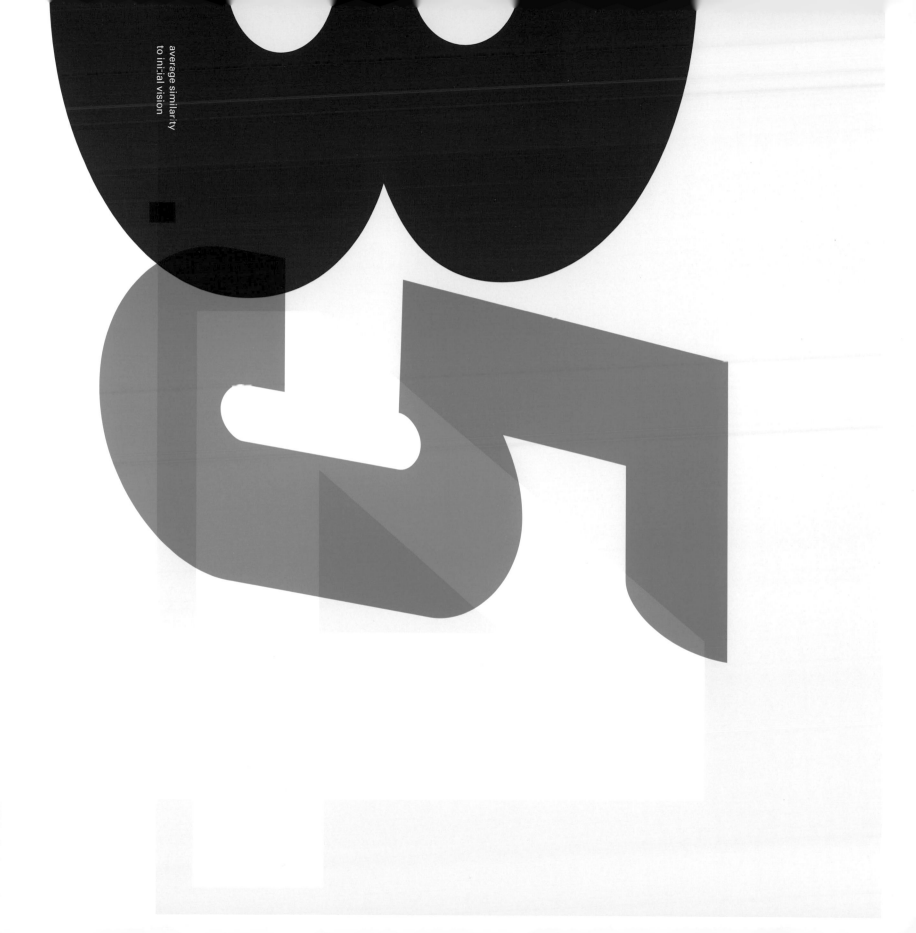

average similarity
to initial vision

# AIGA 2001 Activities

**January**

- *Trace: AIGA Journal of Design*, volume 1, number 1: Surprise (20)
- 1/17–3/30 365: AIGA Annual Design Exhibition (AIGA Communication Graphics 21)

**February**

- 2/24–26 Looking Closer: AIGA Conference on Design History and Criticism, Lighthouse International, New York

**March**

- 3/10 Verge: AIGA Seminar on Experience Design, Parsons School of Design, New York

**April**

- 4/18–20 DFTV.002: AIGA Conference on Design for Film and Television, New York
- 4/11–7/27 ¡Propaganda! Cuban Political and Film Posters

**May**

- *Loop* number 2 (22)
- AIGA/Aquent Survey of Design Salaries 2001 (21–20)
- A Client's Guide to Design: How to Get the Most Out of the Process (18–17)

| June | July | August | September | October | November | December |
|------|------|--------|-----------|---------|----------|----------|
| 30 | 31 | 31 | | | | |
| 29 | 30 | 30 | | | | |
| 28 *Trace: AIGA Journal of Design, volume 1, number 2: Exposure* | 29 | 29 *8/29–11/21 AIGA 50 Books/50 Covers of 2000 Exhibition* | | | | |
| 27 | 28 | 28 | | | | |
| 26 | 27 | 27 | | | | |
| 25 | 26 | 26 | | | | |
| 24 | 25 | 25 | | | | |
| 23 | 24 | 24 | | 31 | | |
| 22 | 23 | 23 | | 30 | | |
| 21 | 22 | 22 | | 29 | | |
| 20 | 21 | 21 *Gain: AIGA Journal of Design for the Network Economy, volume 2, number 1* | | 28 | | |
| 19 | 20 | 20 | 30 | 27 | | |
| 18 | 19 | 19 | 29 | 26 | | |
| 17 | 18 | 18 | 28 | 25 | | |
| 16 | 17 | 17 | 27 | 24 | | |
| 15 | 16 | 16 | 26 | 23 | | |
| 14 | 15 | 15 | 25 | 22 | | |
| 13 | 14 | 14 | 24 | 21 | | |
| 12 | 13 | 13 | 23 | 20 | | |
| 11 | 12 | 12 | 22 | 19 | | 31 |
| 10 | 11 | 11 | 21 | 18 | 30 | 30 |
| 9 | 10 | 10 | 20 *Cancelled: Voice: AIGA National Design Conference* | 17 | 29 | 29 |
| 8 | 9 | 9 | 19 | 16 | 28 | 28 |
| 7 | 8 | 8 | 18 | 15 | 27 | 27 |
| 6 | 7 | 7 | 17 *Trace: AIGA Journal of Design, volume 1, number 3: Voice* | 14 | 26 | 26 |
| 5 | 6 | 6 | 16 | 13 | 25 | 25 |
| 4 | 5 | 5 | 15 | 12 | 24 | 24 |
| 3 | 4 | 4 | 14 *Loop number 3* | 11 | 23 | 23 |
| 2 | 3 | 3 | 13 *AIGA Ethics Series* | 10 | 22 | 22 |
| 1 | 2 | 2 | 12 | 9 | 21 | 21 |
| | 1 | 1 | 11 | 8 | 20 | 20 |
| | | | 10 | 7 | 19 | 19 |
| | | | 9 | 6 | 18 | 18 |
| | | | 8 | 5 | 17 | 17 |
| | | | 7 | 4 | 16 | 16 |
| | | | 6 | 3 | 15 | 15 |
| | | | 5 | 2 | 14 | 14 |
| | | | 4 | 1 | 13 | 13 |
| | | | 3 | | 12 | 12 |
| | | | 2 | | 11 | 11 |
| | | | 1 | | 10 | 10 |
| | | | | | 9 | 9 |
| | | | | | 8 | 8 |
| | | | | | 7 | 7 |
| | | | | | 6 | 6 *365: AIGA Annual Design Exhibition, part 1* |
| | | | | | 5 | 5 |
| | | | | | 4 | 4 |
| | | | | | 3 | 3 |
| | | | | | 2 | 2 |
| | | | | | 1 *AIGA Website and Design Forum relaunch* | 1 |

**January** *Trace: AIGA Journal of Design, volume 1, number 1: Surprise* Issue one of the relaunched AIGA journal examined the possibilities of creating moments of surprise in a culture that's predicated on irony and cynicism. Features included an in-depth exploration of camouflage and other designs for deception; humorous incidents of typographic misquotations in Hollywood blockbusters; a comparative look at the ways in which creative epiphanies are depicted in movies; a motion graphic designer's exploration of film and television's greatest "A-ha!" moments; and a photo portfolio of Vietnam War re-enactors in Virginia.

**365: AIGA Annual Design Exhibition (AIGA Communication Graphics 21), January 18–March 30, 2001** Presenting the selections from the 2000 competition judged by Gayle Christensen (Federal Express, Memphis), Karin Fong (Imaginary Forces, Los Angeles), Tom Geismar (Chermayeff & Geismar Inc., New York), Russ Haan (After Hours Creative, Phoenix), Maira Kalman (M&Co., New York) and Margaret Youngblood, chair (Landor Associates, San Francisco).

This country's premier design competition, "AIGA Communication Graphics" sets the standards for the profession. "Communication Graphics" addresses AIGA's commitment to evaluating design in the broader context of commerce and culture, exhibiting the selections that the jury felt represent excellence in design in terms of function, strategy and communication, while maintaining a high sense of aesthetics.

1 "365" exhibition brochure designed by Spot Design, New York 2 "365: AIGA Annual Design Exhibition" at the AIGA National Design Center, designed by Spot Design, New York

**February** **Looking Closer: AIGA Conference on Design History and Criticism, Lighthouse International, New York, February 24–26, 2001** This two-day conference was based on the assumption that increasing numbers of designers and students take an interest in design history and criticism – many even write themselves. One of AIGA's initiatives is to "become a primary information resource for the history of graphic design." This new biennial conference aimed to establish a core community of members who wish to advance discussion about the role and relevance of design history and design criticism and to explore how historical analysis and criticism and journalism intersect. Attendees received a binder containing reference materials that assist in the creation of a design history program at their schools. The conference was moderated and cochaired by Steven Heller and Alice Twemlow, and featured presentations by The New York Times film critic Elvis Mitchell, British design critic Rick Poynor, No Logo author Naomi Klein, design theorists Johanna Drucker and Matt Soar, plastic.com editor Steven Johnson, cultural historian Neal Gabler, Walker Art Center design director Andrew Blauvelt, design historians Maud Lavin, Ellen Lupton, Victor Margolin and Jeremy Aynsley, typographers Tobias Frere-Jones and Jonathan Hoefler, and design academics Meredith Davis and Jack Williamson.

3 Title slide from "Looking Closer," designed by Paul Elliman, New Haven

**March** **Verge: AIGA Seminar on Experience Design, Parsons School of Design, New York, March 10, 2001** "Verge" was a one-day convergence on experience design that presented several seemingly divergent individuals' theories and pragmatic approaches to shaping experiences, where meaning is the only true currency.

Designer, performer, researcher and writer Brenda Laurel moderated the event and presentations were given by diverse practitioners including science fiction writer Vernor Vinge, photographer Rodney Smith, magician Ryan Oakes, musical montager DJ Spooky, experience producer Scott Ault, WWF Entertainment creative director Debbie Bonnanzio, director of attraction development at Universal Studios Recreation Group's Dale Mason and exhibition guru Ralph Appelbaum.

4 Title slide from "Verge," designed by Nancy Nowacek, New York

**April** **¡Propaganda! Cuban Political and Film Posters, April 12–July 27, 2001** The first exhibition of its kind in New York, "¡Propaganda! Cuban Political and Film Posters" presented 100 original silk-screened political and film posters dating from the 1950s to the late 1990s. The exhibition represents the importance of the Cuban poster both in promoting the revolution and in demonstrating Cuba's art culture as a thriving international force. A special highlight of this show was a rare collection of film posters designed by Cuban artists for both Cuban and foreign films.

5 "¡Propaganda!" exhibition at the AIGA National Design Center, designed by Mark Randall, World Studio, New York, and Stefan Hengst and Klaus Kempenaars, xSITE, New York

**DFTV.002: AIGA Conference on Design for Film and Television, New York, April 18–20, 2001** "DFTV.002" was AIGA's second conference devoted to design for film and television. Cochaired by Emily Oberman and Bonnie Siegler of

Number Seventeen and moderated by author, med a critic and -ad o host Kurt Andersen, the conference explored the terri ory at the intersection between the film, television and grap nic design professions. Presenters included Jonn Canemaker cf NYU's Tisch School of the Arts, Razorfish's Lee Hunt David Wild of Wild Scientific, Jeffrey Keyton of MTV, Randy Balsmeyer of Balsmeyer & Everett, Jonathan Notaro of Brand New School, Beth Urdang of Agoraphone and Michael Horsham and Graham Wood of the British design studio Tomato.

Additionally, Steven Heller interviewed Pablo Ferro about his legacy as a pioneering filmmaker-designer. The discussion was followed by a screening of The Thomas Crown Affair, for which Ferro developed an innovative multiple-screen method for the title sequence. Presenting Sponsor: Aquent.

**May** L oop number 2 Loop's second issue was up on the web in May with a packed roster that featured an ongoing sub-theme of "collaboration." Articles included three information design lessons taken from the films of Charles and Ray Eames; in-depth looks at design curricula at Art Center's "Mok Institute," Sweden's Hyper Island and Carnegie Mellon University; interviews with Terry Swack (TSDesign), H arry Sadler (Metadesign) and Karen Mahony (Xymbiol; and reviews.

**AIGA/Aquent Survey of Design Salaries 2001** This year's survey results were mailed to professional and associate members in May. The publication is also available in pdf format on AIGA's website. Presenting Sponsor: Aquent.

**A Client's Guide to Design: How to Get the Most Out of the Process** Just added to AIGA's website in May, this content was developed by Lana Rigsby and fills a need expressed by many members over the years. It is targeted at the business community, which needs to better understand how and when to engage designers appropriately in projects.

**June Trace: AIGA Journal of Design, volume 1, number 2: Exposure** Issue two took on the timely theme of exposure, and examined such diverse design phenomena as the creation of celebrity-likeness dolls; the person as pixel in mass stadium graphics; the proliferation of mammoth design monographs; the art of the Cuban propaganda poster; the evolution of Hollywood testimonials in advertising; the origins of the teen magazine format; and a photo portfolio depicting the design details of classic "Bollywood" film studios in Bombay. Presenting Sponsor: Mohawk.

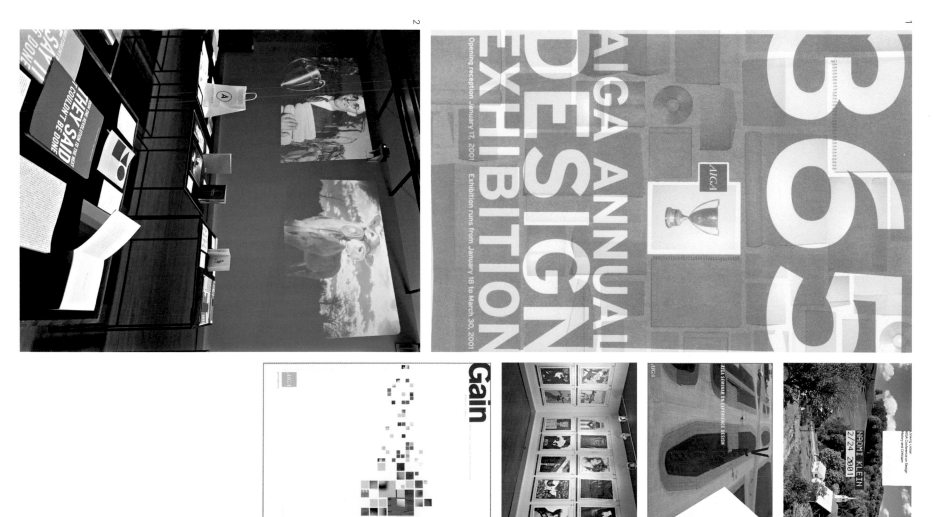

**July** Gain: AIGA Journal of Design for the Network Economy, volume 2, number 1 The second issue of Gain continued the evolution of both print and web formats of the publication, and featured an extensive profile on Alan Cooper; case studies on united.com and a trio of philanthropic nonprofit sites; an article exploring the marketplace concept of "inreach", and a detailed analysis of the state of the interactive design business "after the fall." Presenting Sponsor: Sapient.

6 Gain, designed by Sapient, San Francisco

**August** AIGA 50 Books/50 Covers of 2000 Exhibition: **August 29–November 21** Since 1923, the "AIGA 50 Books/50 Covers" competition has recognized excellence in book design and production. Entries include books and book covers designed between January 1 and December 31 of the previous year. Categories range from trade, reference and juvenile books to university and museum publications and include limited-edition and special-format books. 7, 8 "AIGA 50 Books/50 Covers of 2000 Exhibition" at the AIGA National Design Center, designed by Chermayeff & Geismar Inc., New York

**September** Voice: AIGA National Design Conference AIGA scheduled its national design conference, on the role of design in contributing to civil discourse, for September 23–26 in Washington, D.C. The conference would have included more than 100 speakers and culminated in a day of advocacy on Capitol Hill, articulating the importance of information design in strengthening a participatory democracy. The tragic acts of terrorism on September 11, however, required that AIGA cancel the conference, although the content created for the conference will find its way into other activities in the upcoming year.

9 "Voice: AIGA National Design Conference" reminder postcard, designed by James Victore Inc., Beacon, New York 10 "Voice: AIGA National Design Conference" registration mailer, designed by Oh Boy, A Design Company, San Francisco

**Trace: AIGA Journal of Design, volume 1, number 3: Voice** Issue three was meant as a companion guide to AIGA's "Voice" conference. Features include articles about the origins of the speech bubble; the apparent neutrality of stock photo images; and the crisis of cultural clutter. Artist Ward Sutton also contributed a six-page cartoon about the history of media pranks. Presenting Sponsor: Mohawk.

11 Trace, designed by 2X4, New York

Loop number 3 This issue featured a number of articles on user-centered design, including professional position papers on user-centered design methods; a report on "Designing User-Centered Experience," a workshop held at Arizona State University with Katherine and Michael McCoy; inside views on working methods from SmartDesign, SonicRim and Thirst; a provocative essay on the fallout from recent dotcom failures; and a review of Nathan Shedroff's new book, Experience Design I.

**AIGA Ethics Series** In September, AIGA inaugurated a new range of publications that deal with ethical standards and practices for designers and their clients. These design ethics brochures include A Client's Guide to Design: How to Get the Most Out of the Process; Business and Ethical Expectations for Professional Designers; Use of Fonts; Use of Software; and Use of Illustration. New topics will be added to the series regularly, and additional copies can be downloaded from www.aiga.org. Presenting Sponsor for the series: Aquent. Paper Sponsor for the series: SMART Papers. Presenting Sponsor for "Use of Fonts": Agfa/Monotype. Presenting Sponsor for "Use of Software": Business Software Alliance.

**November** AIGA Website and Design Forum relaunch The second phase of AIGA's web strategy was completed with the addition of the Design Forum. The Design Forum proved its value in the wake of the 9/11 tragedies, providing a place for designers to come together to share their grief and inspiration. The forum and its content received immediate acclaim from around the world and were featured in such diverse publications as Le Monde, Surface magazine and Communication Arts. The entire site was relaunched shortly thereafter with additional functionality created by Thirdwave and a new look and feel created by Lance Rutter. The additional functionality included the launch of the National Job Bank and member profiles enhanced with online portfolios through Adobe Studio.

**December 365: AIGA Annual Design Exhibition, part 1, December 5, 2001** Design excellence is the result of a process involving creativity, inspiration, skill, experience, intuition and discipline. AIGA is committed to using the selections from the competitions to demonstrate the process of design, the role of the designer and the value of design. The selection criteria include aesthetic judgments as well as communication effectiveness and appropriateness. Presenting Sponsors: Aquent, Sappi.

# AIGA 2001 People

**Director of corporate partnerships**
Deborah Aldrich

**Director of production**
Pamela Aviles

**Director of events**
Kelley Beaudoin

**Project manager**
Molly Beverstein

**Editorial director**
Andrea Codrington

**Information management associate**
Maureen DeLorenzo

**Membership coordinator**
George Fernandez

**Executive director**
Richard Grefé

**Customer service associate**
Melissa Lum

**Director of competitions and exhibitions**
Gabriela Mirensky

**Program director**
Alice Twemlow

**Finance and administration associate**
Marc Vassall

**Facility assistant**
Johnny Ventura

**Director of new media**
David Womack

**Chief experience officer**
Denise Wood

**President**
Clement Mok
Michael Bierut

**Secretary/treasurer**
Sam Shelton
Beth Singer

**Executive director**
Richard Grefé
Richard Grefé

**Directors**
Dana Arnett, John Chuang, Marc English, Peter Girardi, Bill Grant, Nigel Holmes, Terry Irwin, John Maeda, Jennifer Morla, Terry Swack, Gong Szeto, Petrula Vrontikis, Margaret Youngblood

Bart Crosby, Marc English, Peter Girardi, Bill Grant, Eric Madsen, John Maeda, Clement Mok, Jennifer Morla, Emily Oberman, Mary Scott, Sam Shelton, Thomas Suiter, Petrula Vrontikis

**Chapter presidents' council representative**
Amy Strauch
Douglas Powell

**WA  Seattle**
Tan Le and Laura Zeck
Tan Le and Laura Zeck

**OR  Portland**
Catherine Healy and Ron Dumas
Susan Agre-Kippenhan

**HI  Honolulu**
Stacey Leong
Jon Sueda

Staff

Board of directors

Chapters and chapter presidents

White type denotes individuals who hold positions in 2001–2002

Black type denotes individuals who held positions in 2000–2001

**UT  Salt Lake City**
Ryan Mansfield
Linda Sullivan

**CA  San Francisco**
Brian Jacobs
Diane Carr

**Orange County**
Yamini Prabhakar
Yamini Prabhakar

**Los Angeles**
Noreen Morioka
Noreen Morioka

**San Diego**
John Dennis
MaeLin Levine

**NV  Las Vegas**
Alfred Herczeg
Alfred Herczeg

**AZ  Arizona**
Laura Von Gluck
Laura Von Gluck

---

**NE  Nebraska**
Joel Davies
Brenda Lyman

**CO  Colorado**
Stuart Alden
Clare Kelly

**KS  Wichita**
Jeff Pulaski
Jeff Pulaski

**OK  Oklahoma**
Casey Twenter
Casey Twenter

**TX  Dallas**
Bill Ford
John J. Conley

**Austin**
Sherri Whitmarsh
Sean Carnegie

**Houston**
Dylan Moore
Dylan Moore

---

**MN  Minnesota**
Joelle Anderlik
Joelle Anderlik

**WI  Wisconsin**
Ken Hanson
Ken Hanson

**IA  Iowa**
Antje Gray
Karen Beach

**MI  Detroit**
Bruno Hohmann
Bruno Hohmann

**IL  Chicago**
Marcia Lausen
Lance Rutter

**OH  Cleveland**
Linda Brown
Linda Brown

**Cincinnati**
Rondi Tschopp

**IN  Indianapolis**
Lori Long
Lori Long

**MO  Kansas City**
Joseph LaCrue
Michael Lamonica

---

**KY  Knoxville**
Dan Lipe
Kenneth White

**AL  Birmingham**
Beth Santoro
Jennifer Tatham

**GA  Atlanta**
Kathi Roberts
Peter Borowski

**LA  New Orleans**
Roderick Lemaire
Christy Bracken

**FL  Jacksonville**
Bonnie Barnes and
Steve Shepherd
Bonnie Barnes and
Steve Shepherd

**Orlando**
Jenise Oberwetter
Steve Shepherd

**Miami**
Jonathan Gouthier
Jonathan Gouthier

---

**MA  Boston**
Leigh Mantoni
Amy Strauch

**NY  Upstate New York**
Mari Crum
Mari Crum

**New York**
Janet Froelich
Janet Froelich

**PA  Pittsburgh**
Larkin Werner
and Paul Schifino
Bernard Uy
and Paul Schifino

**Philadelphia**
Gilman Hanson
Rosemary Murphy

**MD  Baltimore**
Brigitt Thompson
Carl Cox

**DC  Washington, D.C.**
Gerette Braunsdorf
Michael Hilker

**VA  Richmond**
Jason Burton
Donald McCants

**NC  Raleigh**
Christy White
Christy White

**Charlotte**
Patrick Short
Patrick Short

# AIGA Medalists

The medal of AIGA, the most distinguished in the field, is awarded to individuals in recognition of their exceptional achievements, services or other contributions to the field of graphic design and visual communication. The contribution may be in the practice of graphic design, teaching, writing or leadership of the profession. The awards may honor designers posthumously. Medals have been awarded since 1920 to individuals who have set standards of excellence over a lifetime of work or have made individual contributions to innovation within the practice of design. Individuals who are honored may work in any country, but the contribution for which they are honored should have had a significant impact on the practice of graphic design in the United States.

White type denotes past recipients of the AIGA Medal

Black type denotes past recipients of the Design Leadership Award

**1920s**

29 William A. Dwiggins
27 Timothy Cole
   Frederic W. Goudy
26 Burton Emmett
25 Bruce Rogers
24 John C. Agar
   Stephen H. Horgan
22 Daniel Berkeley Updike
20 Norman T.A. Munder

**1930s**

39 William A. Kittredge
35 Rudolph Ruzicka
   J. Thompson Willing
34 Henry Lewis Bullen
32 Porter Garnett
31 Dard Hunter
30 Henry Watson Kent

**1940s**

48 Lawrence C. Wroth
47 Elmer Adler
46 Stanley Morison
45 Frederic G. Melcher
44 Edward Epstean
42 Edwin and Robert Grabhorn
41 Carl Purington Rollins
40 Thomas M. Cleland

**1950s**

59 May Massee
58 Ben Shahn
57 Dr. M. F. Agha
56 Ray Nash
55 P. J. Conkwright
54 Will Bradley
   Jan Tschichold
53 George Macy
52 Joseph Blumenthal
51 Harry L. Gage
50 Earnest Elmo Calkins
   Alfred A. Knopf

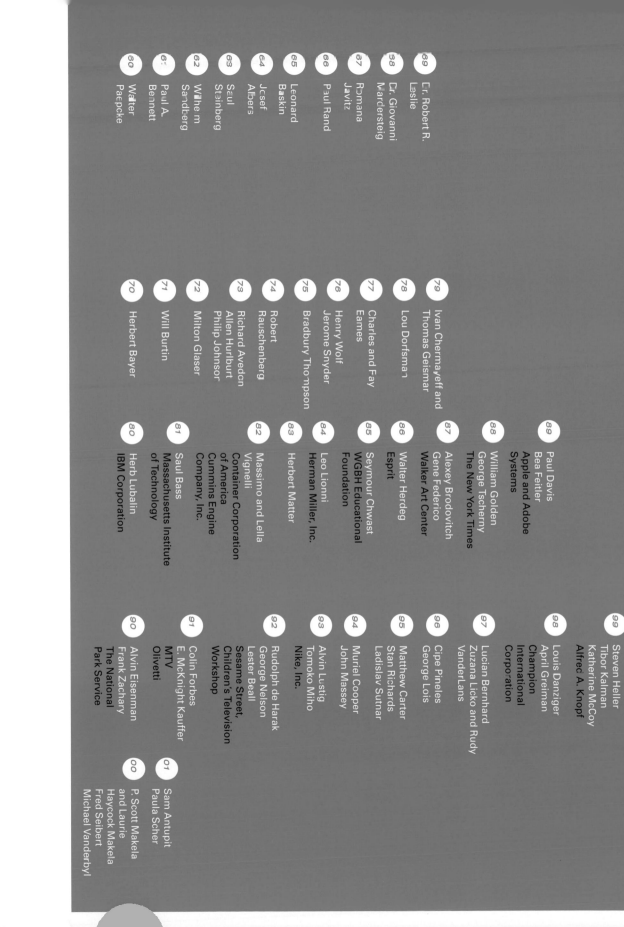

PAU
LA
SCH
OR
ER

The first time I interviewed Paula Scher, she protested: "This should not be a profile! This should be three paragraphs about my work. That's all."

That Scher should have an opinion – a brutally frank opinion – was not surprising, considering what I already knew about her. I knew that she once designed a poster for her own lecture that depicted a cigarette (brand: Paula) and came with a warning: "Paula Scher in Raleigh" (fig. 1). I knew through an op-ed piece she published in The Times that she thought the 2000 presidential election debacle in Palm Beach County was a predictable sham caused by bad design. Furthermore, I knew that she once riled the entire design community by superimposing a Swatch watch onto a Herbert Matter poster (fig. 10) and that she married her hero, the illustrator Seymour Chwast – twice. I only found out later that the designer has no use for cell phones or voice mail, that she takes her dog to work and that she only now, after a lifetime of loathing it, has started to appreciate Helvetica.

Rather than call herself a designer – a term that doesn't express the exuberance and idiosyncrasy of her work – Scher prefers the term "visual environmentalist." "I've always walked the other way," she says with a grin. Scher is sitting in a conference room at Pentagram, where she had been the only female partner for 10 years until April Greiman joined in 2001. On the wall behind her is, in all likelihood, the 100th poster she's designed for the Public Theater. At her feet is Mattie, one of her two Australian Shepards, who comes to Pentagram every day.

The slender-framed blond with piercing blue-green eyes is no stranger to awards. She's won hundreds of them, including four Grammy nominations. And they continue to pour in. But lately, the awards are of the lifetime-achievement variety, the kind you get at the end of a career. In 1998, for instance, she was named to the Art Directors Club Hall of Fame, and in 2000 she won the coveted Chrysler Award for Innovation in Design. More recently, she was granted an honorary doctorate from Corcoran College of Art and Design. And this year, at age 52, Scher will be the seventh woman in 71 years to win an AIGA medal.

WARNING: Paula Scher in Raleigh
Presented by AIGA, Sponsored by FGI
Thursday, February 24, 1994, 7:30pm
100 Hamilton Hall, University of
North Carolina, Chapel Hill

The medal is the highest honor in the field whose past recipients have included Ben Shahn, Josef Albers, Charles and Ray Eames, Herbert Matter and, of course, Seymour Chwast.

The onslaught of awards is a surefire way to prompt the visual environmentalist to rebel. "I'm not done yet! I'm not going to say sayonara and walk into the sunset," she says.

Eventually she defers to the interview and offers, "If there's one thing that has not been addressed and has to do with the AIGA medal is my persistence in graphic design." In fact, for 31 years, Scher's career has followed a path that winds through both intensely personal and highly public terrain. "She's a powerhouse from a completely personal perspective," says Janet Froelich, art director of the The New York Times Magazine. Only a few graphic designers have been as successful as Scher at integrating a personal style with a broad appeal while over and over reinventing her work. Over the years she's brought her own brand of eccentric and sophisticated design to the mainstream – no small feat. Her lifelong goal has been to "make elite culture popular and popular culture elite," a phrase Scher picked up from George Wolfe, playwright and director of the Public Theater, who had used it to describe his vision for the organization. This leveling of the playing field and the passion for popular culture, evident in Scher's best work, developed when she was a girl.

Scher grew up near Washington, D.C., in Virginia and Maryland in the 1960s. Her mother was a schoolteacher and her father a mapmaker. As a child she was an outspoken tomboy and a self-described "scrappy student" who drew and painted constantly. "I designed posters for the proms I never went to," she says with a mixture of irreverence and pride. Scher immersed herself in a youth culture that sang of rebellion and challenged the status quo.

The Vietnam War was raging when Scher enrolled at the Tyler School of the Arts in Philadelphia. "It was the '60s and I was in art school. I was a hippie," she says. "I loved the Beatles and the Rolling Stones and my teacher [Polish designer Stanislav Zagorski] designed the Cream cover. It was something we all wanted to do."

When Scher graduated from Tyler in 1970, she saw the Swiss International Style as the enemy. "Part of the reason I hated the Swiss International Style was because I associated it with American corporate power that was pro-Vietnam," she says with characteristic candor. "What was cool for me was the Revolver cover." So she walked in the opposite direction of Swiss-school stricture and right into the offices of Seymour Chwast, whose Pushpin Studios – the antithesis of the International Style – was at the height of its fame. Presented with a college portfolio, Chwast recalls: "Her thinking was better than her illustration." Says Scher, "I wanted to work for him, not date him."

Chwast didn't hire her; he married her. Chwast was 42 and Scher was 25; she would marry him again when she was 40. For all the peace, love and harmony espoused in the '60s, the two never could work together without butting heads. "I was the art director and publisher of Pushpin Graphic and whatever she wanted to do had to be done," bellows Chwast in a telephone interview. "If I didn't like it, the hell with me." Nonetheless, Scher steadfastly credits Chwast for being her single most important influence, the person who taught her how to see. It's difficult to find the superlatives to describe her," Chwast continues after a pause. "She's a fascinating person who keeps me on my toes and keeps me young."

Scher couldn't draw – a fatal liability for an illustrator. Instead she gravitated toward typography. "She was a latter-day Pushpin eclecticist who took it beyond," says Steven Heller, the prolific author and art director of the The New York Times Book Review. "She married Russian constructivism with Victoriana and created a hybrid style. People paid attention to her work." What has been called Scher's "postmodern" sensibility is really her unwillingness to be pigeonholed. For 31 years she has freely raided the typographic larder, fusing aspects of popular culture – like Zigzag rolling papers packages, Zap comics and Billy Wilder films – with Alexandr Rodchenko, El Lissitzky, Fluxus, Dada and De Stijl.

"It's the idiosyncrasies that give a design its special character," she told a rapt audience at AIGA's 1999 "Cult and Culture" conference in Las Vegas. It's a lesson Scher has always known instinctively.

Scher's first significant job was at CBS Records, first designing ads and later record covers. (She briefly left CBS to work for Atlantic where she designed covers for Sonny & Cher and Charles Mingus, among others.) By 1975 she returned to CBS as art director, designing some 150 album covers a year for bands like Boston, Cheap Trick, Billy Joel and numerous classical and jazz artists (figs. 2–7). Scher worked at CBS for most of the 1970s, drawing on typographic styles from the past and hiring outside illustrators and photographers to provide the images. In 1979, her Best of Jazz poster (fig. 9), a constructivist juxtaposition of wood type, was initially rejected by annuals and later lauded and widely imitated. "It became a stylistic noose around my neck," she once said. An economic crash in the late 1970s forced her to use type to convey the same content that previously was conveyed through image, a twist of fate that would ultimately inform her mature work. "It was a period of self-discovery," Scher reflects. "I was developing my own vocabulary."

One aspect that didn't need fine-tuning was her sharp wit. All the while she was at CBS, Scher kept one foot in Pushpin Graphics, writing satire for its humor magazine. In 1977 she wrote "Gastric Aggression or Why Germany Went to War," a hilarious parody that blamed German fascism on a diet of red meat. Ironically, she herself was once spoofed in Spy magazine as the world's most hated woman in graphic design.

"Humor is my way of being generous," she says, revealing a quest to give something back to the public. "It exists in my work because it exists in my life," she once said. Though Scher was talking about her graphics, not her writing, one clearly informs the other. One of Scher's funniest pieces is a 1985 spoof in Print

2

7

5

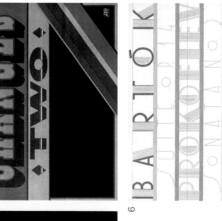

4

3

6

called "Anal Retentiv Speaks His Mind." The piece is an interview with the legendary Swiss designer, Anal Retentiv, whose work is "extremely borink." Says Retentiv: "Each circle and square I design first in my own mind. Not from simple geometry but from my own dreams!" Scher laughs when she recalls the article. "I was still goofing around with parody."

Ironically, it was at CBS, while producing materials for a raging youth culture, that Scher learned everything about corporate culture. Here, turning out hundreds of record covers, she had to be quick and decisive. "In the music business even Stevie Wonder and Ray Charles have cover approval," she is known to quip. The lessons would prove invaluable, for soon after she left CBS she started her own firm with Terry Koppel, a former schoolmate at Tyler with whom she was reunited while freelancing for Time, Inc. From 1984 to 1989, Koppel & Scher designed projects for clients that included Swatch, Champion, EMI Records and numerous book publishers.

Scher continued to draw from eclectic sources, fostering an idiosyncratic style that was seldom outright political, although it often contained a spirited irreverence that critics have called "generational." "I was still rebelling against Herb Lubalin's ITC typefaces and ligatures," Scher remembers. "I hated the typefaces they drew. They took away the eccentricities of the faces and homogenized them. I liked big and powerful type." When it was her turn to design a promotional piece for Champion papers, she chose to publish a collection of period faces no longer sold at type houses. "Beautiful Faces," unlike the ITC fonts, could be reproduced for free. For an early Swatch Watch campaign she parodied 1950s advertising; she cals it "Leave it to Beaver" with watches." For a Manhattan Records identity program (fig. 8) she freely adapted Piet Mondrian's painting Broadway Boogie Woogie — a map of Manhattan seen through distinctly De Stijl eyes. She called the appropriation a visual pun.

It was 1984 and Swatch, needing a new ad campaign, held a meeting at the Swiss International Business Building on Fifth Avenue in New York. When Scher

2 Japanese Melodies LP,
CBS Records, 1978
3 Heads LP, CBS Records,
1977 4 H LP, CBS Records,
1977

5 Changes Two LP, CBS
Records, 1974 6 Bartók,
Prokofiev, Lees LP, CBS
Records, 1973 7 "Trust
Elvis" poster, CBS/
Columbia Records, 1981

walked into the building her eyes were immediately drawn to the posters on the walls, all of them designed by Herbert Matter. "I said, 'These posters are screaming out for watches!'" she recalls. Soon, Scher wrote to Matter's widow, Mercedes, and obtained permission to reproduce her husband's hallowed Swissair poster. The famous poster depicts an idealized Teutonic skier on which Scher overlaid two Swatches (fig. 10). Her design credit on the bottom edge of the poster read: "Koppel & Scher with Herbert Matter." The Swatch poster was a response to a specific design problem, but it was also a prank – another parody – that ignited what could only in hindsight be called a madcap controversy.

"A faction of the design world thought they owned Swiss Modernism. Paula was an outsider. She wasn't Swiss. She was poaching on their sacred iconography," explains Ellen Lupton, curator at the Cooper-Hewitt Design Museum. "It's a poster about a poster. It's a joke!"

Today the to-do seems parochial, but at the time, designers didn't mess with sacred cows – particularly if they were Swiss men. "So much is accidental. You don't know how people on the outside will perceive your work," Scher reflects. "The poster's been controversial forever, but there's never really been a debate about it. If there's a failure to the poster it's that it was above its audience."

The Swatch episode was devastating. "I wasn't sure where my work was going. I felt vulnerable," she recalls. Scher's work was getting noticed, but it was also being labeled "postmodern," "new wave" and "historicist" – terms she loathed. "To me modernism is Richard Nixon; postmodernism is Ronald Reagan," she once said. The historian Phil Meggs dubbed her style "retro." By 1989, some of her colleagues, particularly the late Tibor Kalman (with whom she was friends), began to publicly criticize her style. "In 1985 the historical stuff still looked cool," says Scher. "Things look cool in their time."

She retreated inwardly and her design took another turn. During this period she designed her famed Ambassador Arts "Big A" poster (fig. 15). She also started noodling around with illustration. For the cover of the 1991 AIGA annual (fig. 13),

8 Identity for Manhattan
Records, 1984 9 "The
Best of Jazz" poster, CBS
Records, 1979

10 Poster for Swatch Watch
USA, 1984

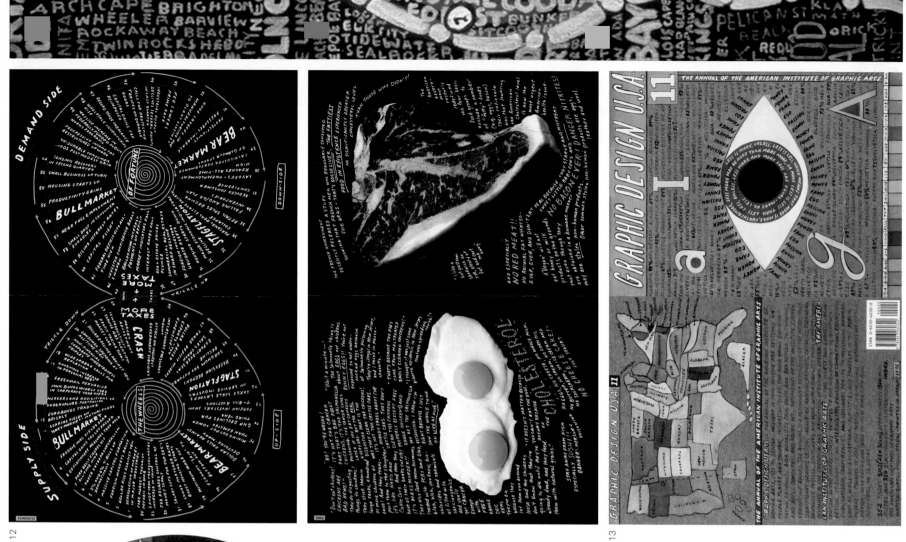

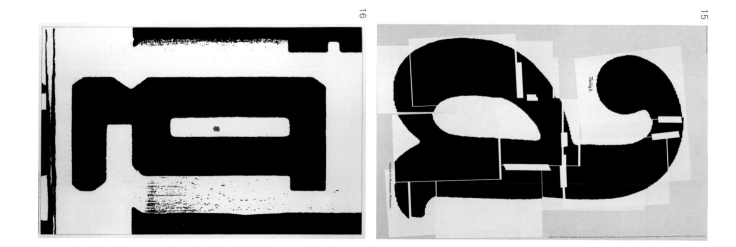

she drew obsessively. The drawing depicted an eye with lashes made of words (money, power, fame, ego, passion, ennui) over a backdrop of proper nouns (the name of every American state interspersed with the word "Helvetica") – a strategy that would be echoed the following year in an illustrated self-portrait (fig. 11). "I was getting vilified and doing this AIGA cover at the same time," she says. "I wanted to do the opposite of what was going on, and that was the computer," she says. "I had a clear sense of rebelling against something and it became a style."

Nonetheless, a recession at the end of the 1980s nearly bankrupted Scher. Koppel & Scher amicably broke up. Koppel took a job as art director for *Esquire*. Scher ran the shop solo for a while before she was offered a partnership at Pentagram in 1991. Though she calls herself "the only girl on the football team," Scher is no cheerleader. "More than anyone else I know," says Pentagram compadre Michael Bierut, "Paula embodies the spirit that got me and so many other people into design in the first place. She makes it look so easy it would be depressing if it wasn't so inspirational."

At Pentagram, Scher took on high-profile projects that would have been difficult for a woman designer to land on her own. "I was able to take on any job that a big, fat man could," she says with relish. She was also able to charge big, fat fees. Citibank, Anne Klein, the Museum of Natural History, Sony, the Brooklyn Museum, Ballet-Tech (fig. 21), *Metropolis* (figs. 20, 22), and *The New York Times Magazine* comprise some of her clients. But it is her work for the Public Theater (1994-present, figs. 17–19) that has become the high point of her career, earning her numerous awards. The posters are widely collected by leading museums, including the Museum of Modern Art and the Cooper-Hewitt. "With the Public Theater, she became a really great designer," says Lupton.

In an excellent article on the Public Theater campaign, Steven Heller describes the impact of Scher's "call-to-arms typography" on herself, on the Public Theater and on New York. For it is here that Scher's wit, humanity, boldness and love of

Victorian wood type came together in a remarkable display of graphics that was somehow more contemporary and classic than her previous work. Heller wrote: "Scher's cacophony of wood types, silhouetted photos and bright flat colors is more akin to the two-color rag bond or oak tag bills produced by job printers or run off at Kinko's to advertise circuses, country fairs, prizefights and dance bands, then stapled and wheat-pasted to every available outdoor space." For the Diva is Dismissed poster (fig. 18), for example, a gigantic propeller of words literally screams from the mouth of actress Jenifer Lewis. Again, Scher's work was as popular as it was personal.

With the Public Theater, Scher's graphics wallpapered every conceivable surface of the city with shouting type. What was next was to overtake the buildings themselves. Her latest work is signage, but not in the usual sense of the term. Instead, Scher is taking architecture and using it as a canvas. "Cities are like magazines," she said in a recent profile. "Some spaces are editorial, some are advertising."

At Pentagram, Scher leads me into a narrow hallway that is filled with slide trays and grabs a tray labeled "Paula #2." She takes me on a virtual walking tour of the buildings she has covered with type: the Duke Theater (fig. 24), a school for the New Jersey Performing Arts Center (fig. 23) and an office tower, 770 Broadway. "This is the next rebellion, but it's a hard fight," she says. "Architects don't like it. Architects are antipopulists who are very proprietary." Again, Scher is faced with criticism and labels.

At the same time, Scher continues to paint obsessive maps (fig. 14), reminiscent of the AIGA annual cover. They are intensely personal and just plain intense. Loose and hand-scrawled, they are the opposite of the corporate graphics she "produces" (her verb of choice) at Pentagram.

"Paula's had all these phases of her career and she keeps coming up with new ideas rooted in the same impulses and humor," say Lupton.

"The reinvention is deliberate and not accidental and I'll have to do it again, every

**BALLET·TECH**

A NEW COMPANY FROM ELIOT FELD

30 PERFORMANCES ONLY

MARCH 4 – APRIL 13

The Joyce Theater / Chelsea 175 Eighth Ave. at 19th St.

CALL JOYCECHARGE 212-242-0800

THE PUBLISHERS OF METROPOLIS MAGAZINE & CITY & COUNTRY

NET @ WORK

MAY 19-21 2000

Things will never be the same again

METROPOLIS MAGAZINE PRESENTS

WONDERBRANDS
(west)

AT THE PRESIDIO IN SAN FRANCISCO NOVEMBER 12 & 13

BRANDING BY STRATEGY AND DESIGN
JOIN THE WORLD'S FINEST BRANDERS FROM ARCHITECTURE TO ADVERTISING, DESIGN TO E-COMMERCE. MEMBERS OF THE INTERNATIONAL ARCHITECTURE, DESIGN AND MARKETING PROFESSIONS WILL CONVENE IN SAN FRANCISCO TO EXAMINE 2000 YEARS OF BRANDS AND IDENTITY. FOR TWO INTENSE DAYS SPEAKERS, RESPONDENTS AND THE AUDIENCE WILL EXPLORE THE PROCESS AND CREATION OF WONDERBRANDS

24

five years," she says. There is a tone of dread in her voice as she considers the prodigious effort involved in creating a really new body of work. She acknowledges how easy it is to become lazy. She describes the pain involved in reevaluating your position in society as you get farther and farther from the youth culture. "An award locks your place in history, but it can also deny your place in the present," she admits.

She pauses and with a wry smile adds, "It's great. It's nice. I'm USDA approved!"

23 Environmental graphics for New Jersey Performing Arts Center, Lucent Technologies Center for Arts Education, 2001 24 Interior environmental graphics for New 42nd Street Studios/ The Duke Theater, 2000

# Less is more, more or less: Sam Antupit by Darcy Cosper

The jacket of a large, handsome monograph on the work of architect I.M. Pei (fig. 1), designed by Sam Antupit during his long tenure as art director of Abrams Books, features an unusual portrait. The focus of the photograph is sharp, but in the middle ground, at the center of the image, Pei's face is very slightly blurred, as if he had turned away from the camera at the moment its shutter dropped. "There were other exposures where everything was in focus," Antupit says, "but he's a very reticent, self-effacing person. I guess self-effacing is what that image is, in a real sense."

Such unusual and risky choices speak volumes about Antupit's design sensibility, which is at once subtle and bold, literal and transcendent. And they illuminate something about the man and his work that in our era of celebrity designer and signature style seem very much of another time. Antupit's deferential charm, quiet graciousness and humility are that of a gentleman in the old style; his work is fresh and startling in its almost revolutionary purity, and in its self-effacement. His book and editorial designs – from the glory days of Esquire in the 1960s and Abrams in the art-boom '80s to the projects he creates these days for his own company, CommonPlace Books – appear not designed, simply complete. They are a poetic synthesis of form and content in which Antupit is not a presence but a lens, his sensibility not the thing we see, but that through which we see.

Antupit began his career at Yale in the 1950s, where he majored in English with plans to become a writer. It was there, by chance, that he met Josef Albers, who was at the time the head of Yale's School of Design and Architecture. "I didn't know who he was," Antupit admits, "but I used to see him around, this really elegant guy with a grown-up child's face and beautiful, silvery-white hair. One day I went up to him in the dining hall and started chatting, and he invited me to stop by his school and take a look. I went over and became absolutely fascinated with it." In his senior year, Antupit was admitted to the design school as a special student. "I had no idea what I was getting into," he says with a laugh. "I thought, I really like this graphic design business, this doodling with type. The curiosity was to see

# I.M. PEI

## A PROFILE IN AMERICAN ARCHITECTURE

### CARTER WISEMAN

what designers did with what you wrote. I really thought that would be as much as I would get into." But Antupit ended up attending the master's program, where he studied with Alexey Brodovitch, Herbert Matter, Alvin Lustig, Paul Rand, Lester Beall, Norman Ives, Alvin Eisenman and Rob Roy Kelly. "It was a real awakening," Antupit says gleefully. "I felt like I was in first grade, and had started my education all over again."

In 1956, Antupit was drafted, and left Yale for the army, where, because of his design training, he ended up in a training-aids division. "The best thing I ever did was teach drivers to use these big trucks without a single word, using only sequential diagrams," he says. "That was just great training." The influence of this early experience is manifested in much of Antupit's work, from the simplicity of his early editorial designs to his 1984 redesign of Harper's magazine – elements of which were featured in Edward Tufte's book, Envisioning Information. For Antupit, it seems, all design is information design, and his oeuvre is largely characterized by such utilitarian directness and clarity.

On leaves, Antupit returned to Yale to work on his thesis project. In 1958, when his service was completed, the young designer moved to New York, where Henry Wolf, who had recently left Esquire to become the art director of Harper's Bazaar, hired him. After three years, Antupit followed Wolf to Show, a new entertainment magazine. Wolf praises Antupit's sense of humor and the joy he brought to his work. "I took it seriously, and he laughed," Wolf says. "He once met the editor of Bazaar in the hall on a weekend, and she said 'What are you doing here on a Saturday?' and he said, 'It's not a job, it's a hobby!' And that's how he did everything."

In 1962, Antupit made what he describes as his only career mistake: he went to work at Condé Nast under Alexander Liberman. "It was horrendous," Antupit remembers. "He had absolutely no design sense whatsoever. He was nothing but an accommodator. I worked on features for all the magazines – Vogue, Glamour, House & Garden, Mademoiselle, whatever – I would do these layouts

1 Book jacket of I.M. Pei:
A Profile in American
Architecture, Harry N
Abrams, 1990, portrait by
Marco DeValdivia

and the magazine would come out and the layout would be totally different. All the decisions were politically based; they had no standards at all."

After one year, Antupit fled to Pushpin Studios. He describes it as one of his best professional experiences, largely for the opportunity it afforded him to work with founders Milton Glaser and Seymour Chwast, as well as Paul Davis, Norman Green, Isadore Seltzer and Myrna Mushkin. "As collaborators they were unmatched," Antupit says, "and the range of projects was terrific. Whatever they asked me to do I did, and was grateful, and enjoyed it." Glaser returns the compliment. "Sam was a lot of fun," he declares. "He knows how to work well with others, probably because he is intrinsically a courteous and gracious man. He has a wonderful sense of taste. He's very editorial in his thinking; inevitably he thinks first of the content, and then the most appropriate way of expressing it."

These qualities were honed at Pushpin, where his projects included a design update for Art in America (fig. 3) and the creation of the New York Review of Books (fig. 2). "It was during the newspaper strikes," Antupit remembers. "Jason and Barbara Epstein got a bunch of their friends together, real writers, and they asked me to do the design. I used to go to their house every Tuesday and lay the whole thing out in four hours in their living room. We thought we'd only do a few issues, until the strike was over, but then they started getting ads and it just kept going." Nearly 40 years later, NYROB's basic design – rigid grids, serif typefaces and signature illustrations by David Levine – has altered little (though Antupit describes the current cover design as "a disgrace"), a testament to the enduring strength of Antupit's work.

Antupit was so happy at Pushpin that when in 1962 he was offered the position of art director at Esquire, he was deeply conflicted about accepting it. He turned to Henry Wolf for advice. "Henry said something like, 'Keep moving,'" says Antupit, "so I went to Esquire. And it was a super-duper time, the golden age. All the people were terrific, a good idea could come from anywhere, and everyone was respected for their ideas. It was brilliant. *Esquire* is the best place I've ever wo-ked." Antupit heaps praise on his colleagues, including editor-in-chief Harold Hayes, "who he describes as a legend; assistant art director Walter Bernard ("an absolute delight, my right arm and my right leg"); and fiction editor Robert Brown. It was here that he first had a chance to fully flex his muscles as an art director – which in Antupit's case meant developing intensely close collaborative relation- ships with editors, illustrators and photographers, a modus operandi that remains central to his work to this day. "The result was," as one young designer put it, "the *Esquire* that you think of when you think of *Esquire*" – designs characterized by wry wit and stealthy irreverence, which twist iconic images in wholly unex- pected ways. One cover features a Richard Hess illustration of Lyndon B. Johnson as a paint-by-numbers president (fig. 4); a story on model Jean Shrimpton, the Christy Turlington of her day, depicts the beauty as Michelangelo's ideally pro- portioned human (fig. 7); the religious overtones of an excerpt from Thomas Pynchon's novel *The Crying of Lot 49* are suggested by a classical triptych com- missioned from illustrator Philip Hays (fig. 5).

After six years at the magazine, Antupit decided to heed Henry Wolf's dictum and keep moving. In 1969, he joined forces with Richard Hess, an illustrator and designer with whom he had worked at *Esquire*, to form their own studio, Hess and/or Antupit. After two years, the partners separated, and Antupit and Others was founded. The staff included Raymond Hooper, Andrea Da Riff and Hiroshi Morishima; they produced posters, annual reports and a number of Grammy- winning album covers.

Antupit also created a book packaging division, Subsistence Press; he had poach- ed *Esquire*'s assistant fiction editor Jamie Shalleck, and she became his primary partner in the development and production of their publications. Shalleck, who went onto a career as a bookbinder and designer, says of Antupit, "My whole sense of how a book should look and feel I developed by working with Sam. He wasn't just visual; he thought about the size of the book, the shape, the weight,

On following spread:
2 *The New York Review of Books*, cover art by David Levine, 1964 3 *Art in America*, cover art by Alexander Calder, 1964

4 *Esquire*'s famous LBJ cover, cover art by Richard Hess, 1967 5 Spread from *Esquire* story by Thomas Pynchon, art by Phil Hays, 1967 6 Spreads from *Esquire* story by Gay Talese on building of Verrazano bridge, photo essay by Bruce Davidson, 1966

7 Page from *Esquire* featuring the proportions of supermodel Jean Shrimpton, photo by Melvin Sokolosky, 1965 8 Poems by Robert Brown from *Esquire* using only the top row of type- writer keys, photo by John Paul Endress, 1968

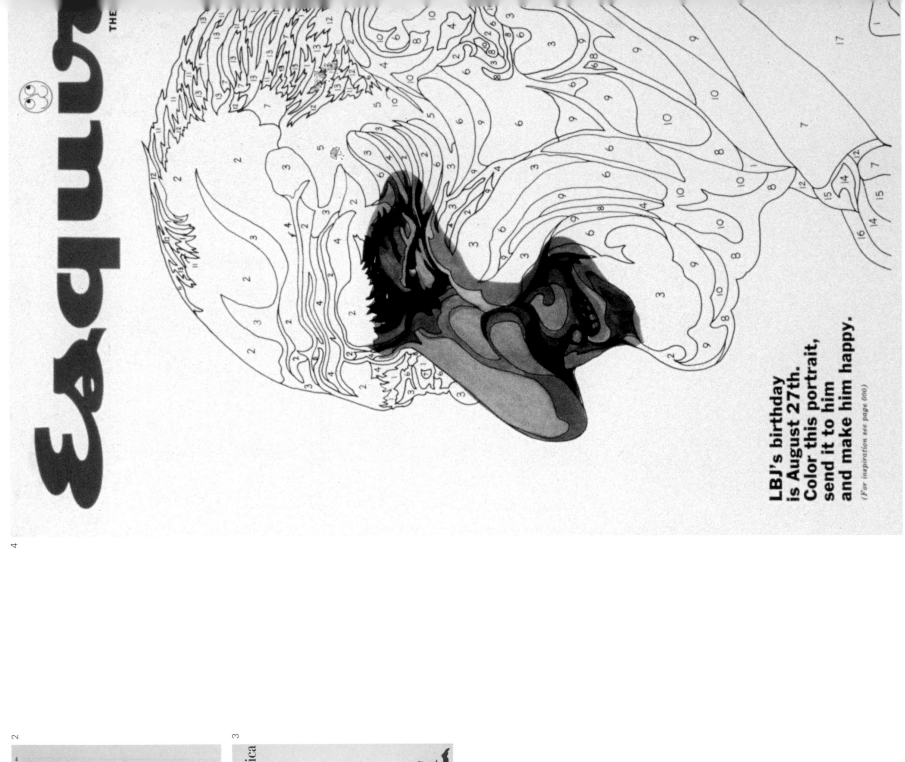

**ESQUIRE** THE

LBJ's birthday
is August 27th.
Color this portrait,
send it to him
and make him happy.

*(For inspiration see page 000)*

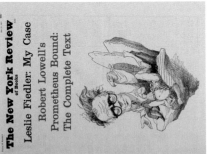

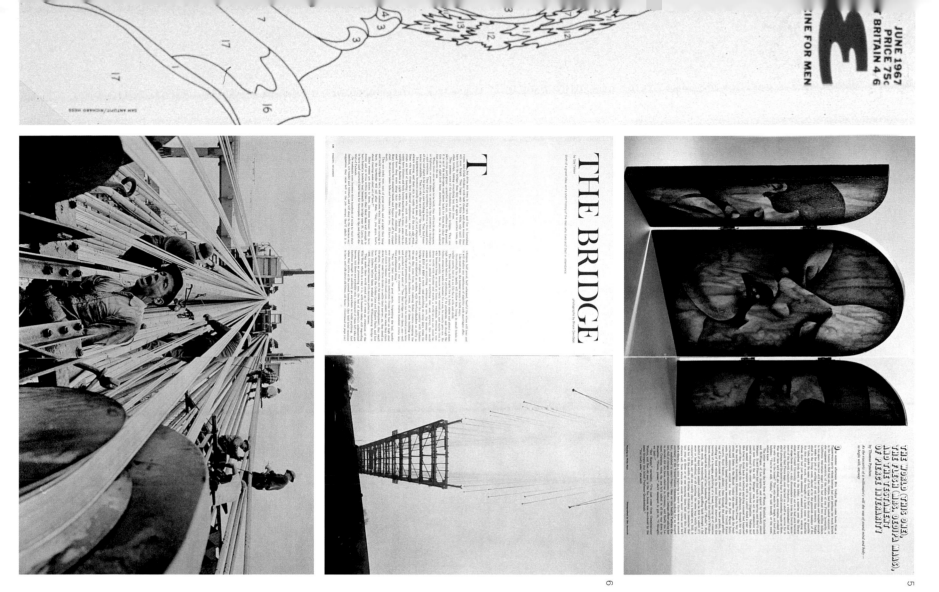

# THE BRIDGE

*photographs by Sheng Camaban*

## THE WORLD (THIS ONE), THE FLESH (MRS. OEDIPA MAAS), AND THE TESTAMENT OF PIERCE INVERARITY

*by Thomas Pynchon*

## The Imposing Proportions of Jean Shrimpton

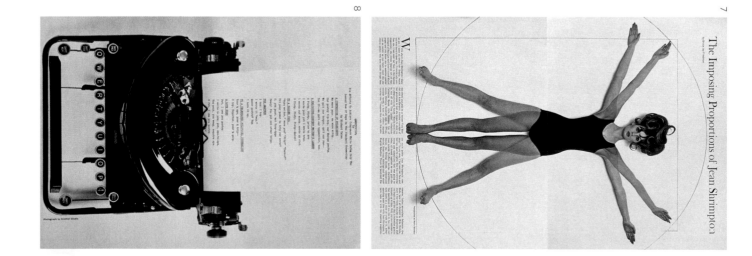

Tea.
Jamie Shalleck

THE SORROW AND THE PITY
A FILM BY MARCEL OPHULS

INTRODUCTION BY STANLEY HOFFMANN

THE SORROW
AND
THE PITY
A FILM BY MARCEL OPHULS

OUTERBRIDGE
& LAZARD

PRISON
INTERVIEWS BY LEONARD J. BERRY

the way, it felt in your hands, the sense of the piece, how it should be read. He's one of those designers who really reads and comprehends text."

This sensitivity to content is abundantly evident in the Subsistence books. The cover of their first effort, on the history and ceremonial uses of tea, features a photograph of a tiny ship going under in a teacup (fig. 10). "We got a soup tureen and glued it to a big platter with a giant serving spoon," Antupit explains, "and then got a model ship and sank it in the tea." The tempest-in-a-teacup image, perhaps a subtle reference to the problematic colonialist culture from which the Western cult of tea arose, both amuses and disturbs. More powerful is the cover Antupit designed for the script of *The Sorrow and the Pity* (fig. 11), which features, or the front, a photograph of a French flag with the swastika cut out of it. "I just thought of what the Germans had done to France, and cut the swastika out of the flag, and was going to end with that," Antupit says. "But I couldn't throw the swastika away afterward." Instead, he used it on the back cover, laid across several photographs of French collaborators – a remarkable and unsettling evocation of French complicity with the Nazis.

Among the most compelling of these publications, from a design standpoint, is *Prison* (fig. 9). The book is a composite record of an average day in a prison, comprising interviews with inmates, wardens, guards and other members of prison commun ties across the country. Filled with photographs that Antupit culled during extensive photo research, and set in an inelegant sans-serif typeface, the book is so plain as to appear undesigned – until one realizes that it looks, very intentionally and authentically, like a court document.

Also published by Subsistence was the companion volume to the beloved record and the television special *Free to Be You and Me*, which Antupit art directed – in antic collaboration with dozens of illustrators and photographers – and for which he won an Emmy.

In 1977, after having consulted for Book of the Month Club on the organization of its art department, Antupit was offered the position of art director. Initially he refused; the company tendered the offer again a year later, stipulating that Antupit could bring in his staff and continue to do outside work, and (after running it by Henry Wolf) he agreed.

Four years later, Antupit went over to Harry N. Abrams, the country's premiere publisher of fine art books, where he reigned for 16 years as art director, and as a member of the editorial board and publishing committee. During his time there, Antupit oversaw the production of nearly a hundred books, many of which he conceived and designed himself.

Though Abrams specialized in art, Antupit's pet projects involved more vernacular designs: a book based on a show at MoCA in Los Angeles about the automobile and culture (fig. 12), featuring original photographs of car parts and details in such extreme close-up as to render them abstract; a catalogue for an exhibition of contemporary chair designs with an introduction Antupit commissioned from renowned art critic Arthur Danto; and a facsimile of Kate Greenaway's Mother Goose (fig. 13) with margins larger than the images themselves. (Antupit, a father of four, said this was so children could draw in the book without marking up the illustrations.)

One of Antupit's all-time favorite Abrams books is a monograph on George Herriman's comic strip "Krazy Kat" (fig. 14), a childhood obsession of his. The text is set in slim columns recalling the art's original context in daily newspapers. The images, many available only on ancient newsprint, were reproduced without retouching. Antupit's faithful use of these artifacts – faded colors, yellowed paper and all – points up the passage of art through time, the comics' place in a particular historical moment and the nostalgic relation readers have to "Krazy Kat."

The fine-art books Antupit did work on – notably two volumes on the work of artist Roy Lichtenstein (figs. 16, 17) – were unorthodox in their conception and execution. One is a collection of crayon and pencil sketches designed to resemble an artist's sketchbook – stiff pale blue-gray cloth covers, the corners and spine bound in black, the images beautifully reproduced on heavy white paper. The other book documents the creation of Lichtenstein's Mural With Blue Brushstroke for the lobby of the Equitable Life Insurance Building in New York City; its design sug-

12 Front jacket and spread from Automobile and Culture, Harry N. Abrams, 1984, photos by Henry Wolf 13 Spread from Kate Greenaway's Mother Goose, Harry N. Abrams, 1988, photos by Color Wheel 14 Spread from Krazy Kat, Harry N. Abrams, 1986, art by George Herriman

AMERICAN AUTOMOBILE DESIGN

AUTOMOBILE AND CULTURE

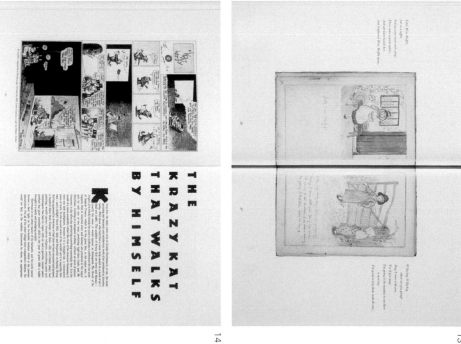

THE
KRAZY KAT
THAT WALKS
BY HIMSELF

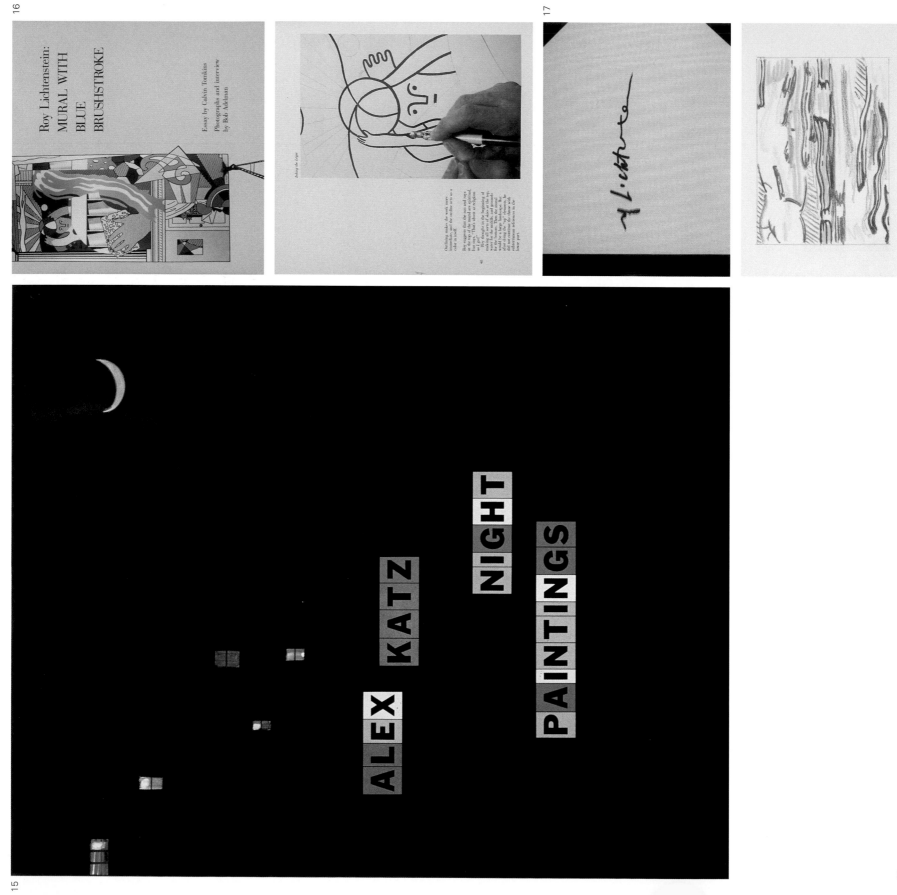

15 Book jacket from Alex
Katz: Night Paintings, Harry
N. Abrams, 1991 16 Book
jacket and page from Roy
Lichtenstein: Mural with
Blue Brushstroke, Harry
N. Abrams, 1987 17 Cover
and page from Roy Licht-
enstein: Sketchbook, Harry
N. Abrams, 1985

gests a very elite how-to book, with close-up photographs of materials, palettes
anc the artist's hands at work.

For a designer so invested in simplicity, Antupit, by his own admission, rarely leaves
well enough alone. Most of his Abrams books include endnotes on type, witty
embossing on cloth covers that might never be seen, color-contrasting endpapers
and French folds to reinforce paper jackets. Yet somehow, his elaborate attention
to detail never seems fussy, only lovingly thorough. One sees, in Antupit's work,
his profound ability to create, with hundreds of deft gestures and subtle choices, a
design not merely appropriate to a document's content, but a visual narrative that
shapes and becomes integral to the reader's experience.

In 1994, Antupit took a leave of absence and, with the aid of an NEA grant, traveled
the country for a month, recording storytellers of various Native American tribes
and printing their tales in limited editions at Cycling Frog Press (fig. 18), the letter-
press shop he founded in 1960 using type and equipment from the late 19th
century. Galvanized by the experience, and unable to do enough challenging work
at Abrams to keep him satisfied, Antupit began to consider other outlets for his
nary project ideas, and in the fall of 1995 formally established CommonPlace Publishing,
based in New Canaan, Connecticut, where he works with writers and artists
from all over the country and produces three original books a year for organizations
from Simon and Schuster to the Jewish Theological Society. "At CommonPlace
I have total freedom," he says, "but it's also very scary, because for the first time
I have total responsibility for the content. I'm just now beginning to understand
how much is on the shoulders of an editor," he continues. "It's made me realize
what an insignificant part of the project design is. Of course it's important, but
not as important as designers think it is. Designers should get a life, get out there
and see the other aspects of the project. If the bones don't work, you've just
got a pile of skin."

Now well into his 60s, Antupit is still learning, still willing to be humbled and shows no signs whatsoever of slowing down. When asked about plans for retirement, he pauses as if baffled, and then declares, "Not now. Not in the foreseeable future." As at the beginning of his career, design is now not so much a job for Antupit as a hobby that brings him – and to which he brings – all the joy in the world.

Asked to describe Antupit's work and its significance, Milton Glaser says, "Most graphic design these days is about transgression, violence and brutal gestures. Sam is another kind of guy. His issues are coherence, classicism, balance, proportion, appropriateness, clarity. As far as I can see, Sam's work is about manifesting respect for the narrative, making it as accessible as it can be. It has always had a certain modesty – it attempts to do things with respect, and without using everything as a vehicle for some narcissistic expression of self. To me that is a very powerful and bold characteristic, and one very much missing from a lot of design that one sees about."

Antupit, summarizing his approach to design, says he tries "to do as much as possible with as little as possible." Then, in an utterly characteristic move, he gives someone else their say, and the credit for it. "One of my students once was asked to characterize my design philosophy," he says, "and she described it as 'Less is more, more or less.' And that's great – she got it right on the button."

18 Spreads from *How the Parrots Came to Be at Acoma*, Cycling Frog Press, 1993, art and text by Wanda Aragon 19 Spreads from *Dover Beach*, Cycling Frog Press, 1971, art by U.S. BankNote Co., poem by Matthew Arnold

20 Two books from the Turning Point Invention series: *Clock, Lightbulb*, CommonPlace/Atheneum, 1991–2000, photos by Sally Andersen-Bruce

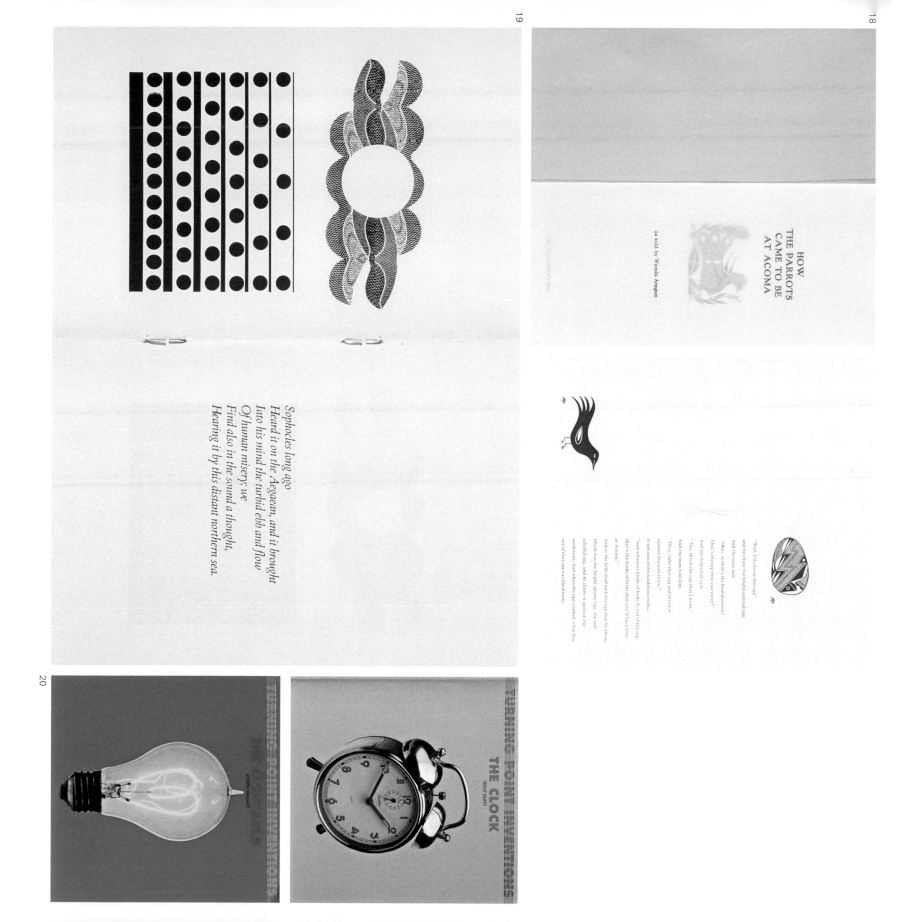

Question J
On a scale of 0–10,
how much control
did you feel you
had over the final
product's outcome?
0 = no control
10 = total control

Catalogue numbers
A = anonymous

9.6

average level
of control

# BRANDING STRATEGIES

**Jurors Jack Anderson** HornallAnderson, Seattle **Nathan Shedroff** San Francisco **Gael Towey** Martha Stewart Omnimedia, New York

Over time, branding approaches have evolved from packaging concepts to corporate identities to consumer experiences, and continue to adapt to the New Economy.

Jurors will focus on the strategy behind the branding, rather than only on the finished product. Work that challenges branding formulas and strives to develop a new vocabulary for the practice should be entered in this category.

Beautiful and interesting logos, corporate identities and other designs for branded names and images may be what most people think of when they think of branding, but brand strategy is a breed apart. It must be delivered in more than just one medium and address how people understand and build meaning in their minds and lives. The best of these solutions operate more subtly and humanely, and treat people as if they're capable of thought and dialogue.

In this year's branding strategy competition, only about half of the entries included any description of the strategy behind these design solutions. In order to merit inclusion, the brand couldn't just be beautifully designed and the strategy shouldn't be merely to show it off in as many places as possible. The strategy – what was described or what could be inferred – had to communicate a plan for how these brand messages were going to affect the company itself, its employees, products, sales, customers and values.

There were some exemplary solutions, of course, that strove to communicate human values throughout the chain of people from CEO through employees to customers and beyond. The winners here show that brand strategy can apply to whole company image restructuring as well as to very small projects that need to accomplish only one goal well. All of these winners, however, found ways to communicate important messages in sensitive and strategic ways.

Question J
How much control
did you feel you had
over the final
product's outcome?

Response, cat 7

## ULTIMATELY WE MAKE NO DECISIONS, BUT EVERYTHING THEY'RE CHOOSING FROM COMES FROM US.

Trends in this year's entries included an emphasis on people imagery, and a notable attempt by companies to personalize their messages and connect to their audiences and customers in "real" ways instead of overtly digital or technological ones. All of these strategies were exceptionally clear and straightforward. This isn't to say that they were all obvious or lacked substance. On the contrary, most touched important issues and communicated powerful messages rather than relied on tricks or too much ornamentation.

Several entries also seemed to make an explicit attempt to reach people in multiple media, and not just through traditional collateral and corporate-identity manuals. Landor's decks of cards for Hewlett-Packard (cat. 6) not only allows employees to interact with the brand physically – shuffling pictures, colors and phrases that exemplify HP's "invent" brand – but enables them to customize it as well, picking out the elements that speak to each employee and creating a personal vocabulary that each can then use to describe the company in their terms.

Most companies try to align their goals with higher human values and emotions, and the petroleum company BP Amoco has done this exceptionally well (cat. 5). The company has redefined "BP" to stand for a bundle of phrases, each typifying a variety of different issues, concerns and messages: bold people, better products, big picture, beyond petroleum. As with Hewlett-Packard's strategy, this allows all employees to connect with a message that builds personal meaning. It also extends the number of brand messages into a larger group that would otherwise be unmanageable. These two companies are obviously trying to communicate effectively throughout their organizations first before they communicate out to their customers, partners and competitors – and they're doing so successfully. This strategy also allows them to innovate from the inside at all points within their companies and not merely from the design office.

Another trend that emerged seemed to indicate that the best of these strategies were careful, reasoned approaches with realistic long-term expectations. The last few years of dotcom mania have bred a generation of designers and business people who think that brands can emerge and evolve in 6 to 12 months, and that the only real tool to build a brand is to repeat it loudly and often enough for it to be remembered and regurgitated in a market-research poll. The reality is that brand strategies must plan at least one year, but more like three to five years, ahead to be effective.

Of course, there are companies not represented in the following selections because no one bothered to enter them into the competition. Target's brand strategy, for example, has been a brilliant category-defying one that has catapulted its brand not just into the designers' stratosphere, but has affected a 180-degree turn in the minds of consumers as well. Prada, Mercedes-Benz and Jaguar are brilliantly turning their brands from the well known but somewhat boring "quality" and "luxury" attributes they've always had into exciting and energetic brands without losing these standard associations. They are, in effect, redefining what quality and luxury can be in order to affect their companies' products, customers and, of course, futures. This is, at its best, the power of good brand design. Nathan Shedroff

Each branch of the United States Armed forces had its own base exchange (retail store) and separate credit card system. It was determined that our country's major military services would, for the first time, join together to share and utilize a common credit program. Since each of the five branches, the United States Army, Air Force, Navy, Coast Guard and Marines have enormous pride in their defining insignias, the main objective was to create diversity within unity. A star was created — a unique cobranding credit card program was developed. Each point of the newly named "Military Star" represents the emblem of each of the five branches of the Armed Forces.

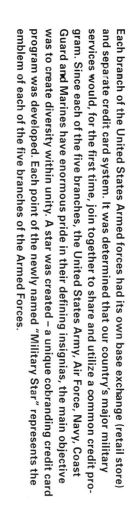

The Armed
Forces' Exchange
Credit Program
identity

Design firm
BrandEquity
International, Newton,
Massachusetts
Creative director
Joe Selame
Designer BrandEquity
Design Team

1

As Nickelodeon has grown and expanded over the past 15 years, the brand message has changed. The initial assignment included strategy and positioning of the Nickelodeon brand and components like Nick Jr. and Nick at Nite. The internal audience's perception of the brand was correlated with information from the external audience. Once determined, the on-air visual reface was produced to provide a clearer and proprietary voice for Nick. The reface elements were coordinated with off-air needs to provide a holistic communication system for Nickelodeon. After the initial launch, the reface kit-of-parts needed to be implemented by the Nickelodeon creative departments. The system had to be flexible, inspire creativity and encourage ideas and concepts.

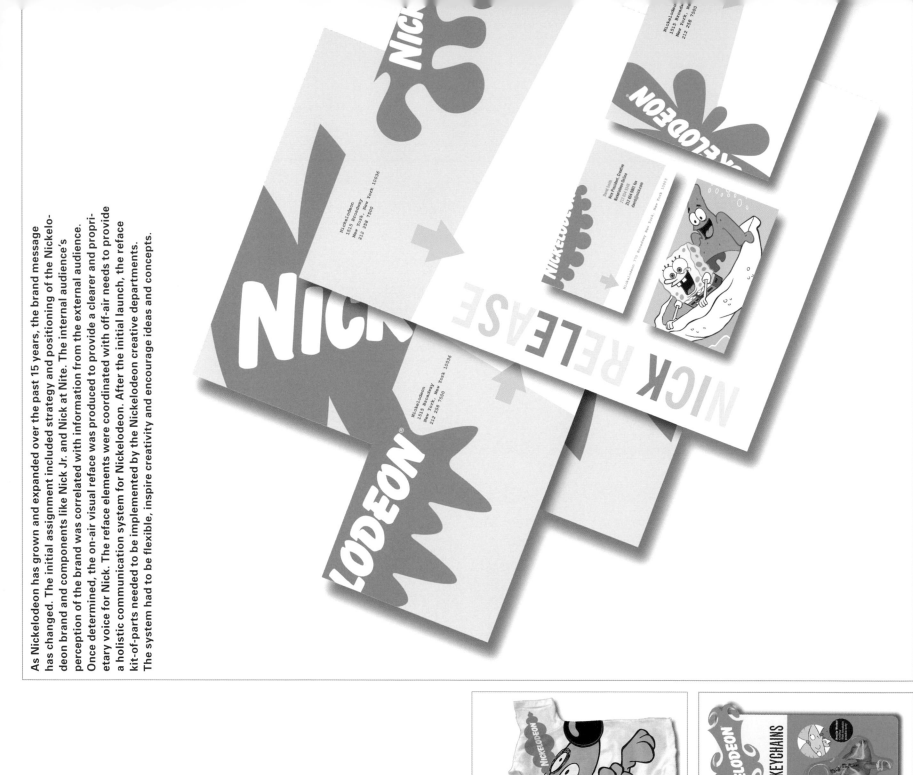

**NEW ON NICKELODEON**

**MAY 8 TAINA**
The whole world is gonna know who Taina is—according to Taina, anyway! Premieres Tuesday, May 8 at 7:00pm

**MAY 9 AS TOLD BY GINGER**
Watch her go from shy to A-list. Premieres Wednesday, May 9 at 8:00pm

**NICKELODEON LOCAL EVENTS**

**SWIMMINGLY**
Nickelodeon's SpongeBob SquarePants can make your life like a day at the beach.

Generate local ad sales revenue and become a hometown hero when you sponsor The SpongeBob SquarePants Squishy SweepStakes and send a family to Los Angeles and Nickelodeon Animation Studios!

THE SPONGEBOB SQUAREPANTS SQUISHY SWEEPSTAKES

NICKELODEON™

SPONGEBOB SQUAREPANTS 7PM MONDAYS

**Nickelodeon
identity reface**

Design firm
AdamsMorioka,
Beverly Hills

Creative directors
Sean Adams,
Noreen Morioka

Designers
Sean Adams, Noreen
Morioka, Volker Dürre,
David Van Riper,
Matthew Dunteman,
George Guzman

Print production Terry
Stone, Michelle Gray,
Karen Dragotto

Illustrators Chip Wass,
Michael Mabry

Writer Eric McPaul

On-air producer
Lu Olkowski

Audio Andy Caploe

Client Nickelodeon

2

BUY A XOOTR
ACCESSORIES
SERVICE
ABOUT US
XOOTR NEWS
EYE SPY XOOTR

URBAN
TRANSPORT

*This site provides detailed information on the Xootr scooter as well as a secure shopping cart for purchasing a scooter on-line. Xootr scooters are designed by a team of engineers with several years of experience in high-performance vehicle design and industrial designers with a sensitivity to the human and aesthetic qualities of products.*

When Xootr first launched, there wasn't time or budget for a traditional brand identity and marketing communications program. It was critical that any branding elements create an understanding of the Xootr brand as the "BMW of scooters" (as opposed to the Razor). At the product's launch, we intuitively aimed the graphics efforts toward males aged 17–24. As sales climbed, we found a majority of the buyers to be in the 25-35 age range. The same "extreme" aesthetic emphasizing speed and status was needed, but we added "urban landscape" as a literal and metaphoric background. The Xootr logo is designed with a mix of motion, nostalgia and performance in mind. Its unique word mark has the ability to live within a number of different environments; showing up in a single color on the deck and with more complex bracketing elements when shown in multiple colors on badges and labels.

Xootr
Scooter brand
development

Design firm
Lunar Design,
San Franc sco

Art director
Kristen Bailey

Designers
Becky Brcwn,
Florence Bautista

C ient
Nova Cruz
Products LLC

3

**H&R Block identity revitalization**

Design firm
Landor Associates,
San Francisco

Creative director
Margaret Youngblood

Senior design director
Eric Scott

Designers Kistina
Wong, Cameron
Imani, Tina Schoepflin,
Irena Blok, David
Rockwell, Mary Hayano

Writers
Daniel Meyerowitz,
Susan Manning

Account directors
Russ Meyer, Liz
Magnusson

Project management
Bill Larsen,
Stephen Lapaz

Realization
Tom Venegas

Client H&R Block

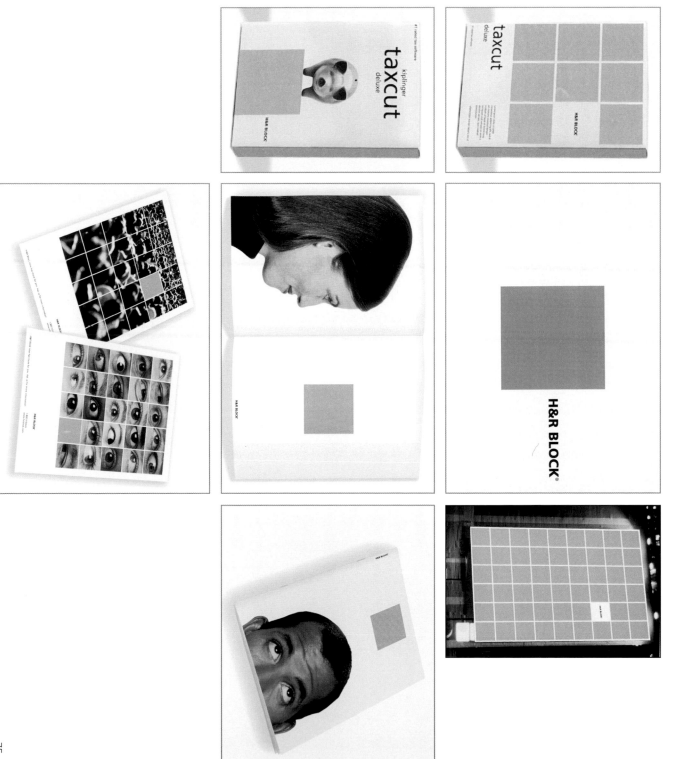

H&R Block was revitalizing its organization with a new vision to expand well beyond its traditional role as a reliable, approachable tax expert. Through acquisitions and new business development, H&R Block had developed a portfolio of diversified product and service offerings designed to meet all of the financial needs of current clients, as well as prospective clients. From home mortgages to financial planning and investing, H&R Block's vision was to become an approachable provider of financial services to Main Street America. Landor developed a new corporate identity system, anchored by the green block. The block – an obvious graphic representation of the company's name – expresses the solid relationship between H&R Block and its customers. Overall, the contemporary identity system communicates a dynamic, new and expanded H&R Block that is emotionally engaged with its financial services clients.

British Petroleum (EP) and Amoco merged in 1998 to form BP Amoco, which went on to acquire ARCO and Burmah Castrol. We recommended that BP be the name of the newly merged company: bold people, better products, big picture, beyond petroleum. The lowercase logotype makes a break from the past and is more modern, open and friendly. We also developed a symbol that communicated BP's commitment to environmental leadership and the development of alternative energies. The Helios mark reflects BP's determination to create products and services that respect human rights and the natural environment. The interlocking parts of the Helios mark form one vibrant whole, symbolizing the collective power of the individual companies coming together. The symbol also resembles the sun, a priority in BP's search for new sources of energy.

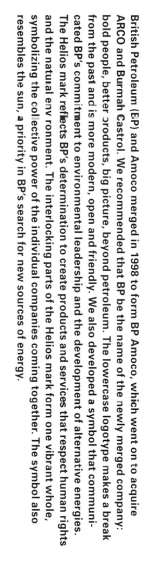

BP Amoco
merger identity

5

Design firm
Landor Associates,
San Francisco

Creative directors
Margaret Youngblood,
Nancy Hoefig,
Courtney Reeser

Senior brand strategist
Peter Harleman

Design director,
environments
David Zapata

Design director,
interactive Brad Scott

Designers Cynthia
Murnane, Todd True,
Frank Mueller, Michele
Berry, Cameron
Imani, Ivan Thelin,
Ladd Woodland,
Maria Wenzel

Writers Jane Bailey,
Susan Manning

Account director,
interactive Wendy Gold

Project management
Greg Barnell, Stephen
Lapaz, Bryan Vincent

Realization
Russell DeHaven

Client BP Amoco

**HP Invent
identity system**

Design firm
Landor Associates,
San Francisco

Creative director
Margaret Youngblood

Senior design director
Patrick Cox

Designers
Frank Mueller,
Paul Chock, Christian
Guler, Jean Loo

Writers Mark Welte,
Daniel Meyerovich,
Susan Manning

Account directors
Hunter Marshall, Peter
Mack, Brett Mangels,
Liz Magnusson

Project management
Scott Briefer

Realization
Wayne DeJager,
Brian Green, Monica
Lee, Rose Robinson,
Russell DeHaven,
Judy Wurstler,
Emma Rybakova

Client Hewlett-Packard
Company

The overarching goal for the HP identity program was to revitalize and reestablish Hewlett-Packard as the leading technology brand through a powerful, single brand identity. HP led this change with an advertising campaign by Goodby, Silverstein & Partners that included a new signature that simplified and added dimension to the familiar HP symbol, and a new clean and uncluttered typeface. With this foundation, Landor developed a system that is open and honest. The words and pictures that tell HP stories are captured in a holding device called an "idea unit," and the shape of this unit is founded on the rectilinear, soft-cornered shape of the familiar HP symbol. The distinctiveness and power of the design system comes from the orderly and purposeful repetition of this shape, a unique approach to imagery, a dynamic and broad color palette and the combination of clear yet thought-provoking words, graphics and images.

Audrey isn't a computer, it's an Internet appliance, and our challenge was to market sophisticated technology for the home in a distinctive and unintimidating way – to make people think of Audrey the way they would a dishwasher or toaster. We used neglected communication opportunities like the user manual and packaging to make even the most technology-challenged consumers comfortable with Audrey. The approach of engaging and explaining using clarity and wit was continued in point-of-sale displays designed to look like a slice of a kitchen, brochures covered in the familiar junk from kitchen drawers and invitations that used a blender to explain Audrey's functions. Packaging had to be merchandised on shelves of limited space so box height and depth were a concern. Also stackability, ease of shipping and ease of shelf replenishment were taken into consideration. We also worked with a packaging specialist to design the interior foam that protects Audrey.

7

**Audrey branding**

Design firm
Turner Duckworth,
San Francisco

Creative directors
David Turner, Bruce
Duckworth

Designers David Turner,
Mark Waters, Sara
Geroulis, Mary Foyder,
Allen Raulet, Jonathan
Warner, Lian Ng

Photographers
Stan Musilek, Lloyd
Hyrciw

Illustrator Brian Cronin

Client 3Com Corp.

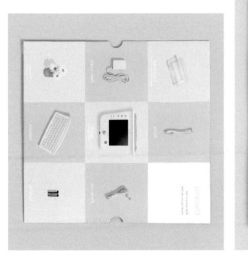

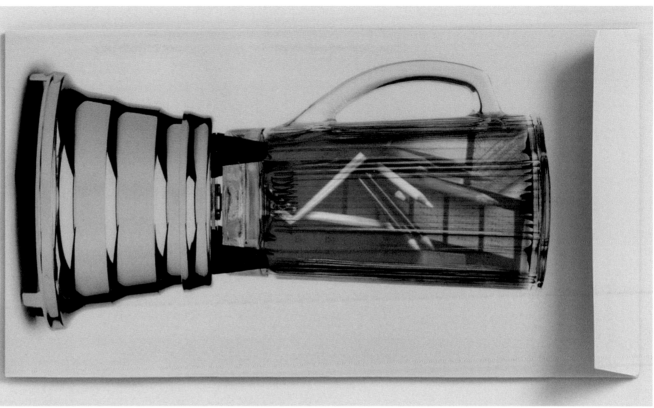

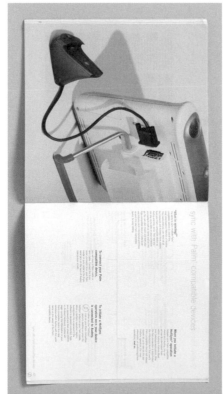

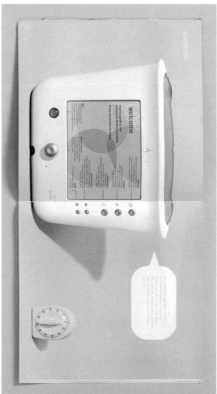

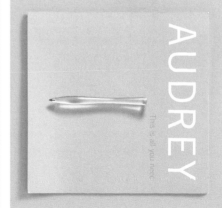

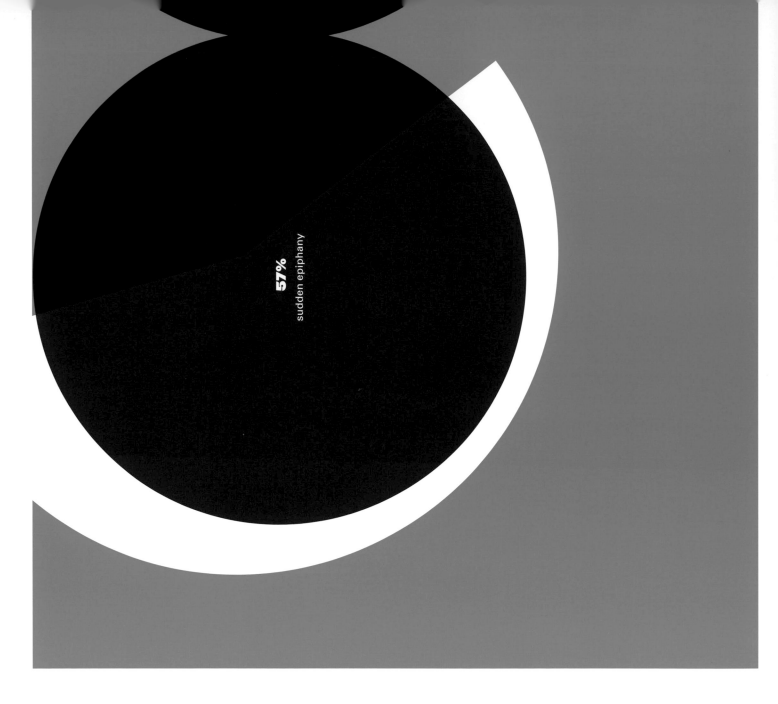

**57%**
sudden epiphany

Question P
Was the project's
design the result of a
sudden epiphany or
a slow build of small
alterations?

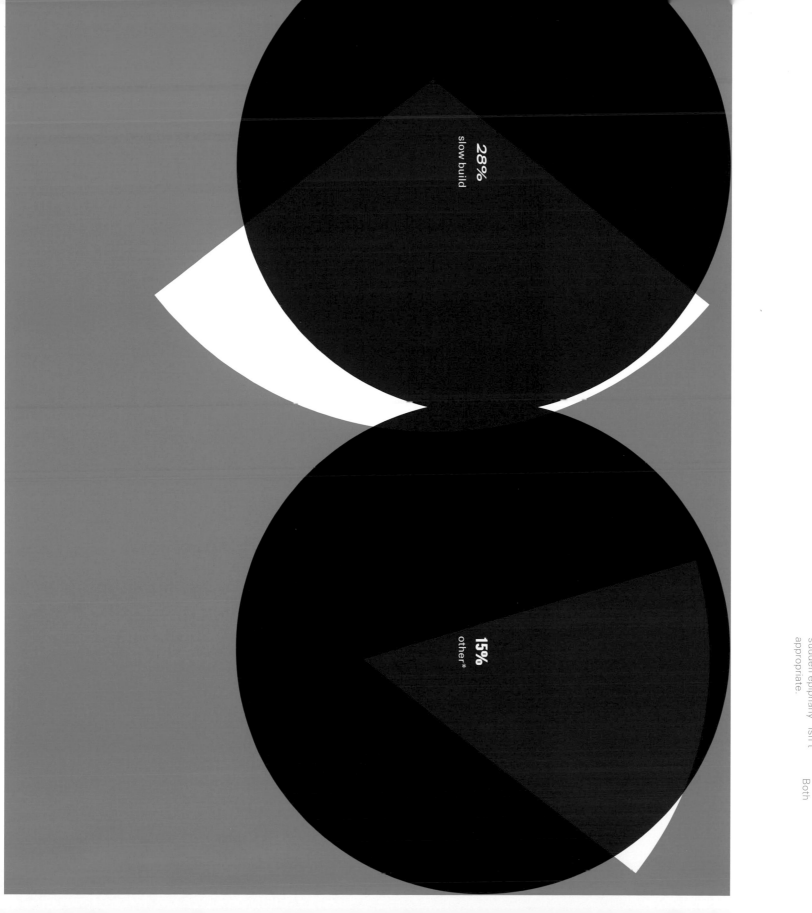

**28%**
slow build

**15%**
other*

* Other responses:

They are all fairly quick
due to budget: and
schedule — but most still
are developed with 2–3
concepts presented so
"sudden epiphany" isn't
appropriate.

"Sudden epiphany"
is way too swell, like
always I just did my
homework

Just the result
of lots of drawing

Both

# BRANDING APPLICATIONS

**Jurors Jack Anderson** Hornall/Anderson, Seattle **Michael Donovan** New York **Lana Rigsby** Rigsby Design, Houston

Branding has become increasingly important and diversified as companies and products vie for more share of customers' minds. Entries in this category should be thought of as brand experiences and could take the shape of packaging, identities, environments and experiences. They can represent newly developed brands, repositioned legacy brands or established brands evolving in new ways. Corporate identity campaigns, logos, stationery systems and annual reports should be entered in this category.

As companies and products vie for a greater share of customers' minds and pocketbooks, branding has become increasingly important and diversified. Indeed, "brand" seemed to be the buzzword of 2000, mainly used in the marketing industry and consequently spilling into the design field. Still, an absolute definition of what constitutes a brand continues to elude us.

This year, AIGA's call for entries directed entrants to think of branding applications as "brand experiences that could take the shape of packaging, identities, environments and experiences," and the jury embarked on its task of reviewing the 1,200 entries expecting to see work that portrayed the approach of a company toward its marketplace through stationery, signage, annual reports, websites and other vehicles of corporate identification. They were eager to see thoughtfully designed systems like those spun out by such highly visible companies as Red Envelope, IBM, PeopleSoft, Williams-Sonoma, Fidelity, Charles Schwab, Martha Stewart and Blue Fly. What they found instead were individual and isolated examples of corporate communications and consumer goods packaging.

A focused analysis of the call for entries left the jury to believe that the lack of actual systems was a consequence of the way the category was defined, which in turn made its task two-fold: making selections that were part of branding systems in absentia of the complete system and redefining the category so that the

Question G
While researching,
what–if anything–
did you do differently
from your normal
design process?

following year this problem would be avoided. Keeping this in mind, the 16 selections in the following pages represent outstanding examples of communications as part of larger branding systems.

One selection that clearly exemplifies this is VSA's annual report for IBM (cat. 23) – a piece of corporate communications that functions as part of a large branding system that we are all familiar with, but that was not entered. The type used on the cover and throughout the contents, the ubiquitous blue and the trendy yet corporate overall treatment of the piece relays IBM's entire branding strategy, even when seen by itself.

Doyle Partner's case study of the Martha Stewart packaging and store displays (cat. 16) was another example of a great piece of communication design. From the format – an elegant booklet with gatefold covers – to the muted color palette consistent with the Martha Stewart brand, every detail is thoroughly thought out without being over-designed.

The identity systems selected this year demonstrate a wide spectrum of possibilities; from utter simplicity and extraordinary execution, as is the case with AM ⊃M Design (cat. 14), Merge (cat. 12) and Red Canoe's stationery (cat. 11), which use bold colors and blind embossing with type only; to the creative use of photography where you would least expect it, as in the stationery for the Orthopaedic Surgery and Sports Medicine Specialists (cat. 10), which incorporates X-ray-reminiscent imagery. Duffy's color-coded stationery system (cat. 13) also demonstrates the successful integration of information design and corporate identity.

There are two hybrids among this year's selections. In the case of the direct mail piece for the de Young Museum in San Francisco's Golden Gate Park (cat. 15) and in the catalogue for Takashimaya (cat. 17), a high-end retail store in New York, the branding aspect is just as purposeful as the promotional intent. Although there is no doubt that these are paramount examples of communications that exude the originator's branding approach, an equally important purpose of

Response, cat. 22

## WE FORCED OURSELVES TO WRITE ABOUT THE COMPANY, ITS MESSAGE AND ITS INDUSTRY FOR TWO WEEKS BEFORE WE EVER SKETCHED A THING.

these pieces is to promote the services or products of the client institutions. The year 2000 showed relative economic well-being in the U.S., and the design field, as well as most sectors (at least at the beginning of the year), enjoyed an abundance of projects, generous budgets and clients who paid their bills. Perhaps this is the reason behind the dearth of self-promotional entries.

Consumer packaging entries presented another dilemma. The current structure of the competition binds packaging with branding applications, but the jury felt strongly about a need to separate them in the future. There were only two consumer packaging selections this year – NapaStyle (cat. 9) and Thomas E. Wilson Foods (cat. 8) – a worthy though narrow representation since these are both gourmet products sold in supermarkets. It would appear from these selections that luxury items are the only ones in which close attention has been paid to design. Taking into consideration that the volume of packaged goods to the consumer in the market is much larger than any of the other forms of branding selected, the representation is far from accurate.

Packaging is a vehicle for conveying brand identity that is as valid as any piece of corporate communications. A package designer must deal with a very precise and highly legislated host of requirements specific to this discipline, information that "outsiders" would never know. This is one of the reasons that AIGA has decided to hold a separate competition for packaging next year.

At the end of the day, it is still the consumer who decides where his or her loyalties lie. Then again, there's always design to persuade... Gabriela Mirensky

IBP approached Duffy about creating a brand of fresh and added-value meats, the first national brand for beef and pork. Our audience consists of mothers who are not always confident in knowing how to prepare meats correctly. A brand rooted in heritage, with a modern feel, was created and implemented in packaging, point-of-purchase displays and trucks. Many of the parameters are set by the food industry, including some type sizes, descriptors and package dimensions that conveniently fit in standard-sized freezers. We started with three viable, but different directions. The final solution combined elements of each.

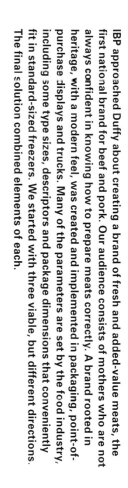

Thomas E. Wilson
Foods cooked
meat packaging

Design firm
Duffy Minneapolis

Creative director
Alan Colvin

Design director
Kobe Suvongse

Designers
Kobe Suvongse,
Joe Monnens,
Craig Duffney

Production artist
Mike White

Print production
Bridget Schumacher,
Anne Hughes

Photographer
Deborah Jones

Art buyer Katie Cook

Writers Mark Wirt,
Scott Barger

Client IBP, Inc.

NapaStyle is a specialty food and lifestyle product line, sold exclusively online and through a catalogue. The products are handcrafted to bring out the richness and quality that is synonymous with California's Napa Valley. NapaStyle needed to launch its product line as a unique brand in a highly competitive field. The goal was to establish a simple, emotional tie between these products and the customer. The design solution was to create a simple and elegant graphic system that ties together different product categories into a cohesive presentation. The system is flexible enough to work across a variety of unique bottle shapes and containers, allowing the product line to be expanded. We chose a color palette that reflects Napa Valley's balance of nature, and since the products are sold exclusively through the company catalogue and online, we were able to pursue more unconventional packaging solutions.

**NapaStyle packaging**

Design firm
Pentagram Design,
San Francisco

Art director Kit Hinrichs

Designer Erik Schmitt

Project manager
Jon Schleuning

Client NapaStyle

The challenge was to create an identity system that would be different from the typical clinical medical industry identities. The intention was to design a series that was inviting, with a classic/contemporary feel. The design used a six-color printing process to create the warm brown hues. The color palette and warm sepia-toned photography was selected as an inviting solution to the cooler hues more frequently found in the medical industry. Actual X-rays of various bones were tinted and used as the photography in the identity system, with the intention to portray the body as an art form in order to soften the medical experience. The versatility of the elements created numerous possibilities for design outcome. The business cards were designed as six different cards – each with a different bone. Each employee received multiple series of all six bones, which created additional flexibility and interaction.

**10**

**Orthopaedic
Surgery and Sports
Medicine Specialists
corporate identity**

Design firm
Renée Rech Design,
Norfolk, Virginia

Art director/designer
Renée Rech

Client Orthopaedic
Surgery and Sports
Medicine Specialists

A design cabin/studio in the woods above a river, Red Canoe incorporates both "work" and "play" into one existence, hence the evolution of the mission statement into the trademarked tag line of "as we live – so we work." The identity utilizes three warm colors used consistently, yet in both simple and bold contrasting manners. The actual red canoe in the identity is used sparingly, with more of a reliance on consistent type and color treatments to convey the Red Canoe identity. Words also proved to be a significant identity element. The various labels are used in a wide range of packaging applications; the "Connect" card functions equally well as a generic note card, thank-you card or as a large business card (with the Red Canoe mission statement printed on the back side). Other small cards carry the weight of many identity assignments.

**11**

**Red Canoe
identity system**

Design firm
Red Canoe, Deer
Lodge, Tennessee

Creative director
Deb Koch

Designer
Deb Koch

Writer Deb Koch

Client Red Canoe

In this stationery system we aimed to conceptually capture our multidisciplinary nature and the intelligent and unique approach we take to our craft. We wanted a completely modular letterhead system that could also serve as a sales or proposal kit. We developed a series of stickers that were half verbs and half nouns. The verbs and nouns could be combined in dozens of ways allowing each combination to communicate a relevant idea about our approach. This system allows us to customize and tailor virtually every component of our stationery system to fit the application and the audience. We devised multiple die cuts and perfs to accommodate sales information, personal memos and business cards. If the kit is used for a proposal, the perf enables people to tear off the proposal portion to file or pass around.

**12**

**Merge Inc.
identity system**

Design firm
Merge, Atlanta

Art director
Ash Arnett

Creative director
Michael Taylor

Designers Ali Harper,
Rebecca Klein

Illustrator
Rebecca Klein

A name change from Duffy Design to Duffy and global expansion was the catalyst for rebranding Duffy's stationery system. Past equities of the prior system, such as the metal card, were retained while the entire system was modernized. The Duffy stationery system consists of a color-coded translucent envelope that reveals the office location, and a letterhead that is die-cut to insure quick and accurate folding and filing.

**Duffy identity system**

Design firm
Duffy Minneapolis
Creative director
Alan Colvin

Designers
Alan Leusink,
Tom Riddle

Print production
Bridget Schumacher,
Becky Arrell

Production artist
Tracy Hogenson

Client Duffy

**13**

The purpose of this project was to update an existing identity by embracing a new philosophy of transition, mobility and forward thinking while maintaining the company name. The original mark was an icon combination of a sun and moon representing day and night to represent AM PM Design. The new mark consists of three individual circles that illustrate the transition from sun to moon in a vertical plane. It was a challenge to introduce the new mark to our existing clients without causing confusion or concern. That vehicle of introduction came from the mark itself – a mobile of the three circles that represent the new mark.

**14**

**AM PM Design
identity system**

Design firm
AM PM Design,
Centreville, Virginia

Designer/writer
Tamera Lawrence

This direct-mail brochure was designed in response to public comment on the proposed plans for the new de Young Museum in San Francisco's Golden Gate Park. The idea "We've Listened" acknowledges that the architects, contractors and curators have implemented the public's ideas and that the new museum will be a place for everyone.

We've listened.

**de Young Museum brochure**

15

*Design firm*
Cahan and Associates,
San Francisco

*Creative director*
Bill Cahan

*Designer*
Michael Braley

*Project manager*
Katie Kniestedt

*Illustrators*
Nanette Biers,
Walter Hood

*Photographer*
Jock McDonald

*Writers*
Peterson Skolnick,
Dodge

*Client*
de Young Museum

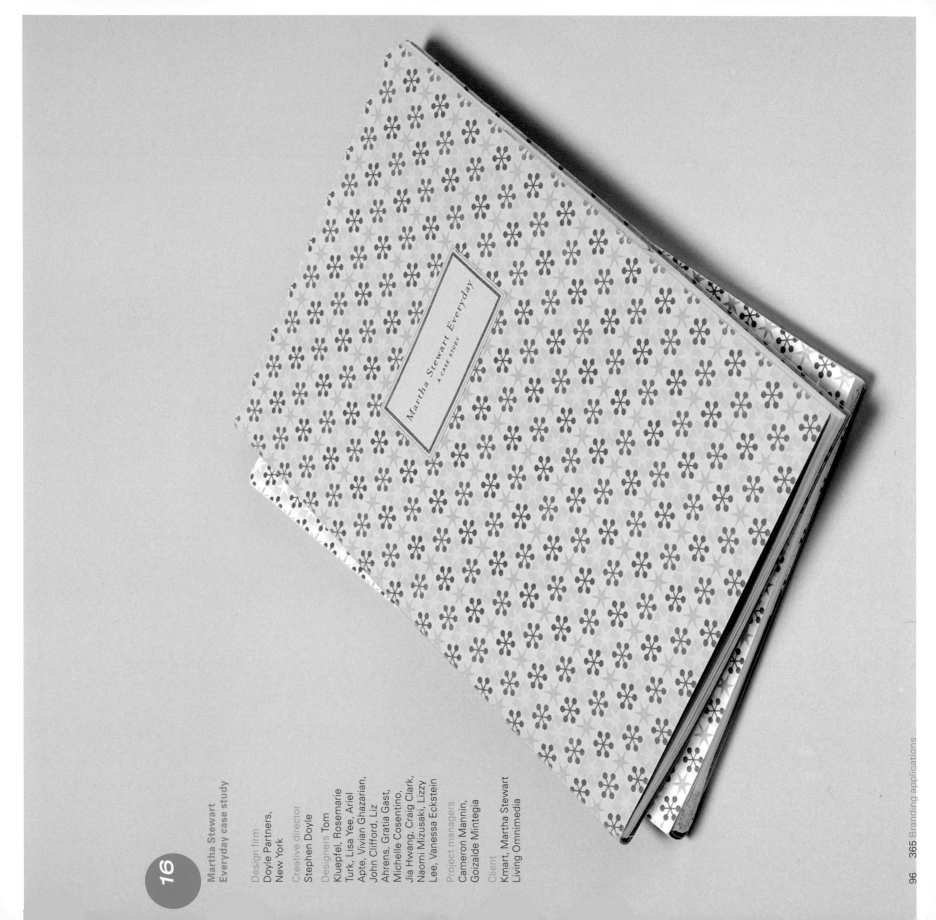

**16**

**Martha Stewart**
**Everyday case study**

Design firm
Doyle Partners,
New York

Creative director
Stephen Doyle

Designers Tom
Kluepfel, Rosemarie
Turk, Lisa Yee, Ariel
Apte, Vivian Ghazarian,
John Clifford, Liz
Ahrens, Gratia Gast,
Michelle Cosentino,
Jia Hwang, Craig Clark,
Naomi Mizusaki, Lizzy
Lee, Vanessa Eckstein

Project managers
Cameron Mannin,
Goizalde Mintegia

Client
Kmart, Martha Stewart
Living Omnimedia

The mission was to create a visual identity and cohesive packaging program for thousands of products made by hundreds of vendors that explains the product assortment, highlights the beautiful product design and is "magnetic" to shoppers in Kmart's mass-market environment. The Martha Stewart Everyday design program is comprised of a simple logo and an overall clarity that is synonymous with Martha Stewart's brand, all delivered in a wide assortment of bold colors and accessible type. Packaging was constructed to highlight the product attributes, allowing light to shine through the glassware packages, letting customers feel the weight of flatware or even presenting uninterrupted surfaces of plates in a subtle range of colors. The sheer volume of the Kmart housewares department allows numerous 40-foot runs of products, a branding reinforcement unsurpassed in the industry.

Doyle Partners created the graphic identity for the Martha Stewart Everyday brand in 1997. Since the launch, we've created extensive packaging, in-store signage and shopping environments as the brand rapidly grew.

As a brand, Martha Stewart Everyday is equal parts information and inspiration; the package design

brings these core concepts to the retail experience. Simple typography, beautiful colors and accessible design show each product to its best advantage. Carefully conceived bright photography and information such as recipes, how to's, and cross merchandising references educate shoppers and encourage them to enjoy and explore the brand.

In a mass-market category, the authority and exuberance of the Martha Stewart Everyday packaging commands consumer attention and trust—and record-breaking sales. In just three years, the program has achieved annual sales of $1.4 billion.

Takashimaya is a unique shopping environment, and each year we endeavor to make the catalogue an experience to savor. Our aim this year was to create a journey through a discrete world. Various short sheets and die cuts create a cinematic continuum, a quiet accretion of insights. The resulting juxtapositions allow for new combinations of textures and products, embodying the retail experience of the store. The papers were chosen to reflect the myriad textures and neutral tonality for which Takashimaya's merchandise mix is known. The subtle shifts in sheen, sparkle, translucency and iridescence also contribute to the fluidity of the brochure.

**Takashimaya
Volume 8
catalogue**

Design firm
Design: MW, New York

Creative directors
Allison Williams,
J.P. Williams

Art director
Allison Williams

Designers Allison
Williams, Yael Eisele

Photographer
Gentl and Hyers

Writer Laura Silverman

Client Takashimaya
New York

17

When 3Com came to us to do the report, the company had just finished launching its new brand personality. With that new brand came a new message of "Radical Simplicity" that needed to be conveyed to shareholders, customers and employees. The contents of the report had to include 3Com's product, customers and new message. Our concept, "Radical Simplicity, Rich Connectivity," illustrated how things we take for granted everyday are actually very complicated and, like technology, took many years to develop into their current simple forms. 3Com products have become equally transparent in our lives, due to the fact they are so simple to use. We confirmed that fact through customer testimonials that followed the big-picture message.

Radical Simplicity,
Rich Connectivity

18

**3Com 2000
annual report**

Design firm Howry
Design Associates,
San Francisco

Art director Jill Howry

Designer Calvin Jung

Print production
Shellie Cohen

Photographer
Tom Feiler

Writer Ethan Place

Client
3Com Corporation

MATCH.
Fusing wood
and sulfur to
light a fire.

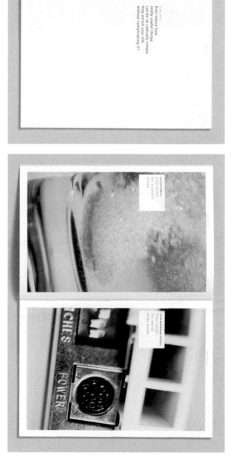

Ever notice how
really useful things
can be so radically simple
they enrich your life
without complicating it?

3COM IP TELEPHONY.
Fusing voice
and data
to spark
productivity.

At-a-Glance

$3.3 billion in FY2000 ongoing sales
$3.1 billion in cash and short-term investments
400+ million customer connections
47 million hits per month at www.3com.com
10,597 employees around the globe
163 worldwide locations
48 countries of operation
356 U.S. patents issued

Consumer Market

year in review

arrivals

a brief history of how the international terminal came to be

04 | 1992

11 | 1997

gate

The San Francisco International Airport 2000 annual report commemorates the opening of the new international terminal. Morla Design documented a visual history of airport construction milestones over the past eight years. The "pocketbook" size format is a compendium of site photos, art installations, icons and graphs that highlight the building's progress and completion.

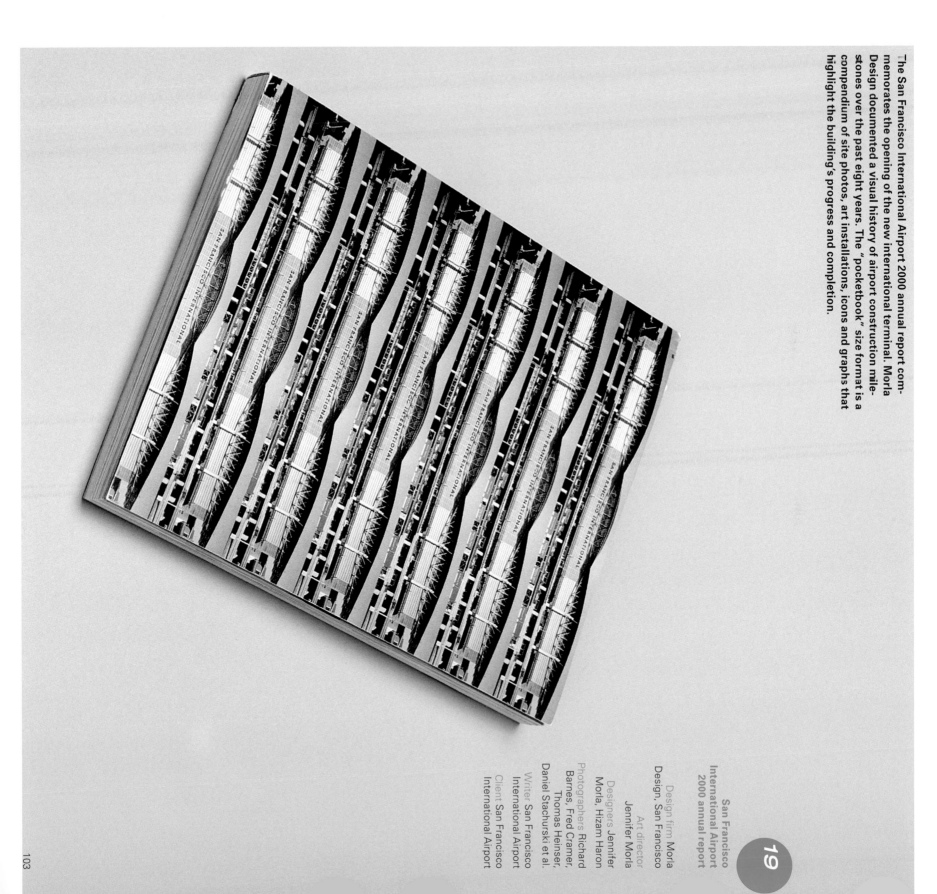

San Francisco
International Airport
2000 annual report

Design firm Morla
Design, San Francisco

Art director
Jennifer Morla

Designers Jennifer
Morla, Hizam Haron

Photographers Richard
Barnes, Fred Cramer,
Thomas Heinser,
Daniel Stachurski et al.

Writer San Francisco
International Airport

Client San Francisco
International Airport

20

**The George Gund Foundation 1999 annual report**

Design firm Nesnadny + Schwartz, Cleveland

Creative director Mark Schwartz

Designer Michelle Moehler

Photographer Douglas Lucak

Writers David Bergholz, Deena Epstein

Client The George Gund Foundation

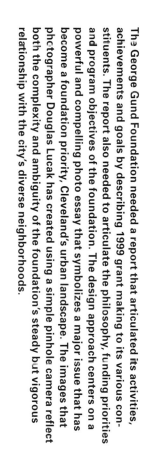

The George Gund Foundation needed a report that articulated its activities, achievements and goals by describing 1999 grant making to its various constituents. The report also needed to articulate the philosophy, funding priorities and program objectives of the foundation. The design approach centers on a powerful and compelling photo essay that symbolizes a major issue that has become a foundation priority, Cleveland's urban landscape. The images that photographer Douglas Lucak has created using a simple pinhole camera reflect both the complexity and ambiguity of the foundation's steady but vigorous relationship with the city's diverse neighborhoods.

This annual report uses the beautiful detail inherent in Swiss Army Brands' products to deliver the message that the company is paying close attention in all aspects of product design and operations. The book's diminutive format adds to the "details" theme. The final report is identical to the original concept.

**21**

**Swiss Army Brands Inc. 1999 annual report**

Design firm
SamataMason, Inc.,
Dundee, Illinois

Art director
Dave Mason

Designers
Pamela Lee,
Dave Mason

Print production
Pamela Lee

Photographer Victor
John Penner

Writer Steve Zousmer

Client Swiss Army
Brands Inc.

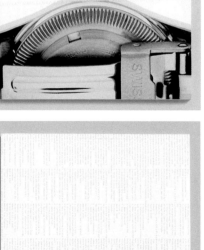

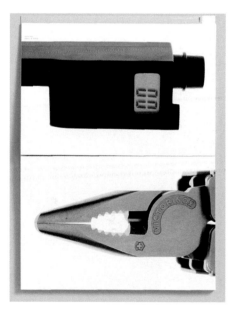

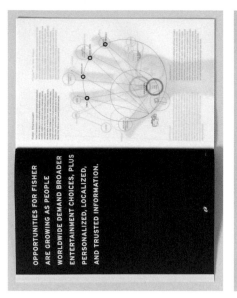

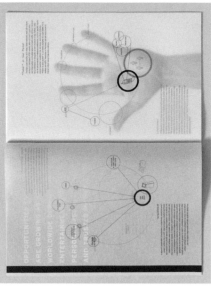

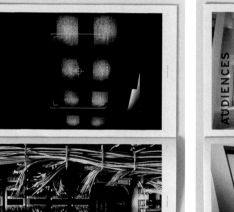

The goal in this project was to produce the 1999 annual report for an audience consisting of investment analysts, shareholders and employees. Historically, Fisher has been involved in several disparate businesses. Recently, it has focused on becoming solely a communications and media company. Our idea was to create a manifesto-like report that acts to unequivocally clarify where the company is headed, what business it's in and where the potential opportunities lie. Limited color, gritty photos and newsprint-like paper are used as signals for a company reinventing itself. A bold pictorial section describes industry conditions and opportunities, while a diagram deconstructs itself, page by page, in a section of vellum overlays.

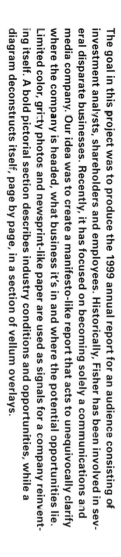

FISHER COMPANIES INC. ANNUAL REPORT

WE ARE
SHARPENING
OUR FOCUS.

WE ARE
BROADENING
OUR REACH.

**Fisher 1999
annual report**

Design firm
The Leonhardt
Group, Seattle

Art director
Steve Watson

Designers
Steve Watson,
Ben Graham

Project manager
Lori Kent

Photographer
Don Mason, stock

Writers Steve Watson,
Chris Wheeler

Client
Fisher Companies, Inc.

22

23

IBM 2000
annual report

Design firm
VSA Partners, Inc.,
Chicago

Creative directors
Curt Schreiber,
Jeff Walker

Designers
Scott Hickman,
Michelle Platts

Photographer
Christian Witkin

Client/publisher
IBM

2000 the IT industry was going through a volatile and transformational year. IBM partnered with VSA to develop a "story" that captured this wild roller-coaster ride – a story that only a company with the breadth, depth and technological presence of IBM could tell. Working with IBM, VSA created a novel approach to the report, capturing the spirit of the industry and one year in the life of a company within it by building a colorful and engaging story that highlights IBM'ers who are facing a wide range of challenges, battles and successes. Simple, clean typography offers a classic approach with contemporary energy, coupled with artwork that opens up grand themes in each of the five chapters. The report has both a traditional tone of IBM stability and a contemporary energy that captures the dynamics of the world's largest IT company.

THE LEADER'S
DILEMMA

CHAPTER 1

REPORTS OF OUR
DEMISE

IN MARKETS WE ONCE LED
(OR SHOULD HAVE)—HIGH-END STORAGE,
UNIX SERVERS AND DATABASE
SOFTWARE—WE'RE BATTLING BACK
AND MAKING UP LOST GROUND.

$77

$69

$70

$5

$0

28%

221%

Question M
On a scale of 0–10,
how much did
budget affect this
project's design?
0 = no effect
10 = total effect

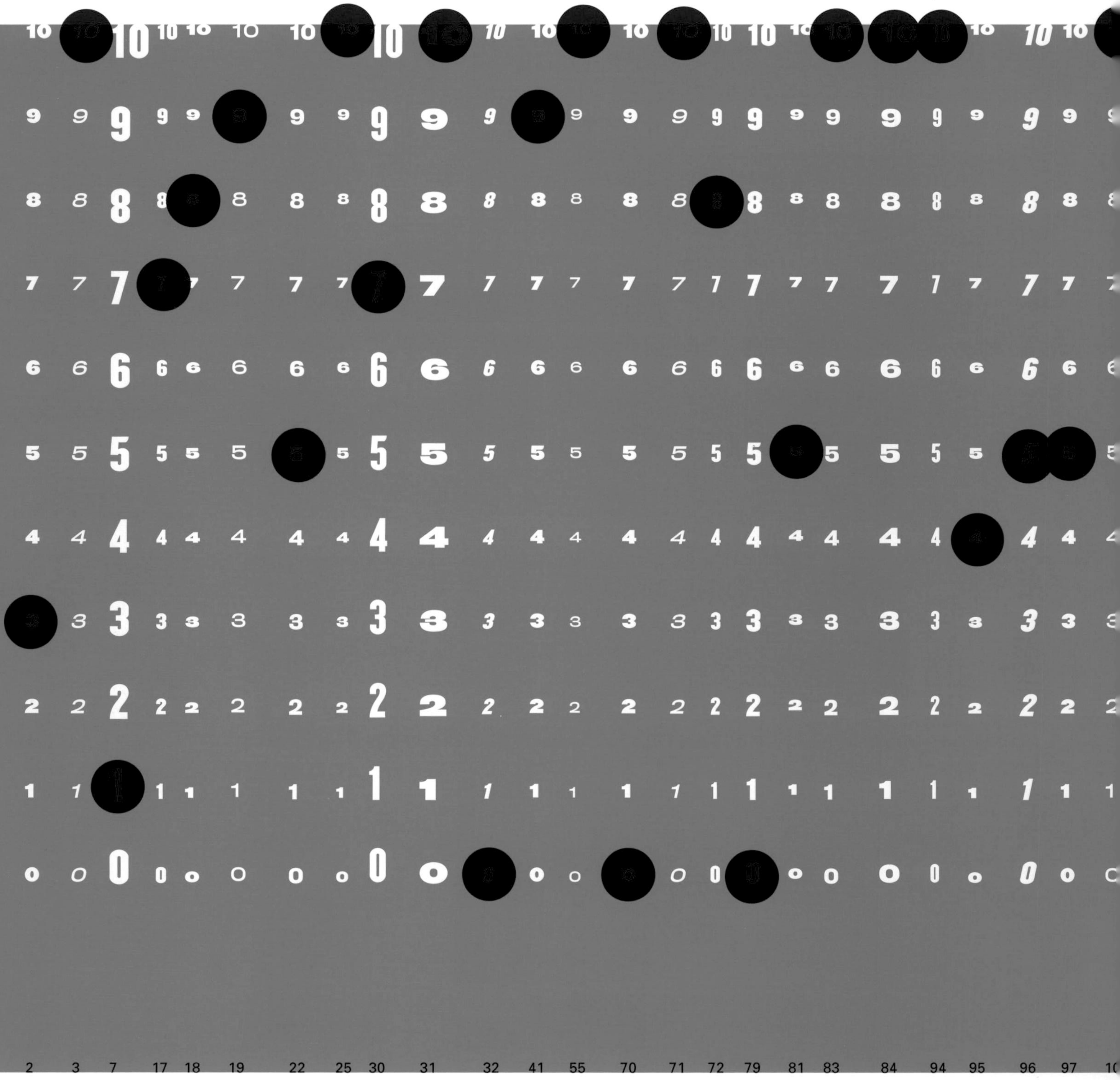

2 3 7 17 18 19 22 25 30 31 32 41 55 70 71 72 79 81 83 84 94 95 96 97 100

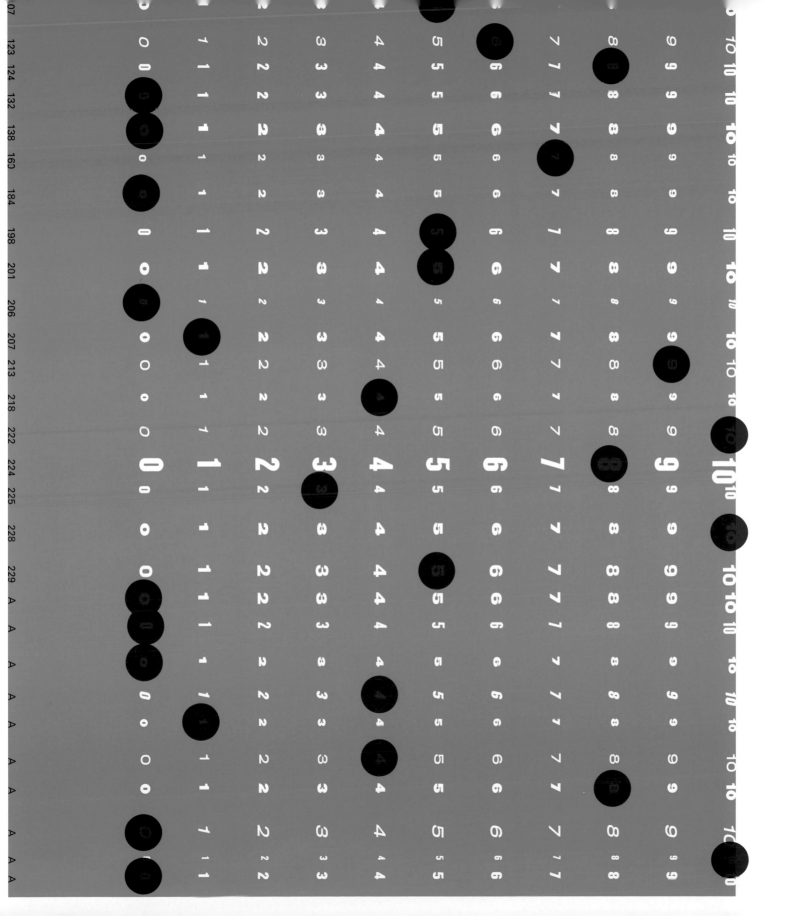

Jurors **Michael Ian Kaye**
Ogilvy & Mather, New
York **Lana Rigsby** Rigsby
Design, Houston

The jurors of this category
will consider work in which
the primary purpose is to
introduce, sell or display a
product, idea, concept or
company. Print ads, interactive banners, press kits,
giveaways, posters, invitations, announcements,
merchandise catalogues
and the like are eligible.

The past few years have shown a remarkable pendulum swing toward the use of subtle, elegant gestures in the world of advertising – a distinctly commercial neo-minimalism in the service of corporate culture that has featured clean type, docu-mentary photography and an abundance of white space. (Just think of anything from IBM's campaign.) This year's competition results, however, reveal a visual sea change. Suddenly, there are little tears in the surface of modernism's deadpan perfection that reveal idiosyncratic tendencies and an increasing preference for work that bears the mark of the hand.

"There's a lot of expressionistic movement," pointed out Michael Ian Kaye of this year's 17 selections. "It's a reaction to minimalism. I bet we'll be seeing Victorian all over again." While Victorian style has not yet emerged in full force, James Victore's recruiting piece for Atlanta's Portfolio Center (cat. 37) demonstrates what could best be called the new maximalism. Measuring in excess of 23 by 16 inches and bearing hand-scribbled text, eclectic imagery and Victore's hallmark visceral illustrations, this brochure-writ-large avoids what the jurors termed the "typical art school trope." "It does a great job of conveying a big personality," noted Rigsby. "It's clearly going to take up the most real estate on the table, which will garner it a lot of attention."

This is not to say that minimalism hasn't had a lasting effect on the current visual

Question G
While researching,
what–if anything–
did you do differently
from your normal
design process?

# I CONCEPTUALIZED OUTSIDE THE FRAME.

Response, cat. 31

environment. "There's not one piece here that has type touching type or layering," said Kaye of the 17 selections. "Only five of these pieces have a four-color process or higher," Rigsby added. "Almost everything is in a limited palette and really simple." Notable for its combination of restraint and exuberance was the Fall/Holiday Nike ACG catalogue (cat. 38), which impressed jurors with its muted palette of blues, yellows and moss, robust vertical navigation system and tactile butcher paper. "To me, this is well done in the same way that the Takashimaya catalogues are," noted Rigsby, "there's more design sensibility that went into this than had to. It makes you feel that every detail of the products will be imbued with the same sensibility, whether it contributes to the performance or not."

Also indicative was Slaughter Hanson's Simple Truths (cat. 40), an annual report for the Greater Alabama Council of the Boy Scouts of America. A small blue book that bears beautiful black-and-white photos of scouts of all ages contrasted with graphic overlays and icons for virtues like courage (Superman), loyalty (Lassie) and strength (Popeye), the annual report impressed jurors with its design integrity and high aesthetic values. The fact that the organization has taken a public stance against homosexuals, however, led the jurors to debate the merits of projects that are, in Kaye's words, "so beautiful, but so politically incorrect." Rigsby admitted that she would never let cigarette packaging into a show, no matter how beautifully designed it was; Kaye – admittedly a smoker – said he would, although he was reluctant in this instance to award a project that so went against one of this country's most valued virtues: tolerance.

More remarkable than maximalism or the remaining traces of minimalism, however, was the predominance of silkscreened pieces – an astonishing six in all. The return of serigraphy seems poetic and entirely appropriate, given its origins as the country's first explicitly commercial medium. (Although silkscreening goes back 2,000 years, it was first patented in this country in 1908 and used for making posters advertising the San Francisco Flag Company.) Long a favored medium in college print shops and artist studios, silkscreening has been considered rough and somehow vulgar in recent years, which makes its triumph, according to the jurors, all the sweeter. This year's "sleeper" selection was a series of flash-card promotions for a screenprinting company called Art Real (cat. 32) – a traditionally lowly trade with high aesthetic standards. Made of cheap, stiff cardboard that bear green, blue and yellow shapes reminiscent of Joan Miró and Paul Rand, the cards charmed the jurors. "I like that it's done in a material that a lot of designers would say 'Ick' about," commented Rigsby. "And this kind of funky, jiggy typography goes really well with being silkscreened. I love it." Silkscreening seems to be a particularly good vehicle for subversion, or so it was in the case of one particular poster (cat. 24) advertising a spring show at the CAE art gallery in Fort Greene, Brooklyn, that matched elements of Massimo Vignelli modernism and, well, personal anatomy. "It's the triumph of information graphics," said Rigsby, tongue firmly in cheek, of the subway map knock-off that, upon close inspection, turns out to exchange the southern tip of Manhattan and Brooklyn for the male member. "It falls into that category that we shouldn't like," added Kaye, "but it's got so much whimsy that we haven't seen lately." Andrea Codrington

The task was to design an eye-catching poster for Cosmic Art Enterprises' art show in spring 2000. The well-known New York subway map was altered by replacing New York City with a scientific illustration of male genitals. While the conception took only one hour of desperate staring at a map in a deserted New York Subway station at 4 a.m., finishing the design in an accurate way required a lot more patience.

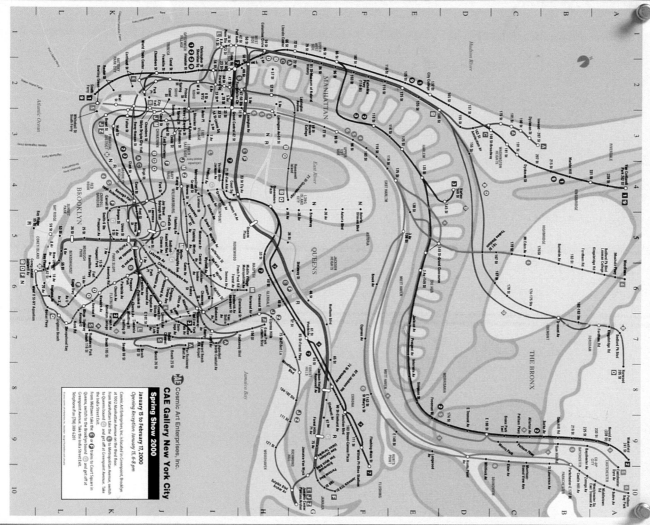

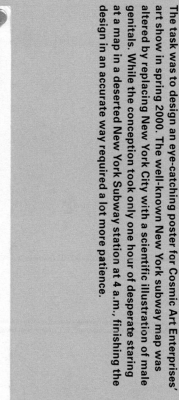

CAE Spring Show
2000 announcement

24

Design firm
Cosmic Art Enterprises,
Inc., Brooklyn

Illustrator/designer
Veit Schuetz

**For this assignment Parsons needed a poster announcing the dates/degree offerings for the semester and art that echoed its new spring catalogue. I wanted the design to induce general creative thought yet reflect the school's maverick program. Since it was going to be a small run, we opted to silkscreen, posting several on the street and selling the rest to recoup the cost.**

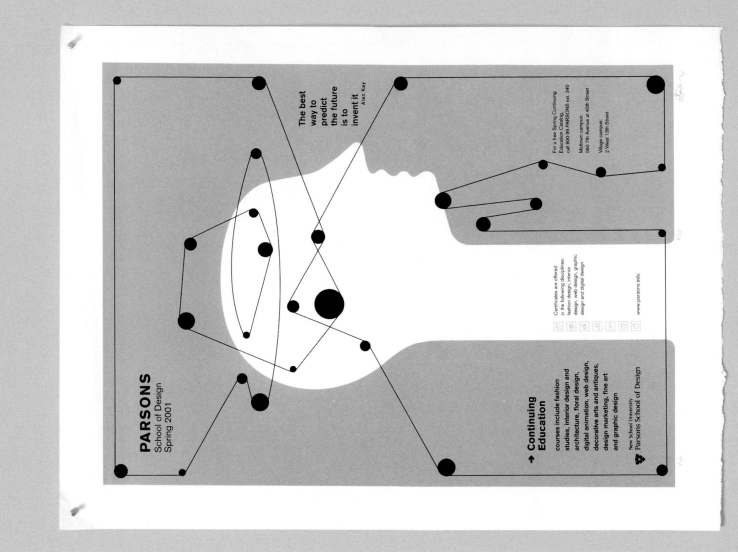

**25**

**Parsons Spring
2001 poster**

Design firm
Felixsockwell.com,
New York

Art director Evelyn Kim

Designer/Illustrator
Felix Sockwell

Client Parsons School
of Design

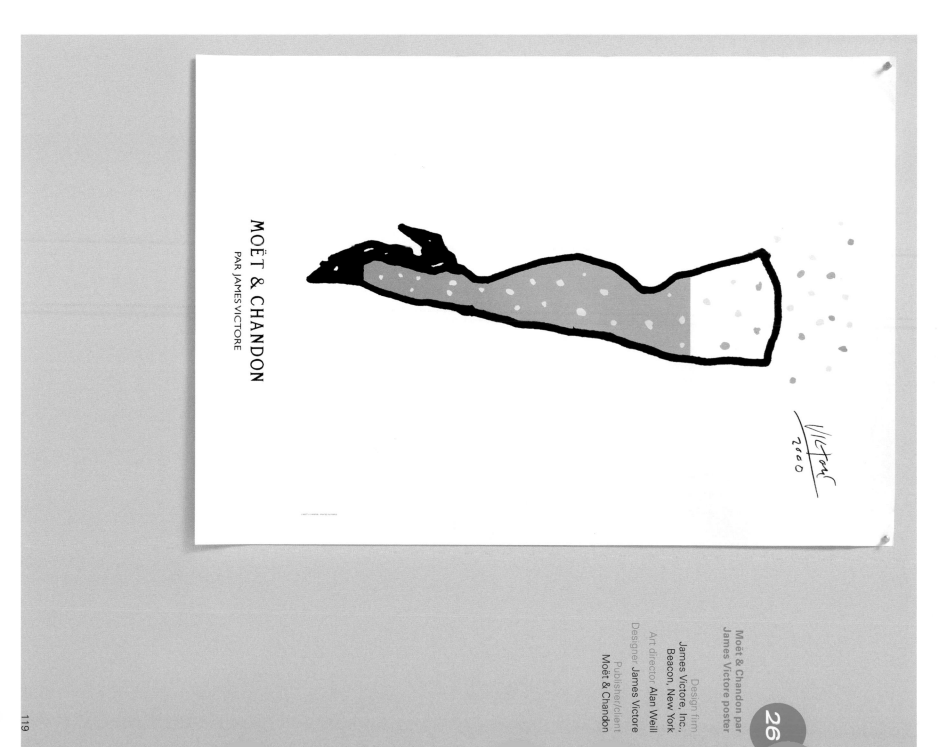

**MOËT & CHANDON**

PAR JAMES VICTORE

Moët & Chandon par
James Victore poster

Design firm
James Victore, Inc.,
Beacon, New York

Art director Alan Weill

Designer James Victore

Publisher/client
Moët & Chandon

26

The design problem was to create a poster that promoted a concert at the University of Wisconsin by the band Spoon. Taking cues from one of the band's songs, "The Fitted Shirt," which speaks of longing for simpler times, the vintage illustration of the shirt was an easy choice. The intentional disconnect of the image of a shirt and the word "Spoon" ultimately made this poster memorable to students and faculty. The poster had to be created on almost no budget, and was limited to two colors to be screen printed. Since I was allowed total creative freedom, the end product was consistent with the original concept.

**27**

Spoon poster

Design firm
Planet Propaganda,
Madison, Wisconsin

Designer
Michael Byzewski

Client University
of Wisconsin

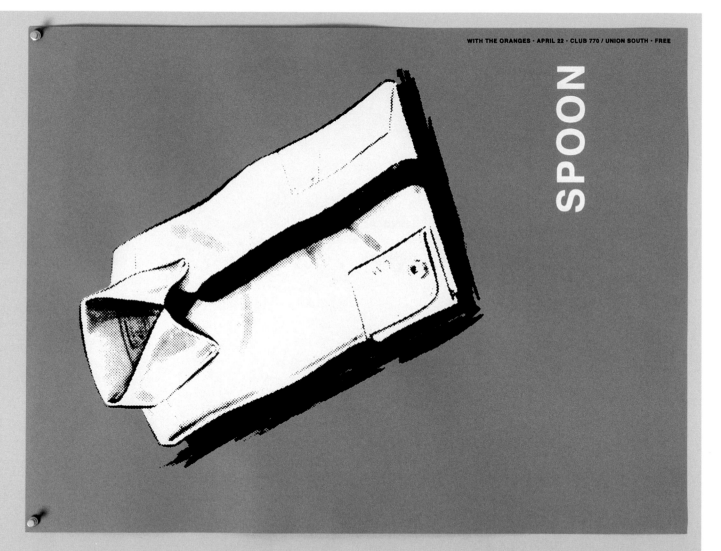

WITH THE ORANGES · APRIL 22 · CLUB 770 / UNION SOUTH · FREE

SPOON

I was asked by a friend to design some posters for a series of plays written by one of her colleagues. The plays dealt with various issues affecting young adults. Jack's Destiny portrays the story of a young man whose involvement with a drug-addicted friend leads him to an unfortunate and early demise. Since these posters were to be distributed on local college campuses, they needed to make a strong visual impact and attract the attention of this young demographic audience. The use of simple line illustrations set on a solid field of color cuts through the usual advertising clutter and gives the posters a strong visual presence.

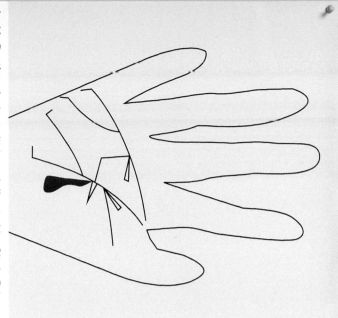

**Jack's Destiny.** A play written and directed by Gloria Prieto. Lee Park • San Antonio, Texas • Friday August 18, 2000 Free Admission • 8:00PM — 10:00PM

*Jack's Destiny*
poster

Design firm
Edward Tamez,
San Antonio, Texas
Art director/designer
Edward Tamez
Illustrator
Edward Tamez
Writer Gloria Prieto
Client Nicole Kobs

---

I was asked by a friend to design some posters for a series of plays written by one of her colleagues. The plays dealt with various issues affecting young adults. Falling For Her depicts a man wandering through life searching for the answers to his obsession with the opposite sex. Since these posters were to be distributed on local college campuses, they needed to make a strong visual impact and attract the attention of this young demographic audience. The use of simple line illustrations set on a solid field of color cuts through the usual advertising clutter and gives the posters a strong visual presence.

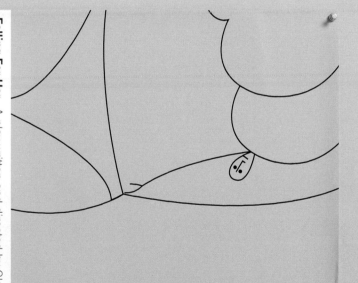

**Falling For Her.** A play written and directed by Gloria Prieto. Lee Park • San Antonio, Texas • Friday August 4, 2000 Free Admission • 8:00PM — 10:00PM

*Falling For Her*
poster

Design firm
Edward Tamez,
San Antonio, Texas
Art director/designer
Edward Tamez
Illustrator
Edward Tamez
Writer Gloria Prieto
Client Nicole Kobs

**This invitation announces "Design Culture Now," a lecture at MIT's Media Lab presented by Ellen Lupton, adjunct curator at the Cooper-Hewitt Design Museum. Using the medium as the message, the post-it note contains all the essential information (allowing the receiver to stick it directly onto his/her date book or computer monitor) and also serves as a commentary on information overload in contemporary culture.**

**The poster's intention was to create awareness of the future release of the band Feathered's audio recording entitled Where The Better Half Live. The poster's development was to be cost considerate, as there was nearly no budget. The first run was a lithograph, which was printed by hand, producing some rich and textured results. From the initial first run, the printing preference of black ink on white Mylar was established. The poster was later reprinted commercially, maintaining the original parameters.**

---

**30**

**Lupton Lecture invite**

Design firm
Visual Dialogue, Boston

Art director
Fritz Klaetke

Designers
Fritz Klaetke, Ian Varrassi

Client AIGA/Boston

**31**

*Where The Better Half Live* poster

Design firm
Vanka, Montreal

Creative director/ designer
Matthew Vanka

Print production
Matthew Vanka, Danielle Belanger

Client Feathered

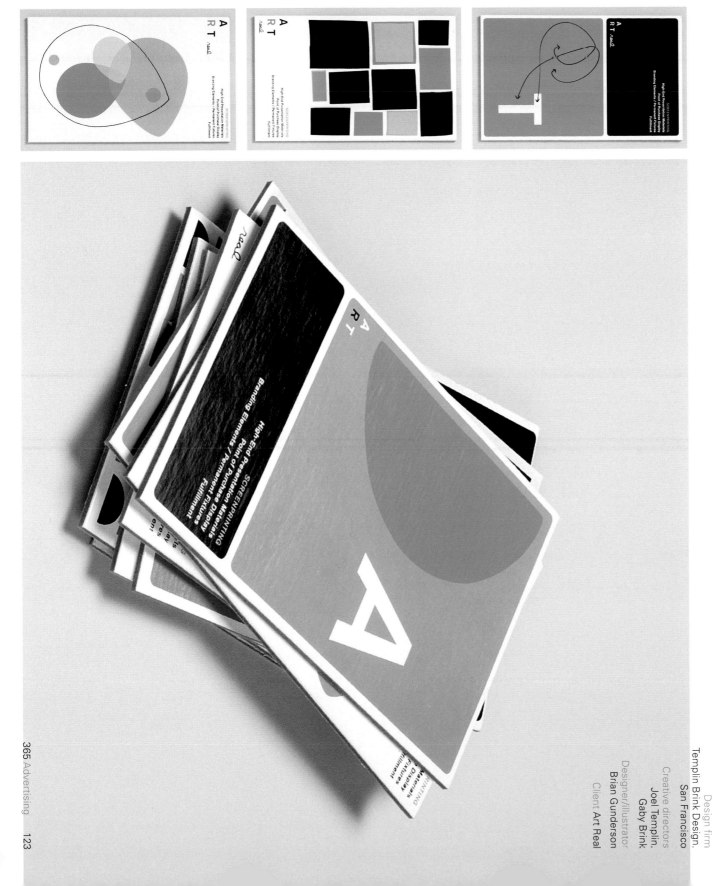

Art Real, a screen printer, approached us for a promotional campaign that could be used over the next year. Given that there were no parameters – except that it had to be screen printed – and limitless creative freedom, we came up with more than 100 directions that were ultimately narrowed down to 12 different postcards. They were printed on a heavy industrial chip board to give the promotion some keepsake value for existing and potential clients.

**Art Real postcards**

Design firm
Templin Brink Design,
San Francisco

Creative directors
Joel Templin,
Gaby Brink

Designer/Illustrator
Brian Gunderson

Client Art Real

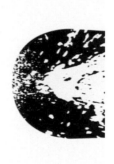

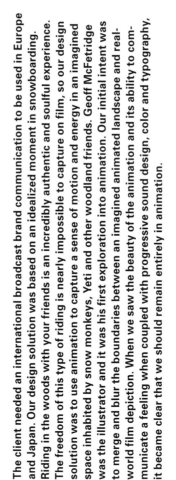

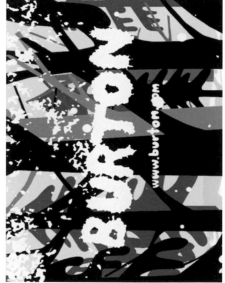

**33**

**Burton "Snow Monkey" animated advertisement**

Design firm Jager Di Paola Kemp Design, Burlington, Vermont

Creative director
Michael Jager

Art director/designer
Jared Eberhardt

Project manager
Leslie E. Dowe

Illustrator/animator
Geoff McFetridge

Producer
Leslie E. Dowe

Client
Burton Snowboards

The client needed an international broadcast brand communication to be used in Europe and Japan. Our design solution was based on an idealized moment in snowboarding. Riding in the woods with your friends is an incredibly authentic and soulful experience. The freedom of this type of riding is nearly impossible to capture on film, so our design solution was to use animation to capture a sense of motion and energy in an imagined space inhabited by snow monkeys, Yeti and other woodland friends. Geoff McFetridge was the illustrator and it was his first exploration into animation. Our initial intent was to merge and blur the boundaries between an imagined animated landscape and real-world film depiction. When we saw the beauty of the animation and its ability to communicate a feeling when coupled with progressive sound design, color and typography, it became clear that we should remain entirely in animation.

Our intent was to create a website that was both informative and easy to use and an active experiment in interactivity that demonstrated the power with which mathematics drives programming and design. The fact that the website was our own made it intensely difficult to be satisfied with the final product. Knowing that it was going to be a promotional tool that marketed us to unknown individuals, we wanted and expected the website to represent the best quality we are capable of. As a result, we took several months to complete the project and came out with a finished site that was better than we had ever imagined possible.

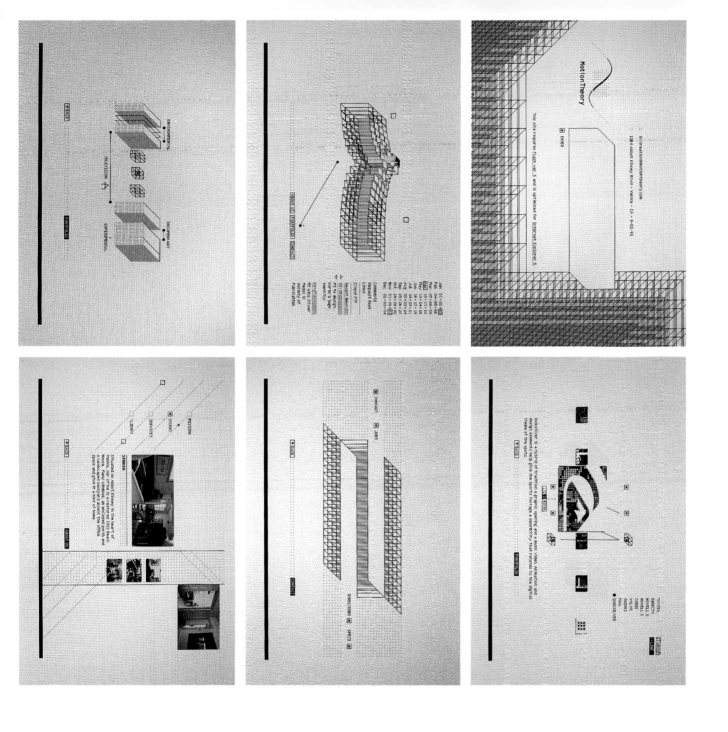

Design firm
Motion Theory, Venice,
California

Creative director
Mathew Cullen

Designers Mathew
Cullen, Ryan Alexander

Photographer
Javier Jimenez

Writer Carm Goode

Programmer
Ryan Alexander

Client Motion Theory

Target approached Kirshenbaum about the creation of a campaign that would help build its image as an upscale, trendy retailer to an audience that might not have traditionally considered Target cool. One specific goal was to showcase fashion items to an urbane audience that was not aware of Target, or did not even think of it previously as fashionable. The ads feature everyday items that combine with each other and play off the model in a novel way: a sleeping bag as a skirt; a vacuum cleaner as a set of bagpipes; a cat bed as a stylish hat. Prices are included to prove the value of the goods, but are kept in relatively small proportion so as to allow the ads to remain a branding mechanism. This combination proves Target can be both practical and stylish at the same time.

**35**

Target Fashion/
Housewares print ads

Design firm
Kirshenbaum Bond &
Partners, New York

Art director
Minda Gralnek

Designers Scott
McDonald, Mike Hahn

Project manager Karen
Preston, Bill Barrett

Photographer
Karina Taira

Writer Ryan Blank

Client Target Stores

2-pack tartan boxers $8.49
dirt devil hand vac $39.99
For the Target store
nearest you: www.target.com

The goal of this series of ads was to evolve Target's "Sign of the Times" branding campaign into print. We decided to take Target's red-and-white world outside, adding blue sky and pool water.

Target "Sign of the Times" Spring print ads

36

Design firm PMH
Art directors Minda Gralnek (Target), Dave Peterson (PMH)
Print production Gary Tassone (PMH)
Photographer Meyers Robertson
Associate Creative director/copywriter Amie Valentine
Client Target Stores

127

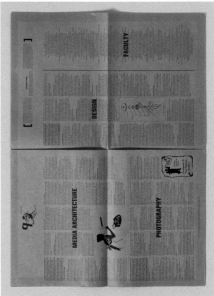

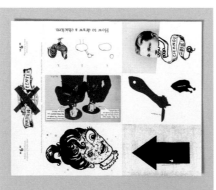

**Portfolio Center**
**Change catalogue**

Design firm
James Victore, Inc.,
Beacon, New York

Art director
Gemma Gatti

Designer James Victore

Project manager
Hank Richardson

Writer Dan Monroe

Fabricator
Graham Thorpe

Publisher/client
Portfolio Center

37

**Nike ACG's Pro Purchase Program is a seasonal selection of product offered to key outdoor industry professionals and athletes. This self-mailing catalogue showcased the Fall/Holiday 2000 collection. We shot for something clean and simple – a look that focused primarily on product. With a minimalistic approach, space and shape were allowed to take precedence.**

**38**

Nike ACG Pro
Purchase catalogue

Design firm Nike, Inc.,
Beaverton, Oregon

Creative director
Michael Verdine

Art director/designer
Angelo Colletti

Print production
Ann Riedl

Project manager
Susan Roy

Photography Marcus
Swanson, Sean
Reynolds (product);
Trevor Graves,
Mark Gallup, Tammy
Kennedy (athlete)

Copy Naomi Gollogly

Client Nike, ACG

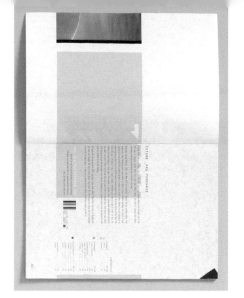

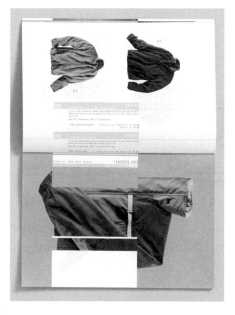

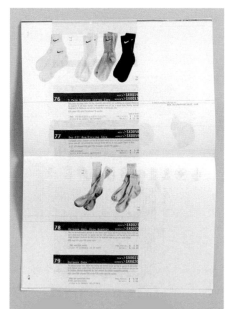

**This Spring/Summer 2001 fashion brochure for New York designer Anni Kuan features rather personal stories about the designer printed on fresh, cheap newsprint and wrapped in crisp aluminum foil. The audience consists of fashion buyers/stores in the U.S., Asia and Europe. The end product was exactly the same as the initial presentation – in fact, we printed the comps. (It helps when the client is your girlfriend.)**

**39**

**Anni Kuan**
**Spring/Summer 2001**
**fashion brochure**

Design firm
Sagmeister, Inc.,
New York

Art director/designer
Stefan Sagmeister

Illustrator/photographer
Stefan Sagmeister

Writer
Stefan Sagmeister

Client Anni Kuan
Design

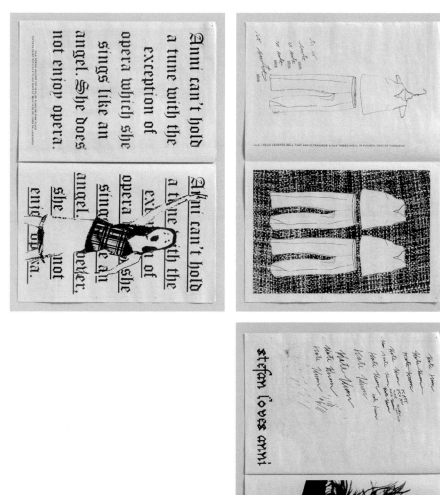

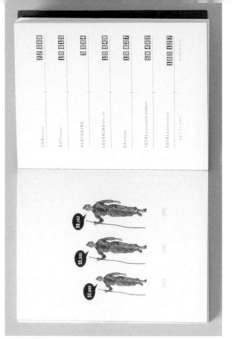
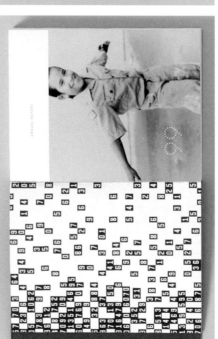

bravery

**Simple Truths**
**1999 annual report/
fundraiser**

Design firm
Slaughter Hanson,
Birmingham, Alabama

Art director
Marion English Powers

Project manager
Stacy Pope

Illustrator David Webb

Photographer
Don Harbor

Writer Kathy Oldham

Client Greater Alabama
Council/Boy Scouts

# SIMPLE TRUTHS

The Greater Alabama Council chooses a theme each year on which to base the year's activities. The theme for 2000 was to coincide with Colin Powell's national public school program emphasizing strong values. Titled **Simple Truths**, the annual report details a scout's story with a simple truth, and a character that once represented that truth: loyalty=Lassie, strength=Popeye, compassion=Bambi, etc. The annual report's usage is twofold: to report the numbers and activities of the year, and as a fundraiser for the next year. All print, paper, design and photography are donated, so that of course played a significant part in both the design and the production.

AT THE COMPUTER **19%**

WHILE EXERCIS

SMALL, PRIVATE PLACE

MOMENT O

SKETCHBOOK **2%**

CONFERENCES **%** AT CC

**2%** WHILE NURSING MY

MY PARTNER **2%**

THE NEW YORK SUBWA

MY BRAIN **2%** BRAINS

6:00 WHEN THE PHONES

THOSE LUCID FIRST MOM

HOME **2%** THE INTER

A TRAIN **2%** WALKING TO

Question D
Where do you do your
best creative thinking?
[Note: many respondents
chose more than one
option, wrote in a unique
answer, or both.]
at the computer
in the shower
while driving
while exercising
when falling asleep
in a small, private place
at home
other

THE SHOWER 17% WHILE DRIVING 22%

13% WHEN FALLING ASLEEP 26% IN A

% AT HOME 19% NOT ANY PARTICULAR

LOCATION 4% EVERYWHERE 4% IN MY

A 2% IT CAN STRIKE AT ANY TIME 2% AT

CERTS AND PLAYS 2% WHILE RUNNING

ON TO SLEEP 2% WHILE TALKING WITH

HILE TALKING WITH MY SPOUSE 2% ON

V TRAIN 2% WHILE WATCHING TV 2% IN

RMING 2% WHILE WALKING 2% AFTER

TOP RINGING 2% IN THE GARDEN 2% IN

NTS AFTER WAKING UP 2% AT WORK/AT

TIAL MOMENTS 2% OUTSIDE ME 2% IN

WORK 2% TOTALLY UNPREDICTABLE 2%

# ILLUSTRATION

**Jurors Janet Froelich** *The New York Times Magazine,* New York **Milton Glaser** Milton Glaser, Inc., New York **Patrick Mitchell** *Fast Company,* Boston

Illustration is as essential as ever to effective communication design, and entries in this category should reflect not only high-quality original illustration(s) but also an appropriateness of occasion for the use of illustration in the design. Please submit entries in context (i.e., as articles or individual tear sheets.

In many ways, the year 2000 saw a dawning of the age of graphic authorship – or at least of the media's attention to it. Illustrators like Chris Ware and Maira Kalman have hit the relative mainstream, their work splashed on the covers of magazines like the *New Yorker* and filling shelves in bookstores across the country. Ware's graphic masterwork *Jimmy Corrigan: The Smartest Kid on Earth,* published by the heavy-hitting literary house Pantheon, has gone into a fourth printing, giving the underground Chicago illustrator an almost overnight mainstream success. Despite this climate of ascendance, jurors this year noted that there were relatively few entries in AIGA's new Illustration and Design competition – a fact that they attributed both to the country's economic downturn and the suspicion that illustrators wouldn't necessarily think of entering an AIGA show since it has traditionally been associated with only graphic design.

In an age of image, however, visual storytellers are needed more than ever, and it seems only logical that the collaboration between art director and illustrator take on a certain primacy. This relationship, once described by hybrid illustrator/art director James McMullan as "an implicit tug-of-war," yields at its best visual expression that not only depicts a person, object or idea, but casts it in a new and often startling light. Janet Froelich was quick to point out, however, that the same can be true of contemporary photography. "We have become comfortable with the manipulation of images and with staged photography," she said, "so that we can now accomplish with photography what used to be only available to illustration or to painting – conceptual imagery."

Mediating between the two media has become a fine art of sorts. This has certainly been the case with Rolling Stone art director Fred Woodward, who has done his fair share of balancing photography's dominance in rock editorial spreads with powerful uses of illustration. The jurors selected three pieces commissioned by Woodward that go a long way in demonstrating the contemporary illustration community's diversity of styles and media. Created for an article about the late rap star Notorious B.I.G.'s posthumous record Born Again, Jason Holley created a painting that bears all the signs of a religious icon, sacred heart and all (cat. 43). Matt Mahurin, known for his darkly lush photographic and video work, delved into the profane with a disturbing digital illustration for a piece about the neo-metal band Slipknot (cat. 44). And Roberto Parada, with all the precision and surrealism of a latter-day Magritte, rendered Stevie van Zandt's metaphoric journey from guitar hero to mafia thug on HBO's hit series The Sopranos (cat. 45).

Asked whether there seemed to be any trends emerging in the year's selections, the jurors pointed out the intrinsic differences between design and illustration. "The work seems to be more or less the same as it's been the last 10 years," noted Milton Glaser. "In illustration the notion of an identifiable system is more necessary for survival than in design, where a matter of thinking is more significant than the final form." That said, the year's best illustration did bear a conceptual clarity that was in evidence despite its visual vehicle. The moral corrosion and hypocrisy of the lead character in Shakespeare's Richard III is rendered by illustrator Lanny Sommese via a Janus-headed figure whose torso and head are comprised of weapons of mass destruction (cat. 41) – an appropriate characterization for a modern remake of this tale of treachery.

Interestingly, two illustrations this year seemed to unwittingly echo each other in their use of a single visual metaphor. Mirko Ilic's The New York Times Book

# I GREW UP IN THE COLD WAR AND I'VE MARRIED A NUMBER OF CRAZY PEOPLE.

Review cover illustration for a story on prison guards (cat. 46) depicts a guard who is trapped by the vertical stripes on an inmate's garb as if behind bars. In David Plunkert's collage for a poster advertising Lorca's The House of Bernarda Alba (cat. 42), the play's grieving widow is seated on a chair whose base forms bars against a young woman's face. (The play recounts the story of a widow who announces to her five daughters that they will observe a mourning period of eight years without leaving the house.) In both instances, the simple play of vertical and horizontal elements depicts a condition of the soul that is visceral and immediately recognizable.

Sometimes it is the graphic virtuosity of an image that catches the eye, as in the case of Anita Kunz's illustration for a Time magazine article called "Teens Before Their Time" about the increasingly early pubescence of girls in this country (cat. 47). A girl with pigtails blows a bubble, the roundness and size of which are echoed not only in her teddybear's head but in the full breasts she prematurely bears. In some strange way, Kunz's hapless Lolita, sexualized before her time, is caught in between the human states explored two centuries ago by William Blake, the archetypal graphic storyteller, who created a series of poem-and-picture cycles called Songs of Innocence and Songs of Experience. Blake, like today's breed of visual interpreters, believed in the apt juxtaposition of word and picture. If the endurance of his oeuvre is any indication, a picture can still speak a thousand words. Andrea Codrington

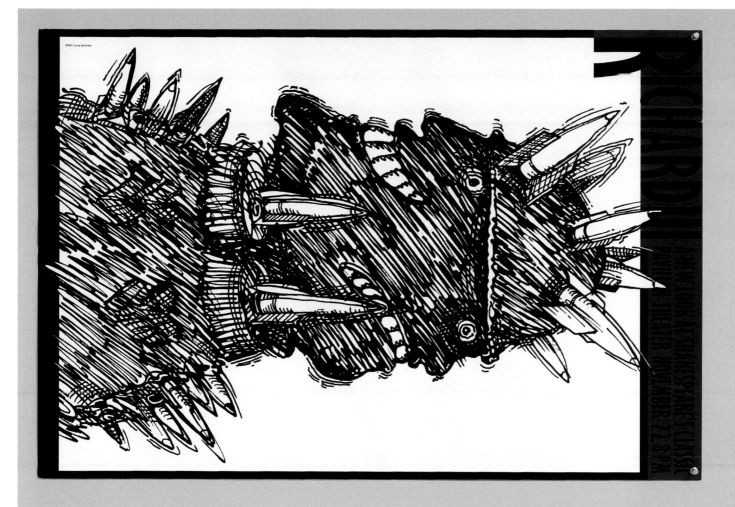

The problem was to create a poster for an updated version of the Shakespeare classic Richard III that would appeal to the population of the Penn State University community. I created the graphic to suggest the production's modernized interpretation of the Shakespeare play. The ironic juxtaposition of the classic's title with the imagery of modern weapons of mass destruction proved to be very effective at appealing to an academic audience that was, for the most part, well aware of the original time frame of the play. Rather than flooding the campus with cheaply printed flyers, we chose to produce a limited number of large posters using one of the large-format computer plotters available to us on campus. These were strategically positioned in order to reach the largest number of people.

*Richard III poster*

Design firm Sommese
Design, State College,
Pennsylvania

Art director/
creative director
Lanny Sommese

Designer/illustrator
Lanny Sommese

Digital production
Matt Flick

Client
Penn State University

41

**The House of Bernarda Alba is one of a series of seven posters announcing the 2000–2001 series of the Madison Repertory Theatre. Each poster needed to feature the same stylistic treatment and also accurately represent the varied themes and tones of each play. The audience was the general live theater crowd in the Madison area. Spur was to design each of the title treatments and illustrate each play. The solution shows the title character of the play sitting ramrod straight on a chair that also symbolizes a cage. The final poster needed to work in black-and-white as well as in color, and be reproducible at a small scale.**

**42**

*The House of Bernarda Alba poster*

Design firm
Spur Design, Baltimore

Art director/
creative director
Chad Bollenbach/
Lindsay, Stone & Briggs

Designers
David Plunkert,
Chad Bollenbach

Illustrator
David Plunkert

Client/publisher
Madison Repertory
Theatre

"Notorious B.I.G." illustration

Design firm *Rolling Stone* magazine

Art director
Fred Woodward

Illustrator Jason Holley

Client *Rolling Stone*

43

# RECORDINGS

**JUVENILE, P and BIGGIE rule hardcore from the South and from the beyond.**

*By* TOURÉ

## The Notorious B.I.G.
*Born Again*
BAD BOY/ARISTA
★★★

*By* ROB SHEFFIELD

I N MOST CASES, IF THE MUSIC IN AN artist's vaults were great, it probably wouldn't have gone into the vaults in the first place. This may be especially true of the Notorious B.I.G., who was the first MC to drop an album and then get ubiquitous on us, releasing an unending slew of singles, remixes and cameos, each one better than the last.

*Born Again,* the Notorious B.I.G.'s third album (after 1994's *Ready to Die* and 1997's *Life After Death*), is the product of a long-awaited vault opening. As well [*Cont. on 56*]

## Master P
*Only God Can Judge Me*
NO LIMIT/PRIORITY
★★★

## Juvenile
*Tha G-Code.*
CASH MONEY/UNIVERSAL
★★★

M ASTER P LIKES TO CALL himself the ghetto Bill Gates, but he's really the ghetto Regis Philbin, a glad-handing game-show host peddling a fantasy of big money. 'To be a millionaire in this game, you don't need finesse or even musical talent – just luck, hustle and a final answer. (In Master P's case, the final answer would be "Jungle!") With his blockbuster No Limit empire, P has used this fantasy to turn the South into hip-hop's land of dreams, inspiring scenesters all over the region to play up their loudest, liveliest cartoon visions of fame and fortune. Along with his New Orleans neighbor Juvenile (of the Cash Money posse), P sells tons of records with no concessions to pop, R&B or even the national hip-hop audience. These [*Cont. on 59*]

"Slipknot"
**illustration**

Design firm
*Rolling Stone*
magazine, New York

Art director
Fred Woodward

Illustrator Matt Muhurin

Client *Rolling Stone*

44

**"Steve Van Zandt"**
illustration

Design firm
*Rolling Stone*
magazine, New York

Art director
Fred Woodward

Illustrator
Roberto Parada

Client *Rolling Stone*

45

The purpose of the illustration is to represent a book written by a former prison guard about prisoners coming and going. If being a guard is your life's profession, you basically become a full-time prisoner yourself since most prisoners' sentences are shorter. The guard is in the negative space between the stripes of the prisoner's uniform, which become bars of the guard's own prison. The black stripes are exactly the same size and shape as the white prison bars – a strange kind of Yin and Yang.

The New York Times
Book Review
May 14, 2000 $1.25
Copyright © 2000 The New York Times

Impersonating an Officer

In 'Newjack: Guarding Sing Sing,' Ted Conover tells how he went under cover at New York's notorious penitentiary.
*Reviewed by Daniel Bergner* **4**

Richard Eder on Michael Ondaatje **7**    Special Children's Books section **17-32**

0  354813

**46**

"Impersonating an Officer" Illustration

Design firm
Mirko Ilic Corp.,
New York

Art director
Steven Heller

Illustrator Mirko Ilic

Client/publisher
*The New York Times
Book Review*

This was an illustration I produced to accompany an article in *Time* magazine entitled "Teens Before Their Time." It explored the recent phenomenon of young girls reaching puberty far earlier than their predecessors did – sometimes as early as six years old. The article attempted to find reasons for this oddity.

yes

Question R
Have you ever
had a useful idea
while lying in bed
or in a dream?

# TYPOGRAPHY
# AND DESIGN

**Jurors Michael Bierut**
Pentagram Design,
New York **Barry Deck**
The Attik, New York
**Barbara Glauber** Heavy
Meta, New York

Type and typography play essential roles in effective communication design. Entries in this category should use typography as the principal feature of the work's visual language and demonstrate an understanding of the possibilities for authentic typographical experimentation.

"I don't think type is where it's at in design right now."
This was not a particularly encouraging start to a type-related discussion amongst the typography jurors of AIGA's annual design competition. But Barry Deck went on to qualify his statement by explaining that new media – especially the fusion of television and the Internet – is changing the design environment so fundamentally that type is just not the current focus of attention. "What is interesting about design today is that now, more than ever, it is about editing and directing, architecture and user experience." Barbara Glauber took up the theme: "New media is an inhibited typographic art; there's not much you can do typographically at 72 dpi for a phone or a PDA screen. I'm still waiting for typefaces to become active players in new media."

This year's competition entries, however, reflected the activity of designers who express themselves through their selection and composition of type rather than by actually making typefaces – whether for screens or the printed page. And so conversation turned to a less pessimistic topic: designers with a propensity toward letterforms. "If you're a type-oriented designer, type is the vehicle where you locate all the meaning," said Michael Bierut, "and when you get it right it's satisfying on a level that is above all else." Glauber agreed. "Being able to fit the tools to the needs of your message – that's what distinguishes the type-oriented graphic designer from other designers."

There was a pervading sense of the authentic personal voice of this "type-oriented designer" in the selected entries – from the carefully rendered lettering in Rolling Stone spreads and silkscreen printing in Paul Sahre's poster, to a playful perceptual gimmick in the InformationArt business card and Alan Hori's distinctive typographic filigree.

It was its well-resolved page layouts and the use of classic typography – albeit with a contemporary twist – that brought VSA Partners' IBM 2000 annual report (cat. 52) to the jury's attention. Hyperbolic prose set in centered Jansen is used to tell the five-chapter story of "one year in the life of a company." The jury also noted the successful transference of the visual and verbal language of cult literary journal McSweeney's into the context of the business arena.

The business card of an information architect working in digital media (cat. 51) was selected not only for its effectiveness and appropriateness as a piece of communication design, but also for the delightfully physical and interactive experience it affords. A telephone number is laser die-cut out of the card and back-to-back registered with exacting care so that the flipside reveals a cell-phone number. Paul Sahre's silkscreened poster (cat. 50) makes similar perceptual play with type. The jury admired the simplicity of what Glauber referred to as "whacked out barcode typeface," especially since the poster – illegible until tipped obliquely – promoted the designer's own lecture.

All the judges remarked upon the consistency of Rolling Stone's visual sensibility, achieved, they believed, not through a typographic house style but via the fastidious maintenance of high-level craftsmanship. The two winning spreads demonstrate different aspects of this craftsmanship. The Axl Rose spread (cat. 49) employs HTF Requiem overlaid with floral patterns to ironic decorative effect, while the black-and-white DMX spread (cat. 48) with its crude shadow lettering evokes the high school study-hall aesthetic of felt-tip pen doodles. Glauber and Bierut both remarked upon the white outline around the Albert Watson photograph of the hip-hop artist's back, creating the appearance of a glowing aura.

Two of Allen Hori's posters were elected – one announcing a symposium at MoMA (cat. 53), the other an ACD call for entries (cat. 54). "Fairly inscrutable and fussy." "Extraordinarily controlled and precise." "Considered." "Lavish confections." Deck elaborated upon the jurors' diverse responses in personal terms: "I love eye candy and with Allen's work I can indulge in something beautiful and complex without it having to be a guilty pleasure, because it doesn't let you down on an intellectual level." The posters are intricate typographic diagrams of information. As Glauber notes, "Usually text is lumped at the bottom of a poster, but here it's beautifully integrated." Bierut added to the eulogy: "It's not just the way it's formally resolved," he said, referring to the "Things in the Making" poster, "but the architectural event it promotes was a big deal and the poster added its own commentary to the shadings of meaning."

Interestingly, there was little evidence of one of the year's prevailing trends: systems-based design. With their personalities firmly removed, many designers have been embarking upon coolly analytical investigations of form and visual codes incited, perhaps, by impetuses in contemporary art, photography and music. The work of Paul Elliman, Andrew Blauvelt, Daniel Eatock and Experimental Jetset, to name a few, exemplify this tendency to foreground process and organizational structure. Perhaps due to the subdued and utilitarian nature of the typography found in this genre, its proponents didn't see fit to enter it in the typography section of AIGA's competition. Alice Twemlow

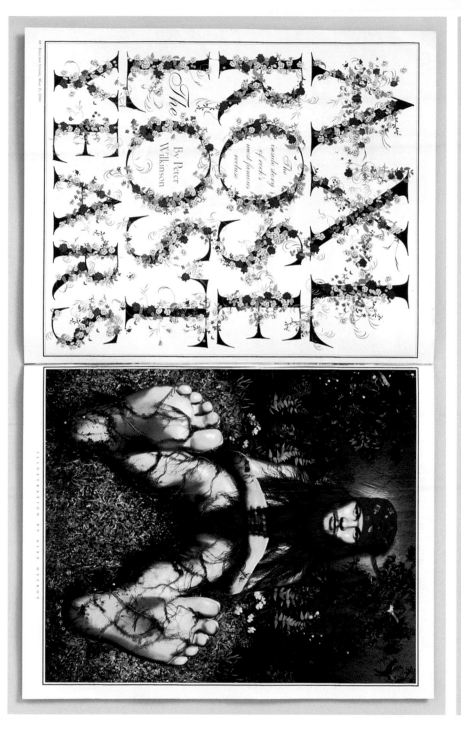

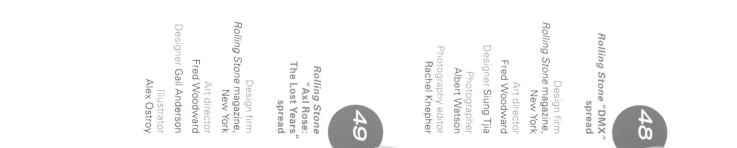

**49**

*Rolling Stone*
"Axl Rose:
The Lost Years"
spread

Design firm
*Rolling Stone* magazine,
New York

Art director
Fred Woodward

Designer Gail Anderson

Illustrator
Alex Ostroy

**48**

*Rolling Stone* "DMX"
spread

Design firm
*Rolling Stone* magazine,
New York

Art director
Fred Woodward

Designer Siung Tjia

Photographer
Albert Watson

Photography editor
Rachel Knepfer

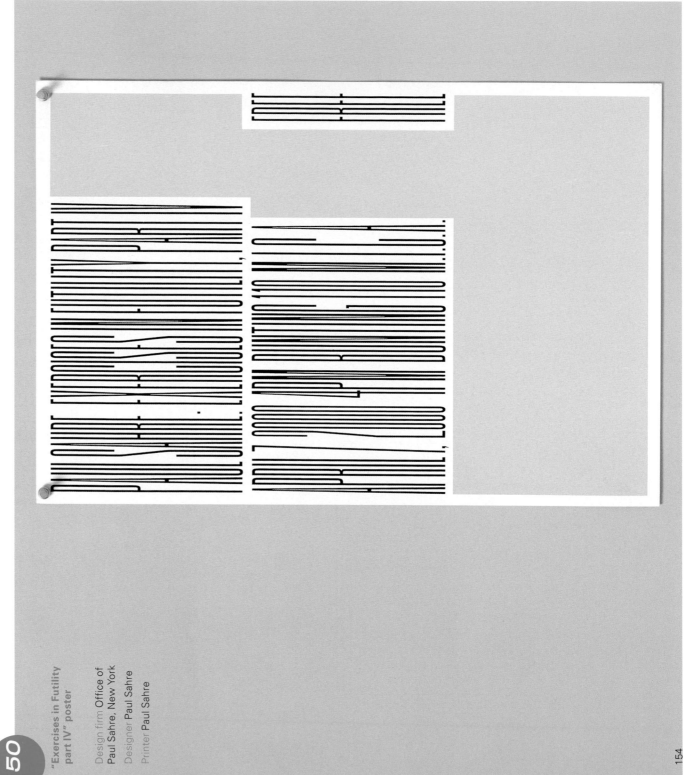

**50**

**"Exercises in Futility part IV" poster**

Design firm Office of
Paul Sahre, New York

Designer Paul Sahre

Printer Paul Sahre

The client is a digital artist whose work is driven and informed by data. As she was starting up a new business in an essentially nonexistent field, she needed an identity system to assist in making contacts. In keeping with her vision to inject art into the otherwise purely functional, the solution elevates the content of each piece over any form of traditional "identity." "We deconstructed the word "informationart" across three separate folders and distributed her contact information across four separate business cards, each embodying her approach and aesthetic in print form. This phone card, with a different number on each side, was a particularly difficult production problem, requiring perfect back-to-back and laser die-cut registration. The client has found these cards to be an ideal springboard for discussion about her work.

INFORMATIONART

InformationArt
phone number card

Design firm
Elixir Design, Inc.,
San Francisco

Creative director
Jennifer Jerde

Designers
Nathan Durrant,
Holly Holmquist

Print production
Christopher DeWinter

Client InformationArt/
Lisa Strausfeld

**51**

In 2000 the IT industry was going through a volatile and transformational year. IBM partnered with VSA to develop a "story" that captured this wild roller-coaster ride – a story that only a company with the breadth, depth and technological presence of IBM could tell. Working with IBM, VSA created a novel approach to the report, capturing the spirit of the industry and one year in the life of a company within it by building a colorful and engaging story that highlights IBM'ers who are facing a wide range of challenges, battles and successes. Simple, clean typography offers a classic approach with contemporary energy, coupled with artwork that opens up grand themes in each of the five chapters. The report has both a traditional tone of IBM stability and a contemporary energy that captures the dynamics of the world's largest IT company.

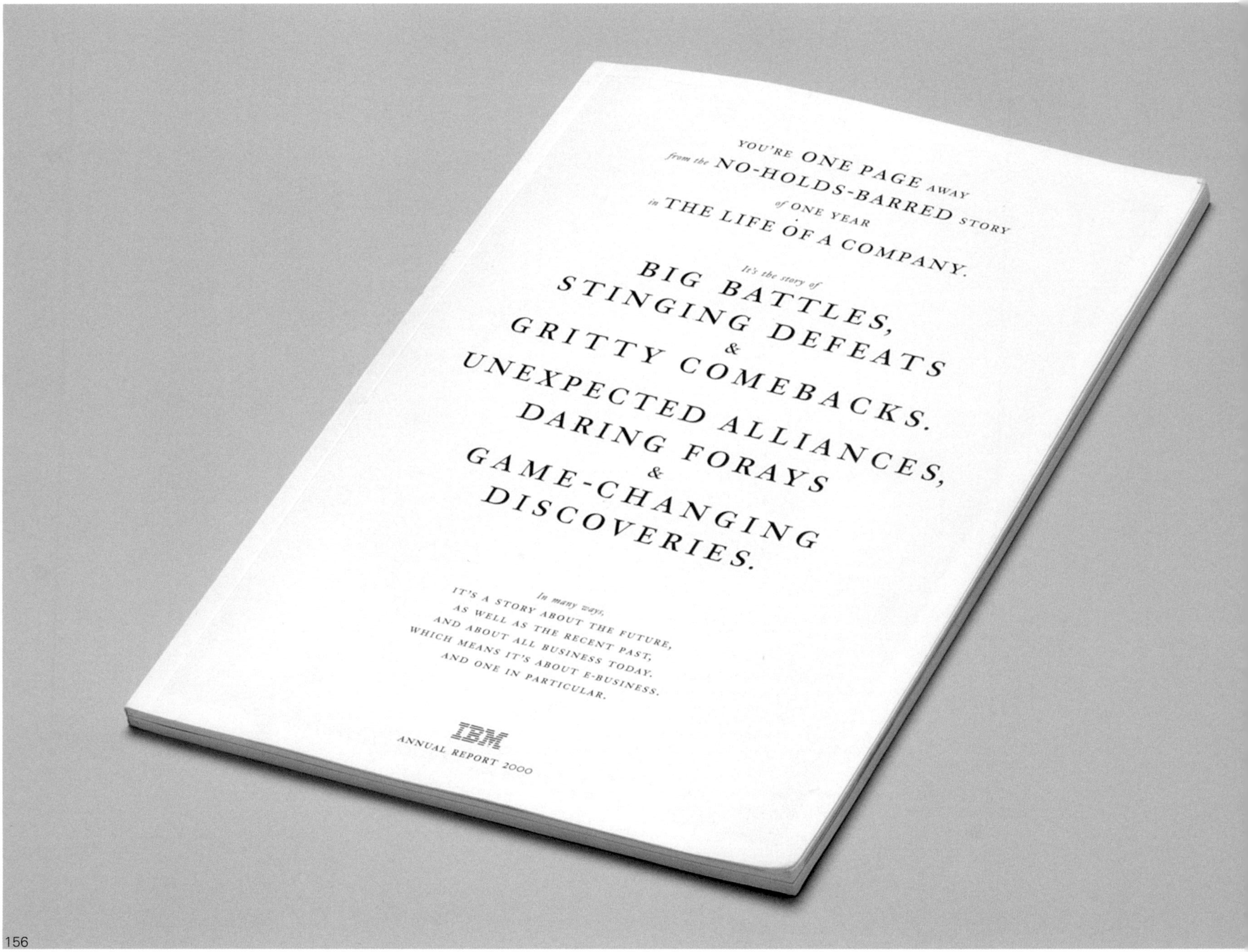

YOU'RE ONE PAGE AWAY from the NO-HOLDS-BARRED STORY of ONE YEAR in THE LIFE OF A COMPANY.

It's the story of

BIG BATTLES,
STINGING DEFEATS
&
GRITTY COMEBACKS.
UNEXPECTED ALLIANCES,
DARING FORAYS
&
GAME-CHANGING
DISCOVERIES.

In many ways,
IT'S A STORY ABOUT THE FUTURE,
AS WELL AS THE RECENT PAST,
WHICH MEANS IT'S ABOUT BUSINESS TODAY,
AND ONE IN PARTICULAR.

IBM

ANNUAL REPORT 2000

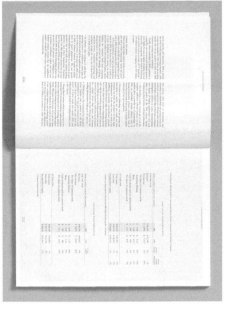

**IBM 2000 annual report**

**52**

Design firm
VSA Partners, Inc.,
Chicago

Creative directors
Curt Schreiber,
Jeff Walker

Designers
Scott Hickman,
Michelle Platts

Photographer
Christian Witkin

Client/publisher IBM

"Things in the
Making" poster

Design firm
Bates Hori, New York

Creative director
Ed Pusz

Designer/photographer
Allen Hori

Client Museum of
Modern Art

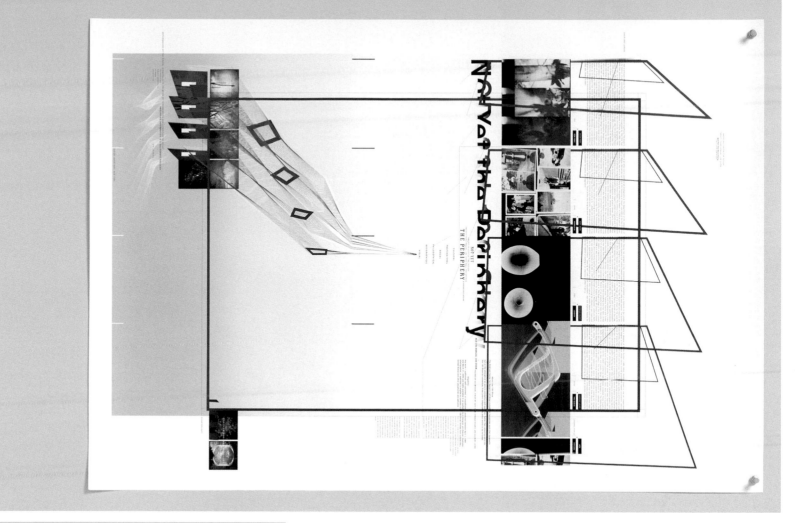

**"Not Yet the
Periphery" poster**

Design firm
Bates Hori, New York

Designer Allen Hori

Photographers
Allen Hori, Gaye Chan,
Siobhan Keaney,
Harmine Louwé

Client American
Center for Design

54

Question N
On a scale of
0–10, how much
did the project's
deadline affect
the final product?
0 = no effect
10 = total effect

Catalogue numbers
A = anonymous

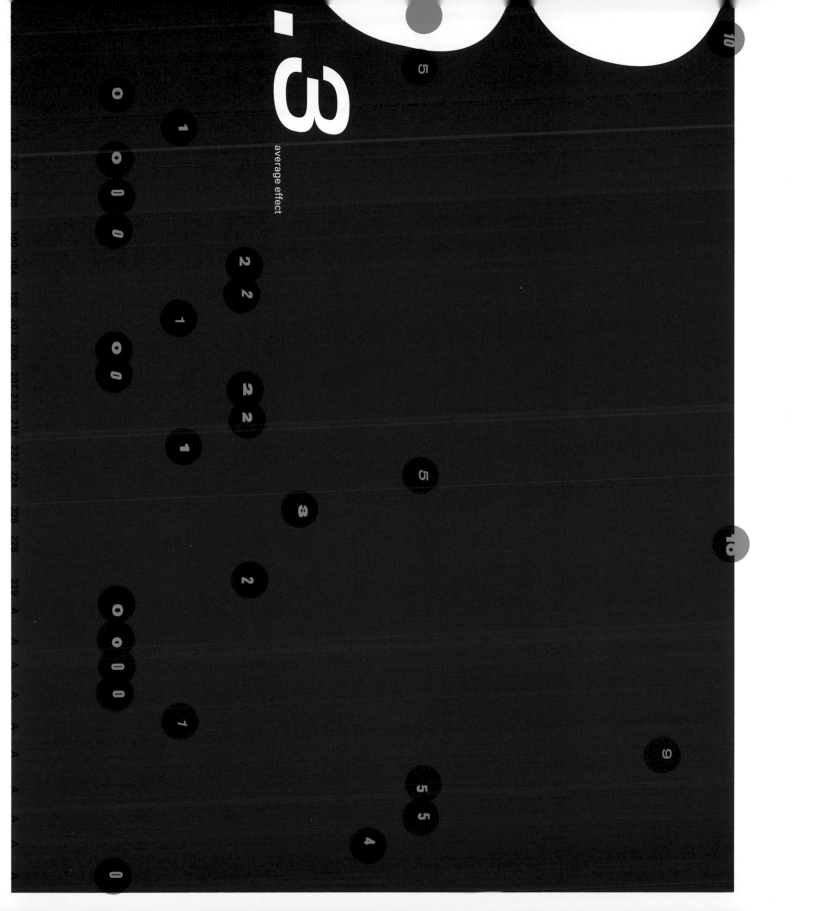

.3

average effect

# EDITORIAL DESIGN

**Jurors Nicholas Blechman** New York **Luke Hayman** *Brill's Content*, New York **Patrick Mitchell** *Fast Company*, Boston

The editorial designer creates a visual framework for the written word that illuminates and informs the content while contributing his or her own perspective to the overall piece. Entries in this category may include magazines, newspapers, journals and newsletters, submitted as complete issues or individual tear sheets.

The year 2000 saw the willing adoption of a "new sobriety" in the field of editorial design. As the millennial hangover set in, and the impact of an economic downturn and a new administration began to be felt, there was a tangible shift away from visual excesses that had characterized the late 1990s. In their interpretations of editorial content – the choice of illustration, photography, typography and composition – art directors were revealing a fascination with the quotidian, the unslick, the awkward, the amateur, the human.

Viewed optimistically, the pendulum swing was toward honesty – manifested in a concern for craftsmanship and respect for editorial content above visual pyrotechnics and even, for some designers, a heightened sense of awareness of the social implications of their work. Skeptics, however, might have seen the newfound interest in non-beautiful, awkward and amateur images and typography as just another trend or another attempt to put some more distance between editorial and advertising. Among the reasons that the AIGA editorial design jury cited for this move away from complexity – or what Patrick Mitchell termed "David Carsonization" – were a lack of resources, the influence of a particular genre of spontaneous, unstaged and snapshot photography and a weariness with the tricks of the computer. In short, work becomes more interesting when you can see mistakes, clumsiness and sense the maker's handprint.

The dual drive toward simplicity and the mark of the maker's hand was neatly exemplified in Critique's "Simplify" cover (cat. 59) – through its use of one color, white space, a witty customization of Thoreau's quote and its hand-lettered masthead. Another expression of this unostentatious mood was the proliferation of low-key, low-budget self-published zines. Among the jurors' selections in AIGA's competition was Peter Arkle News (cat. 55), a home-grown newsletter of stories printed on 8 1/2 x 11 paper at a Brooklyn copy shop by its titular hero, Peter Arkle. The stories – rendered in hand-lettered text and illustrated with stylized cartoons, painterly sketches and graphic doodles – are the author's observations on the mundane details of his everyday life: the irony of singing a song by The Clash whilst ironing a pair of jeans, incongruous T-shirt slogans sighted and snippets of conversation overheard on his daily jaunts through the neighborhood. Nicholas Blechman was impressed by the "relentlessness" of Arkle's voice. "When an artist or a designer has a vision and pushes it to the extreme," he said, "it achieves a certain kind of integrity." Another low-budget self-published production is the Pushpin Group's The Nose (cat. 57), dealing with issues such as the pros and cons of the death penalty and featuring the illustration and design of Seymour Chwast.

A low-key but considered piece was a small-format, one-color literary journal called Insurance (cat. 66). Set in utilitarian-looking brown Akzidenz Grotesque, it displayed a kind of restrained conservatism offset by occasional quirky features such as page numbers that slide down the outer edge of the book as you flip it. "Traditionalism is definitely in the air," said Blechman. "Dave Eggers uses Garamond and it seems fresh all of a sudden. It's really classical – you can't be more conservative than that – but it feels satisfying."

Another more long-term trend that the jurors noted was the way in which the maturation of the profession allows now not just for the design of editorial but for the ed itorialization of design. Rolling Stone's "Crosby, Stills, Nash & Young" spread (cat. 62), for example, uses no headline, simply a sequence of full-page

## WATCHED HORSESHOE CRABS MATING ON A BEACH IN BROOKLYN.

Question G
While researching, what – if anything – did you do differently from your normal design process?

black-and-white photographs of the featured artists, punctuated by a full-page ampersand. Luke Hayman enthused, "There's a genius to this visual joke." Mitchell agreed, saying "I love the idea that the art director can say 'We don't really need words on this' and the editor agrees and then it happens. They think more highly of their readers than other magazines do." Similarly, illustrator Maira Kalman was given complete freedom to record her impressions of the world of Parisian couture in her three-spread personality-filled "Couture Voyeur" story for The New York Times Magazine (cat. 56). The demarcations between photographer, illustrator, art director and editor, therefore, become increasingly blurred.

Among the magazines not entered into AIGA's competition, Hayman was sorry not to see titles like Time and Business Week – the unsung heroes of the magazine world. "While they may not always provide beautiful solutions," he said, "they are incredibly well crafted and resolved and use smart information graphics. They're easy to ignore because they're part of the background fabric." Alice Twemlow

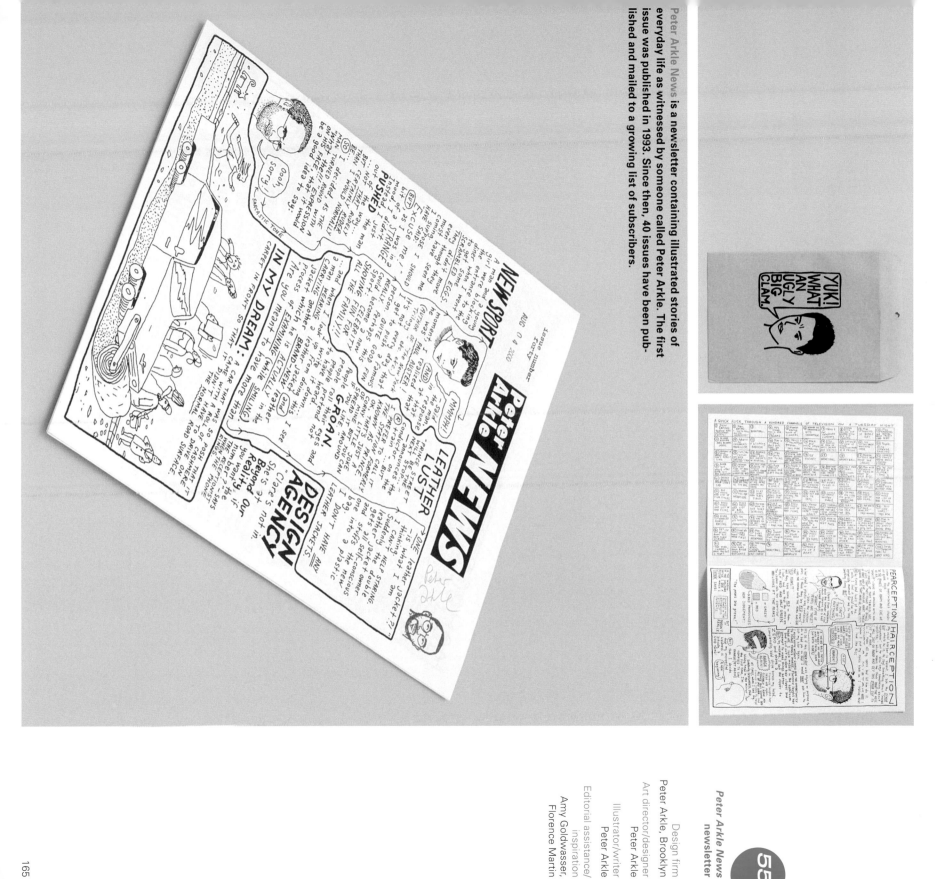

**Peter Arkle News** is a newsletter containing illustrated stories of everyday life as witnessed by someone called Peter Arkle. The first issue was published in 1993. Since then, 40 issues have been published and mailed to a growing list of subscribers.

Design firm
Peter Arkle, Brooklyn

Art director/designer
Peter Arkle

Illustrator/writer
Peter Arkle

Editorial assistance/
inspiration
Amy Goldwasser,
Florence Martin

*Peter Arkle News*
newsletter

**55**

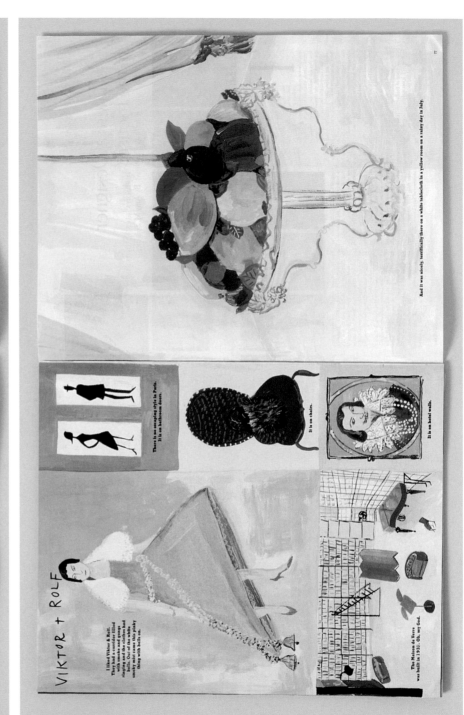

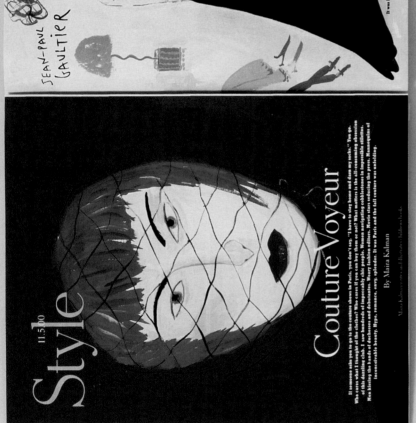

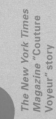

## 56

*The New York Times Magazine* "Couture Voyeur" story

Design firm
*The New York Times Magazine*, New York

Art director
Janet Froelich

Designer
Claude Martel

Illustrator
Maira Kalman

**The New York Times Magazine reports on the European collections several times a year. This season we sent Maira Kalman to Paris to record her impressions and gave her complete freedom. As an outsider, Kalman decided to record her impressions of the entire couture experience, not just the fashion shows. She came back with wonderful drawings and a charming story and we didn't have to do much to complete the package.**

The Nose is a semiannual publication produced by the Pushpin Group that presents material of a controversial and/or social nature and is sent to friends, clients and those who might be interested in the subject. This issue presented both sides of capital punishment (but slanted against) and centered around an article by Christopher Hitchens. Aside from being an expression of the designer's and editor's social consciences, the purpose of The Nose is to present the designs and illustrations of Seymour Chwast, so it may be considered a series of promotional pieces. To that end, a wide range of illustration and photography is shown.

The Nose #4,
Electric Follies
publication

Design firm
The Pushpin Group,
New York

Art director/designer
Seymour Chwast

Print production
The Actualizers

Illustrator
Seymour Chwast

Photographer
Jonathan Atkin

Writer
Christopher Hitchens

Editor DK Holland

57

We set out to create a modern visual look for a series of classic New York stories. The theme of the issue was the classic New York arrival story – people driven by politics, ambition and dreams to come to this city. The city itself was a source of inspiration for the design and we tried to create design elements that referenced its rich vernacular. Our original concept was much more traditional (using illustration), which at first we thought fit the classic nature of the subject, but our editor encouraged us to push the design to another level in order to make the approach more contemporary and unfamiliar.

**58**

*The New York Times Magazine "My First Year in New York" issue*

Design firm
*The New York Times Magazine*, New York

Art director
Janet Froelich

Designers
Claude Martel,
Andrea Fella

Photo editor Kathy Ryan

Photographer
Sacha Waldman

Speak, Memory

By Peter Landesman

After an accident gave her amnesia, she came to New York to remember who she was.

His Only Address Was an E-Mail Account

A gay teenage runaway... he decided he'd rather face the streets of New York than...

The Difference A Year Makes

The Difference A Year Makes

Simplify, simplify.
—Thoreau

ECONOMY
WINTER 2000

**59**

*Critique*
*"Simplify" cover*

Design firm
James Victore, Inc.,
Beacon, New York

Art director
Marty Neumeier

Designer
James Victore

Print production
Christopher Chu

Writer
Henry David Thoreau

Publisher/client
*Critique*

The cover had to present two stories, both of which spoke to the personal drama of politics and history between Cuba and the United States. The concept was to photograph the ocean that separates Key West and Cuba – a physical, political and emotional boundary. The type floats in the water, expressing the danger and depth of that water. The type references memory by being a transparent layer. This solved the problem of conveying the message of the story with a headline that did not impose on the poetry of the photograph.

The overall theme of the issue was "How Americans Spend Their Money" – a kind of "you are what you spend" look at life in this country. The initial image was of Carly Roney, a 32-year-old Internet entrepreneur. We chose a very literal solution by making Carly out of all the money she spent in one year. The shades of gray created levels and depths and allowed the reader to move in and out of what Carly spent and what Carly looks like. This effect gives the reader the ability to contemplate how our spending defines us.

**60**

The New York Times Magazine "Love in the Time of Castro" cover

Design firm
The New York Times Magazine, New York

Art director
Janet Froelich

Photo editor Kathy Ryan

Designer Joele Cuyler

Photographers
Virginia Beahan,
Laura McPhee

**61**

The New York Times Magazine "Spending" cover

Design firm
The New York Times Magazine, New York

Art director
Janet Froelich

Designers Joele Cuyler, John Fulbrook

**David Crosby, Stephen Stills, Graham Nash & Neil Young** sit shoulder to shoulder on wooden stools around a forest of microphones. On the far left, Stills plays a gentle riff on a snow-white, wide-body electric guitar. Across from him, Young, wearing a red flannel shirt and a black baseball cap, strums an acoustic guitar and sings "Old Man," from his 1972 album *Harvest*.

Young's shivery tenor sounds fragile in the cold, dark space of the Convocation Center in Cleveland. But when the other three enter the chorus with swan-diving harmonies – "Old man, look at my life/I'm a lot like you" – the song blooms with fresh meaning. Crosby, Stills, Nash and Young are no longer the four young bucks who overwhelmed rock in 1969 with pedigree and promise. They are in their fifties, and they sing "Old Man," a reflection on passing youth and lost opportunity, with electrifying honesty. Unfinished business runs deep in those bruised gold voices.

There is no applause at the end – because there is no audience. CSNY are in final rehearsals for their first concert tour since 1974. Opening night in Detroit is four days away. But to hear this band in a big, empty room is to experience magic in its native state. Everything that makes CSNY one of rock's premier melodramas – drugs (Crosby's 1994 liver transplant and new celebrity as a sperm donor for lesbian moms Melissa Etheridge and Julie Cypher; Nash's boating accident BY DAVID FRICKE >> PHOTOGRAPHS BY MARK SELIGER >

**62**

*Rolling Stone*
"Crosby, Stills,
Nash & Young"
story

Design firm
*Rolling Stone*
magazine, New York

Art director
Fred Woodward

Designers
Fred Woodward,
Siung Tjia

Photographer
Mark Seliger

Photography editor
Rachel Knepher

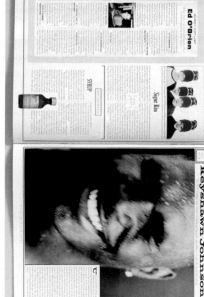

**63**

*Rolling Stone*
"The Hot Issue"
special issue

Design firm
*Rolling Stone*
magazine, New York

Art director
Fred Woodward

Designers
Fred Woodward,
Siung Tjia

Photographer
Mark Seliger

Photo editor
Rachel Knepher

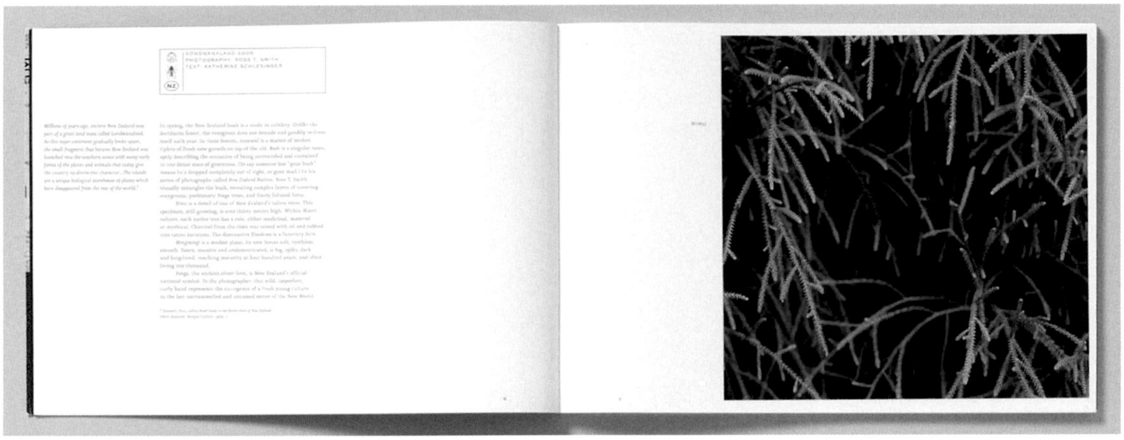

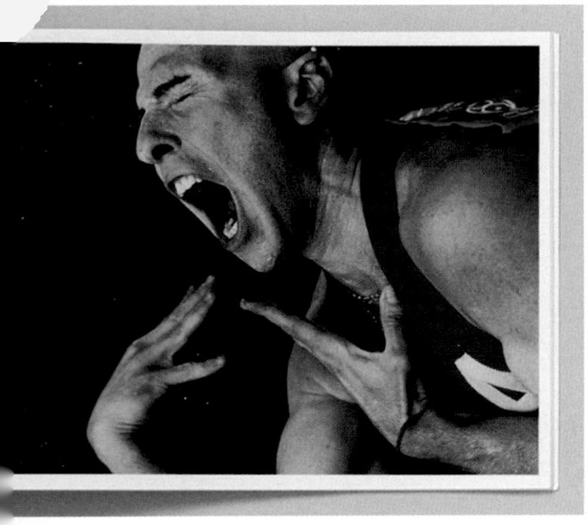

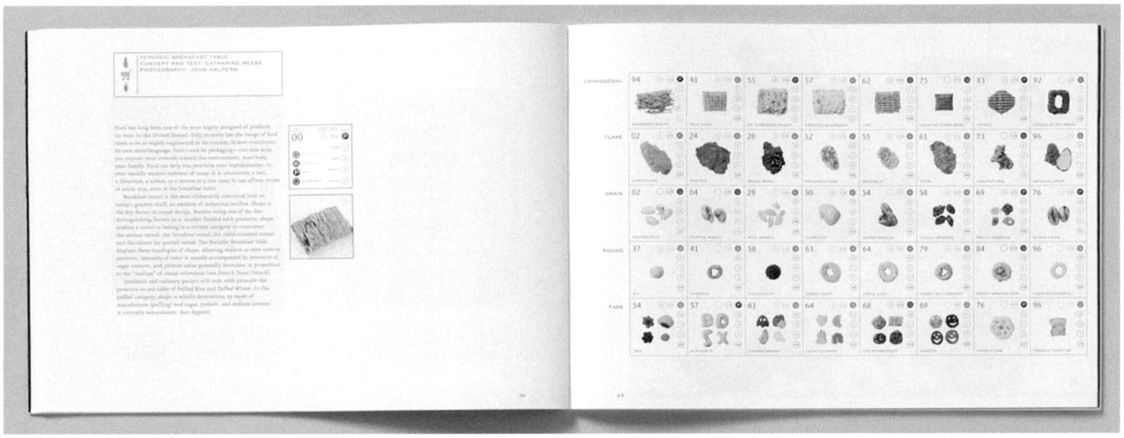

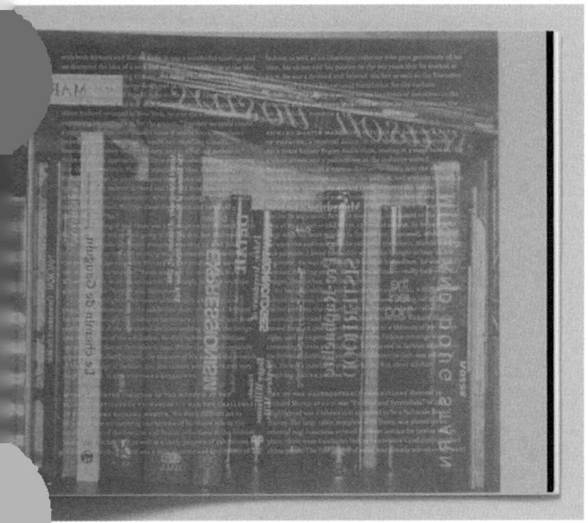

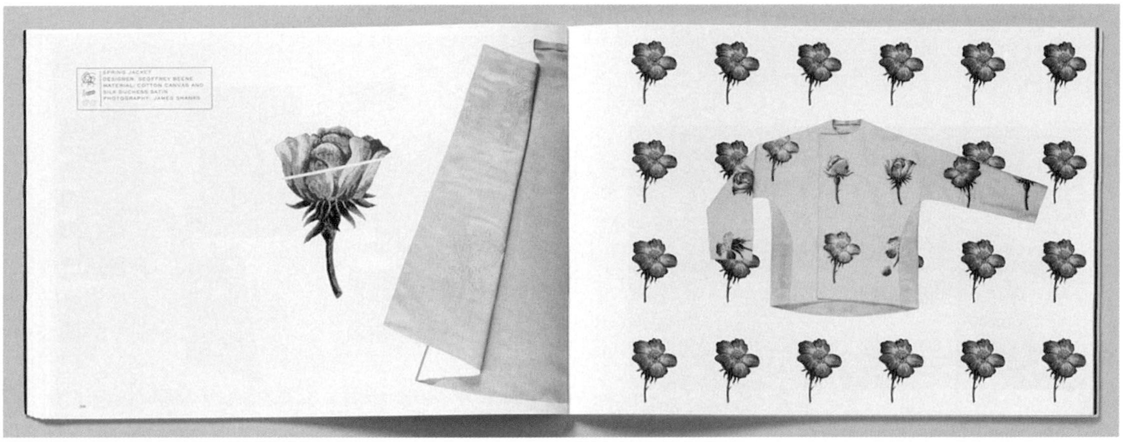

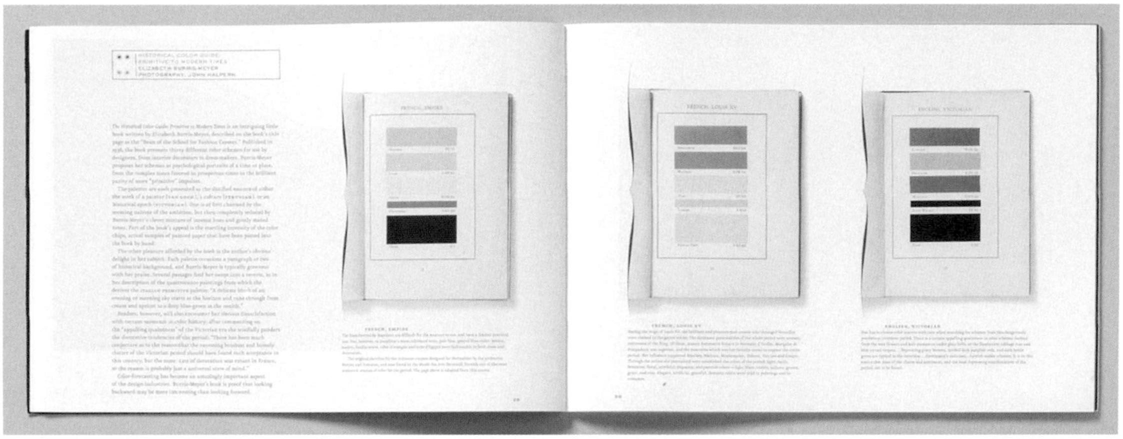

This twice-yearly publication takes a different theme for each issue. Our audience is a particular one, interested in the intersection of performing and visual arts. The "Rites of Spring" issue followed a few especially dark topics, and the publisher wanted a deliberately brighter perspective. "Eye candy" is a disparaging term, but that was what we especially set out to address; things that look pretty, that are undeniably attractive. It also, obviously, coincided with the arrival of spring, so there was a sense of growth, renewal and an athletic sense of "springing." The coordination of – and relationship between – several different photographic scenarios is complex.

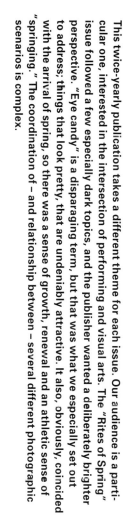

Design firm
Pentagram Design,
New York

Creative director
J. Abbott Miller

Designers J. Abbott
Miller, Roy Brooks

Project manager
John Porter

Client 2wice Arts
Foundation

*2wice* "Rites of
Spring" issue

64

This twice-yearly publication deals with the intersection of performing and visual arts. The "Ice" issue explored cryogenics, literary representations of ice, photographs of icebergs and the importance of ice in cuisine, as well as our mainstay of performance and choreography images. Metallic silver ink, holographic foil, snowflakes and letters with ice caps were all employed to confer the chilliness of the topic. Putting a dancer on an ice rink, painting another entirely in silver body makeup and getting a great ice sculptor involved were critical to the issue.

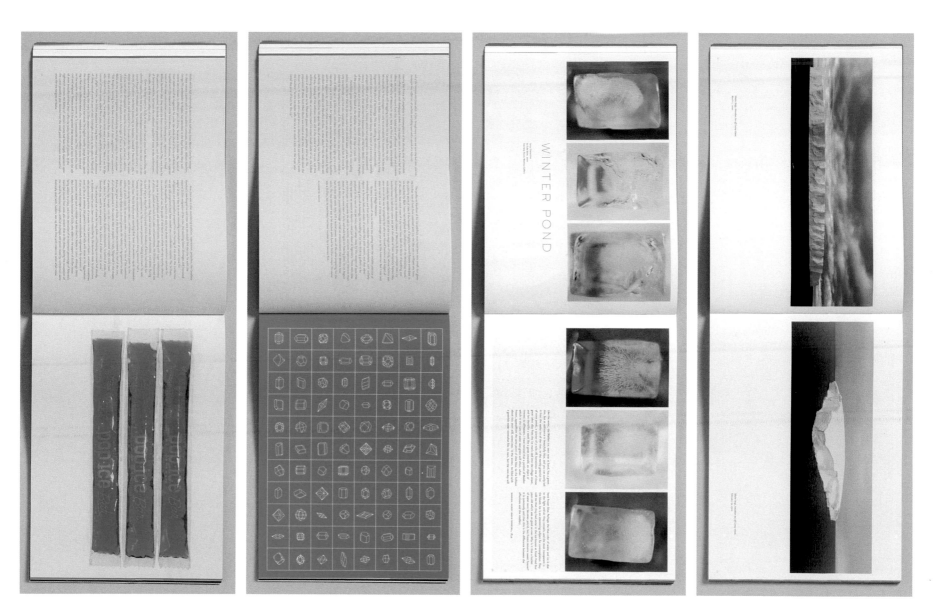

WINTER POND

2wice "Ice" issue

65

Design firm
Pentagram Design,
New York

Creative director
J. Abbott Miller

Designers
J. Abbott Miller,
Jeremy Hoffman

Project manager
John Porter

Client 2wice Arts
Foundation

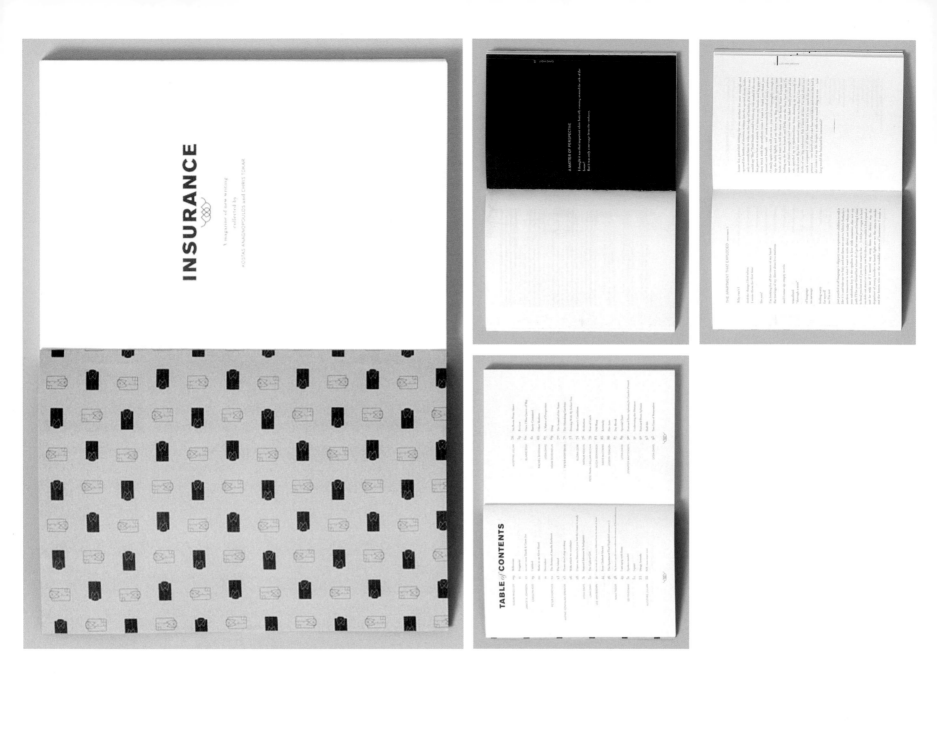

**66**

*Insurance* magazine

Design firm
goodesign, New York

Art director/designer
Diane Shaw

Editors
Kostas Anagnopoulos,
Chris Tokar

Client
*Insurance* magazine

The client wanted to publish a literary journal of new works of poetry and prose that did not look like existing literary journals on the market. The client also wanted the journal to look consistent as a series, like a collection of encyclopedias. This being the premiere issue, we took the name as inspiration and decided to give it the look of a 1950s insurance salesman, complete with plain brown suit. Following issues will have a similar design, each with its own color. The budget for this project was tight, so production was low tech. The printer offered to donate leftover paper from another job, however the only uncoated available was cream. Originally we had envisioned a soft white, but the shade of brown we chose ended up working well to enforce the worn aesthetic of the journal.

Question S-2
On a scale of 0–10,
please rate the
level of pleasure
experienced in
the thick of the
project.

Question T-2
On a scale of 0–10,
please rate the
level of anxiety
experienced in
the thick of the
project.

0 = no
pleasure/anxiety
10 = total
pleasure/anxiety

Yellow numbers
indicate pleasure

Magenta numbers
indicate anxiety

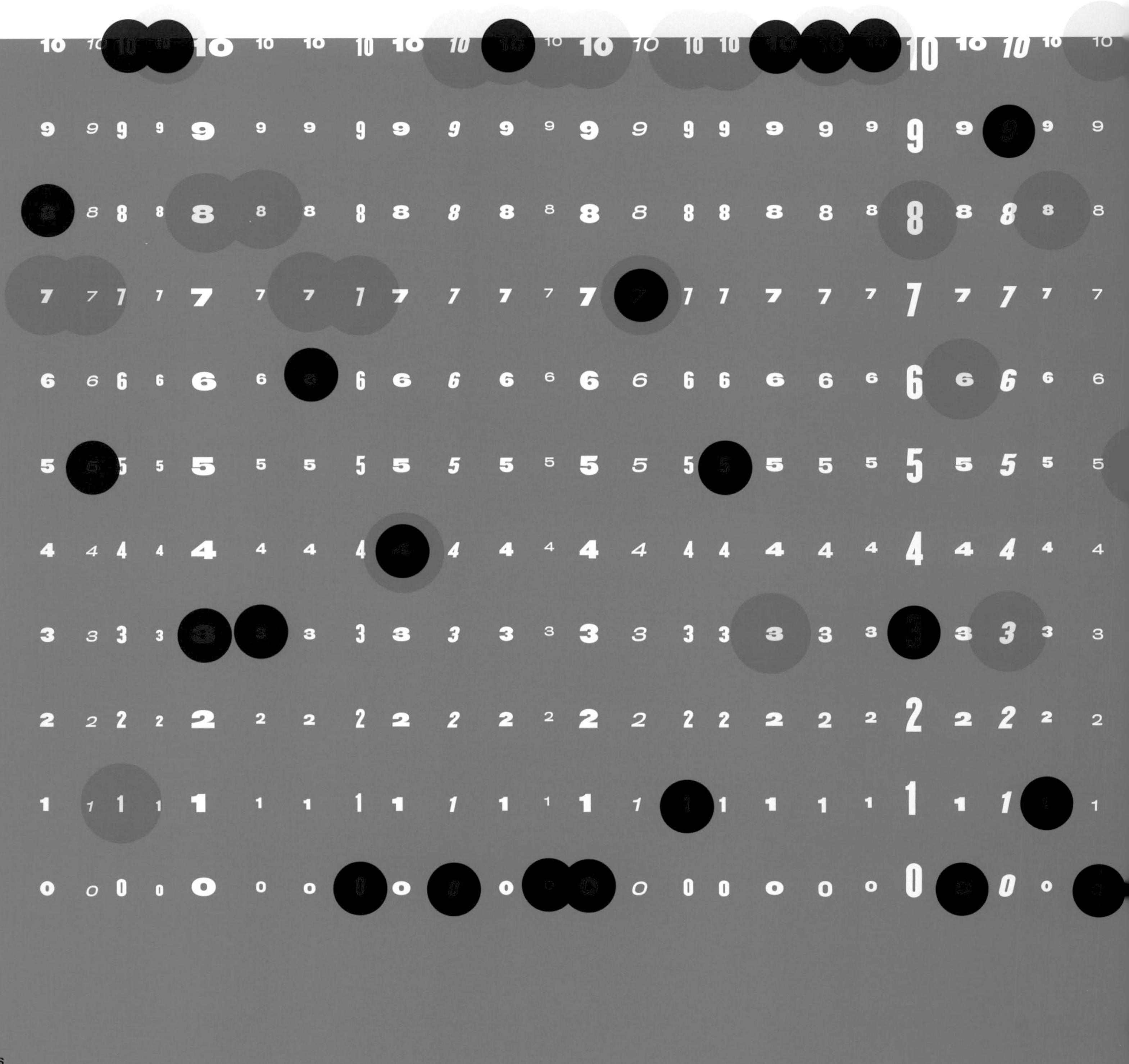

Catalogue numbers
A = anonymous

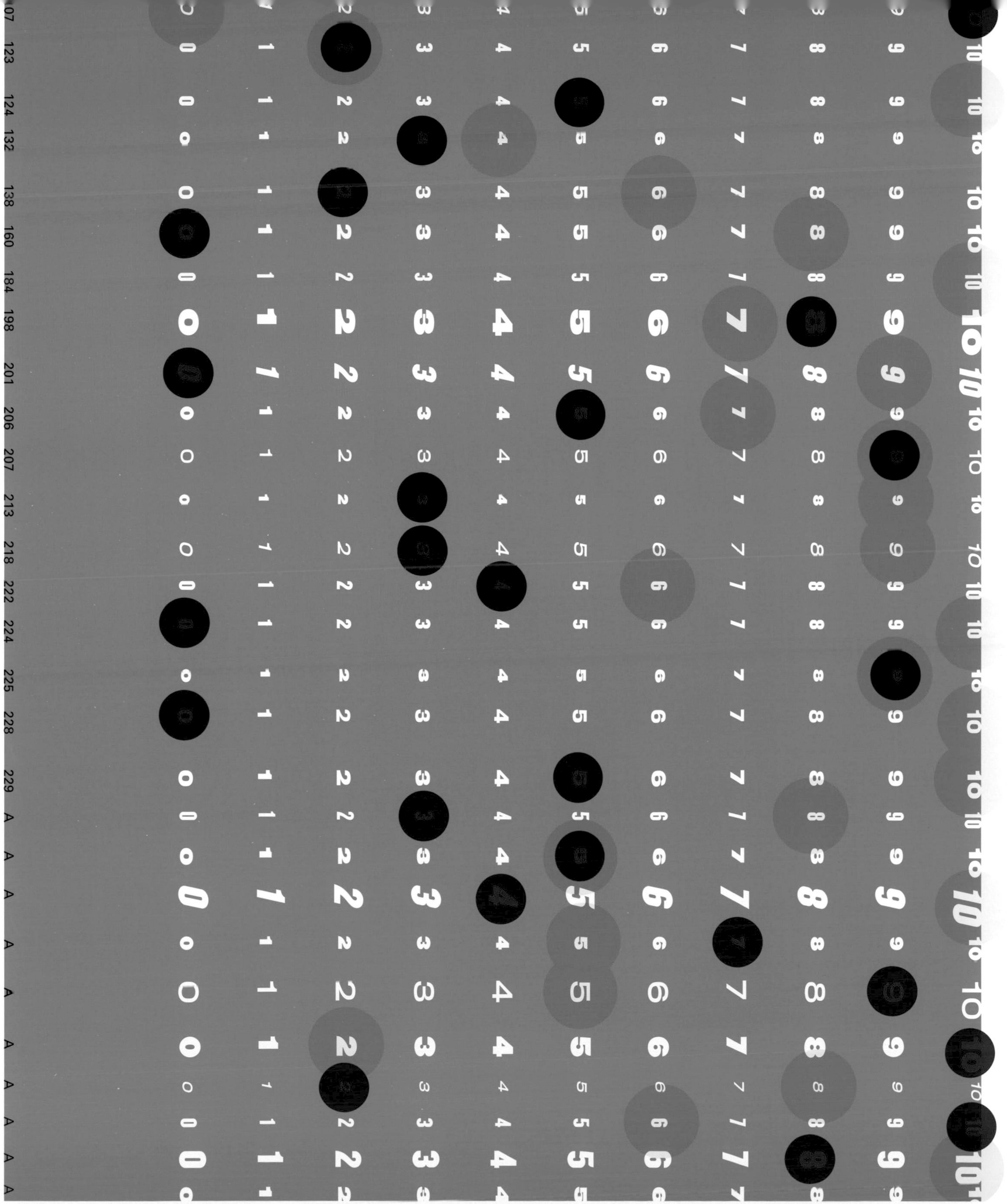

107
123
124
132
138
160
184
198
201
206
207
213
218
222
224
225
228
229
A
A
A
A
A
A
A
A
A
A

For the purposes of this competition, a book must be at least 48 pages long (except for children's books) and bound between covers – either casebound or paperbound – and not a portfolio of loose pages. Except in the case of limited-edition books, print runs should be in excess of 250 copies.

The book should be for sale to the general public or, if offered gratis, should not be a publication whose primary purpose is to advertise or serve as an annual report (such publications should be submitted to the appropriate section from the ones described above). Instruction manuals and textbooks will be accepted.

**Chaired by Eric Madsen** The Office of Eric Madsen, Minneapolis **with Harriett Barton** HarperCollins, New York **Walter Hamady** The Perishable Press, Mount Horeb, Wisconsin **Anita Meyer** plus design, Boston **Rodney Phillips** New York Public Library, New York **Jill Shimabukuro** University of Chicago Press, Chicago

In a year when money bought pardons and ballots didn't count, getting a "free ride" seemed to be the order of the day. This was not the case for this year's 50 Books/50 Covers competition; jurors rewarded work that was conceived through a holistic approach, where the result was not only aesthetically beautiful, but possessed a strong concept and visual wit – books in which minute attention was paid to every detail, from cover to bar code.

This year's jury focused on honoring work that successfully integrated all the "physical" elements of book design – margins, typography, materials, binding, production quality, layout, structure, flow, rhythm, visual and tactile texture – with those conceptual and intellectual qualities that give a book its soul.

Strategic changes in the book-selling industry – what jurors termed the wide-spread "supermarket" approach – have presented book designers with an additional challenge: negotiating with marketing departments. Marketers these days have the authority to make design-determining decisions – from the selection of paper stock to the use of gold hot stamping for titles by certain authors – while possessing no knowledge of design whatsoever. It is increasingly a critical skill of the current book designer to navigate the marketing maze in order to save the integrity of the book and his or her work.

Question F
Briefly describe the
research methods
used for preliminary
design on th s project.

# TALK TO LOU REED.

Response, cat. 107

Perhaps not surprisingly, in the first year of the new millennium, the dotcom aesthetic still ruled. HTML-reminiscent icons, flat images and colors and the ubiquitous square, plastic see-through cover that mimics the familiar computer screen appeared frequently, if not appropriately, among this year's 900 entries. Full-bleed photography was still a widely used visual trope, with the addition of very small type situated in a corner of the image. Thankfully, the tiny, manic, hard-to-read type that was so characteristic of 1999 entries was barely detectable amidst these submissions. After a year of experimentation, the change could be a testament to the creed that form must follow function – books are, for the most part, meant to be read.

Some of the trends that became apparent this year can be attributed to the continuous improvement of digital design programs as well as the wide availability of stock photography, which cuts back on production time and money, leaving more budget for materials, binding and intricate printing processes. Digital technology has had some negative consequences on book design, however. As one of the jurors observed, designers are now expected to be de facto typesetters, despite the fact that they generally lack the experience and deep understanding of the field. As a result, although many of the entries reviewed provided appropriate design solutions, a certain typographic deficiency prevented them from being included in the final selection. This was also the fate of over-designed entries in which expensive materials seemed to be used in lieu of content-driven solutions.

One impressive example of both beauty and brains is Sugimoto: Theatres (cat. 84), a book about the photographer's work, whose form the jurors considered to be perfectly defined by its content, from cover to cover. The book's binding – glow-in-the-dark hard covers contained in a brushed aluminum s lpcase – is as dramatic as theater itself.

But it wasn't only lavish productions and sexy materials that found a place amidst this year's selections. The cover of Genealogies, Miscegenations, Missed

Generations (cat. 124), introducing an exhibition catalogue published by the University of Connecticut, is a great example of maximum impact with limited means. The full title can be read through the overlay of a vellum dust jacket-like sheath that is printed on both sides over a white cover with black letters, a visual play on the literal and hidden meaning of the words. This solution is proof of the designer's deep understanding of the subject matter and audience, paired with talent and witty use of resources – a winning combination that the jurors deemed worth celebrating.

Loyal followers come to survey AIGA's "Book show," as it is commonly known, looking for the unusual. Among this year's refreshing surprises were two intimate, small-format pieces: Kate Spade's Contents (cat. 101) and the Brooklyn Museum's Artists' Books (cat. 67). Each at opposite ends of the spectrum when it comes to production budget, Contents is carried in a felt bag, more reminiscent of the fashion than publishing industry. Artists' Books, on the other hand, formatted at just under 5 x 5 inches, connects us with those qualities so inherent to books: concreteness, texture, intimacy and treasure.

It was particularly interesting to note how in this age of information overload, when the fate of the printed book has seemed so bleak – its end supposedly hastened by the advent of electronic books – the publishing industry is actually reporting a high increase in sales. Could it be that nowadays books have become more than reading material – that they are, in fact, artifacts? This year's competition showed that books continue to be a reflection of curiosity. In spite of the economic slowdown of 2001, they may become that indulgence we just can't live without. Gabriela Mirensky

With so many Brooklyn-based artists producing innovative books, the Brooklyn Museum decided to mount an exhibition of them. The special challenge was to create a catalogue that was an actual artists book in itself. The solution was to show how the very idea of the contemporary artists book grew out of the kind of innovative catalogue design propagated by the museum earlier in its history, specifically in an El Lissitzky-inspired book called Modern Art created in 1926. The binding materials of Artists' Books – corrugated board with gold foil stamping – were chosen to reflect the rough-and-ready brilliance of Brooklyn. Within the small, pocketsize format of the book, a rich density of text and images was smoothly and elegantly accommodated in a lucid, legible design concept. The three categories of books in the exhibition – unique works, limited editions and multiples – were divided into three distinct sections by "guillotine" tabs.

Design firm
Brooklyn Museum
of Art, Brooklyn
Creative director
Deirdre Lawrence

Designer
Stacey Wakefield, Evil
Twin Publications
Photographer
Pak Fung Wong
Production coordinator
Stacey Wakefield
Compositor
Stacey Wakefield
Author
Deirdre Lawrence
Editor James Leggio
Publisher Brooklyn
Museum of Art

Tony Millionaire's cartoons seem to be artifacts from a Victorian Era that got over its hang-ups and learned how to tie one on – "Popeye" as written by Eugene O'Neill. My goal was to make it look like something you'd unearth in your grandmother's attic, just after she'd been shipped off to the Better Days home for the elderly.

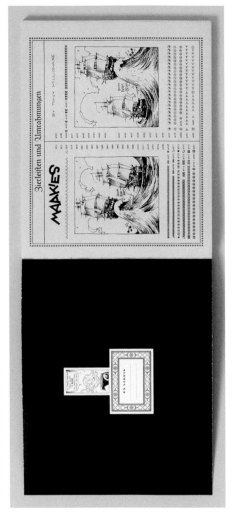

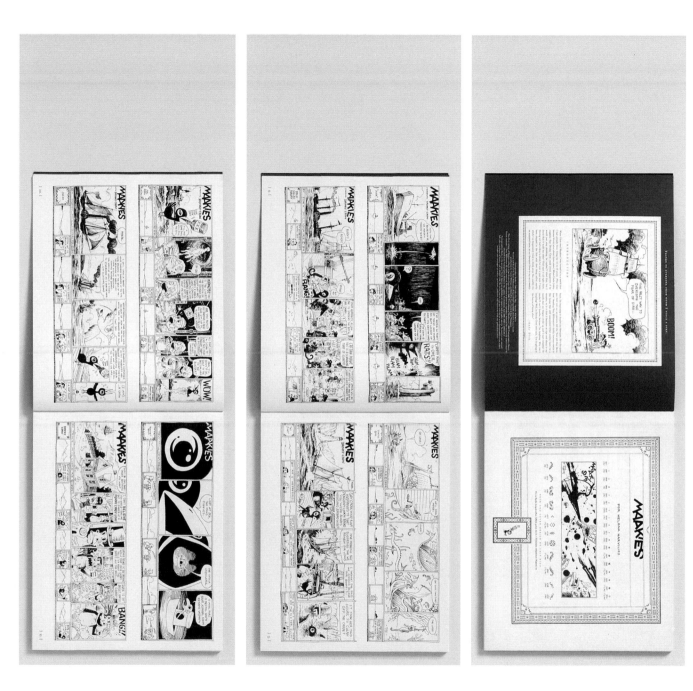

Art director/designer
Chip Kidd

Illustrator
Tony Millionaire

Production coordinator
Eric Reynolds

Author
Tony Millionaire

Publisher
Fantagraphics

*Maakies*
book

68

As editor of this book, my role was to leave Chris Ware free of the dull restrictions and hand-wringing anxieties that are usually imposed on book designers working for large corporations. In this respect I was mostly successful, but not without hair-raising moments – such as gently explaining to the editor-in-chief of Knopf why this jacket not only omitted the author's name from the front (Mr. Ware is famously self-effacing) but also deconstructed the title into a kaleidoscopic whirl. Ultimately he agreed that it was so beautiful and ingeniously conceived that it didn't matter. And we were right – the book is in its fourth printing.

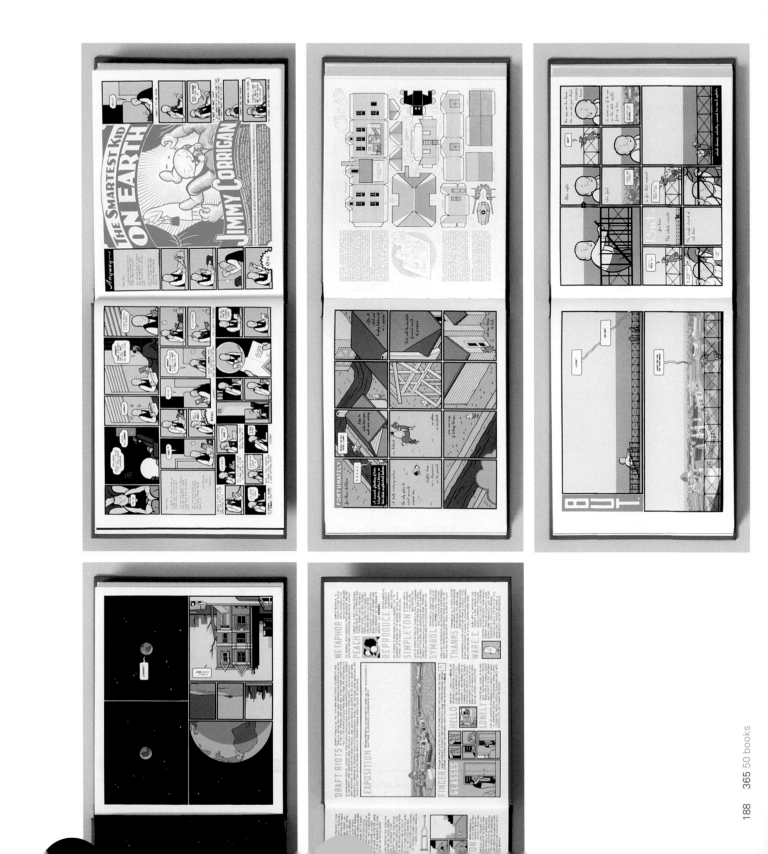

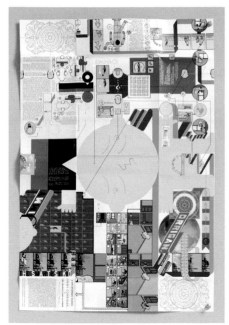

**69**

*Jimmy Corrigan:*
*The Smartest Kid*
*on Earth book*

Design firm
Alfred A. Knopf, Inc.,
New York

Art director Chip Kidd

Designers
Chip Kidd, Chris Ware

Illustrator Chris Ware

Production coordinator
Andy Hughes

Compositor Chris Ware

Jacket designer
Chris Ware

Author Chris Ware

Publisher
Pantheon Books

**The challenge, as always, is to get the design out of the way so the photography can be viewed at its best.**

*listening to cement*
*robert stivers*

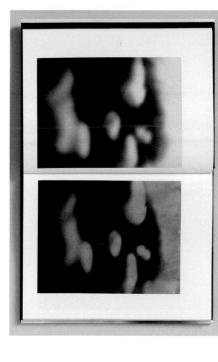

Design firm
Arena Editions,
Santa Fe

Creative director
Elsa Kendall

Designer/compositor
David Skolkin

Photographer
Robert Stivers

Production coordinator
Lara Colombarolli

Author John Stauffer

Publisher
Arena Editions

*Listening
to Cement book*

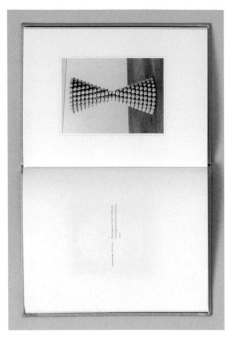

The cabinet of curiosities was a 16th-century precursor to the contemporary museum, a collection of objects assembled to instill a sense of wonder and awe. The design of the catalogue alludes to collecting by having the art reproductions printed as separate stickers that are placed in the book by the user. (The stickers were not a cost-saving measure.) The art – by such artists as Damien Hirst, Katharina Fritsch and Yasumasa Morimura – supplies the wonder. The idea of an assembly is carried through to the section dividers, which are antique anatomical illustrations and pages from a catalogue of typographic decorative material. The concept even works down to the text face, a custom remix of one of my fonts, New Clear Era.

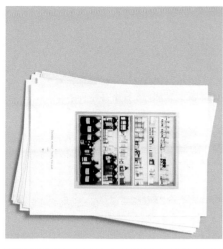

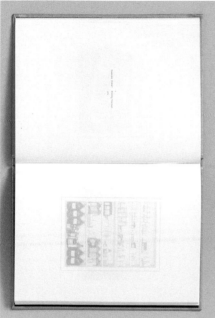

**71**

A Contemporary
Cabinet of
Curiosities book

Design firm
Aufuldish & Warinner,
San Anselmo, California
Designer Bob Aufuldish
Production coordinator
Celeste McMullin
Author Ralph Rugoff
Publication manager
Genoa Shepley
Editor Nancy Crowley
Publisher
California College of
Arts and Crafts

**72** *Babylon 1.7* **book**

Design firm
Babylon AG c/o Eclat
NY, Ithaca, New York

Creative director
Robert Kruegel-
Durband

Designers
Gion-Men Kruegel-
Hanna, Elke Schultz

Production coordinator
Arbeitsgruppe
Babylon 1.7

Jacket designer
Robert Kruegel-
Durband

Authors Roland Müller,
Robert Roos, Rolf
Todesco, Emil Zopfi

LIEBES-
ERKLÄRUNG
AN DIE
MEDIEN.

Edition Babylon 1.7

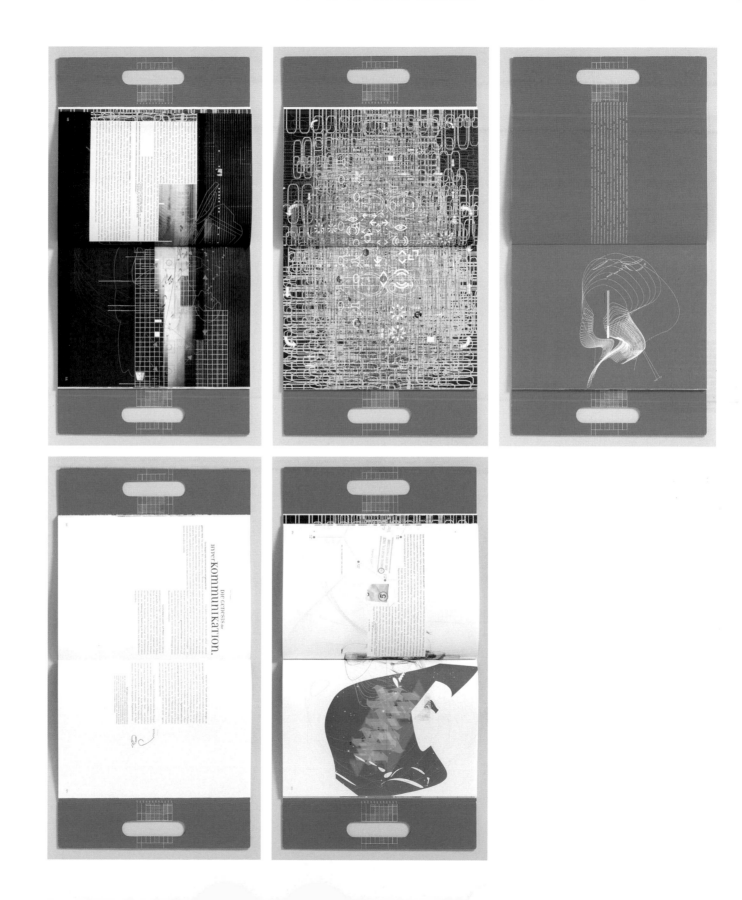

The most challenging portion of this job was to create an interesting pacing that would allow a more organic flow of objects based on conceptual, formal and material decisions. The visual complexity of the design acts as a glue, bringing together material of various levels and qualities and creating a unique language reflective of the energy particular to each region of the country. The flow of the book grows from not only a visual understanding of the images, but from a conceptual engagement of what they represent. The overall system we created to integrate images and typography was an evolving structure that changed as the book progressed and new elements were introduced into the mix. The underlying grid creates a kind of play with the surface elements and grows and becomes visible by the intersecting of images and graphics.

73

*American Contemporary Furniture book*

Design firm
Cabra Diseño,
San Francisco

Art director Raul Cabra

Designers
Santiago Giraldo,
Jeremy Stout,
Raul Cabra

Photographers
Richard Barnes,
Dino Dinco,
James Chian,
Debra Seidman

Production coordinator
Dung Ngo

Editors Raul Cabra,
Dung Ngo

Publisher
Universe Publishing

the great in-between

These designers savor the **isolation and anonymity** the region offers.

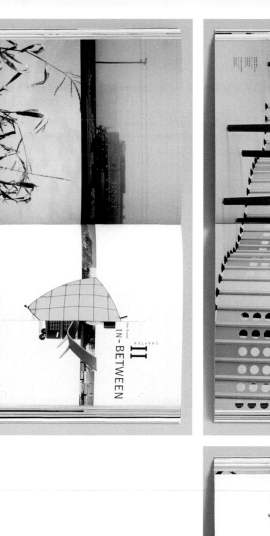

CHAPTER II
the Great IN-BETWEEN

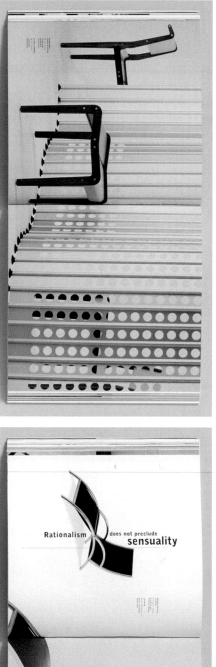

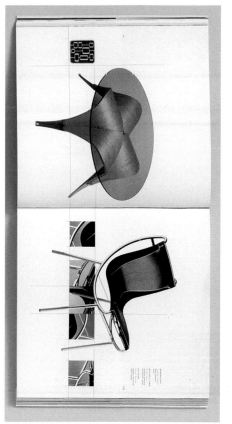

CHAPTER III
the WEST

Rationalism does not preclude **sensuality**

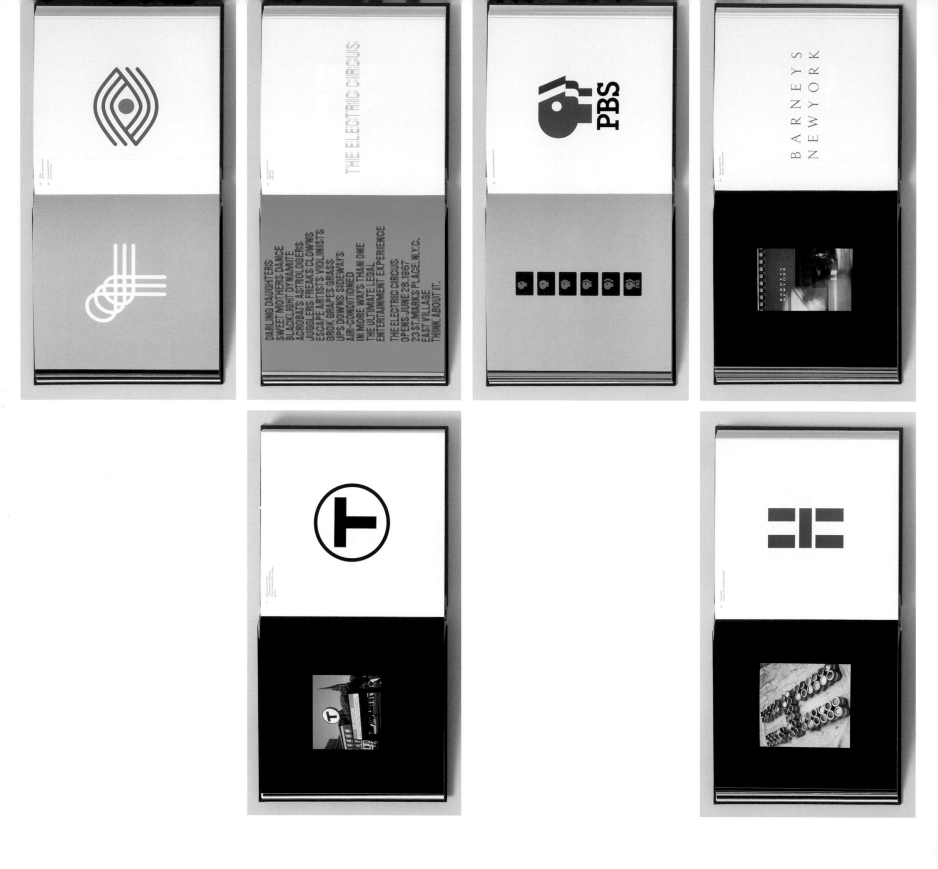

The challenge in designing our own trademarks book was to get it done in-between all our client-related projects. It forced us to digitize all trademarks designed between 1960 and approximately 1989. The trick was to make it a real project and stay with it, editing out the not-so-important marks, adding new ones and staying within the page count established. The most interesting aspect of the book is that we intentionally left out the date for each project. Although the trademarks are organized chronologically by decade, we wanted to make the point that our trademarks are timeless. We tried to match with a four-color process the precise original color for each identity. However, we discovered in the last round of proofs that the printer in Hong Kong was using different inks for CMYK than we do here in the U.S, which changed all our specified tint percentages.

Trademarks designed by
Chermayeff & Geismar

**74**

*TM: Trademarks
Designed
by Chermayeff &
Geismar book*

Design firm
Chermayeff &
Geismar, New York

Art directors
Ivan Chermayeff,
Tom Geismar,
Steff Geissbuhler

Publisher Princeton
Architectural Press
(U.S.), Lars Müller
Publishers (Europe)

Krijn de Koning creates "site-specific" sculptures that raise questions about how architecture conditions and limits us. Experiencing his work entails walking from room to room, looking from window to window, space to space – experiencing the inside/outside. Our challenge was to create a "site-specific design" to de Koning's work. The resulting design is based on the experience of inside/outside by employing interior/exterior and horizontal/vertical grids. The horizontal and vertical grids form overlapping layers. The blue "bars" on the outside of the book indicate the horizontal and vertical grid, and the horizontal structure of the interior is used as a big window, showing all installations and main reading texts. Marked as a page with crop marks, this grid is looped like a video, and the frame shifts throughout the book slowly to the right. The vertical grid is used for all background information, including drawings, models, an interview and traveling pictures.

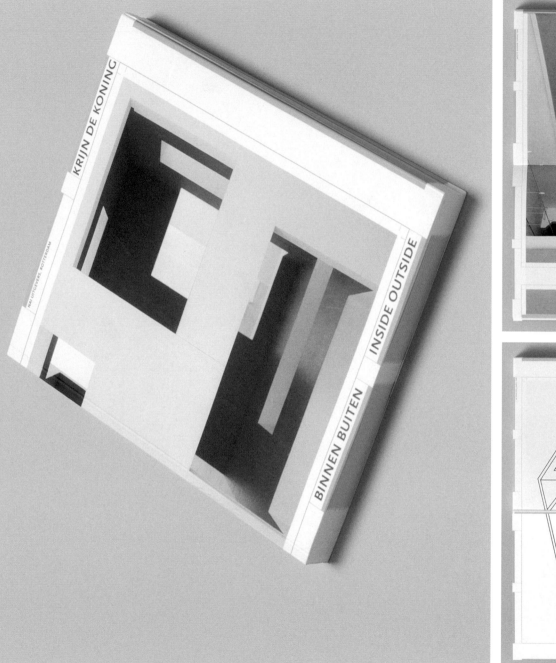

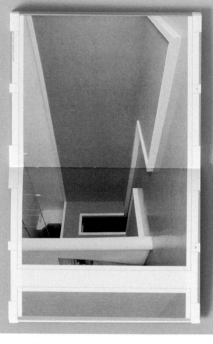

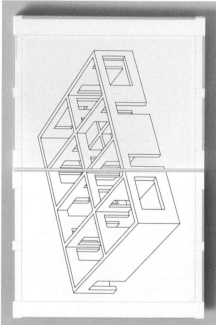

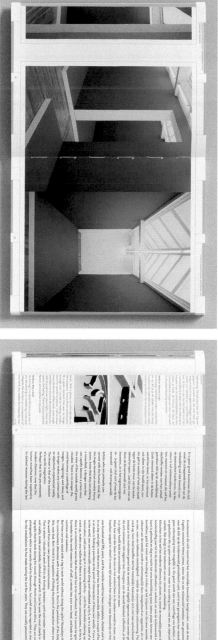

**Krijn de Koning:
Inside Outside
book**

Design firm
Coma, Brooklyn

Designers
Cornelia Blatter,
Marcel Hermans

Illustrator
Krijn de Koning

Photographers
Krijn de Koning et al

Production
coordinator
Barbera van Kooij

Authors
Rutger Wolfson,
Valentijn Byvanck,
Daniel Buren,
Michel Gauthier

Publisher
NAI Publishers

75

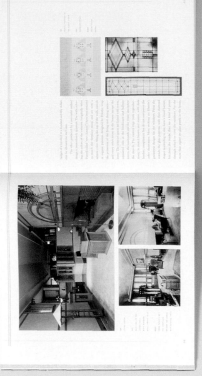

This book is a visual and verbal tour of the Purcell-Cutts house, the "crown jewel" of the Minneapolis Institute of Arts' Prairie School collection. We wanted this to be a unique combination of historical account, house tour and museum guide, a book that captures the modern, innovative spirit of the Prairie School – typified by the often horizontal, geometric and organic qualities of the architecture and design of the time. This was done in several ways through the book's format (square when closed, horizontal when open); the title "box" on the cover that's "transparent", the low, horizontal, open format of the spreads with photos occasionally breaking out; the use of airy letterspacing of modern sans serif type in combination with more traditional serif type; and the creation of a sensory book rather than a purely academic catalogue.

Design firm Deb Miner, Designer, Minneapolis

Art director/designer Deb Miner

Production coordinator Donald Leurquin

Compositor Deb Miner

Author Jennifer Komar Olivarez

Publisher Minneapolis Institute of Arts

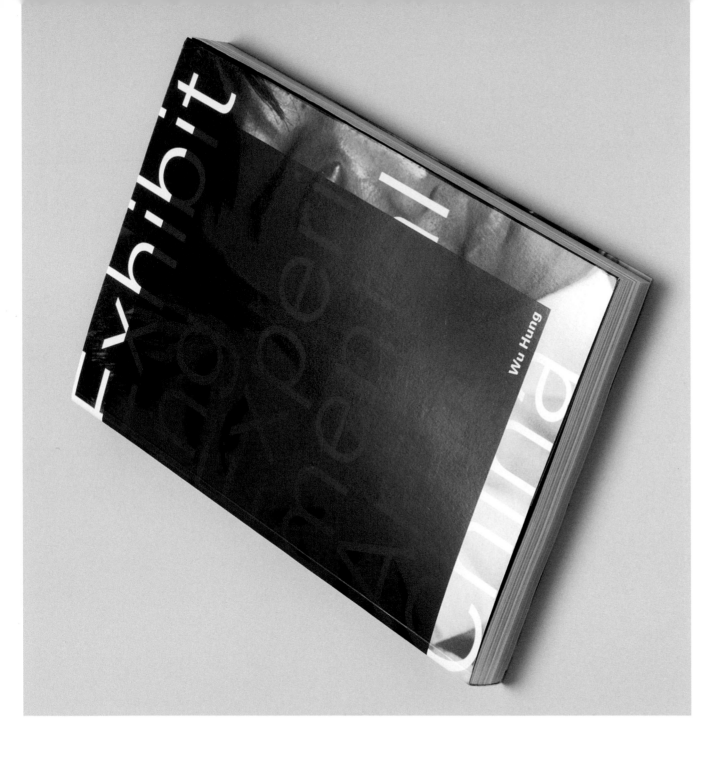

Wu Hung

**77**

***Exhibiting***
***Experimental Art***
***in China* book**

Design firm
Froeter Design, Inc.,
Chicago

Creative director
Chris Froeter

Designer Tom Zurawski

Production manager
Rachel Perez-Stable

Publication manager
Stephanie Smith

Author Wu Hung

Editor Margaret Farr

Publisher
Smart Museum of Art

This book is the first serious study of contemporary art exhibitions and exhibition spaces in China. Questions about censorship, self-censorship and the business of art in China ring true in both Eastern and Western cultures. From a design standpoint, this book needed to address the social importance of the commentary while fulfilling the needs of market sophistication. We were very fortunate in that this book designed itself: the editorial content and detail created the tone.

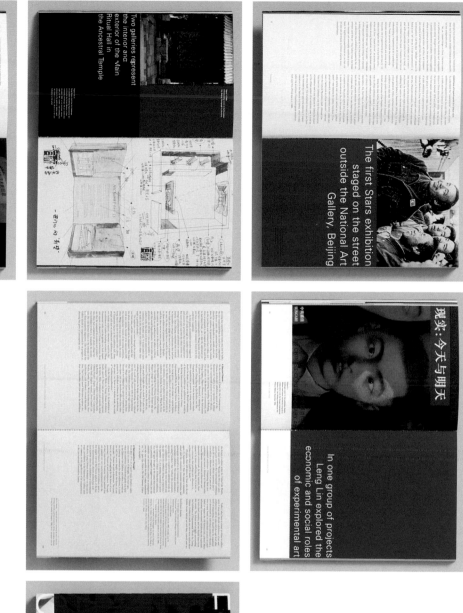

Two galleries represent the interior and exterior of the Main Ritual Hall in the Ancestral Temple

The first Stars exhibition staged on the street outside the National Art Gallery, Beijing

现实:今天与明天

In one group of projects Leng Lin explored the economic and social roles of experimental art

Exhibiting

Wu Hung

The special challenge in Faces was to give a smooth flow from color to black-and-white images, from single photos to spreads. My design solution was to be simple and clean. The publisher determined the book size, which we then revised to better accommodate the 4 x 5 transparency proportions. I am most happy with the quality of the reproductions.

**78**

*Faces book*

Design firm
Gittings Design,
Tucson

Art director
Dana Arnett

Designer
Jane Gittings

Authors/photographers
François and
Jean Robert

Production
coordinator Tera Killup,
Chronicle Books

Publisher
Chronicle Books

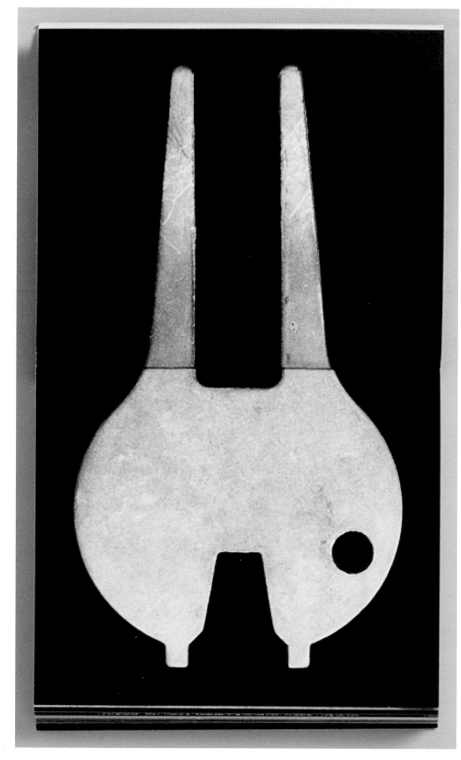
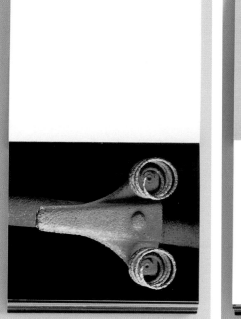

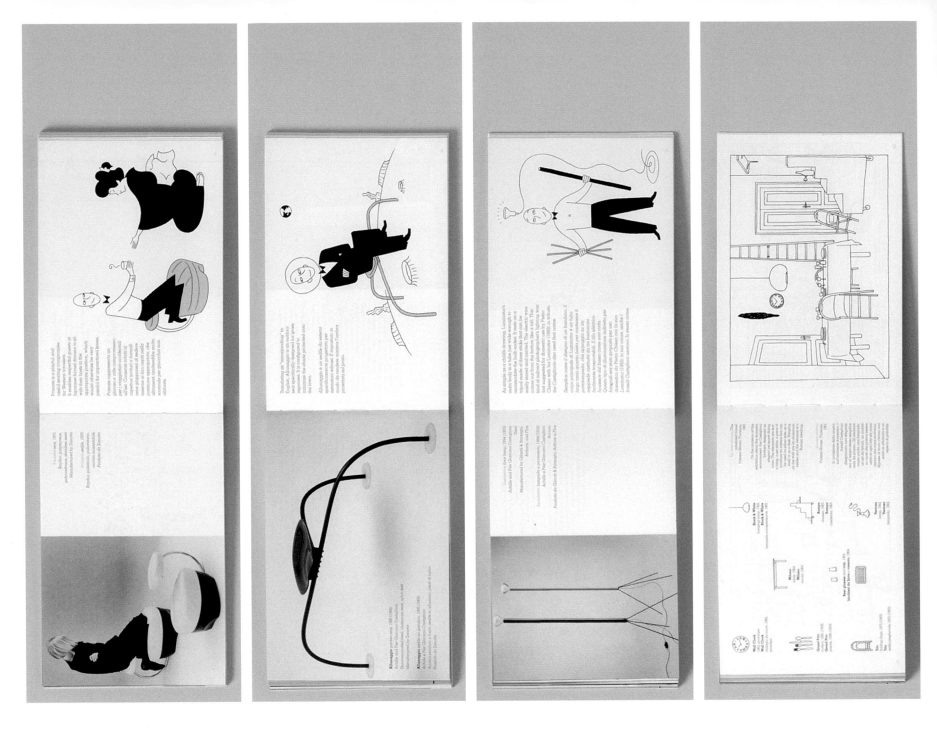

*Achille Castiglioni*
book

Art directors
Marzia and
Maurizio Corraini

Designer
Maurizio Corraini

Illustrator
Steven Guarnaccia

Author
Paola Antonelli

Publisher
Corraini Editore

Seeing the show at the Museum of Modern Art that inspired the book helped drive the design, although it was important to make the book distinct from the show. As the book was published in an Italian/English edition, the challenge was to retain the beauty of the design while contending with twice the amount of text. We were happiest with the front and back cover visual game, and that we were able to produce a book on design quite different from the usual. We were also pleased that the book won an award at the Bologna Children's Book Fair, even though it was not specifically aimed at children.

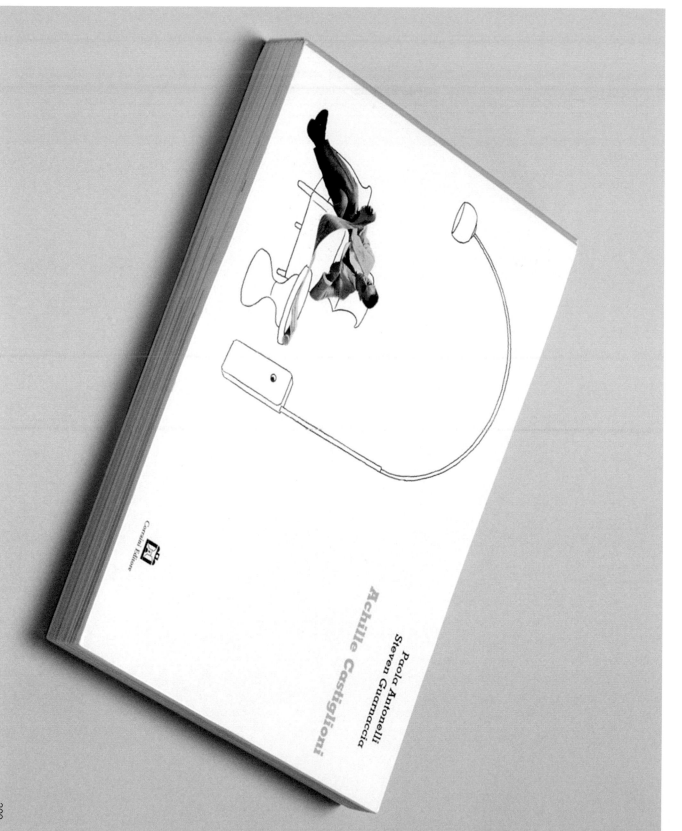

Paola Antonelli
Steven Guarnaccia
**Achille Castiglioni**

Corraini Editore

This publication was intended to display some of the achievements in the fields of calligraphy, type design, book design and typography of the noted German graphic artist Hermann Zapf. It was published to coincide with an exhibition of Zapf's work at the Grolier Club in New York. A special challenge was staying fairly close to the great variety of the original colors, while printing only part of the book in full color and using flat colors elsewhere. The book was set in the elegant Zapf Renaissance type (for the text) with Zapf's latest alphabet design – the script type Zapfino – used for the headings. This is probably the first use of Zapfino for a book-length project. In the end, I think the book achieved its goal of displaying lesser-known Zapf works to a larger audience, thereby giving some hint of the extent of his artistic achievement.

Design firm
Jerry Kelly LLC,
New York

Art director/illustrator
Hermann Zapf

Designer/production
coordinator
Jerry Kelly

Author
Hermann Zapf

Publisher
The Grolier Club

80

*The Fine Art
of Letters* book

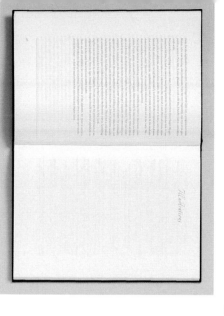

This catalogue design was an attempt to recreate the experience of visiting the exhibition, which explored the relationship between art and the popular image of California in the 20th century. The strategy of the cover and jacket and the sequence of images that begins the book was to demonstrate that many of the popular images of California tend to contradict each other, yet that they are all valid to some extent. The title font for the book, based on letterforms on a 1940 California license plate, was created to give the book a voice that is simultaneously historical and contemporary.

*Made in California*
book

Design firm
LACMA, Los Angeles

Designer Scott Taylor

Supervising
photographer
Peter Brenner

Production
coordinators
Rachel Ware Zooi,
Chris Coniglio

Compositor
Scott Taylor

Authors Stephanie
Barron, Sheri
Bernstein, Ilene
Susan Fort, Michael
Dear, Howard N. Fox,
Richard Rodriguez

Editors Nola Butler,
Thomas Frick

Publisher LACMA
and University of
California Press

MADE IN
CALIFORNIA

ART, IMAGE,
AND IDENTITY,
1900–2000

81

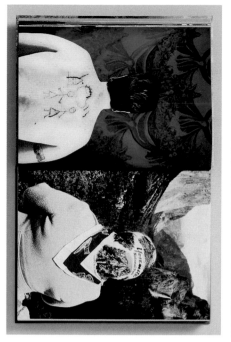

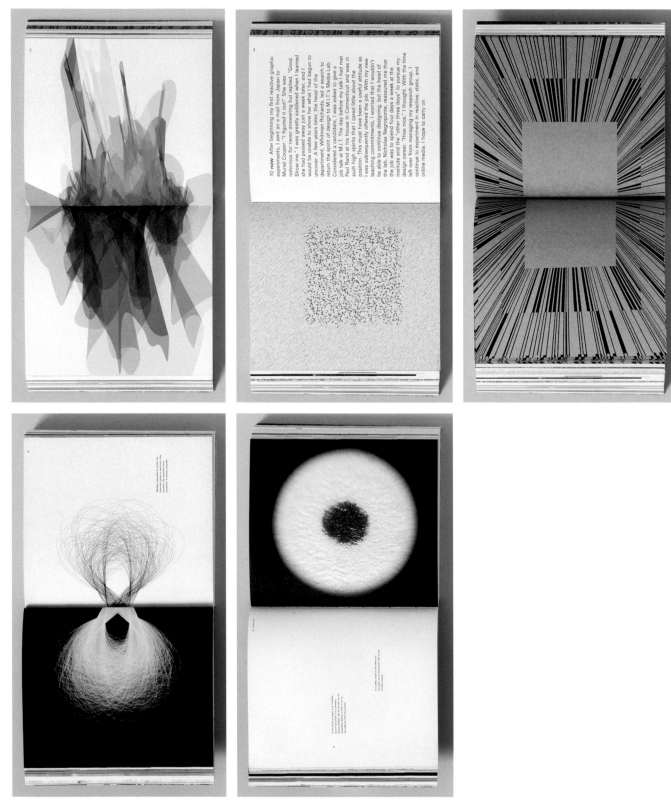

table of contents

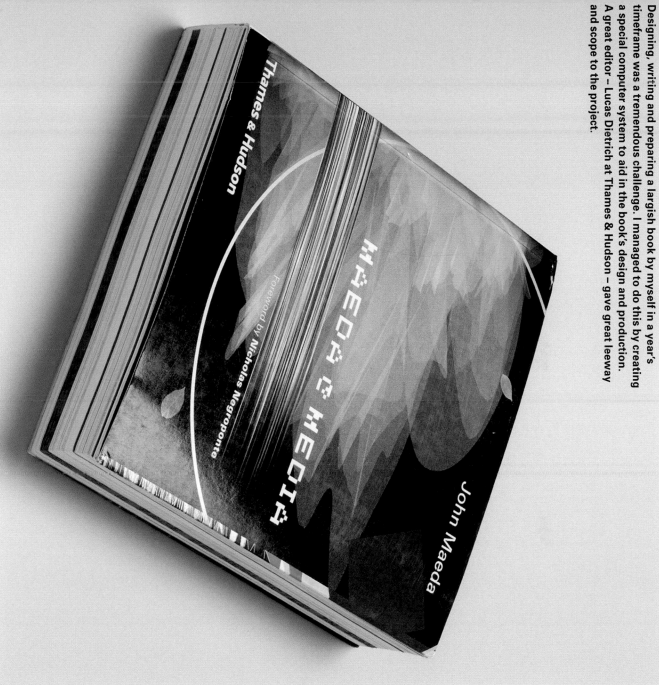

**MAEDA @ MEDIA**

Foreword by Nicholas Negroponte

John Maeda

Thames & Hudson

Designing, writing and preparing a largish book by myself in a year's timeframe was a tremendous challenge. I managed to do this by creating a special computer system to aid in the book's design and production. A great editor – Lucas Dietrich at Thames & Hudson – gave great leeway and scope to the project.

Design firm
Maeda, Cambridge,
Massachusetts

Art director/designer
John Maeda

Production coordinator
Kris Maeda

Compositor
John Maeda

Author John Maeda

Publishers
Thames & Hudson,
Rizzoli, Bangert Verlag,
Digitalogue

This catalogue was published to feature the work of two fine artists, Glenn Ligon and Gary Simmons, at the Fabric Workshop and Museum in Philadelphia. The impressive size of this catalogue was a design decision to directly reflect the importance and power of the subject matter.

GLENN LIGON AND GARY SIMMONS

THE FABRIC WORKSHOP AND MUSEUM

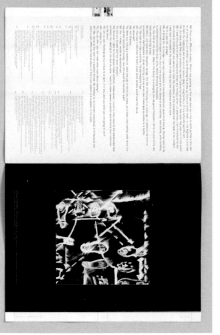

**Thelma Golder:** When did your interest in boxing begin?

**Glenn Ligon:** I don't really remember when I became interested in boxing outside of any other sport spectacle until I was a teenager. I wasn't at all interested in sports, though I knew of the famous fighters and certainly knew and admired Muhammad Ali.

**TG:** When did boxing enter your artwork?

**GL:** It came into my work at the time I made the Mapplethorpe piece, in 1991, titled Notes on the Margin of the Black Book. I was making a series of works dealing with masculinity. This seemed to be another arena in which I could continue this investigation. Actually, I was most interested in Ali as a persona and a public figure and the role he had in his prime of being a spokesperson for the black community, then I was interested in him as an athlete. The sport also entered my work because boxing encompassed so many issues. Boxing is the space of hyper-masculinity, it engages notions of sexuality and relies on the mythology of the brutish black man. Prowess in boxing generates respect despite coming primarily from the physical use of the body, it stows the ambivalent relationship white Americans have to black bodies. All of that is in there. I am attracted to the complicatedness of the fact that, on one level, black people were brought here and subjugated for the physical labor of their bodies. On another level, All becomes a public persona who is respected, listened to, and admired based on his achievement as a fighter, which is based on this same physicality. This admiration allowed him to transcend the stereotypes. This was rather unique.

**TG:** Are you interested in any other sports in relation to these issues?

**GL:** Why?

**TG:** Mike Tyson, for example, does not have that same effect.

**GL:** Because Tyson fits too much into the cultural stereotype of what a black man is. Tyson is a thug. And he always presents himself that way. Ali had the same kind of physical skill but he presented himself as a highly principled man. Tyson does not.

**TG:** Football? Basketball?

**GL:** No, though basketball is another way you could tackle some of these issues. Basketball would allow a discussion of race and class, but with boxing you also have sexuality. The erotic is so much more heightened or hyped in boxing.

**TG:** Is this why you chose to conflate hip-hop culture and boxing in your installation Skin Tight?

**GL:** Yes, I was interested in rappers who were using hip-hop as a means of social critique, which, to me, was very related to what Ali had done. Some of the old-school rappers, Public Enemy and KRS 1 especially, were using their platform to speak in a similar way. The thought process of certain rappers seemed to be: "I'm in this position, so how do I use this position? Do I reproduce the cultural stereotypes? How do I use this space I've created as platform to speak about other political agendas?"

**TG:** It seems that this is the subtext to your interest, this interest in the erotics.

**GL:** The erotics are ever-present. There is a quote from George Plimpton in his writing about Ali where he says Ali glowed. He meant it, perhaps, in an unsexualized way, but the subtext is sexual. This speaks to the kind of desire around boxers, the sense of the physical strength also being a kind of hyper-attractiveness.

**TG:** What does that mean then, talking about boxing in the contemporary moment? Talking about black boxers?

**GL:** Boxing is a safe space. It is a controlled spectacle. People can satisfy their desire in a controlled environment. It is why, perhaps, Ralph Ellison chooses the boxing match as one of the opening sequences of Invisible Man as a way to explore the safety of what would otherwise be socially unacceptable behavior. There are always spaces in the cultural where otherwise unacceptable behavior is sanctioned. Behaviors, speech, Richard Pryor could say the things that he said because he was on stage doing comedy.

**83**

**Glen Ligon and Gary Simmons book**

Design firm
Matsumoto
Incorporated,
New York

Creative director/
art director
Takaaki Matsumoto

Designers
Takaaki Matsumoto,
Thanh X. Tran

Author
Thelma Golder

Publisher
The Fabric Workshop
and Museum

*Sugimoto: Theaters*
book

Design firm
Matsumoto
Incorporated,
New York

Creative director
Takaaki Matsumoto

Art director
Hiroshi Sugimoto

Designers
Takaaki Matsumoto,
Larissa Nowicki

Photographer
Hiroshi Sugimoto

Author Hans Belting

Publisher Sonnabend
Sundell Editions
and Eyestorm.com

The **Sugimoto: Theaters** book was published to feature the complete theater series (including movie theaters and drive-in theaters) by the fine-arts photographer Hiroshi Sugimoto. With the use of the traditional dry-trap offset printing process – by printing one color at a time and allowing the ink to dry in between runs – we have managed to represent the artist's photographs as close to the original as possible in a book form. The cover has been silkscreened with day-glo ink and matte film laminated to conceptually recreate the illusion of light that is portrayed in these photographs. The special edition book is accompanied by a limited edition of Hiroshi Sugimoto's U.A. Walker, New York 1978 photogravure print. One thousand prints were numbered and signed by the artist, and are cased in a custom-made, piano-hinged, brushed-aluminum box.

**Each Wild Idea**
book

Design firm
MIT Press Design
Department,
Cambridge,
Massachusetts

Designer
Ori Kometani

Production coordinator
Terry Lamoureux

Author
Geoffrey Batchen

Publisher MIT Press

This book accompanies an exhibition of works acquired or given to the National Gallery over the past 10 years, and was designed with a dual audience in mind: donors and collectors, as well as general museum visitors. Creating a consistent yet variable format to accommodate the wide scope of works – size, category and medium – and last-minute additions were probably the biggest challenges. In the end, the puzzle pieces fit together and I was pleasantly surprised by the cohesion of the book and by the fine quality of the reproductions on the Xantur paper.

Art for the Nation
COLLECTING FOR A NEW CENTURY

**86**

***Art for the Nation:
Collecting for
a New Century***
book

Design firm National
Gallery of Art,
Washington, D.C.

Art director/designer
Margaret Bauer

Production coordinator
Margaret Bauer

Editor Julie Warnement

Curator Alan Shestack

Publisher
National Gallery of Art

**87**

*The Patricia G.
England Collection
of Fine Press and
Artists' Books*
book

Design firm National
Gallery of Art,
Washington, D.C.

Art director/designer
Margaret Bauer

Photographer
Lyle Peterzell

Production coordinator
Margaret Bauer

Editor Ulrike Mills

Curator Ruth E. Fine

Publisher
National Gallery of Art

This small book was designed to celebrate and document the exquisite collection of fine press and artists books given to the gallery by Patricia G. England, and includes an interview with the donor, a few photographs of choice objects illustrating the range of the collection and – at the back, printed on a different color stock – a complete catalogue of the collection's holdings. The design was conceived as something serious, intimate and a little bit luxuriant, with marble paper dividers taken directly from one of the collection's books; the treatment of these divider pages draws on the idea of the "bookplate."

THE
COLLECTION OF
FINE PRESS AND ARTISTS. BOOKS

S

PATRICIA G. ENGLAND

*National Gallery of Art, Washington*

**Ezekiel's Horse** is not merely a collection of horse photography, it is a body of fine art work roughly organized around the theme of horses. I wanted the book's design to reflect this change in photographer Keith Carter's vision from documentary to art photography and the fact that this is not your run-of-the-mill collection of horse pictures. The book was designed to have a cutting-edge sensibility that would communicate visually that this was a book of art.

*Ezekiel's Horse*
book

Design firm Pentagram
Design, Austin

Art director DJ Stout

Designers/
compositors DJ Stout,
Nancy McMillen

Photographer
Keith Carter

Production coordinator
David S. Cavazos

Authors Keith Carter,
John Wood

Publisher University
of Texas Press,
in cooperation with
the Wittliff Gallery
of Southwestern &
Mexican Photography
at Southwest Texas
State University

4 SPIRITED 1998

EZEKIEL'S HORSE KEITH CARTER PHOTOGRAPHS

AND GOD TOOK
A HANDFUL OF
SOUTHERLY
WIND, BLEW HIS
BREATH OVER
IT AND CREATED
THE HORSE.

BEDOUIN LEGEND

28 STABLE GIRL 1999

This book was one of the first elements to introduce a new graphic identity we produced for the Whitney Museum of American Art, so it needed to set out a typographic territory that the museum would operate within for some time. It also answered a problem typical of many publications that present a range of disparate images, using an uncoated sheet of paper as a divider between each of the artist's work. As one page blocked most of the view of the previous page, it also became a place to present a narrative and caption about the art on the opposite page.

**Whitney Biennial 2000 book**

Design firm
Pentagram Design,
New York

Creative director
J. Abbott Miller

Designers
J. Abbott Miller,
Roy Brooks,
Scott Devendorf

Publisher
Whitney Museum
of American Art

89

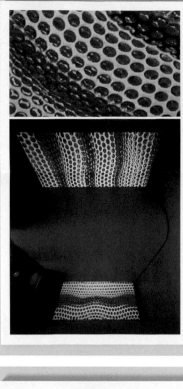

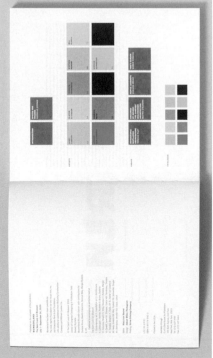

This book had to be produced to coincide with a large exhibition about installation art at the St. Louis Art Museum. The problem was that the installation of the 10 works would not be complete until opening day, so we had to create a slipcase that would then contain a book of essays and previously completed projects by the artists that could then accommodate a sequence of inserts that documented the newly commissioned projects. It was a challenge to make a book package that would be "completed" at a later date, and to make it look deliberate and enriching to the book rather than detracting from it. The slipcase allowed for 10 inserts that take advantage of being able to make larger, poster-like presentations of this very environmental work – something that would be awkward to do in a conventionally bound book.

WONDERLAND

SPACES FOR WONDER

**Wonderland book**

**90**

Design firm
Pentagram Design,
New York

Creative director
J. Abbott Miller

Designers
J. Abbott Miller,
Roy Brooks,
Scott Devendorf

Photographer
Peter Mauss/Esto

Production coordinator
John Porter

Editor
Rochelle Steiner

Publisher
The St. Louis Art
Museum

Parallax is an autobiography 15 distinct ideas the result of a 6 month conversation a handbook $40.00 at a bookstore near you an attempt to organize contradictory "...a must for anyone practicing or studying in a climate affected by light" "...[full of] leaden, humorless meditations" a diary approximately 5" x 7", 350 pages, with over 300 pictures, many in color a philosophical capabilities brochure set in Monotype Grotesque and Berthold Baskerville a design process that enabled a collaboration words and pictures

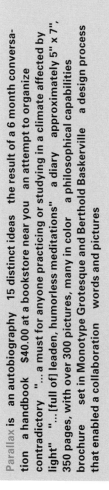

**91**

*Parallax*
**book**

Design firm
2x4, New York

Art director
Michael Rock

Designers Conny Purtill,
Michael Rock

Production coordinator
Clare Jacobson

Author Steven Holl

Publisher Princeton
Architectural Press,
Inc., New York

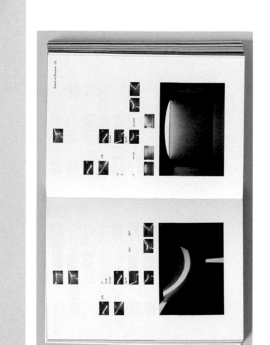

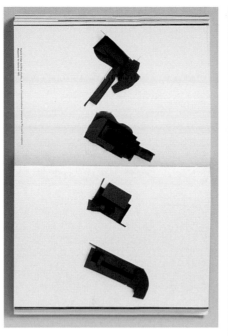

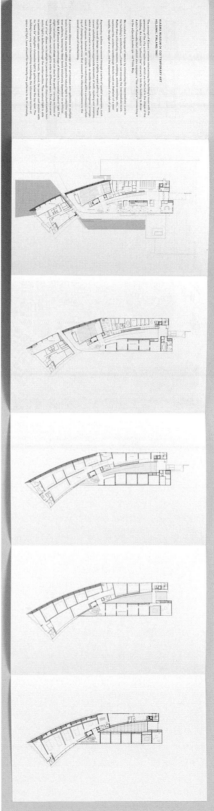

The challenge with the cover was to find a way to graphically present an extensive art collection without relying on one specific iconographic work or artist. For the book interior, the challenge was to create a design that responded to the work of some 75 different artists in a way that allowed the artworks to stand out individually without conflicting with each other. My cover approach investigated the notion of creating a visual field of forms derived from a deconstructed analysis of the book's subtitle. Since the focus of the collection is essentially modernist, I felt typography could be used to reference the parallel development of modernist typographic forms and composition. I also needed to create a design that was at once a bold and graphic statement and a modular and flexible system that could be used as a "brand" for other materials created in conjunction with the book.

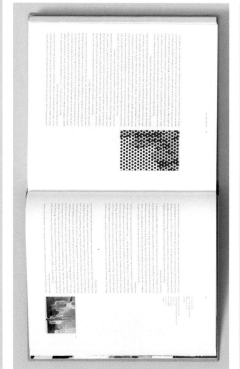

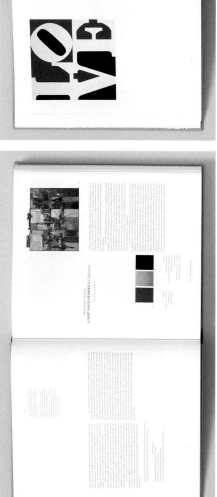

**92**

*Celebrating Modern Art: The Anderson Collection book*

Design firm
San Francisco Museum of Modern Art, San Francisco

Art director/designer
Tracey Shiffman

Photographer
Ian Reeves, et al

Illustrator
Tracey Shiffman

Production coordinator
Kara Kirk

Compositor
Tracey Shiffman

Editor
Gary Garrels, et al

Publisher San Francisco Museum of Modern Art, University of California Press

This catalogue posed dozens of the usual challenges, including developing a grid that would work for all elements, finding the appropriate typographic treatment for each level of information and maintaining the proper relationships between the various pieces. After reading the materials, I looked for a form that could treat disparate entries (size of image, length of text, etc.) equally and attractively. The two most important influences on the design were budget (hence the one-color interior) and the curator (through her text, conversations and review of layout proposals). The book is fairly close to the original concept and presentation. The major change is a more conservative presentation of the images. Originally we proposed pages using small reproductions and occasional enlarged details or silhouettes for each entry. A combination of curator comments and space limitations led us to our final design.

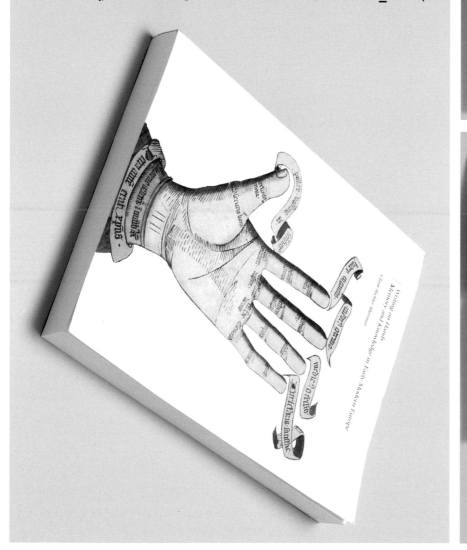

*Writing on Hands:*
*Memory and Knowledge in Early Modern Europe*
Claire Richter Sherman

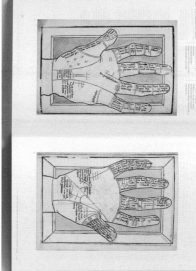

**93**

***Writing on Hands:***
***Memory and***
***Knowledge in Early***
***Modern Europe book***

Design firm Studio A,
Alexandria, Virginia

Art director
Antonio Alcalá

Designers
Antonio Alcalá,
Mary Dunnington,
Helen McNeill

Author
Claire Richter Sherman

Publisher
The Trout Gallery,
Dickinson College

This catalogue accompanied an exhibit of Chinese scholars' stones held at the Art Institute of Chicago. Historically, these stones were thought to embody primordial energy and magical powers. The curator wanted a book that was dramatic, one that captured the fluid energy of the stones, yet was open, spare and somehow contemporary. To accomplish this, we created an opening sequence that spotlights the captive energy of the stones and used Balance, a font that seemed both machine and handmade, typeset so that it had the feel of a Chinese scroll, set tight to the top and loose at the bottom. The book's format and typography draw from traditional Chinese painting, where gaps in visual information and a series of repetitive horizontal or vertical forms are often employed. We created numbers and titling type for the catalogue using the idea of lines that fade in and out.

**94**

**Spirit Stones
of China book**

Design firm
studio blue, Chicago

Art directors
Kathy Fredrickson,
Cheryl Towler Weese

Designers
Cheryl Towler Weese,
Radhika Gupta

Illustrator studio blue

Photographer
Michael Tropea

Typographer
Matt Simpson

Production coordinators
Matt Simpson,
Sarah Guernsey

Author Stephen Little

Editor Kate Steinmann

Publisher The Art
Institute of Chicago,
in association with
University of California
Press

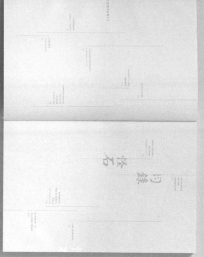

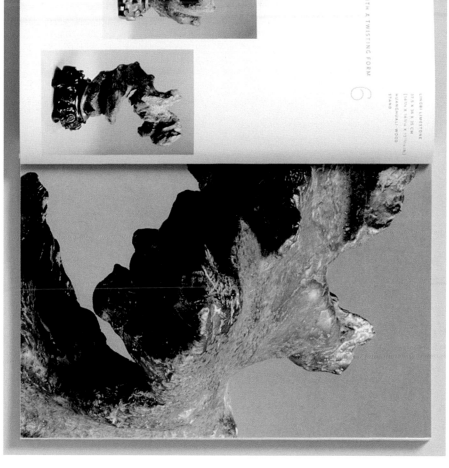

STONE WITH A TWISTING FORM

6

LINGBI LIMESTONE
37.5 × 38 × 20 CM
(14¾ × 14½ × 7⅞ IN.)
HUANGHUALI WOOD
STAND

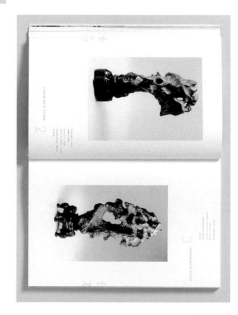

This catalogue is about Marcel Duchamp and his work in multiples – including a good deal of graphic design that very few people have seen before. Duchamp was a type aficionado and loved using a broad range of typefaces in a given work, sometimes varying each letter by font, or sometimes each page. He despised repetition; each work looks completely different from the next, making this difficult subject matter to represent visually. Because the idea of optics, transparency and the ability to look at something forwards and backwards were important to Duchamp, we appropriated the titling type from a Russian eye chart he owned, and repeated it in reverse on the back cover. The chapter openers repeat this theme. The book's structure responds to Duchamp's work by juxtaposing a rigid typographic grid with images that float freely and overlap.

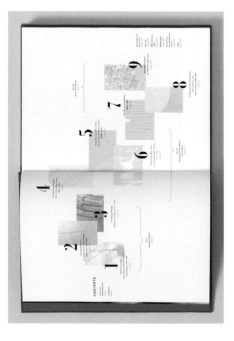

95

*Marcel Duchamp:*
*The Art of Making Art in*
*the Age of Mechanical*
*Reproduction book*

Design firm
studio blue, Chicago

Art directors
Kathy Fredrickson,
Cheryl Towler Weese

Designers
Cheryl Towler Weese,
Heather Corcoran,
Garrett Niksch

Illustrator studio blue

Production coordinator
Matt Simpson

Author
Francis Naumann

Publisher
Ludion (Belgium),
Abrams (U.S.)

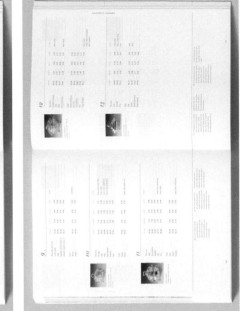

**96**

*Campbell Collection
of Soup Tureens
at Winterthur book*

Design firm
studio blue, Chicago

Art directors
Kathy Fredrickson,
Cheryl Towler Weese

Designers
Heather Corcoran,
Garrett Niksch,
Cheryl Towler Weese

Production coordinator
Matt Simpson

Authors
Donald Fennimore,
Patricia Halfpenny

Editors
Onie Rollins,
Teresa Vivolo

Publisher
Winterthur Museum

240   365 50 books

From the 17th to 19th centuries, soup was a consistent first course for formal meals in Europe and the Americas, and the soup tureen served as vessel, table ornament and prestigious symbol. To provide cultural context, we encouraged the museum to incorporate imagery related to the history of soup and dining in general. We introduced two pale varnishes to organize the tureens by medium, and used small details and maps to flesh out the narrative. It was especially challenging to make the soup tureens engaging, and create graceful structures for a range of complex technical information. The tone of our original design comes through here, but the book's structure evolved over the project's life.

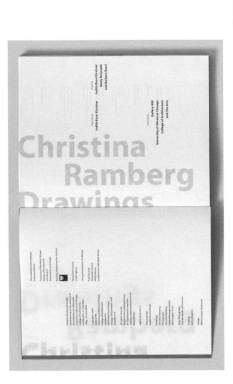

**97**

*Christina Ramberg
Drawings* book

Design firm
Studio/Lab, Chicago

Designer
Marcia Lausen

Illustrator
Christina Ramberg

Photographers
Christina Ramberg;
Tom van Eynde,
Jeff Crisman (copy
photographers)

Author
Judith Russi Kirshner

Publisher University
of Illinois at Chicago

The drawings of Chicago imagist Christina Ramberg center around overtly female themes. On notebook pages and the backs of used index cards, Ramberg repeated images in pencil and ink and catalogued drawn variations of female hands, garments, heads, hairstyles, injuries, bindings, weeping figures, quilts and household objects as inventories of aesthetic possibilities. Critical to the book's design concept is a paper stock that can both conceal and reveal. The translucency of the paper also provides opportunity to demonstrate the complexity of Ramberg's methodology, in which drawings were often traced and retraced to explore nuances of emotion in the exact same pose of a figure or rendering of a garment. The drawings are produced at actual size along with examples of source materials. The inexpensive and lightweight materials of the catalogue are designed to evoke the qualities of a sketchbook and invite the reader to experience Ramberg's rich imagination and complex creative process.

Christina Ramberg
Drawings

Gallery 400
University of Illinois at Chicago
College of Architecture and the Arts

**98**

**The Fairest Fowl:**
**Portraits of**
**Championship**
**Chickens book**

Design firm
The Grillo Group,
Inc., Chicago

Art director
Maria Grillo

Designers
Julie Klugman,
Gabrielle Schubart,
Winifred Gundeck

Photographer
Tamara Staples

Author
Christa Velbel,
Ira Glass

Publisher
Chronicle Books

Tamara Staples has been photographing chickens for many years. One night over a bottle of wine she and I decided they should be in a book and we agreed that our criteria for success would be measured by our ability to respectfully present the chickens and the judging process without losing the distinctly "human" character of each individual bird, ranging from lighthearted to sweet to serious to hilarious. The main challenge was to be sure that the personality of the chickens in the photographs was the main event – not overpowered by any of the other content. We chose to enhance the already wonderful portraits with as much detailed and historic information as possible.

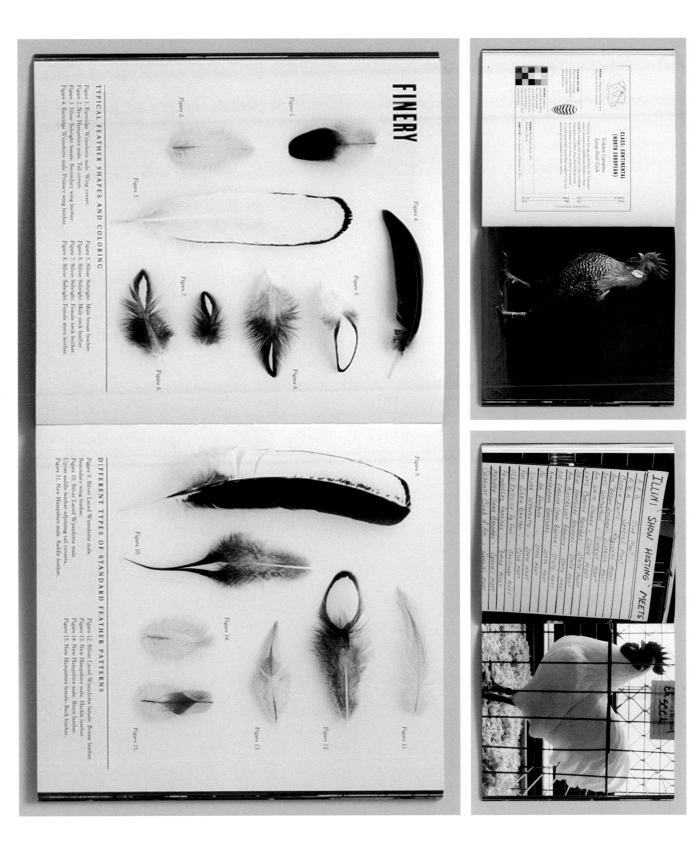

FINERY

TYPICAL FEATHER SHAPES AND COLORING

Figure 1. Partridge Wyandotte male Wing covert.
Figure 2. New Hampshire male Tail covert.
Figure 3. Silver Sebright male Secondary wing feather.
Figure 4. Partridge Wyandotte male Primary wing feather.

Figure 5. Silver Sebright Male breast feather.
Figure 6. Silver Sebright Male neck feather.
Figure 7. Silver Sebright Female neck feather.
Figure 8. Silver Sebright Female wan feather.

DIFFERENT TYPES OF STANDARD FEATHER PATTERNS

Figure 9. Silver Laced Wyandotte male.
Figure 10. Silver Laced Wyandotte male.
Figure 11. New Hampshire male Saddle feather.

Figure 12. Silver Laced Wyandotte female Breast feather.
Figure 13. New Hampshire male Hackle feather.
Figure 14. New Hampshire male Stern feather.
Figure 15. New Hampshire female Back feather.

CLASS: CONTINENTAL
(NORTH EUROPEAN)
Golden Campine
Large Fowl Cock

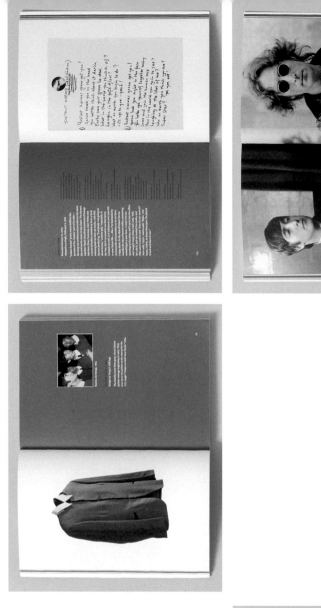

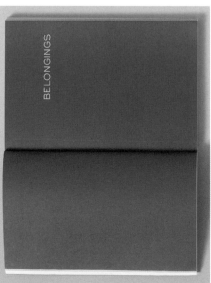

This book needed to be both birthday celebration and memorial, since it was produced for an exhibition we designed on the 60th anniversary of Lennon's birth and the 20th anniversary of his death. We wanted it to focus on Lennon as a literary artist, hence the readerly size of the book. We also wanted it to have an intimate and more modest sense of scale; the look and feel was meant to downplay the celebrity quotient. The white-on-white grid of holes in the cover represents absence and presence, markers and voids. The work of Yoko Ono – her Fluxus projects as well as her collaborations with Lennon – figured prominently in our thinking about the show and the book. The white and honey-colored palette is based on the Milk and Honey album they created together.

LENNON HIS LIFE AND WORK

*Lennon: His Life and Work book*

Design firm
Pentagram Design,
New York

Creative director/
designer
J. Abbott Miller

Editor James Henke

Publisher
Rock and Roll Hall of
Fame and Museum

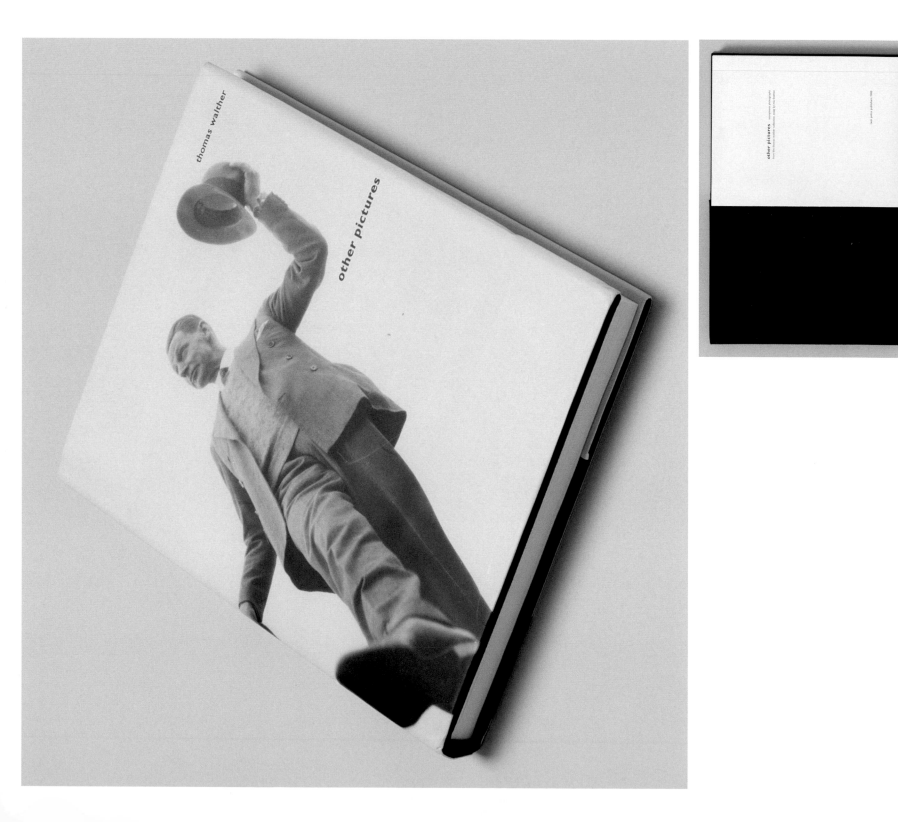

*Other Pictures* book

Design firm
Twin Palms Publishers,
Santa Fe

Art director
Jack Woody

Designers
Jack Woody,
Arlyn Nathan

Production coordinator
Jack Woody

Author
Thomas Walther

Publisher
Twin Palms Publishers

100

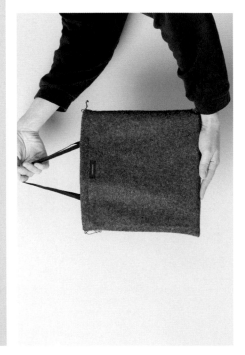

**101**

*Contents book*

Design firm
Michael Ian Kaye,
New York

Creative directors
Kate and Andy Spade

Art director
Michael Ian Kaye

Photographer Dan Bibb

Stylist Jerry Schwartz

Producer Julia Leach

Assistant producer
Jennifer Ruske

Production coordinator
Barbara Greenberg

Assistant designer
Dean Nicastro

Publisher Kate Spade

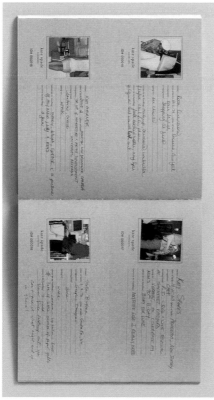

In this book about the contents of people's bags, we wanted to be true to the personalities of the bag holders while maintaining the elegance and sophistication of the Kate Spade ethos. We did this by allowing participants to fill out a form that reveals their own personalities and bag-carrying habits in their own words, and including a pen and these forms in the back of the book. The book appeals to anyone who might be curious as to what people carry with them. including Kate Spade shoppers, voyeurs and kleptomaniacs.

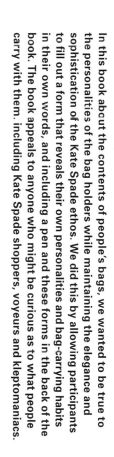

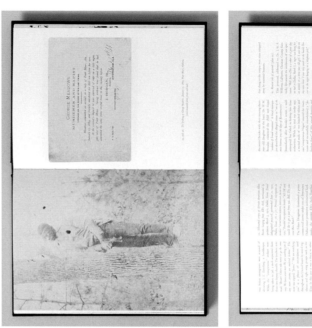

**Without Sanctuary:**
**Lynching**
**Photography in**
**America book**

**102**

Design firm
Twin Palms
Publishers, Santa Fe

Art director
Jack Woody

Designers
Jack Woody,
Arlyn Nathan

Author James Allen

Publisher
Twin Palms Publishers

**103**

*The Boomer book*

Design firm
Alfred A. Knopf, Inc.,
New York

Art director
Chip Kidd

Production coordinator
Roméo Enriquez

Author Marty Asher

Publisher
Alfred A. Knopf, Inc.

The manuscript for Marty Asher's tale of Baby Boomer angst seemed to be just the book that Chuck Anderson's CSA Archive (that magnificent achievement of illustrative archeology) was made for. For me it wasn't even a question, but the author initially had doubts about having illustrations throughout. In the end, it's impossible to imagine the text without the drawings having nearly as much impact.

the BOOMER

a novel

MARTY ASHER

PRINTED IN U.S.A. © 2000 Alfred A. Knopf

**The Accidental Indies book**

Design firm
David Drummond
Design, Athelstan,
Quebec, Canada

Designer
David Drummond

Author Robert Finley

Publisher
McGill-Queen's
University Press

This book combines literature and history to provide a first-hand account of Christopher Columbus's discovery of the New World. The cover has a whimsical quality that conveys the humor and inventiveness of the writing. The book takes the form of a prose poem divided into four sections that covers the entire voyage to the New World. When the pages of the book are turned quickly, a cloud motif can be seen to travel from left to right throughout the entire book.

We wanted to create a beautiful book to sit within the Rumi gift box. Using traditional Islamic pattern design elements as our source, we drew icons and created a sun for the book cover as well as the box cover. Roman capitals circle the sun against a regal purple inset in midnight blue, lending a ruglike simplicity to the flat colors. The two-color interior of rust and dark blue on uncoated stock presents a rich, tactile feel.

**105**

**The Rumi
Card Book book**

Design firm
doubleu-gee,
Petaluma,
California

Creative director/
designer Michele
Wetherbee

Illustrator
Stefan Gutermuth

Production
coordinator
P.J. Tierney

Compositor
Stefan Gutermuth

Author Eryk Hanut

Publisher
Journey Editions

We were charged with producing a book that successfully communicated John Deere's core values, with representation of all its divisions and global operating units. We also needed to cover significant achievements in the firm's 164-year history. Our design solution is based on a rigorous review and selection of images from Deere's extensive archives. The cover image reflects the firm's foundation in the earth, with soil as the uniting factor across all the firm's divisions. We spent much time editing and exploring options to create the best solution, but fundamentally the book remained structured around the original core values we identified: quality, innovation, integrity and commitment.

**106**

***Genuine Value:***
***The John Deere***
***Journey* book**

Design firm
McMillan Associates,
West Dundee, Illinois

Art director
Michael McMillan

Designer/compositor
Megan Kearney

Production
coordinators
Anne McMillan,
Janice Sewell,
Jeanne Thomson

Author John Gerstner

Publisher John Deere

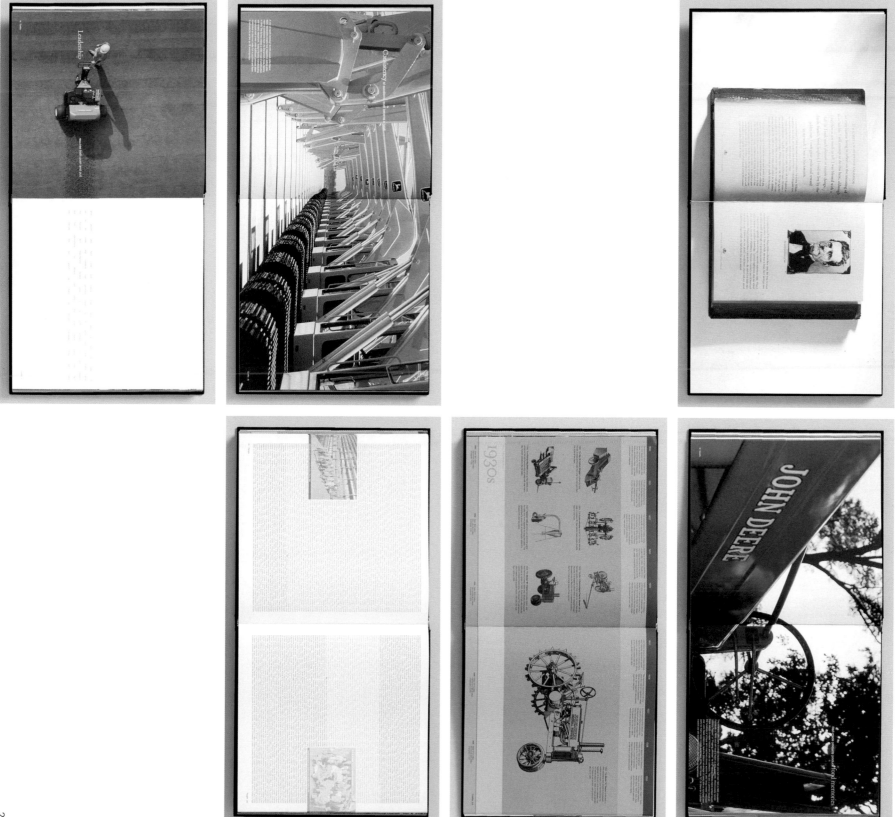

**107**

*Lou Reed:*
*Pass Thru Fire*
**book**

Design firm
Sagmeister, Inc.,
New York

Creative director
Stefan Sagmeister

Designers
Hjalti Karlsson,
Jan Wilker,
Stefan Sagmeister

Photographer
Lou Reed

Production coordinator
Lisa Stokes

Author Lou Reed

Editor Leigh Haber

Publisher
Hyperion Press

This book of the collected lyrics of Lou Reed features a self-portrait with embossed type on its cover. The lyrics are divided into chapters according to each album. Every album has its own typographic style reflecting the overall mood and feel of the words and the music. The steadiness and simplicity of Lou Reed's work is reflected by the use of one single typeface throughout the book. This typeface gets drunk, does drugs, becomes incomprehensible, dresses up, is mean, visionary, gorgeous and glowing. It's Lou's voice personified.

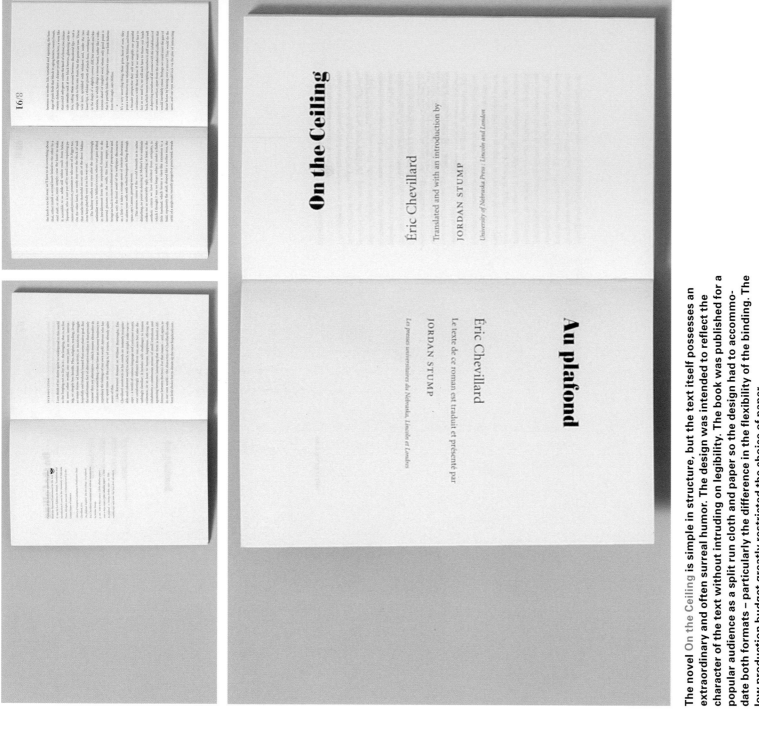

The novel On the Ceiling is simple in structure, but the text itself possesses an extraordinary and often surreal humor. The design was intended to reflect the character of the text without intruding on legibility. The book was published for a popular audience as a split run cloth and paper so the design had to accommodate both formats – particularly the difference in the flexibility of the binding. The low production budget greatly restricted the choice of paper.

108

*On the Ceiling*
book

Design firm
University of
Nebraska Press,
Lincoln, Nebraska

Art director/designer
Richard Eckersley

Illustrator
Richard Eckersley

Production coordinator
Alison Rold

Compositor
Richard Eckersley

Author Eric Chevillard

Publisher University
of Nebraska Press

262

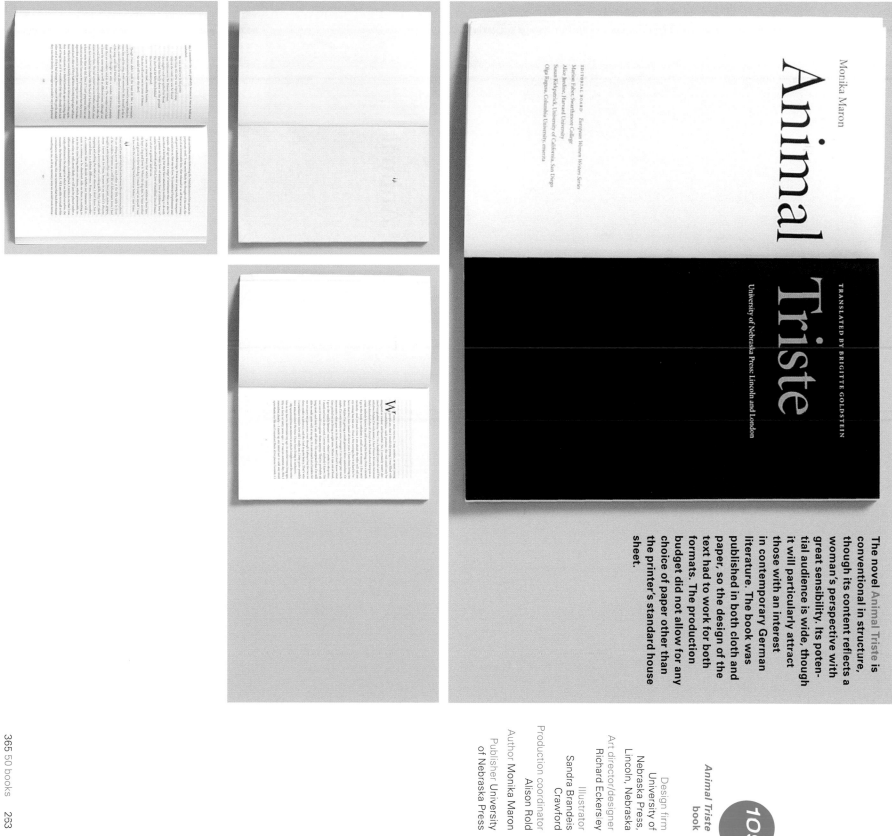

The novel *Animal Triste* is conventional in structure, though its content reflects a woman's perspective with great sensibility. Its potential audience is wide, though it will particularly attract those with an interest in contemporary German literature. The book was published in both cloth and paper, so the design of the text had to work for both formats. The production budget did not allow for any choice of paper other than the printer's standard house sheet.

***Animal Triste***
**book**

**109**

Design firm
University of
Nebraska Press,
Lincoln, Nebraska

Art director/designer
Richard Eckersley

Illustrator
Sandra Brandeis
Crawford

Production coordinator
Alison Rold

Author Monika Maron

Publisher University
of Nebraska Press

This massive book is a compilation of new essays, excerpted texts from letters and novels, Nabokov's lepidopteran findings and various images. A definite challenge was the quantity of different types of texts: lists, letters, doodles and essays; color images, black-and-white photos, captions and poems; scientific graphs, charts and illustrations. It all had to flow smoothly in a coherent, readable and comfortable text without appearing overwhelming. In the end, I had a pile of manuscript bits and pieces about four feet high in my studio. I am pleased I was allowed to keep the generous margins, which were designed to accommodate photos and captions; for many pages, however, they are simply empty, generous and spacious.

**110**

*Nabokov's Butterflies* book

Design firm
Beacon Press, Boston

Creative director
Sara Eisenman

Designer
Lucinda Hitchcock

Photographer
Anonymous,
courtesy the estate
of Vladimir Nabokov

Production coordinator
Dan Ochsner

Author
Vladimir Nabokov

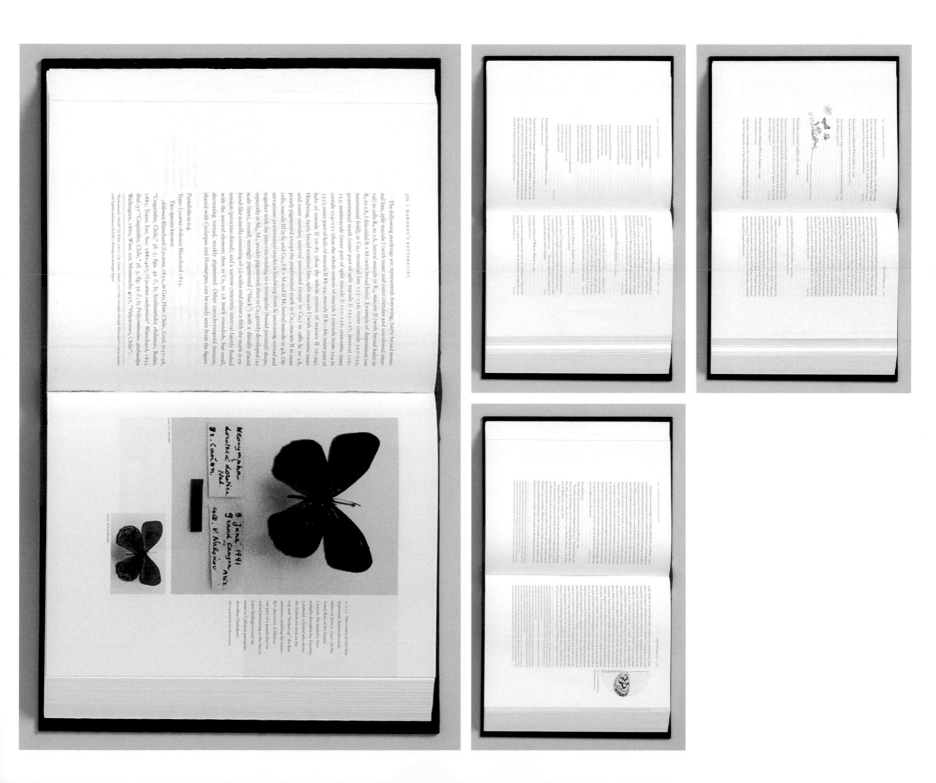

The main challenge with El Capitán was to create a vertical experience without the advantage of four-color images that would have enhanced the grandness of the mountain. The solution was found through the simple pacing of the images as single-page and two-page spreads in an attempt to describe the scale of all that surrounded the climbers. The detailing of the first two lines of text at the beginning of each chapter also serves to suggest the jagged terrain that the climbers would encounter. The photograph on the cover was selected because it basically tells El Capitán's emotional story, and the placement of the type on the cover below the climber implies that the climber is moving up. I am happy with the simplicity of the design as it allows the text and the images to create the drama for the reader. The design does not compete with the storytelling.

**111**

*El Capitán book*

Art director
Sara Schneider

Designer Meryl Pollen

Photographers
Ed Cooper, Tom Frost,
Greg Epperson, Corey
Rich, Eric Perlman

Production coordinator
Steve Kim

Compositor
Meryl Pollen

Author Daniel Duane

Publisher
Chronicle Books

**el capitan**

historic feats and radical routes

by Daniel Duane

**112**

*After the Fall:*
*Srebrenica Survivors*
*in St. Louis* book

Design firm
Design Kitchen, Chicago

Designer
Sam Landers

Photographer
Tom Maday

Production coordinator
Katie Heit

Author
Patrick McCarthy

Publisher
Missouri Historical
Society Press

Combining three separate yet complementary parts to tell one story was the biggest challenge of designing this book. The first part was treated as a chronology of events during the war in Bosnia-Herzegovina using video stills from a documentary called Safe Haven. The second part featured interviews and photographs of the Oric family members in St. Louis. Finally, the third part was a photo documentary of Bosnia-Herzegovina after the war. The use of black-and-white photography was decided upon at the early stages of the project to communicate a stark journalistic approach to capture not just the events of the war, but also the lives of the Oric family. Minimal color (black and red) was used to simply tell the story and not distract from the real events and photographs.

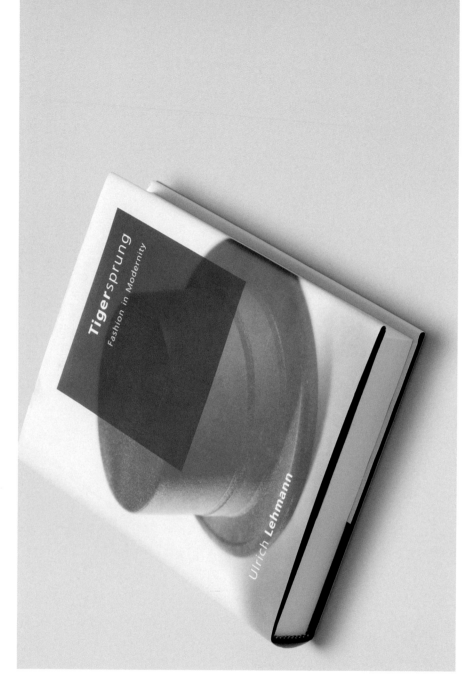

**113**

*Tigersprung*
**book**

Design firm
MIT Press Design
Department,
Cambridge,
Massachusetts

Designer
Ori Kometani

Production
coordinator
Terry Lamoureux

Author Ulrich
Lehmann

Publisher MIT Press

The making of a package for a book about packaging was especially challenging. The use of a "Flow Pack" as a cover for the book became the design solution. The printing facilities that the client offered to us were our only significant parameter. We fully achieved our original concept and found a solution that represents the concept of the book in itself.

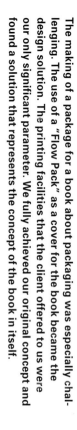

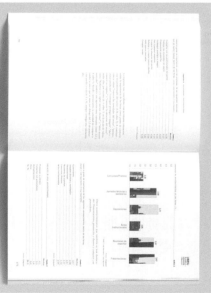

Packaging
White Book book

Design firm
Morillas & Associates,
Barcelona

Creative director
Lluís Morillas

Art director
Francesc Ribot

Designer Ingrid Toran

Photographer
Joan Argeles

Publisher
Fira de Barcelona

114

The primary objective of this piece was to document and promote the first year activity of the "Design Writing" high school program. In the original design brief, it was strongly suggested that I avoid clichéd references to "typical" high school life that might trivialize the work of the students and teachers participating in the program. The images provided as base material for illustrations were very uneven in quality. The design of the book was pared down to a minimal grid structure and a simple hierarchy. A single serif typeface was used as a partial means of referencing traditional book forms and structures. Most of the illustrations and chapter dividers utilized portions of the essays, placing more or less equal emphasis on words and images. In addition, the use of text as part of the illustrations helped to mask the uneven quality of the source images.

**115**

*Design Writing*
book

Design firm
University of Michigan
School of Art + Design,
Ann Arbor, Michigan

Art director/designer/
compositor
Dennis Miller

Editor Jack Williamson

Publisher
Design Michigan

Wörterbuch
der Redensarten

Karl Kraus

Die Fackel

*Fackel Wörterbuch:*
*Redensarten* book

Creative
director/designer
Anne Burdick

Typographic consultant
Jens Gehlhaar

Editor
Dr. Werner Welzig

Publisher Austrian
Academy of Sciences

Graphic Design

Constructing Identities and Mapping Interactions

Fackel Wörterbuch:
Redensarten

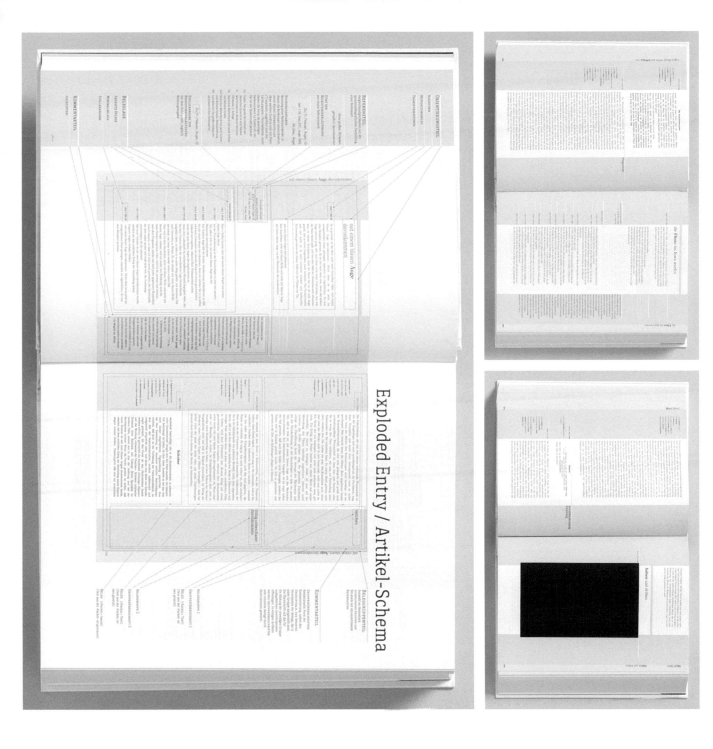

Exploded Entry / Artikel-Schema

The design of this book's interface played an important editorial role in its construction, organization and navigation. Based upon the use of idioms in Karl Kraus's Die Fackel, an early 20th-century Viennese journal of media criticism, the dictionary is intended for use by Kraus scholars, literary theorists and linguists interested in lexicography. The dictionary's unique diagrammatic display helps to identify and organize nine different textual functions for each individual dictionary entry. The primary source material was comprised of excerpts from Die Fackel, which used typography and layout as a rhetorical device. Therefore, images of entire pages became the backbone for the dictionary's organizational flow and helped inform the dictionary's typographic choices. Support texts used unusual and complex writing strategies, so the editors and designer worked in tandem to create a unique punctuation system with multilevel quotation marks and variegated reference strategies.

This book was intended to honor the history of the Hatch Show Print. I decided to design a poster for the book cover. The only criteria was to fit the cover dimensions.

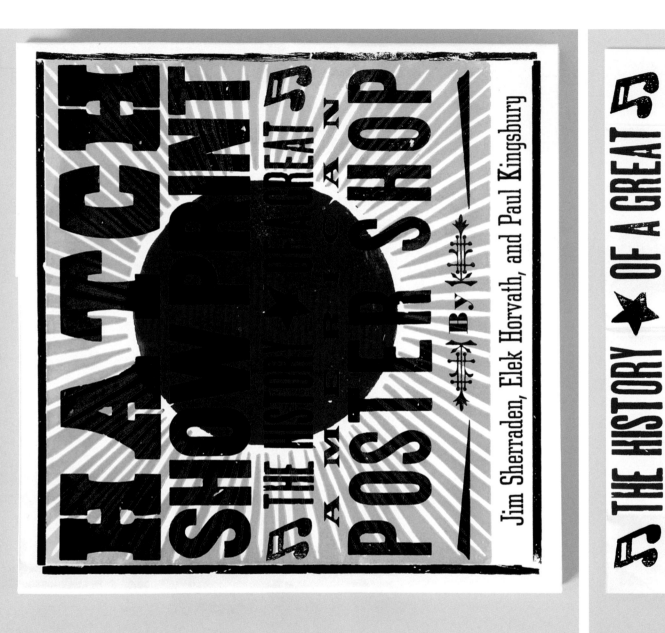

**117**

*Hatch Show Print: The History of a Great American Poster Shop* cover

Design firm
Hatch Show Print, Nashville

Art director
Jim Sherraden

Designers
The staff at Hatch

Authors
Jim Sherraden, Elek Horvath, Paul Kingsbury

Publisher
Chronicle Press

Due to the "collection" nature of this book, it was challenging to create a feel for the poetry without defining a specific genre of poems. I wanted to create a modern cover to introduce this collection as poetry of our modern world. In order to keep it from seeming dated, I chose the sans serif and placed it in a classic format. It needed to feel organic like a poem, thus the scribble and color shift throughout the cover.

THE POETRY OF OUR WORLD

AN INTERNATIONAL ANTHOLOGY OF CONTEMPORARY POETRY

EDITED BY JEFFERY PAINE WITH KWAME ANTHONY APPIAH, SVEN BIRKERTS, JOSEPH BRODSKY, CAROLYN FORCHÉ, AND HELEN VENDLER

WITH EDITORIAL COLLABORATION AND CONTRIBUTIONS BY AGHA SHAHID ALI, BEI DAO, ANITA DESAI, EDWARD DIMOCK, EDWARD HIRSCH, GARRETT HONGO, DENISE LEVERTOV, PERRY LINK, DONALD KEENE, AND BURTON RAFFEL.

**118**

*The Poetry of Our World cover*

Design firm
HarperCollirs,
New York

Art director
Joseph Montebello

Designer
John Fullbrook III

Editor Jeffery Paine

Publisher
HarperCollins

---

The public had to grasp instantly the topic of the book: a look back at 25 years of milk advertising in Quebec. Our solution was to associate an icon with a motto. The icon is a quart of milk made of glass – an image all Baby Boomers can recognize – and the slogan is Quebec's motto, "Je me souviens" ("I remember"). Taken together, they became "I remember milk." The white color of milk became a must. A transparent and perforated book jacket allowed the creation of the desired contrast between the ancient and the modern, the past and the present. The transparent book jacket, produced in San Francisco, arrived at the end of production. It played its part well.

**119**

*Je Me Souviens du Lait cover*

Design firm
Nolin Branding &
Design, Montreal

Art director/designer
René Clément

Production
coordinator
Marie Noël-de-Tilly

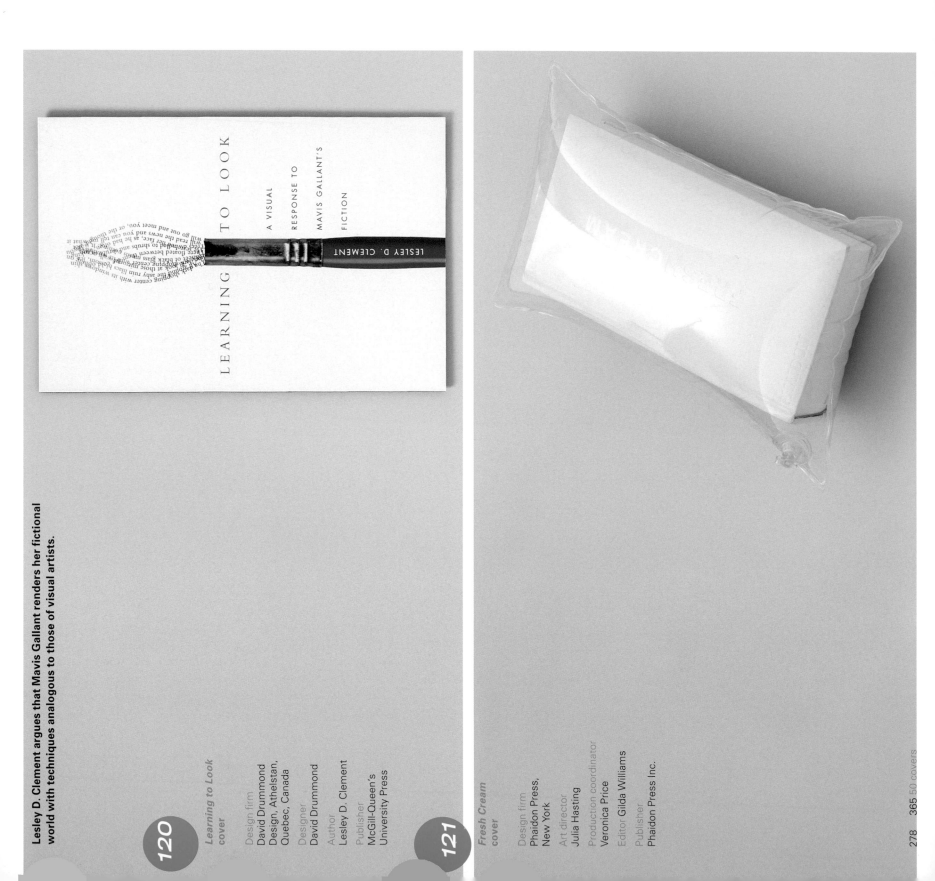

**Lesley D. Clement argues that Mavis Gallant renders her fictional world with techniques analogous to those of visual artists.**

*Learning to Look*
cover

Design firm
David Drummond
Design, Athelstan,
Quebec, Canada

Designer
David Drummond

Author
Lesley D. Clement

Publisher
McGill-Queen's
University Press

120

121

*Fresh Cream*
cover

Design firm
Phaidon Press,
New York

Art director
Julia Hasting

Production coordinator
Veronica Price

Editor Gilda Williams

Publisher
Phaidon Press Inc.

Many of the stories of Demonology have death or violence at their center. The title piece is a sobering meditation on the life and death of the protagonist's sister; other tales include an account of a drive-by shooting at a McDonald's and a narrative about the inner workings of a budget-wedding palace. The levitating Smarties reflect the mood of the title story while suggesting a "collection."

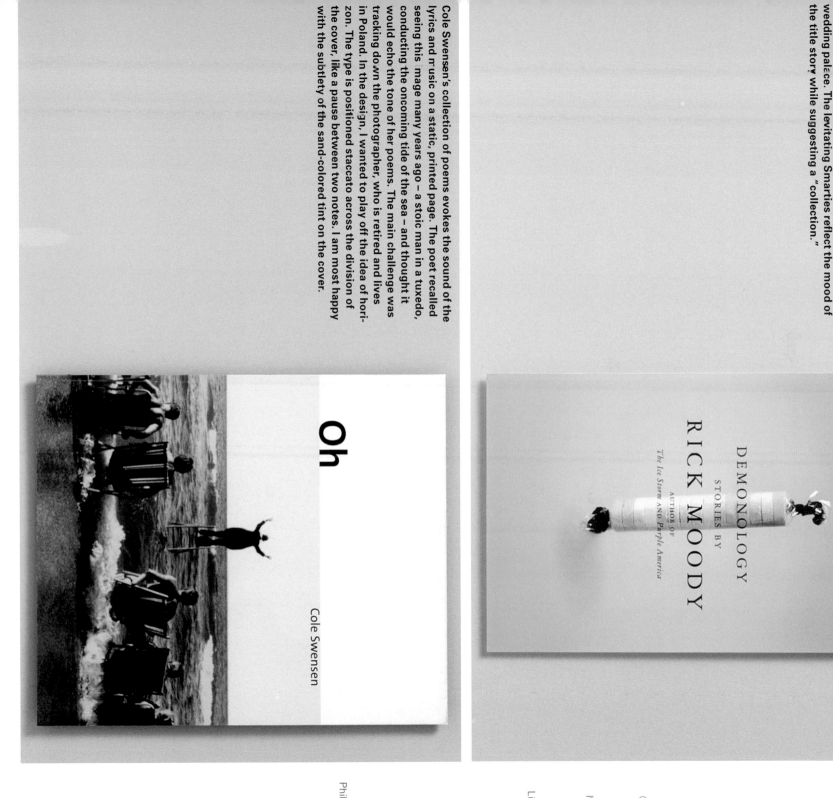

**122**

*Demonology*
cover

Design firm
Office of Paul
Sahre, New York
Creative director/
designer
Paul Sahre
Photographer
Michael Northrup
Author
Rick Moody
Publisher
Little Brown & Co.

Cole Swensen's collection of poems evokes the sound of the lyrics and music on a static, printed page. The poet recalled seeing this image many years ago – a stoic man in a tuxedo, conducting the oncoming tide of the sea – and thought it would echo the tone of her poems. The main challenge was tracking down the photographer, who is retired and lives in Poland. In the design, I wanted to play off the idea of horizon. The type is positioned staccato across the division of zone. The type is positioned staccato across the division of the cover, like a pause between two notes. I am most happy with the subtlety of the sand-colored tint on the cover.

**123**

*Oh cover*

Design firm
Apogee Press,
Berkeley
Designer
Philip Krayna,
Philip Krayna Design
Photographer
Eustachy
Kossowski
Author
Cole Swensen
Publisher
Apogee Press

It was a special challenge to capture the unique content of the art exhibit in the design of the book and cover without interfering with the function of an exhibit catalogue.

*Genealogies, Miscegenations, Missed Generations*
cover

Designer
Jeff Bellantoni

Editor Erin Valentino

Publisher
The William Benton
Museum of
Art, University of
Connecticut

**Yes:** Yoko Ono is a comprehensive scholarly study of Yoko Ono's work from the 1950s to the present. The challenge for the jacket was to capture a sense of her conceptual and visual body of work. We took inspiration from photographs of early events, and Yoko Ono and the Japan Society suggested this 1971 Iain Macmillan image that captures the spirit of her direct and contemplative work. We originally imagined an opalescent background, but the printer helped us find a metallized paper that added reflection to the photograph's glow. Ono's favorite colors are blue, white and black, in keeping with her cool and minimal aesthetic. The blue duotone in combination with the cloud endpapers and flaps reference skies that appear in such works as *Sky Machine*, a vending machine that conceptually dispensed pieces of sky as indicated by a card.

The field of public health law is a vast conglomeration of law, medicine and politics – as evidenced by this book's nearly three-inch thickness. With the cover image, I wanted to reference the book's physical aspects as well as convey the sheer density of material that the author admirably tackles to provide the first systematic definition and theory of this subject.

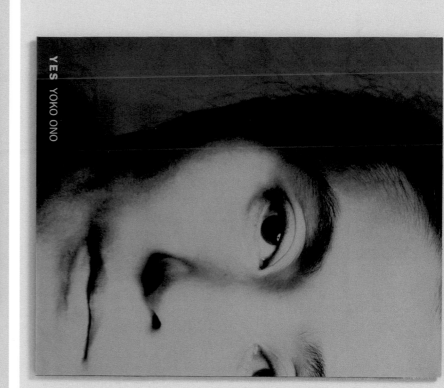

**125**

*Yes: Yoko Ono* cover

Publishers
Harry N. Abrams,
Inc., and Japan
Society, New York

Art director
Michael J. Walsh

Designer/compositor
Miko McGinty

Photographer
Iain Macmillan,
courtesy LENONO
Photo Archive,
New York

Production
coordinator
Hope Kotu'o

Authors/editor's
Alexandra Munroe,
Jon Hendricks

**126**

*Public Health
Law: Power, Duty,
Restraint* cover

Designer/
photographer
Lee Friedman

Production coordinator
Sam Rosenthal

Author
Lawrence O. Gostin

Publisher University
of California Press

The design solution for Leonardo da Vinci was straightforward, except for the question of whether or not to put type on the front. Some people felt that the image was more striking and mysterious without type; others felt that it was necessary to have the title on the front because the image, while highly provocative, would not readily say "Leonardo." I decided to add the title discreetly at the bottom. I like the way the type colors work with the image.

LEONARDO DA VINCI

127

*Leonardo da Vinci* **cover**

Art director
Michael Walsh

Designers
Judith Michael,
Ergonarte

Production
coordinator
Keri Mordue Smith

Author
Pietro Marani

Publishers
Harry N. Abrams,
Inc., and
Federico Motta
Editore S.p.A

The study of econometrics focuses upon the application of statistical and mathematical methods in the field of economics to describe the numerical relationships between key economic forces such as capital, interest rates and labor. While we experimented briefly with more abstract representations as befit these numerical relationships, we felt the design was best approached as a typographic problem, not a mathematical one. Because the author is also a keen typography enthusiast, and because he feared the book could easily look like any other statistical textbook, he agreed that this was an ideal direction. It soon became evident that the author's name and the book's title were each comprised of 12 letters. Our intention was to design a typographic constellation that would at once read as a single concept, yet at the same time could maintain dynamic tension between the letterforms of the book's title and the author's name.

---

**Hillbilly Hollywood** is about the country stars in Hollywood in the '30s and '40s, who, along with their tailors, set the standard for country and western fashion today. The cover needed to immediately convey the glitz and sparkle of the fashions while not forgetting the down-home quality of the musicians. We deliberately made the cover as flashy and gaudy as the costumes were, but behind all the sparkle and rhinestones were simple country performers, one of whom looks out through the die-cut "H." The editor asked for fringe. We gave her rhinestones instead. We all wanted over-the-top, and we got it.

***Econometrics cover***

Design firm
Helfand/Drenttel Inc.,
Falls Village,
Connecticut

Art director/
jacket designer
Sharon Werner

Production coordinator
Betsey Litz

Editor Fumio Hayashi

Publisher Princeton
University Press

**128**

***Hillbilly Hollywood
cover***

Design firm
Werner Design Werks,
Inc., Minneapolis

Art director
Sharon Werner

Designer's
Sharon Werner,
Sarah Nelson

Photographers
Kyle Ericksen et al.

Production coordinator
Signe Bergstrom

Author Debby Bull

Publisher
Rizzoli International
Publications, Inc.

**129**

**FSG's catalogue cover should ideally integrate the ideas "fish" (FSG's logo) and "literary books" (FSG's product). The challenge was to accomplish this objective in an attractive way.**

**130**

*Farrar, Straus and Giroux catalogue cover*

Design firm
Farrar, Straus and Giroux, New York

Art director
Susan Mitchell

Designer
Lynn Buckley

Publisher
Farrar, Straus and Giroux

**131**

*10 x 10 cover*

Design firm
Phaidon Press, New York

Art director/designer
Julia Hasting

Production coordinator
Paul Hammond

Editor
Vivian Constantinopoulos

Publisher
Phaidon Press Inc.

## 132

**The Power Book cover**

Design firm
Pantheon Books,
New York

Art director
Carol Carson

Photographer
Archie Ferguson

Production
coordinator Clare
Bradley Ong

Author
Jeanette Winterson

Publisher
Alfred A. Knopf

## 133

Put simply, this novel is about a speed freak who shoots his mother, torches his house and heads to the local mall with a sack of weapons and a plan for more mayhem. I wanted the cover to work like a small poster and the seemingly simple image to be shocking but not obvious. It takes a second glance to realize you are looking down the barrel of a gun. The title and author text, separated by a typographical bullet, is placed in the center of the barrel to emphasize this idea.

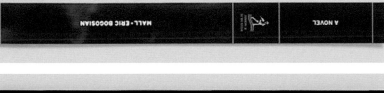

**Mall cover**

Design firm
Spot Design,
New York

Art directors
Drew Hodges,
Jackie Seow

Designer
Kevin Brainard

Photographer
Andres Serrano

Author
Eric Bogosian

Publisher
Simon
and Schuster

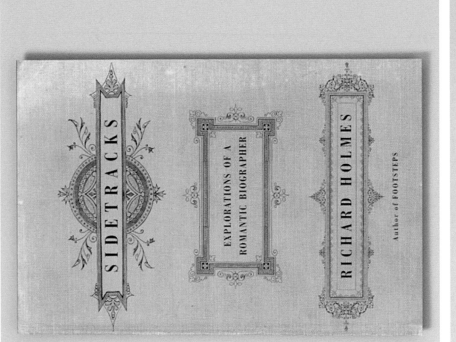

Richard Holmes is a writer's writer. Through himself and other authors he explores the process of biography in this book. By using old book binding and historical type elements I hoped to create something that reflected a sense of literary tradition.

*Sidetracks:*
*Explorations of*
*a Romantic*
*Biographer* cover

Design firm
Pantheon Books,
New York

Art director/designer
Archie Ferguson

Project coordinator
Kathy Grasso

Author
Richard Holmes

Publisher
Pantheon Books

134

---

WHAT She SAW

*in*

A NOVEL

LUCINDA ROSENFELD

WHAT She SAW
*in* Roger Mancuso, Günter Hopstock, Jason Barry Gold, Spitzy Clark, Jack Geezo, Humphrey Fung, Claude Duvet,
Bruce Bledstone, Kevin McFeeley, Arnold Allen, Pablo Miles, Anonymous 1–4, Nobody 5–8, Neil Schmertz, and Bo Pierce
LUCINDA ROSENFELD

RANDOM HOUSE

*What She Saw* cover

Design firm
Random House, Inc.,
New York

Art director
Robbin Schiff

Designer Kapo Ng

Author
Lucinda Rosenfeld

Publisher
Random House, Inc.

135

The challenge of this project was to key the audience into the musical aspect of this collection of short stories. The guitar is such a familiar icon that you can use the smallest section of it and it would still be recognizable. Once potential readers made the connection between the guitar and the author – Ray Davies of The Kinks – they might be persuaded to read more. I wanted the jacket to have a literary feel, since the stories are actually a more fleshed-out version of the already strong narrative of the original songs. Visually, I wanted to suggest a landscape using the curves of the guitar, the type disappearing into the horizon. I wanted to keep the metaphor subtle, and immediately thought of Marc Yankus, who took my simple concept and embellished it beautifully with his unique sensibility of textures and colors.

This is an extremely sensual novel that explores sexual taboos and fantasies in a compelling literary fashion. I tried to create a jacket that spoke to the secrecy, intimacy, subtlety and tactile aspects of our – if not my own – sexuality. I really get off on the melding of the textured stock and diffuse imagery.

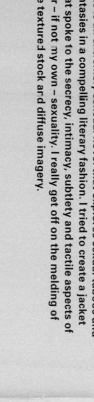

RUPERT THOMSON

THE BOOK OF REVELATION

A NOVEL

RAY DAVIES

WATERLOO SUNSET

stories

Waterloo Sunset cover

Creative director/ designer
David Zachary Cohen

Photographer
Marc Yankus

Production coordinator
John Marius

Author Ray Davies

Publisher Hyperion

136

The Book of Revelation cover

Design firm
Pantheon Books, New York

Art director
Carol Carson

Designer
Archie Ferguson

Photographer
Radek Grosman

Production coordinator
Claire Bradley Ong

Author
Rupert Thomson

Publisher
Alfred A. Knopf

137

This book is directed at readers interested in contemporary Taiwanese fiction. I am most pleased with the moons on the cover.

**138**

*A Thousand Moons on a Thousand Rivers cover*

Design firm
Columbia University Press, New York

Creative director/ designer/compositor
Linda Secondari

Production coordinator
Jennifer Jerome

Author Hsiao Li-Hung

Publisher Columbia University Press

**139**

*Panicking Ralph cover*

Design firm
Doubleday, New York

Art director Ellen Chung

Designer
Rodrigo Corral

Photographer
Stephen H. Sheffield

Author Bill James

Publisher W.W. Norton

The original Carol Carson jacket design had a Breughel painting on the front. For the paperback, my first solution was, of course, to put pancakes on the cover. When the author didn't like that approach I tried a design that had two guys wrestling on the cover. (Editor: Are you sure those guys are, um, wrestling?) Next came the crying baby cover (perhaps this said more about me than the book), then the always-popular "vintage clip art road sign arrows" design and the pancake/Breughel compromise special. Finally, and to great acclaim, we settled on the floating head pictograph design. Believe me, it makes all the sense in the world if you read the book.

remember reading somewhere about people converting messages ntc code and how they'd drop the vowels so they could speed the ro-cess up without losing too much of the information. Faster, a book about the accelerating pace of modern life, has a title and an author name that still make sense using only the consonants, and together with the subtle typography and color scheme of a road sign helps to get across the idea that we'll punch three fives into a microwave instead of a six and two zeroes because we're in a bit of hurry.

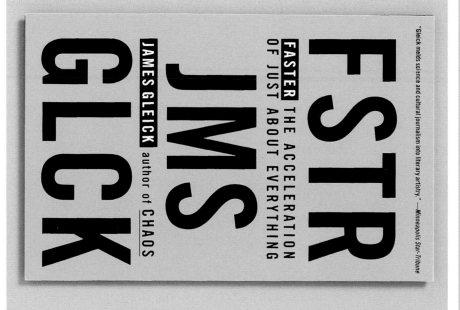

**The Verificationist cover**

Design firm
Vintage Books,
New York

Art director/
designer John Gall

Printer
Coral Graphics

Author
Donald Antrim

Publisher
Vintage Books

**Faster cover**

Art director
John Gall

Designer
Jamie Keenan

Author
James Gleick

Publisher
Vintage Books

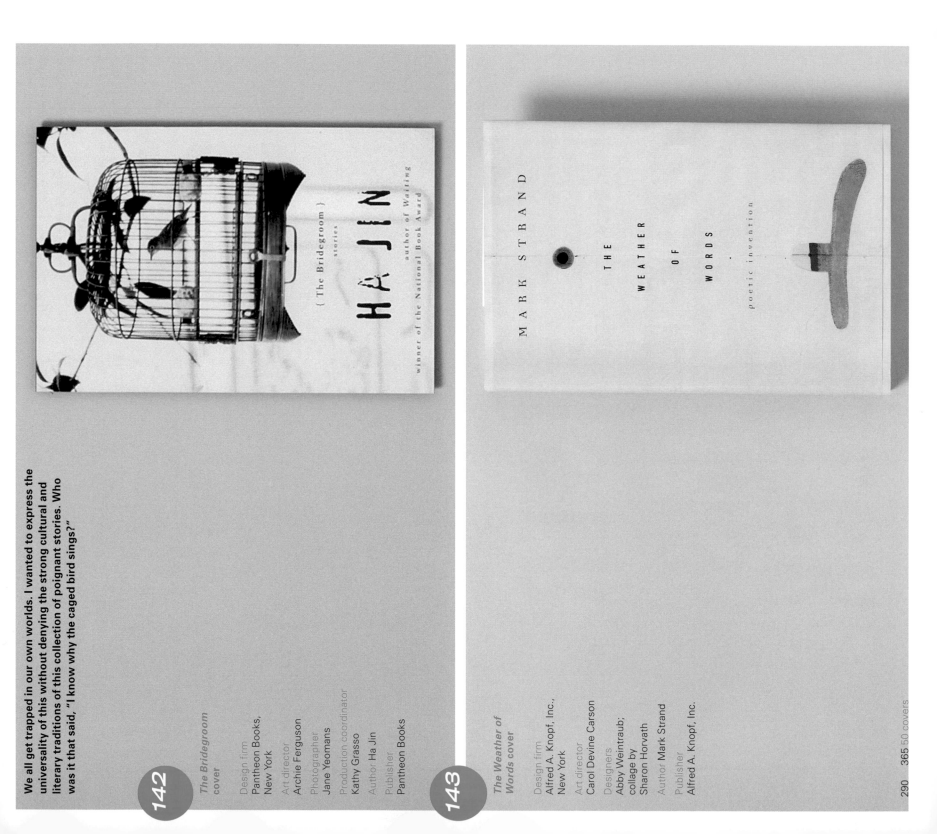

**We all get trapped in our own worlds. I wanted to express the universality of this without denying the strong cultural and literary traditions of this collection of poignant stories. Who was it that said, "I know why the caged bird sings?"**

*The Bridegroom* cover

Design firm
Pantheon Books,
New York

Art director
Archie Ferguson

Photographer
Jane Yeomans

Production coordinator
Kathy Grasso

Author Ha Jin

Publisher
Pantheon Books

**142**

*The Weather of Words* cover

Design firm
Alfred A. Knopf, Inc.,
New York

Art director
Carol Devine Carson

Designers
Abby Weintraub;
collage by
Sharon Horvath

Author Mark Strand

Publisher
Alfred A. Knopf, Inc.

**143**

Evelyn Lau is known as a controversial and poignant author, so what better way to reflect her memoir than by using just words? The design solution is a literal translation of the title, Inside Out. The book itself is the author's outward "reflections" on a life so far," while the dust cover features the "inside" of the book using the author's own prose. The result – a stark and serene book cover with a dash of brilliant red – mimics the reality of Lau's life. Once the concept was approved, the most critical aspect of the book was the use of the transparent dust cover, which allowed the title to be layered. This also allowed for a page from a pivotal moment in Lau's memoir to be exposed and "reflected" on the cover.

The challenge of this project was to match the beauty of André Aciman's spare, haunting, emotional writing with an image and type choice that directly conveyed these qualities. After much research, I found André Kertész's photograph Martinique. It perfectly emulated the two major themes of the book: exile and memory. The type was designed to support the quiet strength of the photograph. After several type experiments, we happily settled on this one.

*Inside Out* cover

Design firm
Pylon Design Inc.,
Toronto

Art director/designer
Kevin Hoch

Author Evelyn Lau

Publisher
Doubleday Canada

144

*False Papers* cover

Design firm
Anne Fink Design,
New York

Art director
Susan Mitchell

Designer Anne Fink

Author André Aciman

Publisher
Farrar Straus
and Giroux

145

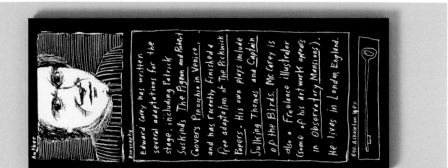

Personally illustrating the initial cover idea was the most challenging part of the Observatory Mansions book cover solution. If I hadn't been able to layout my intention for the cover in the initial sketch, the idea would not have been a viable option. The result was a literal and graphic interpretation that captured and reflected the disturbing content of the story. The most influential component of the cover design was the chosen illustrator, Gary Clement. Gary brought the cover idea to life. Based on my original sketch the cover was to have some color. However, once Gary presented his final illustration it was apparent and mutually decided that color wasn't needed. We were ecstatic that Random House gave us the go ahead to illustrate absolutely everything, including the author's photo.

*Observatory Mansions cover*

Design firm
Pylon Design Inc.,
Toronto

Art director/designer
Scott Christie

Illustrator Gary Clement

Author Edward Carey

Publisher Random
House of Canada

The design for *Wings* was something that happened more easily than most. I've worked with Christopher Myers on all of his picture books at Scholastic Press, and each one is very different in tone. For this book, I immediately felt that a clean, classic design using a serif typeface would be the right way to set off and subtly complement his artwork. I wanted to project a quiet dignity with the typography that reflects the quiet dignity of the main character, Icarus Jackson, a boy who can fly and is ostracized for being different. This picture book is for everyone: it works not only for very young children, but for anyone who reads it. The vertical trim size, generous white space around the artwork inside the book and the plain typography all help to create a quiet space for Myers' artwork to soar.

**Wings cover**

Design firm Scholastic, Inc., New York

Art director/designer David Saylor

Illustrator Christopher Myers

Production coordinator Alison Forner

Compositor David Saylor

Printer/binder Tien Wah

Author Christopher Myers

Publisher Scholastic Press

I think the Poetica cap "T" and ampersand work well with the masterfully executed cover illustration. I am pleased with the type color, too, as it keeps the artwork front and center while remaining legible.

**The Brave Little Tailor cover**

Design firm Harry N. Abrams, Inc., New York

Director Howard Reeves

Typographic designer Barbara Sturman

Illustrators Olga Dugina, Andrej Dugin

Production coordinators Keri Smith, Diane Sahadeo

Compositor Barbara Sturman

Author Retold by Olga Dugina and Andrej Dugin

Publisher Harry N. Abrams, Inc.

RESPO
TH
TY
IN DEVELO
PROJEC
REPORT

Question H
Were any of the
following useful in
developing
preliminary design
for this project?
reading
looking at other work
your own previous work
life experiences
art or music
other

NDENTS RE
EIR OWN PRE
ORK TO BE
PING PRELIMINARY
DESIGNS FOR THE
T, VERSUS WHO
D OTHER PEOPLE'S
ORK TO BE USEFUL

34%

41%

# INFORMATION DESIGN

**Jurors Michael Bierut** Pentagram Design, New York **Terry Irwin** MetaDesign, San Francisco **Clement Mok** Sapient, San Francisco

Information graphics include work whose main purpose is to display information in a clear way in an effort to raise awareness, educate, communicate news, current issues and stories or explain a concept, cause, issue or problem. Examples of work suitable for this category are: labels, charts, maps, newsletters, posters, ads, websites, graphs, specification catalogues, signage and wayfinding systems.

The big information design story of 2000 was, undoubtedly, the fact that the closely fought presidential race was decided by the design – or lack of design – of a ballot card. The impact of information graphics on society had never been felt so forcefully until the primary instrument of democracy was rendered useless by a design flaw. And while the consequences are perhaps not as acute as those of the infamous Florida butterfly ballot, the absence of information design in this year's competition was a prevailing theme as well.

At a time when the average American ingested more data in more diverse ways than ever before, why were there so few examples of the forms of its delivery to choose from? Not because it's not out there, jurors Michael Bierut, Terry Irwin and Clement Mok affirmed. Information design as a discipline has developed dramatically over the last 10 years and it is increasingly valued by business thanks, in part, to the evangelizing work of such pioneers as Richard Saul Wurman and Alan Siegel. As well as improving across the board, it is also mutating in areas. Designers are becoming more involved in large-scale system design and optimization, for example, and less connected to an end product. Ironically, as it becomes less visible and tangible – the visual form or deliverable is often the guidelines that enable someone else to maintain a system – information design actually becomes more integral and vital. In other areas designers are employing ever more creative approaches to data visualization, including innovative uses of sound, and, with digital information, are trying to liberate the user from the experience of sitting in front of screen by integrating it into architecture and the fabric of everyday life.

The paucity of information design in AIGA's annual competition, then, is more a reflection of the way information graphics tends to be treated in design contests than of the health of the industry. In intensive judging situations the subtleties of an edifying chart or diagram are often overshadowed by the sexier qualities of a poster or a glossy image-filled brochure. Furthermore, the collaborative nature of the work means that there is no single author and certainly no design "star" to celebrate. By giving information graphics its own category and its own specialized jury it is hoped that this important sector of graphic design will be better represented in AIGA's year of design.

While the jury acknowledged the large proportion of strong interactive entries and lauded some print pieces teetering on the brink of other categories, they regretted the dearth of everyday examples of well-conceived information organization. Where, they demanded, were the ATM interfaces, train timetables, instruction manuals, web portal usage reports, brokerage house statements, medical diagrams or financial displays such as the Bloomberg screens or NASDAQ data stream in Times Square?

What they did find, though, were some exquisite instances of the ways in which designers had humanized information, both objectively – as in the Harper's map that visually correlates global warming statistics with the number of cholera cases (cat. 156) – and attitudinally, as in AmphetaZINE, a Seattle-based zine providing resources for gay and bisexual men who use crystal meth (cat. 150). The jury concurred when Clement Mok remarked of the zine: "This is a highly entertaining, engaging and useful piece of information design where both the vehicle and the approach are successful."

"In some cases – such as those with ubiquitous public value like the nutrition label

– you can make a claim for neutral information neutrally presented," Michael Bierut said. But most of the examples that the jury zeroed in on demonstrated a point of view, a take on the subject matter being presented.

Another way that the jury evaluated an entry was to consider its success as the conveyor of particular information to a particular audience. The motivated potential user of the IBM Thinkpad Getting Started Guide (cat. 155), for example, contrasts with the jaded recipient of I Reflect, a huge unfolding silver invite for an IDSA conference (cat. 149). Bierut pointed out that just like the crystal meth zine, this audacious production aimed straight at the heart of its target audience and succeeded in communicating information with a point of view.

As for the ensuing year, the jury was optimistic that as the economy continues to weaken it will engender more precise information design that is diverse in media and scope. As Terry Irwin predicts, "circumstances will press design to work harder." Alice Twemlow

Commissioned by IDSA to design a calendar of events as a poster, we chose to use the opportunity to create an inspirational project. To motivate the next generation of designers, we wrote a manifesto addressing what we feel is the most important issue facing the future of design: how to engage in responsible, purposeful projects dealing with fundamental societal issues. The technique of writing in the first person transforms a recurring issue in the profession into a compelling personal statement that literally reflects the person reading it. The manifesto is printed on metalized Mylar, most familiar as the "space blankets" distributed to runners after marathons. Because this material reflects 90 percent of a person's body heat, we propose that it could also be employed to help keep a homeless person warm. In this way the "poster" has the potential to do what the manifesto printed on it says.

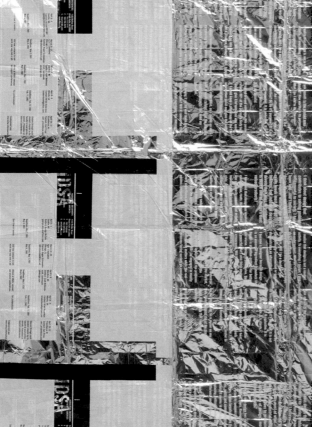

I REFLECT poster

Design firm
The Cultural
Construction Co., Boston

Art directors/designers
Thomas Starr,
Rick Rawlins

Writer Thomas Starr

Publisher
Industrial Designers
Society of America

Client (ELEVEN)

## 149

AmphetaZINE is an HIV-prevention booklet produced for Seattle gay and bisexual men who inject "crystal" methamphetamine. Almost half of this population is HIV positive. Most know that injecting drugs can lead to serious health problems; however, new HIV infections in this population are frequently the result of sexual risk. Crystal enhances libido and decreases concern about sexual safety. Modern Dog was contacted in 1999 because the zines were not being picked up or read by the target population. Our solution was simple: to use humor to diffuse the harshness of the subject matter. The zine format utilizes a "home grown" feel; it appeals where more traditional health pamphlets would fail. Articles are based on principles of harm reduction, health promotion and withheld judgment. Poetry, articles, original artwork and story ideas are contributed by members of the target audience.

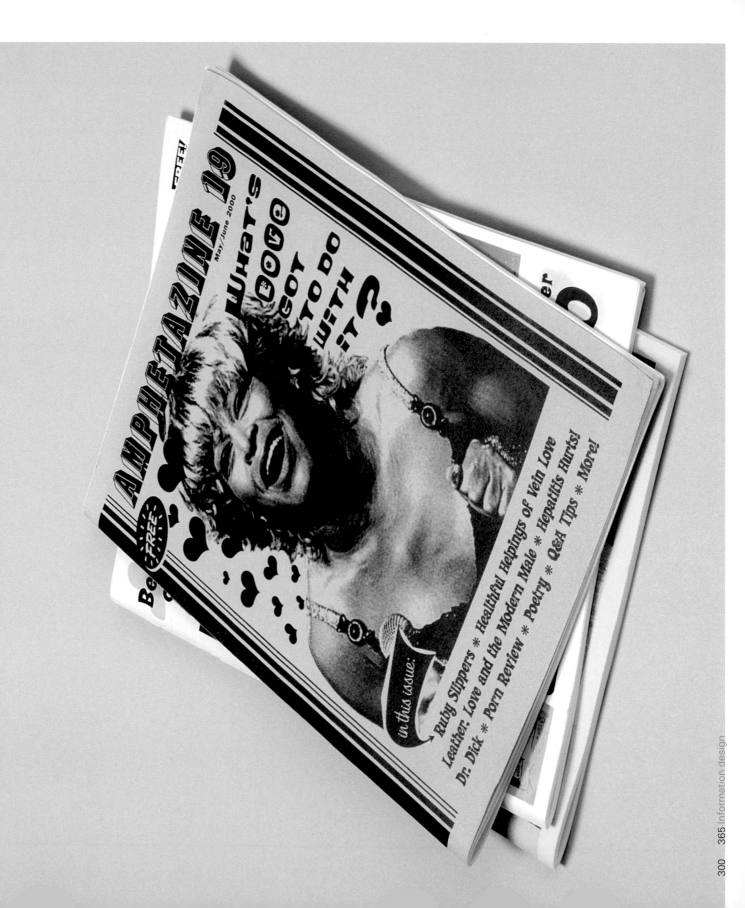

**AmphetaZINE**
zine

150

Design firm
Modern Dog, Seattle

Art director
Michael Strassburger

Designers
Michael Strassburger,
Robynne Raye

Print production
Michael Strassburger

Illustrators
Michael Strassburger,
various

Writers
James Fisher,
Michael Hanrahan,
Susan Kingston,
D.L. Scott

Client Stonewall
Recovery Services

The SamataMason website is built around our mission statement – "we do good work for good people" – and all navigation is keyed to that phrase. We believe this is a simple, elegant and accessible solution for either the best or the worst client in the world – ourselves.

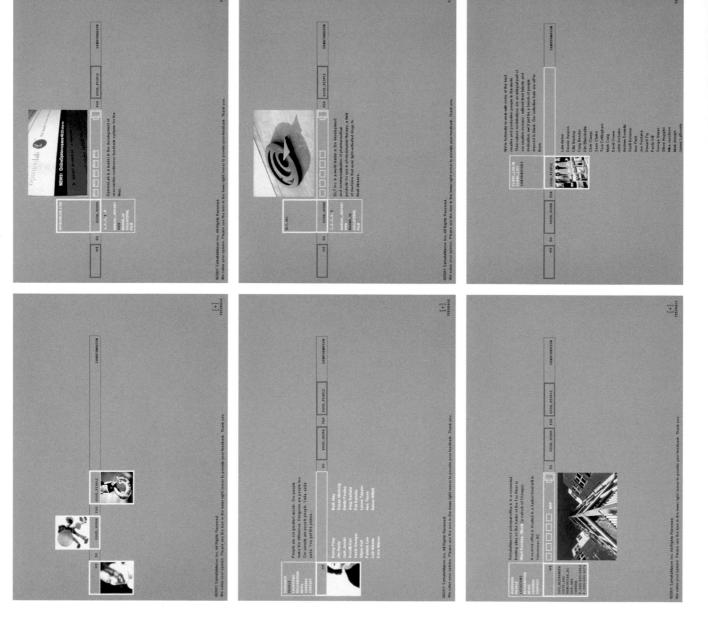

**151**

**SamataMason website**

Design firm SamataMason, Dundee, Illinois

Art directors
Dave Mason,
Kevin Krueger

Designers Kevin Krueger,
Steve Kull

Print production
Kevin Krueger

Photographers
Kevin Krueger,
Rob Schroeder

Writer Dave Mason

Digital video producer
Mike Holmes/
Performance Networks

Client
SamataMason

Gate C22

The next flight from this gate will be flight 3451 to Denver, departing at 7:05am.

4:15am

WELCOME

## UNITED

Flight 1020 from New York La Guardia is scheduled to arrive at 11:20am.

**Houston Intercontinental**

Scheduled departure **12:45**pm

Flight **8234** / **1020**

Boarding in **9 minutes**

11:15am

**Departs 1:00 pm**
Delayed due to weather

### Houston Information

Weather Conditions: **Cloudy skies**

Current Temperature: **82F (28C)**

Local arrival time: **11:58pm**

**Message 2 of 2:** Upgrade List

Customers with the following seat assignments should remain in the gate area for a possible upgrade: 14A, 13D, 23C, 27F and 32E.

## UNITED

Flight 1020 from New York La Guardia is scheduled to arrive at 11:20am.

**Houston Intercontinental**

Scheduled departure **12:45**pm

Flight **8234** / **1673**

11:15am

**Cancelled**

### Alternate Flights

We apologize for any inconvenience.
The following flights may be considered as possible alternatives:

| Carrier | Flight | Gate | Departure Time | Arrival Time | Flight Status |
|---|---|---|---|---|---|
| United | 3456 | 82 | 11:25am | 7:25pm | Limited |
| Virgin Atlantic | 567 | see VA | 1:15pm | 9:15pm | see VA |
| British Airways | 7890 | see BA | 2:05pm | 10:05pm | see BA |
| United | 123 | 83 | 6:15pm | 2:15pm | Available |

**Message 2 of 2:** Rebooking

If you have checked bags for this flight or an electronic ticket, please see a United Customer Service Representative for assistance with a reaccommodation plan.

United Airlines asked Pentagram to design a digital gate information display system that would provide travelers with up-to-date flight and destination information. The gate display consists of two 40-inch rear projection AP/LCD screens mounted side by side above the gate agent at all United gates. By accessing United flight, operational and customer information in real time and allowing manual input capabilities, EasyInfo Gate Display provides the latest flight and destination information in a clear and concise manner. It also provides alerts to changing conditions, reduces complexity by eliminating unnecessary choices and directs customers to their next most likely action. The system was designed using Flash to allow for dynamic content, transitions and animations to alert customers to these changes and action-able items. Because the format and location in the gate environment was predetermined, we developed a system of rotating messages to maximize type size and legibility.

United Airlines
EasyInfo Gate Display
information
display system

Design firm
Pentagram Design,
San Francisco

Art directors Duane
Bray, Brian Jacobs

Designers Matt Rogers

Programmer
Allen Interactions

Interface designer
Duane Bray

Photographer
United Airlines
Creative Services

Client
United Airlines

152

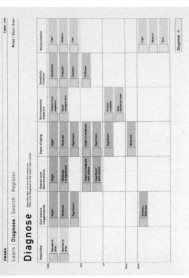

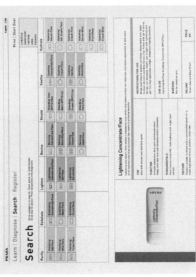

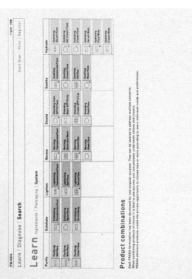

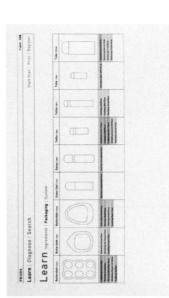

**Prada store kiosk**

Design firm
R/GA, New York

Producer Anja Ludewig

Associate creative
director Vincent Lacava

Art director
Vander Ray McClain

Senior designer
Lesli Karavil

Junior designers
Jesse McGowan,
Dieter Weichman

Production artist
Kohsuke Yamada

Account director
Matt Howell

Account manager
Andrew Rodbell

Senior interaction
designer Ted Metcalfe

Programmer
John Jones

Production coordinator
Sheila Dos Santos

Senior test engineer
Diane Lichtman

R/GA designed kiosks that would enable Prada to promote its new line of skin-care products. The goal was to compose a complete yet utterly simple environment that included the following distinct areas "Learn," "Diagnose," "Search" and "Print." The result is a minimalist design and a groundbreaking user interface. The in-store kiosks enable customers to make more informed product choices, self-diagnose their skin-care needs and learn about Prada's skin-care system. The user is able to select products and print a personal profile from the kiosks, which are located in flagship stores in Tokyo, London and New York.

R/GA's challenge was to create an online version of Richard Saul Wurman's book, *Understanding USA*. The goal was to develop a site that offers a free downloadable version of the book and was in keeping with the book's philosophy: "Public Information should be made public." The experience begins with a quick Flash splash that offers users a symbolic presentation of the book's premise and introduces them to the navigation's graphical and color elements. It dissolves quickly into the home page, with the intuitive navigation prominently displayed to the right. The lower-level pages contain a "zoom" feature encouraging visitors to view detailed data. The color-coded Flash navigation on the home page is mimicked by JavaScript at the top of each ensuing page. Additionally, an interactive site map graphically represents the various sections of the book. Users can rate each page using a simple tool placed globally in the bottom-right corner.

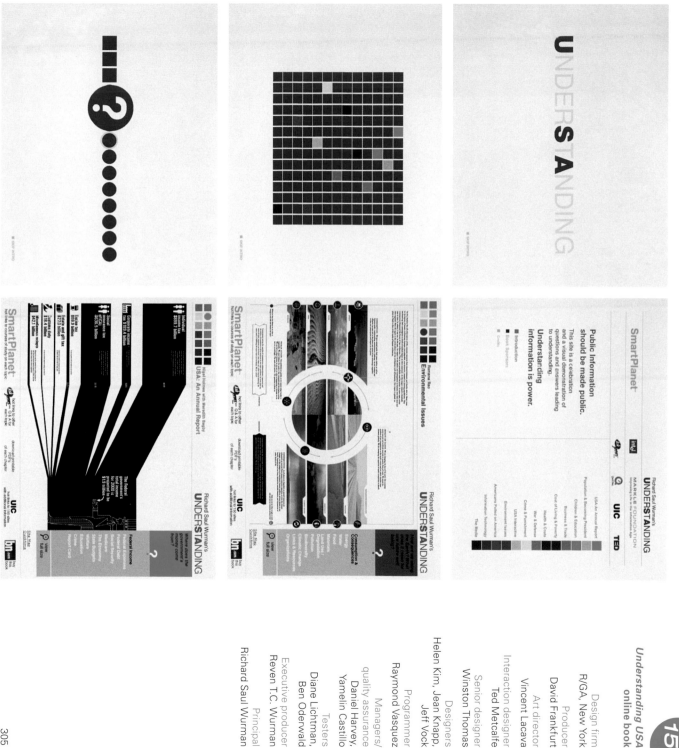

**154**

*Understanding USA*
online book

Design firm
R/GA, New York

Producer
David Frankfurt

Art director
Vincent Lacava

Interaction designer
Ted Metcalfe

Senior designer
Winston Thomas

Designers
Helen Kim, Jean Knapp,
Jeff Vock

Programmer
Raymond Vasquez

Managers/
quality assurance
Daniel Harvey,
Yamelin Castillo

Testers
Diane Lichtman,
Ben Oderwald

Executive producer
Reven T.C. Wurman

Principal
Richard Saul Wurman

Because the TransNote was a new and innovative computer, we wanted the guide to be a departure from typical supporting documentation. The guide ships installed on the writing side of the computer, so we adapted to these physical constraints by creating a publication that was longer than letter size and bound at the top like a writing tablet. The illustration style is soft and sketchy, reminiscent of hand drawn notes and sketches. To orient the user to specific areas of the computer, we created a system that paired a "mini-map" of the overall system with detailed blowups of highlighted areas. The piece was pulled together with a primarily black cover with a quote from Paul Rand, the father of IBM design, and a gloss varnish of the IBM logo "super graphic." Green was used as a secondary color for the cover and throughout the guide to provide highlighting and callouts.

IBM ThinkPad
TransNote: Getting
Started Guide
guidebook

Design firm IBM

Art directors/
creative directors
Amy Dupavillon,
Rebecca Welles

Designers
Amy Dupavillon,
Mary Johnson, Susan
Jasinski

Print production
Amy Dupavillon, Ron
Smith, Masaru Masuda

Illustrators
Luis Elizalde,
Amy Dupavillon

Writers
Michelle Marple
Thomas, Kristine Olka

Client IBM
PCD Mobile Solutions

155

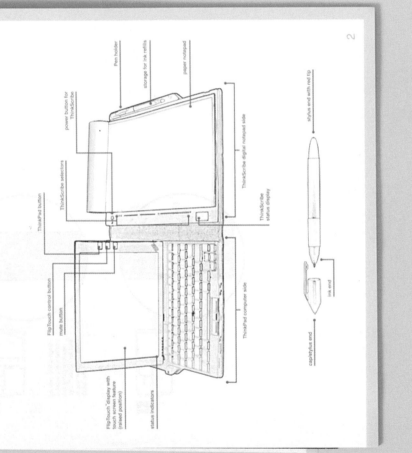

The assignment was to be used for the "Map" section on the back page of each *Harper's*. The design problem was to graphically show the linked relationship between increased rainfall, global warming and the spread of infectious diseases such as cholera. The main challenge was to depict the different layers of information in a complimentary but distinct manner, showing each layer independently but making the correlation evident. Numerical information on the cholera data ranged from less than 10 cases per country to nearly 50,000, requiring an icon system that encompassed the vast margin through scale and color. Information had to be easily read and graphically appealing.

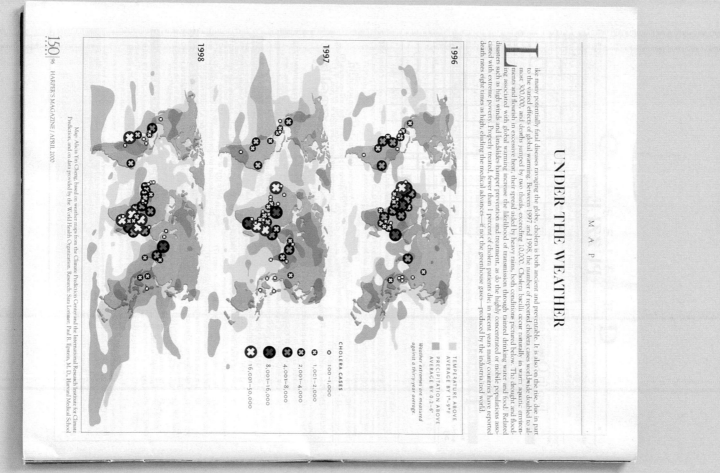

M A P

## UNDER THE WEATHER

L ike many potentially fatal diseases ravaging the globe, cholera is both ancient and preventable. It is also on the rise, due in part to the varied effects of global warming. Between 1997 and 1998, the number of reported cholera cases worldwide doubled to almost 300,000, and deaths jumped by two-thirds, exceeding 10,000. Cholera bacilli occur naturally in warm aquatic environments and flourish in excessive heat, their spread aided by heavy rains, both conditions pictured below. The drought and flooding associated with global warming increase the likelihood of transmission through tainted drinking water and food. Related diseases such as high winds and landslides hamper prevention and treatment, as do the highly concentrated or mobile populations associated with extreme poverty. Properly treated, fewer than 1 percent of cholera patients die; in recent years many countries have reported death rates eight times as high, during the medical advances—if not the greenhouse gases—produced by the industrialized world.

1996

1998

1997

**CHOLERA CASES**

- 0
- 100–1,000
- 1,001–2,000
- 2,001–4,000
- 4,001–8,000
- 8,001–16,000
- 16,001–50,000

TEMPERATURE ABOVE
AVERAGE BY 1°–9°F

PRECIPITATION ABOVE
AVERAGE BY 0.2–6"

*Weather extremes are measured against a thirty-year average.*

150 | 96

HARPER'S MAGAZINE / APRIL 2000

Map: Alicia Yin Cheng, based on weather maps from the Climate Prediction Center and the International Research Institute for Climate Prediction, and on data provided by the World Health Organization. Research: Sara Lorimer. Paul R. Epstein, M.D., Harvard Medical School.

156

*"Under the Weather"*
map

Design firm
mgmt, Brooklyn

Designer
Alicia Yin Cheng

Project manager
Angela Riechers

Writer Charis Conn

Client *Harper's
Magazine*

0 = not well
10 = extremely well

It depends on
who is criticizing.

Depends on
the person.

It depends
on passion.

If it is constructive and or comes from someone
who has knowledge that makes their criticism
relevant, 10. If they are just a jealous asshole, 0.

Depends on who's the critic. If Chwast or Glaser
says it sucks it probably does. On the other hand,
if the new trendy "designer of the month" doesn't
like my work, I probably won't slit my wrists.
I'll just wait and see what happens next month.

7   17   18   25   41

It depends who's
criticizing.

A

# ENVIRONMENTAL GRAPHICS

**Jurors Ayse Birsel** Olive 1:1, New York **Michael Donovan** Donovan and Green, New York **Noreen Morioka** AdamsMorioka, Los Angeles

Environmental graphic design is a diverse field that includes the planning, design and specification of graphic elements in the built and natural environment. Applications include signage, wayfinding systems, mapping, exhibition design, themed environments, retail spaces, sports facilities and special-event atmospherics.

In an age where speed and distraction predominate, the need for clarity in environmental graphics is paramount. Situated in the middle ground between graphic design and architecture, environmental graphics is a little-appreciated discipline that is most often noticed when it doesn't work; it's not just about putting the writing on the wall, it's about making the writing legible at a distance of 50 feet to people who are more likely than not in a rush to move from A to B. This year's jurors were unanimously enthusiastic about this confluence of 2-D and 3-D artistry, and chose projects that, in their words, "told a story" – stories that balanced design, information, scale and content.

"Good environmental graphics are all about essence," explained Michael Donovan. "You have very little time to react because you're in motion." Essence, of course, takes on many different forms and is evident in projects that feature boldly emblazoned super graphics and carefully considered details alike. Several selections this year demonstrated a graphics-writ-large sensibility that matched utility with vitality. Particularly notable was Pentagram's design for the New 42nd Street Studios (cat. 160), a 10-story complex of rehearsal spaces for people in the performing arts. "It's really wonderful," said Birsel admiringly of the project's brightly painted corridors and stairwells. "It reminds me of Mondrian's *Broadway Boogie Woogie*" – a painting created

Response, cat.160

# ANALYZED THE ARCHITECTURE FOR USE AND MADE STYLISTIC ANALOGIES.

Question F
Briefly describe the research methods used for preliminary design on this project.

by the Dutch De Stijl master that captures New York's vibrancy in red, blue and yellow grids. Maureen Norioka agreed, adding that even the most mundane of surfaces – in this instance, a wall next to a broom closet – was activated by the super graphics. "It speaks wonderfully about the whole culture of entertainment and stagecraft," she said. "It absolutely creates that energy."

Morioka's enthusiasm for the energy invoked by splashy environmental graphics extended to the New York offices of the National Basketball Association (cat. 158), which borrows all the iconic visual cues of the game – the shiny lacquered wood floor, the red-and-blue court markings – and combines them with stylish furniture and larger-than-life black-and-white photographs. "There's no question of where you are and what it's about," said Donovan of the office's pitch-perfect atmosphere." Morioka noted that only one thing was missing for that holistic basketball experience: "All they need to do is spill some Coke on the floor so it's sticky when you walk across it."

The subspecies of environmental graphics that garnered some of the liveliest conversation, however, was exhibition design, and this year two examples came to the fore – both dealing with specifically American cultural phenomena. The megaexhibition "Made in California" (cat. 161), which took place at the Los Angeles County Museum of Art and attempted to survey the sweep of California-specific culture, was largely praised for its innovative signage and unconventional graphic flourishes. "With very simple materials the designers have been able to transform this space that is really very difficult to use," noted Birsel of the entrance hall, an unwieldy glass-and-steel atrium that was tamed for the exhibition by a series of huge fabric banners and screens. Morioka, a native Californian, also praised the clever use of materials and hues that read specifically West Coast – particularly the veneer and plywood that came to symbolize L.A.'s famous case-study houses and what Morioka called the show's "Mexican food colors."

The second exhibition, a show called "Cold War Modern" (cat. 162) that took place at Wellesley College's Davis Gallery, sought to explore the intersection between high and low culture during America's Cold War years. Employing distinctly American references like a 1950s-era domestic interior, abstracted nuclear imagery like the concentric sound wave markings that indicate an A-bomb explosion site and clean Swiss typography writ large, the show evokes an atmosphere that says as much about the era as the images and objects shown in the gallery. "All of the surfaces get engaged," said Donovan enthusiastically of the exhibition's multi-layered design. "It's so evocative of that time."

In the end, it was perhaps the most workaday project that conjured the highest praises: Amtrak's signage for its high-speed Acela service (cat. 157). Mediating solidity and speed with a recurrent airfoil shape that proves to be highly visible and well-lit – a must when it comes to displaying constantly changing information for people on the go – the Acela signage evoked cries of "elegant" and "effective" from all three jurors, who have spent enough of their own time in train stations struggling to find their way. "At the end of the day," concluded Birsel, "what we've selected is about clarity. You look and you understand what's going on at a glance. These are instances where architecture and graphic design have come together in a meaningful way." Andrea Codrington

The primary goals of the sign program are to display relevant and real-time information, enhance the customer experience and use the sign system to impose Amtrak's Acela brand identity on the entire passenger experience. Rather than being logotype-driven, the Acela program derives its branding strength from its sculptural forms. A sleekly curved "airfoil" shape became the stylistic nucleus of the entire signage program, which ranges from large ground-mounted pylons to smaller ceiling- and wall-mounted signs. The typical sign body is a double-airfoil shape, featuring two back-to-back curved panels, with some units intersected by a curved vertical fin to evoke movement. Further reinforcing the Acela identity, the sign program's silver and teal colors match those of the new trains. The sign system distinguishes the premium Acela service from regular Amtrak service and is used only at the Acela gates and platforms. The LED displays provide train information to passengers along all points of the travel experience and engender a greater comfort level in passengers.

**Amtrak's Acela specialty station signage**

**157**

Design firm Calori &
Vanden-Eynden,
New York

Creative director
David Vanden-Eynden

Project manger
Jordan Marcus

Designers
David Vanden-Eynden,
Chris Calori, Jordan
Marcus, Denise Funaro

Photographer
Elliott Kaufman

Client
Amtrak/National
Railroad Passenger
Corporation

**158**

National Basketball
Association
New York
office interior

Design firm Gensler,
New York

Project director
Patric O'Malley

Creative director
John Bricker

Design director
Peter Wang

Designers Dicie
Carlson, Susan Merrell,
Dariel Park

Project managers
Julie Applebaum,
Unjoo Noh

Project architects/
managers Kent Hikida,
Lawrence Taormina

Architectural designer
Mary Sze

Photographer
NBA Photos

Client National
Basketball Association

The NBA asked Gensler to develop a master facilities plan. Basketball-themed design elements and a comprehensive graphic program support the project objectives by conveying NBA's strong brand and the kinetic energy of the sport. The experience begins as you step out of the elevator and into a full-scale section of a basketball court where rules and specifications are stenciled on the walls. The media lounge has a cage of basketballs with a coffee bar that adjoins the room. Six backboards form a wall enclosure around a new interconnecting stair. Lightboxes depicting players in action line the corridors, and murals of other memorable NBA moments are arranged on the end walls of work areas. Office signage and wayfinding components were designed as part of the graphics program. Imagery from the NBA archives was used to create photomurals that form a backdrop for the activity in the workplace.

EACH BASKET RING SHALL
HAVE ITS UPPER EDGE
10' ABOVE AND PARALLEL
TO THE FLOOR AND SHALL
BE EQUIDISTANT FROM THE
VERTICAL EDGES OF THE
BACKBOARD. THE RING,
18" IN DIAMETER, SHALL
BE PAINTED ORANGE.

IMAX asked Gensler to develop a prototype design for its theater interiors and communications. The graphic program included product (movie) posters, wayfinding and menus for tickets, movie times and concessions. The client was relying on the environment and graphics as the primary means of repositioning the IMAX brand to customers and prospective development partners on an international level. The overall design approach emphasizes a bold, bright, clean, modern aesthetic that challenges the traditional movie theater. Elements common to movie theaters are either reconceived or eliminated: movie posters become an illuminated wall that addresses the wide and varied IMAX offer and wayfinding relies heavily on a system of icons applied as large-scale graphics integrated with architectural surfaces. Bright colors, high light levels, translucent and metallic finishes signal that this is indeed a different kind of theater for a different kind of movie.

**IMAX Theatre interior**

Design firm Gensler, New York

Creative director
John Bricker

Design director
Peter Wang

Senior graphic designer
Lisa Van Zandt

Designers
Jam e Brizzolara,
Susan Merrell

Project managers
William Staempfli,
Lisa Van Zandt

Client IMAX

The New 42nd Street Studios houses 10 floors of rehearsal space for various performing-arts groups, along with the Duke Theater. The rehearsal studios are very simple, understated spaces that the client wanted to counteract with very active corridors. Throughout the building, De Stijl-inspired graphics perform in the space. Identity and directional signage appears on the floors – an idea inspired by the tape marks put down on stages to indicate performers' positioning. In the elevators, the word "floor" appears inside the car, with the corresponding number positioned at the opening on each level. Doors are painted with strong, simple icons. Billboard-size graphics have moved in from Times Square and taken residence. Typography on the building directory – and in etched mirrored glass on the donor wall – reflects the activity of the building's performers along with the signage and crowds outside.

Design firm Pentagram
Design, New York

Art director
Paula Scher

Graphic designers
Paula Scher, Dok Chon,
Rion Byrd, Bob Stern,
Tina Chang

Print production
Tina Chang

Environmental
production
Rion Byrd, Bob Stern

Architect
Platt Byard Dovell

Photographer
Peter Mauss/Esto

Client Cora Cahan,
New 42nd Street
Studios

**New 42nd Street
Studios/The Duke
Theater interior**

160

**161**

**"Made in California" exhibition**

Design firm
Los Angeles County
Museum of Art

Exhibition designers/
information architects
Durfee Regn Sandhaus
(Tim Durfee, Iris Regn,
Louise Sandhaus)

Designer, graphics
Scott Taylor

Designer,
lifestyle environments
Bernard Kester

Design assistance
Agnes Anderson,
Katherine Go, Jeff
Haber, Petra Michel,
Frederick Nilsson,
Rebecca Rudolph, Tricia
Sanedrin, Giorgos
Sinas, Paul Wehby

Design coordination
Jim Drobka,
Daniel Young,
Rachel Ware Zooi

Curators Stephanie
Barron, Sheri
Bernstine, Ilene
Susan Fort

Client LACMA

The process for developing this sprawling exhibition – the largest ever mounted by LACMA – was to understand the design as an interface that presents, translates and organizes the works and the galleries into a functioning information space. At all levels of this comprehensive design the form emerges from the imperatives of both displaying and contributing to the understanding of the art and ephemeral objects in the exhibition. This conceptual approach is played out in the fabric structure that relines the interior of the plaza, the layered and interactive timelines, the suspended structures at entrances to each section, the shifting wall-objects, the stackable benches and cases, and the wayfinding and exhibition graphics.

MADE IN CALIFORNI
ART, IMAGE, AND IDENTITY, 1900–2000

**162**

**"Cold War Modern: The Domesticated Avant-Garde" exhibition**

Design firm Pentagram Design, New York

Art director
J. Abbott Miller

Designers
J. Abbott Miller,
Jeremy Hoffman

Photographer
Peter Mauss/Esto

Curator
Judith Hoos Fox

Sound consultant
Joel Gordon,
Art of the States

Client Davis Museum
& Cultural Center,
Wellesley College

This museum exhibition, aimed at a general audience, examined the permeable membrane between high and low culture during the Cold War years. Mixing design, art and both avant-garde and popular music, the exhibition had ambitious goals in a small setting. In reference to the exhibition's title, Pentagram put a 1950s-era modern house in the gallery. The house became the locus of sound within the exhibition; the radiating "sound waves" seen on the roof were also the marks on maps that indicate the radius of A-bomb sites. The exhibition mixed the paranoid and utopian elements of the period. The "domestication" of the title was also present in Formica and wallpaper patterns created for the environment. Some of these made patterns out of iconic 1950s furniture, while others used documentary photography to create an environmental backdrop.

An AIGA Minnesota chapter fundraising effort was able to raise sufficient funds to permanently name the primary conference room at AIGA's National Design Center in New York "Minnesota." The assignment was to recognize the firms and individuals from the Minnesota chapter who contributed to the campaign effort. The solution was to design something memorable and symbolic of the Minnesota environment. A snow shovel seemed appropriate. The only available wall space in the conference room was a pair of rather narrow surfaces between the windows facing Fifth Avenue. The shovel solution seemed ideally suited for this space, and two shovels seemed necessary for visual balance. With the exception of the bolts used in fabrication, the shovels are completely custom made. Even the handles were turned on a lathe. The blades are 12-gauge stainless steel. The type engraver and the stainless steel fabricator asked that I not bring them any more projects. The shovels took six months to fabricate.

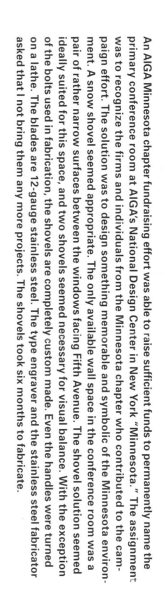

**163**

**AIGA Snow Shovels
donor recognition
artifact**

Design firm
The Office of Eric
Madsen, Minneapolis

Art director/designer
Eric Madsen

Project manager/
fabrication consultant
Steve Beaudry

Fabricator Rainville
Carlson/Panto-Gravers

Client AIGA

Question K
How many rounds
of revision were
involved for this
project?

Catalogue numbers
A = anonymous

average rounds
of revision

# EXPERIENCE DESIGN

**Jurors Clement Mok** Sapient, San Francisco **Nathan Shedroff** San Francisco **Terry Swack** Boston

Entries in this category should utilize digital media to interactively inform, educate or entertain. Eligible entries include websites, CD-ROMs, computer games for any platform, kiosks and other electronic exhibit systems, and software interfaces for mobile devices and networked appliances.

In a network society, communication is not conducted through discrete beginnings and ends, so messages become overwhelmed with meaning.

In 2000, to no one's surprise, it was a web, web, web, web world. This year's jurors were prepared for an overwhelming preponderance of websites over other forms of experience design, and that's just what they got. But in a field filled with the sites of venture capital firms, technology companies and Gen-Z lifestyle peddlers, who would've guessed that the center of attention would be the web-face of haute couture?

Several jurors had been following the genre with interest, and Gucci, Prada, Armani and Issey Miyake were among the entries. The genre's noted staples? Extended animated sequences, wide-screen visuals and a noted emphasis on browsing over buying. Equally of interest was the lack of shopping-cart icons and the organizing principles that typically grease the wheels of e-tailing. Terry Irwin explained, "You're going there figuring out if there's something you'd like to go [to a department store] and buy." Clement Mok concurred that "it's about eye candy and attitude," not information or transactions. "Fashion has its own criteria online, just like it does in print." As the judging proceeded, Mok's statement about fashion proved true of other contexts as well.

In contending that there can be criteria common to web and print, Mok was refuting the digital media exceptionalism of previous years – the idea that there are design rules that define "what works on the web" and don't apply to other media.

As the year 2000 pool made clear, a basic set of principles for web page design has been accepted almost universally. But what the designers recognized this year went beyond such principles to project a new intelligence about the context of their work — the market, industry or culture into which the design would be inserted. This awareness transcends media, and it's at the heart of experience design. It's not just overall user-centeredness, it's shaping interactions that will reward and captivate specific people in a specific setting.

This approach produced selections that were the epitomes of their genres. For example, the jury labored to find the designer's design site in a large field of self-promotional work. They found only one: Red Canoe's website for illustrator Katherine Dunn, which ornaments Dunn's portfolio with hand-drawn interstitial sequences and spoken bons mots (cat. 170). "It's really original and personal. You get a great sense of her," said Shedroff.

Conversely, the sites recognized in the product/services category had graphic vocabularies that jurors found conventional, but appropriate. Jurors especially praised Shutterfly, a clean-looking consumer photo services site that delivered a goal-oriented experience smoothly (cat. 166). They appreciated the instructions that stepped users through sign-in and that enables users to send albums to friends, see if they've viewed them and catalogue their comments. Among fan or community sites, the selected entries were so true to their target users that they actually conjured these people in the jurors' minds. Bthere.TV, a celebrity/ fashion site, evoked for Mok the image of "people who like to watch people… They're probably [surfing the site and] chatting on the phone at the same time (cat. 172)."

None of these sites was selected for having features its competitors didn't have. Rather, they combined tools felicitously, revealing thoughtful user research as well as visual design. On the other hand, the jury found room to recognize entrants that had done something genuinely new and ambitious with technology. They loved Triplecode's MoodLogic Magnet Browser, in which music listeners

# GUESSWORK.

Response, anonymous

can move emotion "magnets" around the screen to "attract" the songs they're in the mood to hear (cat. 174). Mok imagined it as the ideal replacement for Napster's notoriously workmanlike interface.

Perhaps the most contentious categories were "editorial" and "education." The jurors rewarded both longtime centers of opportunity for great interactive work. The jurors rewarded the arts-education efforts of Masterpiece Theatre Online and Continental Harmony for dynamic information design that increased the learning quotient (cat. 175, 169). On the less mainstream side, they also lauded The 1000 Journal Project as "a great concept" in editorial and recognized several of the standout museum exhibit companion sites of the past year (cat. 171). This category also yielded this year's only nonweb selection, TravelBrain's kit of print, audio and CD-ROM-based materials for touring the Gettysburg battlefield by car – a combination that seemed likely to produce a new and uncommonly site-specific travel experience (cat. 173).

And what of the couture website derby? As it turned out, none of the fashion sites were selected. The jurors ultimately decided that while each worked hard at its ambience, none stood out within the genre in an unproblematic way. Said Mok of one such entry, "I love the experimental nature of it ... but experience design needs to be at the very least relevant to the potential customer and place. I don't think she would have the patience." The comment reaffirmed a notion that seems to be on the rise in this interdisciplinary field: Each group that gathers on-line creates its own set of priorities, and the rules of design, where they exist, arise from the designer's attentiveness to who those people are. Andrea Moed

The primary challenge was to showcase more than 150 products on one screen, while continuing to develop and enhance the visual language of the "Workspheres" exhibition. We wanted to develop a not-so-abstract metaphor for the workplace that could visually relate the website to the exhibition. The post-it note – one of the most common elements of the workplace – became this icon. On a technical level, we developed a sorting mechanism to help navigate the user through the massive amount of content, which is accessible on just one page. We feel that the site successfully integrates and continues the design language of both the exhibition and the other marketing collateral. We were able to develop not only a website but also a kiosk that served as a guide within the exhibition.

**Workspheres**
**website and kiosk**

164

Design firm
Method, Inc., New York

Creative director/
lead designer
Olivier Chételat

Designers Alicia Cheng,
Thomas Noller

Interaction designers
April Starr, Ted Booth

Content strategist
Chris Torrens

Site engineering
Jonathan Synder

Producer Natalia Maric

Account manager
Monte Bartlett

Client Museum of
Modern Art

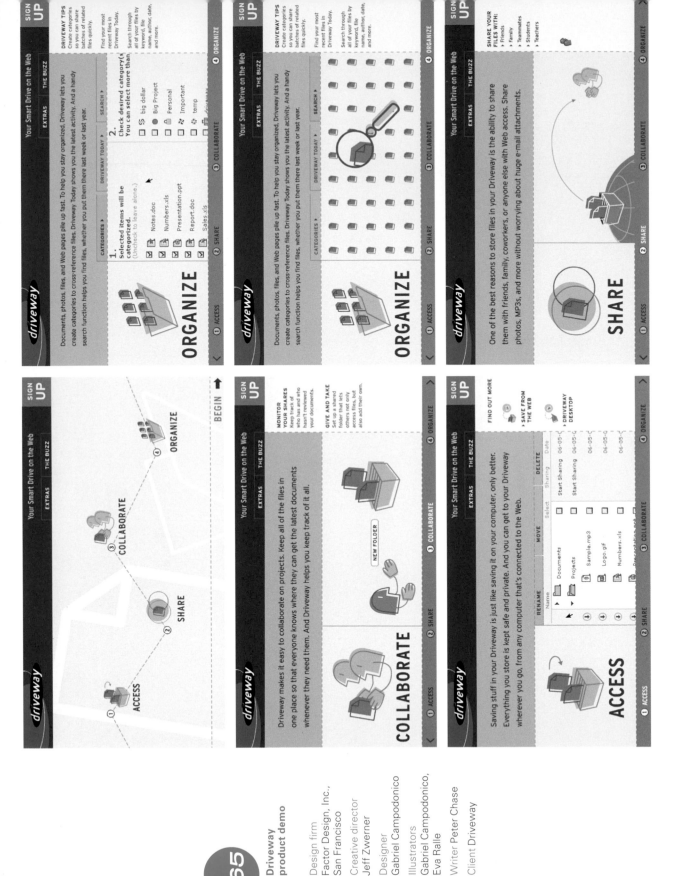

**165**

**Driveway**
**product demo**

Design firm
Factor Design, Inc.,
San Francisco

Creative director
Jeff Zwerner

Designer
Gabriel Campodonico

Illustrators
Gabriel Campodonico,
Eva Ralle

Writer Peter Chase

Client Driveway

On the heels of our successful redesign of its free online file storage site, Driveway asked us to design a Flash-based product demo that would quickly introduce consumers to its service. The Driveway team had originally envisioned creating a step-by-step product tutorial that would walk people through the different facets of the product and its functionality. We suggested that viewers would first need to know the value it offered. We opted to take the approach of focusing on the three primary benefits of the service: accessing files, sharing those files with others and organizing your files. Our solution drew upon the graphic language of the interface, while expanding the illustration style we created for the homepage. Using Flash to guide the user through the primary benefits, we were able to increase the amount of customers who were signing up for the service each day.

Shutterfly is an online photo-processing service. The company was in need of total rebranding to take advantage of the rapidly increasing awareness in digital photography and related digital services. Eleven provided a full compliment of services ranging from identity, collateral, advertising, online marketing, packaging and website design. Targeted mainly toward women who keep and organize family photos, Shutterfly is an easy-to-use service to upload, store and print photos. Clean, intuitive navigation directs users to areas where they can edit, enhance, fix, share and even turn their photos into greeting cards.

166

## Shutterfly website

Design firm
Eleven Inc.,
San Francisco

Creative director/
art director
Michael Borosky

Designer Matt Magana

Photographer
Katharyn Ledner

Copywriter Jay Rendon

Technical directors
Crystal Trexel,
Karen Quek

Account executives
Michele Jacobs,
Betsy Woudenberg

Information architects
Jordan Warren,
John Skidgel

Programmers
Chris Brown,
Joseph Oster,
Sue Quek

Client Shutterfly

The "010101 Art in Technological Times" website for SFMOMA serves as an online gallery, a forum for public discussion and feedback, and an educational resource in conjunction with the museum exhibition. Presented with the unique challenge of designing both the web and gallery presentations, we elected to think of the two venues as two parts of the same design challenge. The curators had introduced us to their idea of conveying the contextual material for the exhibition via quotations. We found we could exploit both the interdependent and independent characteristics of the paired venues if the quotes were dynamic and ever changing. If the quotes included those taken from the website discourse and others chosen by the web audience, a "flattening" of hierarchies could be effectively accomplished. In the absence of any single authoritative voice, the only constant was the sprawl of concepts and interpretations introduced to the exhibition experience via LCD monitors.

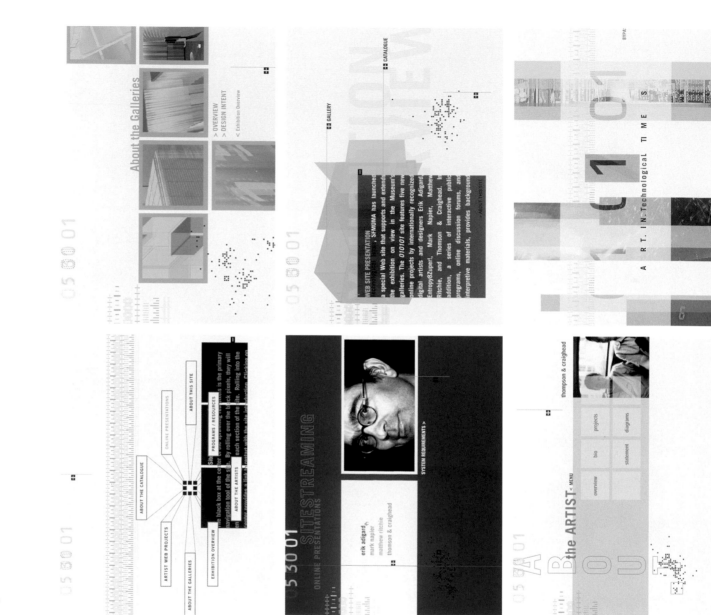

**167**

**010101 Art in Technological Times website**

Design firm
Perimetre-Flux,
San Francisco

Project directors
Anthony Amidei,
Steve Barretto,
Stephen Jaycox

Project team
James Ken Butler,
Curtis Christophersen,
Willow Cook, Vanessa
Dina-Barlow, Judith
Hardy, Sharon Holgado,
Henry Liu, Alex Lord,
Shilla Mehrafshani,
Tim Mohn, Dina Tooley

Client San Francisco
Museum of Modern Art

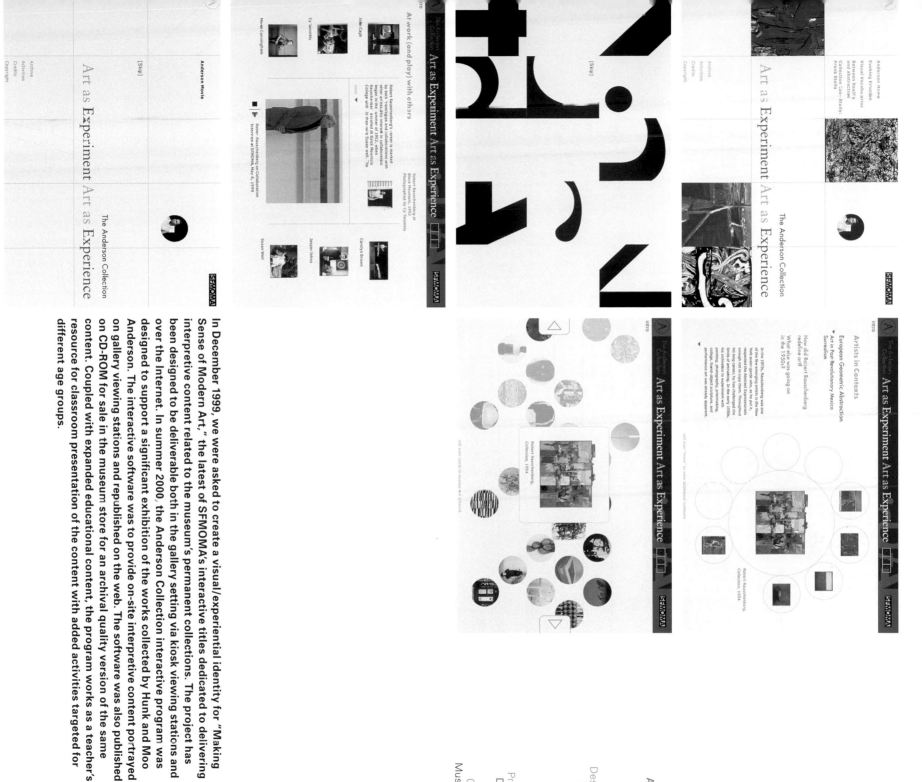

In December 1999, we were asked to create a visual/experiential identity for "Making Sense of Modern Art," the latest of SFMOMA's interactive titles dedicated to delivering interpretive content related to the museum's permanent collections. The project has been designed to be deliverable both in the gallery setting via kiosk viewing stations and over the Internet. In summer 2000, the Anderson Collection interactive program was designed to support a significant exhibition of the works collected by Hunk and Moo Anderson. The interactive software was to provide on-site interpretive content portrayed on gallery viewing stations and republished on the web. The software was also published on CD-ROM for sale in the museum store for an archival quality version of the same content. Coupled with expanded educational content, the program works as a teacher's resource for classroom presentation of the content with added activities targeted for different age groups.

Art as Experiment/
Art as Experience
website

Design firm Perimetre-
Flux, San Francisco

Project directors
Anthony Amidei,
Steve Barretto,
Stephen Jaycox

Project team Vanessa
Dina-Barlow, Sharon
Holgado, Alex Lord

Client San Francisco
Museum of Modern Art

168

Continental Harmony follows 58 composers in different locations across the U.S. as they write and direct music for communities. "Communities In Harmony" allows users to explore the national project and hear the words and music of the 58 commissioned composers. The site also provides information about how to involve your community with music. "Sound Lounge" is a media-rich interactive playground that gives visitors a taste of the composer's experience, as it explores how music influences our daily lives. With sound as the driving medium behind the experience, our challenge was to use the right combination of creativity and technology to engage the user to unlock the magic of the music. Narration and animation are used to invite the user to interact with the site and discover the essences of music. Recordings and images from each composition project can be explored from a map of the U.S.

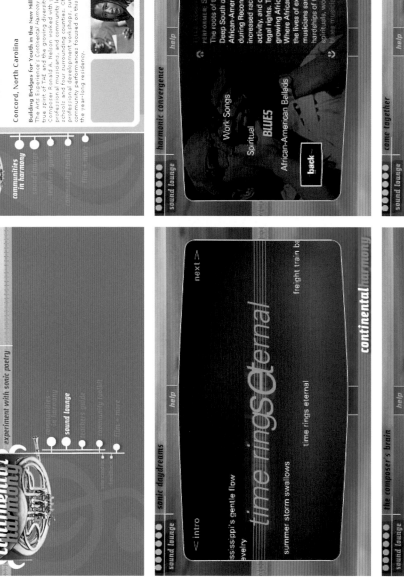

169

**Continental Harmony website**

Design firm
Popular Front,
Minneapolis

Creative director
Laurence Bricker

Design director
Eric Kassel

Project manager
Marny Stebbins

Writer Bill Snyder

Programmer Nate Clark

Producer Mike Keefe

Interface design
Eric Kassel, TJ Shaffer

Flash programming
David Holmdahl,
Rebecca Smith,
Nate Clark

Client Twin Cities
Public Television (TPT),
PBS.org

TPT producer
Erika Herrmann

TPT programming
Chuck Olson

TPT executive producer
Catherine Allan

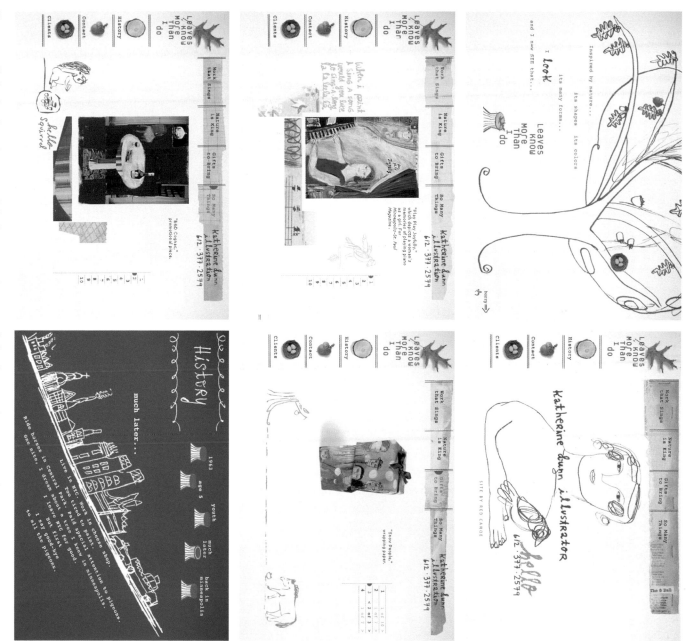

"E&O Cognac," promotional piece.

Katherine dunn illustration
612-377-2579

"Play Play Joyfully," which depicts a woman's memories of playing piano as a girl. For Minneapolis-St. Paul Magazine.

Katherine dunn illustration
612-377-2579

inspired by nature...

i look

its many forms...     its shapes     its colors

Leaves know more than I do

hurry

SITE BY RED CANOE

katherine dunn illustrator
612-377-2579

hello

"Snow People," wrapping paper.

Katherine dunn illustration
612-377-2579

History

much later...

1963          age 5          youth          much later          back in minneapolis

Live in NYC. Work in cheese shop.
Too tired to paint.
Ride horses in Central Park.
One bite: I dream about a tree I knew.
But first. I say good-bye.
I pay special attention to pigeons.
I lease NYC for good.
to all the pigeons.

Illustrator Katherine Dunn's personal desire was to have a website that gently encouraged visitors to think about nature by enjoying it. Red Canoe printed Dunn's illustrations, created three-dimensional prototypes, digitally photographed them and Flash-scripted the site section housing these distinctive pieces. All of the site's sections were named to convey Dunn's charming and playful personality, and each of the four main "portfolio" sections were color-coded and contain unique animations. Photographic navigational elements were used to provide contrast to the illustrative site elements. By rolling over each of these photographic links, visitors are greeted by a distinctive nature-inspired illustration presented as a quick gif animation that prepares guests for the longer intricate Flash illustrations within each section. Thinking of the splash/welcome page as a book cover, we designed it last.

**170**

**Katherine Dunn, Illustrator website**

Design firm Red Canoe, Deer Lodge, Tennessee

Art director/creative director Deb Koch

Designer Caroline Kavanagh

Developers Deb Koch, Benjamin Kaubisch

Flash animator Benjamin Kaubisch

Sound editor Benjamin Kaubisch

Illustrator Katherine Dunn

Writers Katherine Dunn, Deb Koch

Sound Katherine Dunn

Client Katherine Dunn

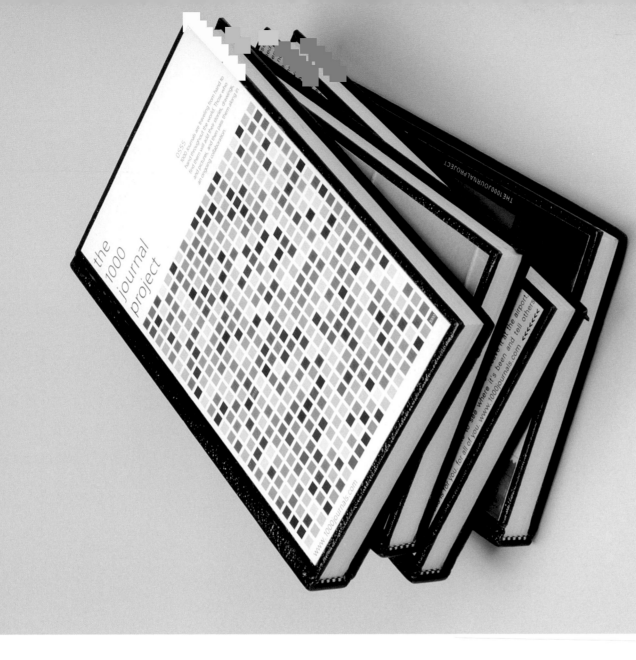

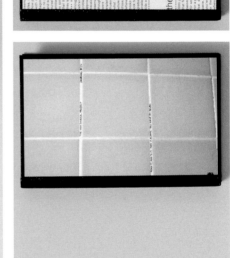

**171**

*The 1000 Journal Project interactive art form*

Design firm Brian
Singer, San Francisco

Project creator
Brian Singer

Contributing
cover designers
Brian Singer, Joshua
Swanbeck, Anders
Hornstrup, Jemma
Gura, Chris Robbins,
Tim Sauder, Vanessa
Enriquez, Greg
Durrell, Simon Powell,
Judith Zissman,
Christopher Pacetti,
Rick Valicenti,
Brian McMullen,
Jon Sauder, Geoff
Ahmann, Amy
Franceschini, Mike
Cina, Shirin Kouladjie

Programmer
Nate Koechley/
Vicksburg Collective

The **1000 Journal Project** is an attempt to follow 1,000 blank journals as they travel from hand to hand around the world. People who find them add stories and drawings before passing them along in an ongoing collaborative art form. The experiment consists of 1,000 physical journals and a website that ties them together. Participants use the site to report on a journal's location and post scans of what was in it. The largest hurdle to overcome is keeping the journals moving and tracked. Different cover designs and instruction sets address this with varying levels of success. The project as a whole is continually evolving. We've had such a huge response from people who want to participate that the website needed to change. Instead of just displaying the artwork and journal info, it's turned into the primary interface between those who have journals and those who want them.

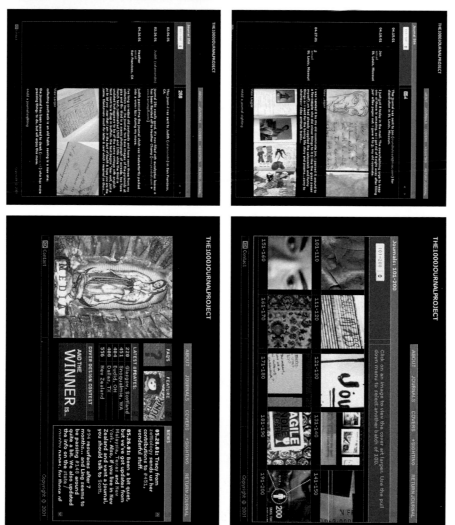

The principal challenge with Bthere.TV was the need to continuously update content and change the featured video clips. Combining Flash and Windows Media with interlinked controls was the major technical challenge. Since the client had no visual identity, we began by developing the Bthere.TV logo, and proceeded to build the site around that. We segmented the clips into subject area "wells" and provided numerous means of accessing individual series. From the home page, you can access the top-five rated clips on the site, see featured clips through the "bBox" and click on the feature video animated descriptions. You can also drill down through the navigation interface to subject areas. The site is constructed to allow our client to access and administrate all content through an HTML interface.

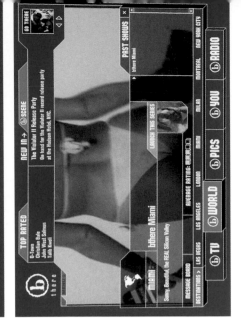

**172**

**Bthere.TV website**

Design firm
Tangram Design,
Charlestown,
Massachusetts

Creative director
Justin Crawford

Art directors
Brian Oakes,
Chris Franzese

Designers
Paul Szypula,
Jenny Woo

Animator
Justin Crawford

Programmers Drew
Millechia, David Chang

Technical director
Damien Morton

Producer
Doug Hoffman

Account supervisor
David Cherry

Client/publisher
bthere.TV

Visitors to the famous Gettysburg Battlefield face a dilemma: they can either find products that teach them about the history of the battle or ones that help them plan their trip. The Gettysburg Expedition Guide combines the power of multimedia with the knowledge of an expert to bring the history of Gettysburg to life. The combination of a multimedia CD-ROM, driving audio tour and companion guidebook gives the traveler a single comprehensive package for visiting Gettysburg. The guide was designed to accommodate multiple layers of interactivity – from a strictly passive learning experience to deeper levels of interaction with the CD-ROM and guidebook, high-impact visual elements, easy-to-use interfaces and directions – all with high entertainment value.

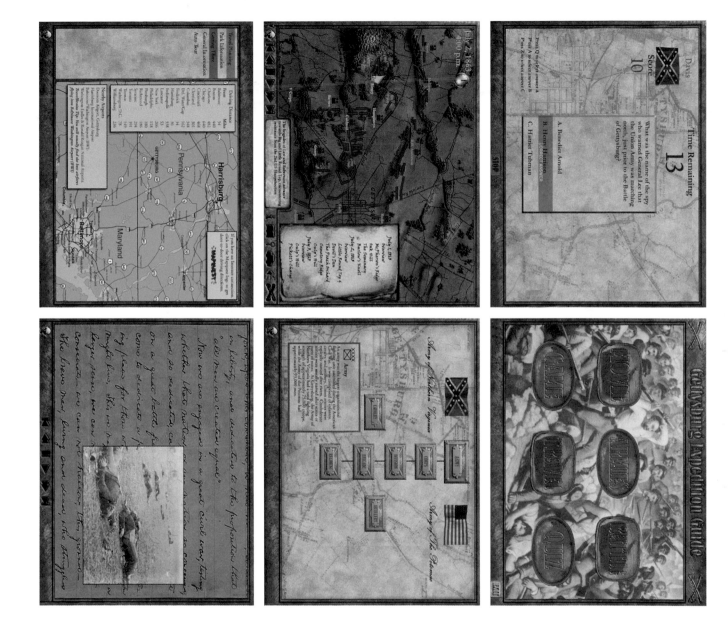

Gettysburg
Expedition Guide
interactive experience

Design firm
TravelBrains, Lake
Forest, California

Creative director/writer
Paul C. Davis

Designer
Catherine R. Davis

Multimedia developer
Victor J. Davis

Historian
Wayne E. Motts

Producer Paul C. Davis

Voice actor Reg Green

173

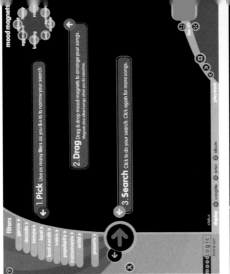

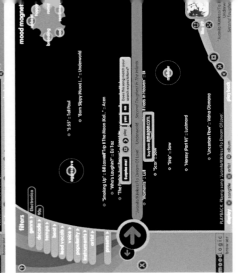

**174**

MoodLogic
browser

Design firm Triplecode,
Beverly Hills

Designers
Lindi Emoungu, Pascal
Wever, David Young

Client MoodLogic, Inc.

The MoodLogic browser allows people to search for songs based on musical characteristics and moods. The primary task was to organize songs based on their relationships and display them in a way that would make sense to the user. Songs were selected from a more than 24-dimensional data space with attributes like song name and title, information about how people perceive the song and abstract signal processing information. It was important that the user's experience be intuitive and simple. We worked closely with MoodLogic to develop an interface concept in which users could search and explore songs using a combination of "filters" and "magnets." Filters limit the songs displayed, and magnets help visually arrange them into meaningful distributions. Visually, the interface plays a secondary role to the content. While there are design elements on the screen, they are less important than the system's content, and so are only minimally treated.

This companion website to "ExxonMobil Masterpiece Theatre," the long-running PBS series, was completely redesigned and relaunched in September 2000. The goals of the redesign were to expand the educational and informational reach of the series; stylistically reinterpret the brand; attract a new online audience to the series and website; honor and celebrate the 30th-anniversary season of the series; and introduce a new collection of films. The design had to be flexible and modular to represent the various styles of the season's productions while maintaining a cohesive overall feel for the series. Using classic typographical elements and imagery in a clean modern way makes reference to the history of the series while conveying the content in a web-friendly way. The site was designed in accordance with WGBH interactive standards, which aim to reach the broadest audience possible, including blind and visually impaired users accessing the content via screenreader technology.

ExxonMobil
Masterpiece Theatre
Online website

Design firm
WGBH Interactive,
Boston

Art director
John Tyler Howe

Designer
John Tyler Howe

Producer Louise Weber

Programmer Molly Frey

Writer Caitlin O'Neil

Editorial review
Julie Wolf

Research assistant
Jessica Cavano

Client ExxonMobil
Masterpiece Theatre

175

Question O
How much time
did this project
require, relative to
an average job?
less than average
average
more than average

less than average

**33%**

average

**44%**

more than average

**26%**

Due to digital graphics programs and nonlinear editing systems, design is increasingly finding its most flamboyant expression on the big and little screen – in TV ads, film title sequences or trailers, music videos, broadcast IDs and interstitial segments. This category is concerned with work that integrates type, image, color, motion and sound over time.

**Jurors Karin Fong**
Imaginary Forces, Los Angeles **Emily Oberman**
Number Seventeen, New York **Joan Raspo**
New York

Capturing a moving image and laying it down in print is a prospect that's similar to trapping an insect in amber: the form may be clear to the eye upon examination, but the way it flies around in real time is all but left to the imagination. This year, however, the problem is less pronounced due to a phenomenon that is best described as a return to flatland. In distinction to the emphatically three-dimensional quality that marked motion graphics a few years ago – just think of all those shiny objects rotating mysteriously in mid-air, those trips into the deep space of the screen's z-axis – many of this year's selections feature intensely pictorial spaces laid out on a two-dimensional plane. As dynamic as they are in motion, take a snapshot of any one of these flatlanders and they seem nothing less than picture perfect on the page.

Since most visual trends tend to correspond these days to technological innovations, the jurors surmised that this overarching tendency has as much to do with web culture and the emergence of Flash animation than with the expected pendulum swing away from the hackneyed illusion of depth. "There's a dimensionality within that flatness," argued Karin Fong, whose own commercials for the investment company Janus have helped pioneer the aesthetic. "There is a two-dimensional grid, but most designers move off it in some interesting way."

Trollbäck and Company's vibrant on-air identity package for the cable station TV Land represented the very best of off-the-grid graphics (cat. 184). With cheerful colors and organic shapes that reference the work of midcentury design giants like Isamu Noguchi, Eero Saarinen and George Nelson, these ID's evoke a retro feeling that's appropriate to the station's programming without resorting to an explicit and cloying TV nostalgia. "There are real ideas behind these spots," noted Joan Raspo, "they're just so conceptually strong." Raspo points to one particular spot for the classic 1970s "shrink" sitcom "The Bob Newhart Show", which features Rorshach-reminiscent patterns of analysands' faces that come in and out of the screen with kaleidoscopic clarity. "Everything we've picked helps to tell a story," she reiterated.

In many instances this year, the stories being told were about branding — or, as in the case with TV Land, rebranding. Taking the flat, normally static logotypes of American corporate culture as a start, motion designers have given birth to a new breed of performative branding. In the instance of a sequence created by Imaginary Forces within an experimental environment for IBM e-business centers, the most iconic of corporate images — the striated "Big Blue" logo by Paul Rand — is reconfigured into an almost architectural space despite its graphic flatness. "You're going through this monumental blue space that ends up with the Rand logo," describes Emily Oberman. "It's the perfect resolution of the 'Big Blue' idea." Similarly, Imaginary Forces has taken the globe-and-skyscraper logotype of Comedy Central and uncoiled its form into an explosive, hyperactive on-screen presence that is a direct commentary on the channel's iconoclastic and energetic programming (cat. 177).

Not all designers in this year's competition were entirely enamored of the flat pictorial space, however. A number of selections featured live-action sequences that expressed a graphic sensibility through clever directorial moves, lush production design or sleight-of-hand editing tricks. A commercial spot for the visually savvy chain store Target, for instance, busted the red bulls-eye logo out of the

## HAD FUN BUT WE ALWAYS DO.

Response, cat. 184

Question G
While researching, what –
if anything – did you do
differently from your normal
design process?

two-dimensional plane and formed it variously through objects at an outdoor bar-becue (cat. 178). And several MTV plugs for its "SoCal Summer" programming feature impressionistic vignettes of West Coast summers – 30-second minifilms that juxtapose simple live-action scenes, graphic overlays and evocative sound design (cat. 181). "They're current and nostalgic at the same time," observed Raspo of the understated spots. "They provided a really beautiful on-air contrast to all that Britney Spears stuff," added Oberman.

Conspicuous for their general absence this year were film-title sequences, which a few years ago seemed to be the pinnacle achievement of the motion-graphics industry. Although the jurors did choose to praise Yu & Co's minimalistic treatment for Lost Souls – in which strings of numbers eerily morph into letters (cat. 180) – they were astonished at the dearth of entries. "Film titles after Seven exploded," commented Fong, "but things are generally more subdued now. Maybe it's a reaction to so many layered things in the past." There was one exception to the prevailing less-is-more mantra in motion graphics, however. Imaginary Forces' new identity for the Lifetime Network features scrapbook-like visual montages of but-terflies, glassine envelopes and soft-focus photographs (cat. 179). While the jurors agreed that the result was beautiful and redolent of a kind of elegiac mood, Oberman noted ironically that exactly the same elements were used "to really scary effect" in Mimic just three years before. Andrea Codrington

Imaginary Forces designed an experience that articulates content as environment. Interactive screens allow for immediate personalization. "Smart" technology guides an audio soundscape that changes with the movement of the inhabitants. The architecture created by Design Office gracefully reconfigures to allow for individual or group experiences. Imaginary Forces and Design Office created a space to reflect and reinforce the e-business prized values of openness, collaboration and flexibility. A fully functional interactive table reshapes the traditional co-nference table deconstructing the hierarchical model. Participants interact and manipulate digital projections that appear on the table's surface in eight distinct interfaces. The tab e configuration encourages collaborative dialogue acting as a local network for shared information.

**176**

Centers for IBM
e-business
Innovation interactive
environment

Design firm Imaginary
Forces, Hollywood

Creative director/
designer Mikon van Gastel

Art director/designer
Matt Checkowski

Animators
Matt Checkowski, Peter
Cho, Chun-Chien Lien

Head of production
Saffron Kenny

Executive producers
Peter Frankfurt,
Chip Houghton

Producer Holly Kempner

Technologist
Jamie Houghton

Editors Carsten Becker,
Jason Kool, Jason Webb

Inferno artists
Kirk Balden, Rob Trent

Coordinator Seri Bryant

Writer Jed Alger

Music Musikvergnuegen

Creative director/
composer/mixer
Walter Werzowa

Additional composers
John Luker, Justin Burnett

Sound designer
Larry Jones

Executive producer
Pat Weaver

Engineers Damien
Chock, Jason Ford

Technical assistant
Benjamin Wynn

Comedy Central felt that its familiar globe-and-skyscraper logo needed some updating, and chose Imaginary Forces to come up with an entirely new on-air package that complimented its bold style of programming. Each piece acts as a mini-graphic story, which shows the updated logo exploding, bending, stretching and uncoiling in wildly unheard of day-glo combinations. With these pieces, Imaginary Forces created a vibe that jumps off the screen and demands that Comedy Central is the place for all brands of comedy. The challenge was to create a strong graphic language that promoted Comedy Central's programming, as well as a bold, updated attitude.

**177**

**Comedy Central
Network redesign**

Design firm
Imaginary Forces,
Hollywood

Creative director
Peter Frankfurt

Art director
Adam Bluming

Designers
Philip Shtoll, Chris Lopez,
Jason Doherty, Joel Lava,
Adam Bluming, Calvin Lo

Executive producer
Saffron Kenny

Producer Candy Renick

Editors Philip Shtoll,
Danielle White

Inferno artists
Kirk Balden, Clyde
Beamer, Don Pascoe,
Sam Edwards, Carie
Chadwick

2-D animators
Joel Lava, Jason Doherty,
Philip Shtoll, Chris Lopez,
Jennifer Lee, Calvin Lo

Coordinator
Brian Kludas

Sr. VP, marketing
(Comedy Central)
Cathy Tankosic

Sr. VP, on-air promotion
and off-air creative
(Comedy Central)
Peter Risafi

Music Musikvergnuegen

Composer
Bernie Locker

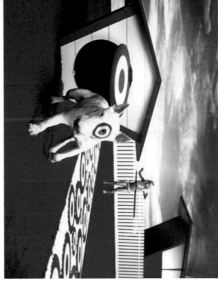

The goal of this series of ads was to evolve Target's "Sign of the Times" branding campaign. We decided to take Target's red-and-white world outside, adding blue sky and pool water. We needed to tie into the "Sign of the Times" theme with pictures, music and, of course, the bull's-eye logo. We also had to make it fresh – this was our fourth execution in the campaign – and seasonally specific for spring.

**Target "Sign of the Times" Spring TV ad**

178

Design firm PMH

Art directors
Minda Gralnek (Target),
Dave Peterson (PMH)

Director Anouk Besson

Associate creative
director/copywriter
Amie Valentine (PMH)

Producer
Gary Tassone (PMH)

Sound design
Hest & Kramer

Editor Brett Astor/
Fischer Edit

Effects Mark Youngren/
Fischer Edit

Client Target

Imaginary Forces created a brand identity for the Lifetime Television Network based on the idea that a woman's journal is where she records and commemorates the special events and the everyday details of her life. To reach the network's broad and ever-expanding audience, the journal concept ties together Lifetime's identity across all of its platforms: broadcast, print and online. In addition to the traditional elements of a network package, Imaginary Forces also wrote, directed and produced a series of interstitials based on the tagline, "In My Lifetime." Covering a range of experience and emotion, these short stories are told by individual women recounting the events that led to a photo or entry in their journal.

**179**

**Lifetime Network redesign**

Design firm Imaginary Forces, Hollywood

Creative director Peter Frankfurt

Directors Michelle Dougherty, Eric Smith, Michael Riley, Kurt Mattila

Codirectors Eric Smith, Sara Marandi, Lynne Gelman, Dana Yee

Art director Michelle Dougherty

Co-art director Eric Smith

Designers Elaine Alderette, Sara Marandi, Dana Yee, Lynne Gelman, Eric Smith, Michelle Dougherty, Peter Cho, Peggy Oei, David Clayton

Branding strategist Anita Olan

Head of production Saffron Kenny

Producer Maureen Timpa Hendricks

Live-action producers Caroline Pham, Brad English, Denise Pouchet

Director of photography Giles Dunning

2-D animators Lynne Gelman, Elaine Alderette, Jennifer Lee, Marcus Garcia

Editors Tony Fulgham, Mark Hoffman, Jason Kool, Philip Shtoll, Carsten Becker, Rich Marchewka

Inferno artists Clyde Beamer, Rob Trent, Rod Basham, Don Pascoe, Kirk Balden

Writers Anita Olan, Kelly Sopp, Nick Frankfurt, Maureen Timpa Hendricks

Editorial assistant Justine Gerenstein

Coordinators Rosalie Concepcion, Eva Prelle, Seri Bryant, Keith Bryant

Music Musikvergnuegen

Composer Walter Werzowa

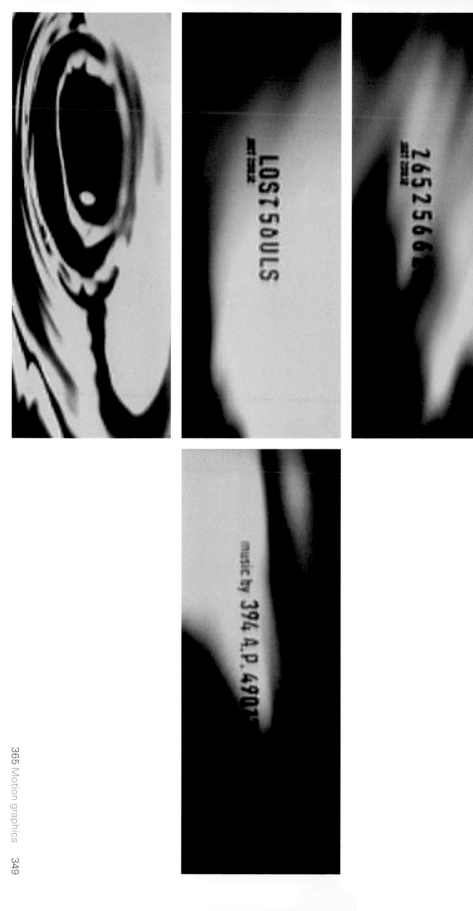

**Lost Souls movie titles**

Creative director/designer
Garson Yu

Designer/animator
Steve Kusuma

Producer Jennifer Fong

180

181

MTV's "So Cal Summer" TV ad

Design firm
MTV Networks,
New York

Creative director
Jeffrey Keyton

Design director
Romy Mann

Director/art director/
senior producer
Jennifer Roddie

Designer Assaf Cohen

SGI Animation
Emily Wilson

Director of photography
Mike Piscitelli

Editor Todd Antonio
Somodovilla

Sound designer
Malcolm Francis/
Popular Beat Combo

The MTV Beach House relocated to San Diego for summer 2000. Since Southern California youth culture has a very specific vibe, we thought it would be distinguishing to show a 15-second moment that would occur on a normal summer day in the life of a SoCal youth. These particular spots were about a group of surfer friends driving down the Pacific Coast Highway looking for some good waves and also "tuning in" to check out what is playing on the radio, and a young adult roller-skating down the boardwalk with headphones on while listening to her favorite tunes.

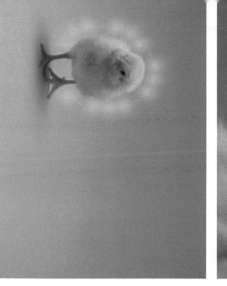

MTV's "Spring Break" packaging was created in the spirit of simplicity and double entendre. The bright background colors acted as dividers on the channel throughout the day. The chicks served the purpose of representing both springtime and the vernacular term for fine lookin' ladies. Star chicks were accentuated with chaser lights as a nod to Las Vegas, the unexpected home of spring break that year.

spring break

SAY WHAT? KARAOKE

**182**

MTV's "Spring
Break Chicks" TV ad

Design firm MTV
Networks, New York

Creative director
Jeffrey Keyton

Design director
Romy Mann

Director/
designer/producer
Keira Alexandra

SGI animation
Emily Wilson

Director of photography
Peter Agliata

Editor Holle
Singer/Consulate
Composer Shay Lynch

We were asked to create three show identities for MTV's "Fashionably Loud" week. We reversed the title to "Loudly Fashionable" and devised a visual world where textile colors, patterns and styles clash. We browsed through the history of fashion and textile design and illustration and came up with two strategies. One strategy was inspired by an old fashion designer and dressmaker's trick, where cutouts of dress shapes serve as masks for trying out textile samples. We created a symbiosis of photographic skin and hair, and flat graphics within the shapes of the clothes and the backgrounds. The second strategy was to shoot with a motor still camera, and then edit the pictures into a sequence. While initially a limited budget forced us to find an alternative to film, we soon appreciated the brilliant quality of these fashion photographs set into jagged motion.

183

MTV's "Fashionably Loud" identity

Design firm Brand New School, Santa Monica

Designers/illustrators
Sean Dougherty,
Jens Gehlhaar,
Jonathan Notaro

Editors/animators
Brumbly Boylston,
Sean Dougherty,
Jens Gehlhaar,
Jonathan Notaro

Copywriter/type designer
Jens Gehlhaar

Photographers Jonathan
Notaro, Pat Notaro

Producer
Angela de Oliveira

Client MTV Networks

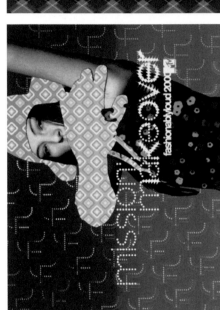

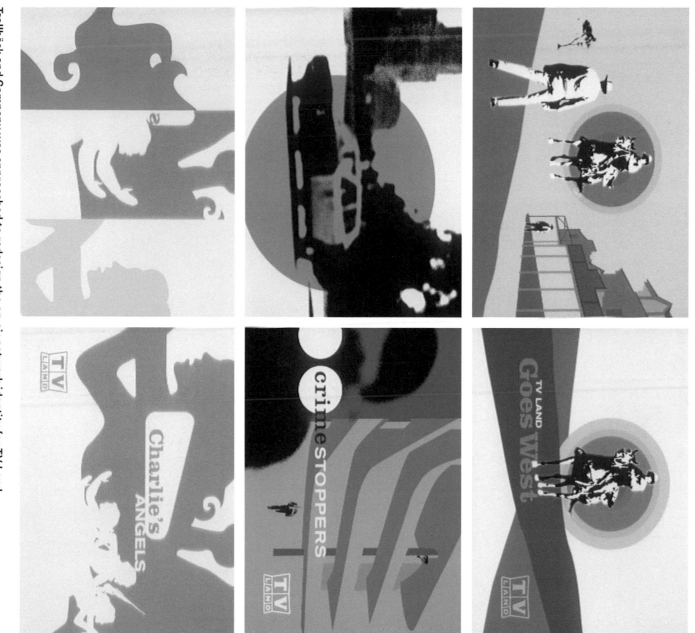

Trollbäck and Company was approached to redesign the on-air network identity for TV Land in an effort to attract the younger range of the demographic (ages 25–54). TV Land asked Trollbäck to tap into the optimism that the 1960s held for the future, particularly as portrayed in the New York 1964 World's Fair. The design solution recalls the essence of this optimism by using colors, designs and graphic shapes that echo the period. But even more importantly, it gives TV Land an intelligent design that respects the creative integrity of the era. The spirit of progress is manifested in a positive color palette and in organic graphic shapes and designs that echo the past while clearly communicating the look of today. Computer graphics enhance the excitement by rendering in a unique "flat" way Saarinen's architecture, Eames' and Noguchi's furniture, Alvin Lustig's graphics and Calder's sculptures.

TV Land Network redesign

Design firms TV Land, New York; Trollbäck and Company, New York
Sr. VP/creative director Kim Rosenblum
Creative director Kenna Kay
Executive producer Gwen Powell
Producer Catherine Mulcahy
Art director Marie Hyon
Creative director (Trollbäck)
Jakob Trollbäck
Art director/designer (Trollbäck)
Nathalie De la Gorce
Producer (Trollbäck)
Meghan O'Brien

184

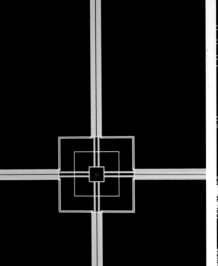

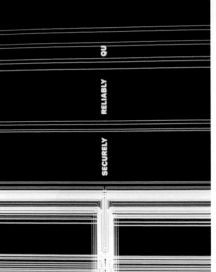

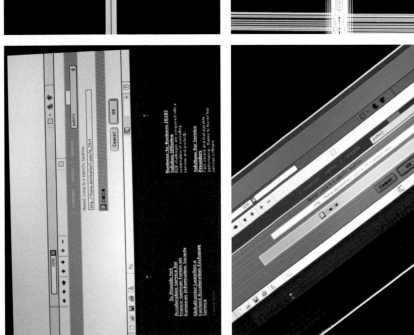

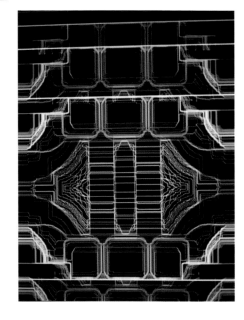

**185**

Novell "Line of
Information" TV ad

Design firm
Motion Theory, Venice,
California

Creative director/
designer
Mathew Cullen

Animators
Mathew Cullen,
Kaan Atilla

Producer
Javier Jimenez

Sound designer
Pete Kneser/Wimbo

Writer
Carm Goode

The goal of the project was to communicate the intricately difficult hurdles
information must travel in today's new technology to get from point A to point
B, and to show how with Novell this process is consistently successful, quick
and safe. Using many layers of interwoven line art that sometimes moved in
unison, but also often separately and conflictingly, we showed a piece of information traveling through a sea of graphically represented hurdles to arrive
at its destined point safely and quickly. We wanted to create a spot reliant
entirely on graphics and enhanced by precise, yet subtle sound design.

Imaginary Forces' concept for Corning was an abstract roller-coaster ride through a fiber-optic tube. As nothing created in the computer has the detailed characteristics of actual light shot on film, several detailed glass models were built that reflected light and carried it in a specific direction. After this, the process was three-fold. First, a series of moves and light effects were shot on the models. Then the footage was manipulated in the Flame, adding exaggerated turns and speed changes. Finally the selects were edited in the Avid, to control the pace of the spot and to hit the appropriate music cues. The constant twists and turns, combined with the selective bullet pointing of information in the form of light, conveys the feeling that Corning's fiber-optic technology is like drinking out of a fire hose of information.

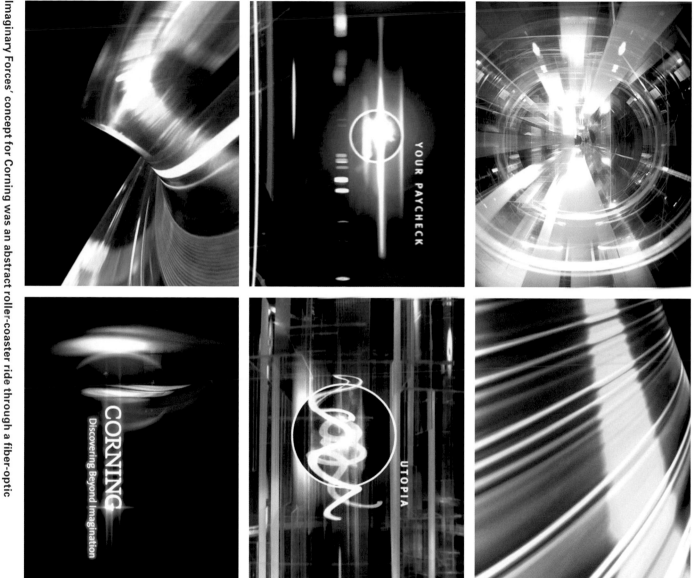

Corning "Future"
TV ad

Design firm
Imaginary Forces,
Hollywood

Creative director
Peter Frankfurt

Director/art director
Adam Bluming

Designers
Adam Bluming,
Philip Shtoll, Joel Lava

Executive producer
Saffron Kenny

Producer Candy Renick

Editors
Philip Shtoll,
Jeff Consiglio

Inferno artists
Kirk Balden,
Clyde Beamer

2-D animator
Josh Graham

Coordinator
Brian Kludas

Agency producer
Kate Ayrton

Agency creative director
Danny Gregory

Agency art director
Guy Marino

Music Tomandandy

186

Question S-3
On a scale of 0–10,
please rate the
level of pleasure
experienced at
the completion of
the project.

Question T-3
On a scale of 0–10,
please rate the
level of anxiety
experienced at
the completion of
the project.

0 = no anxiety/
pleasure

10 = total anxiety/
pleasure

Yellow numbers
indicate pleasure
Magenta numbers
indicate anxiety

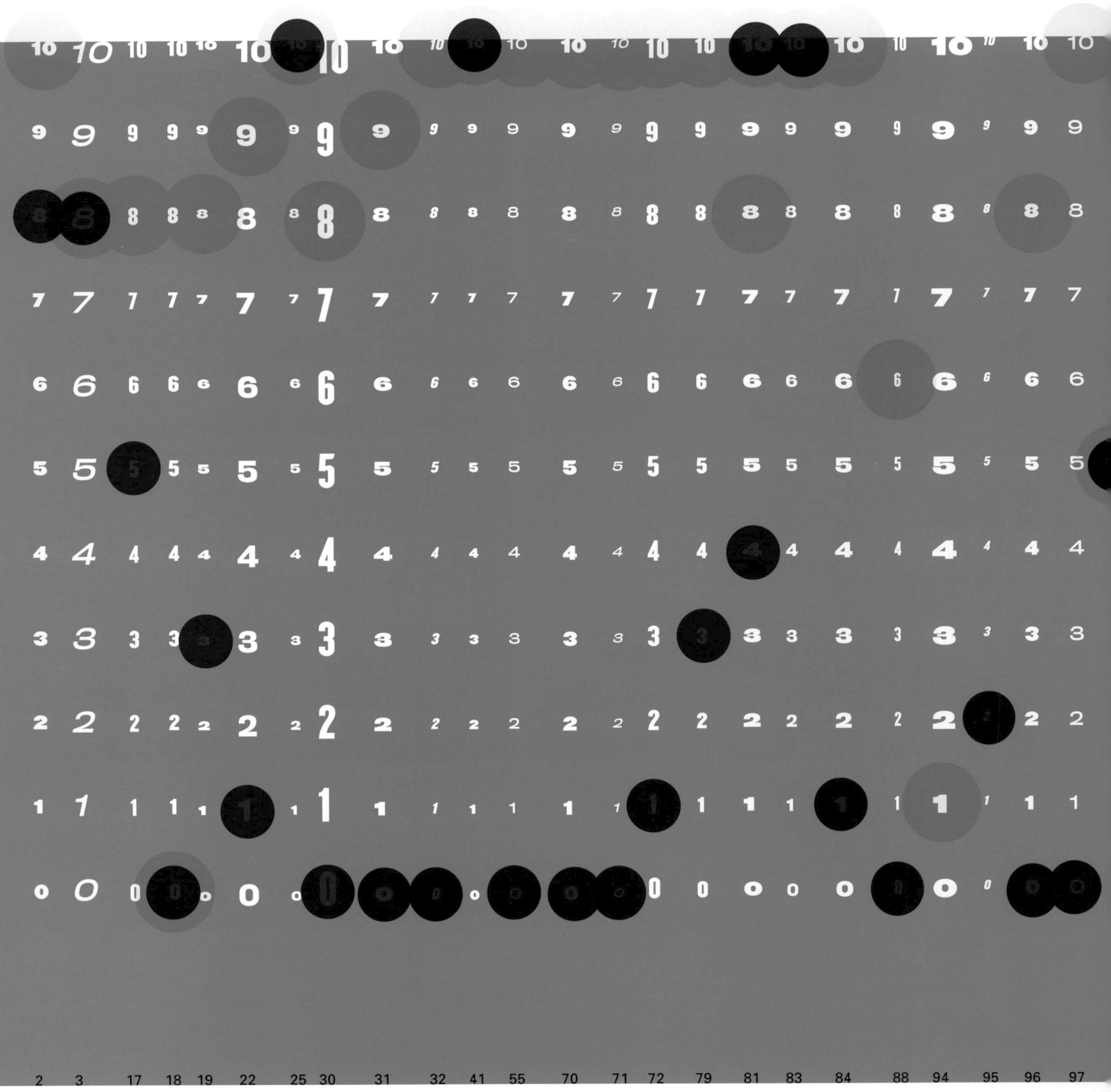

Catalogue numbers
A = anonymous

2   3   17   18   19   22   25   30   31   32   41   55   70   71   72   79   81   83   84   88   95   96   97

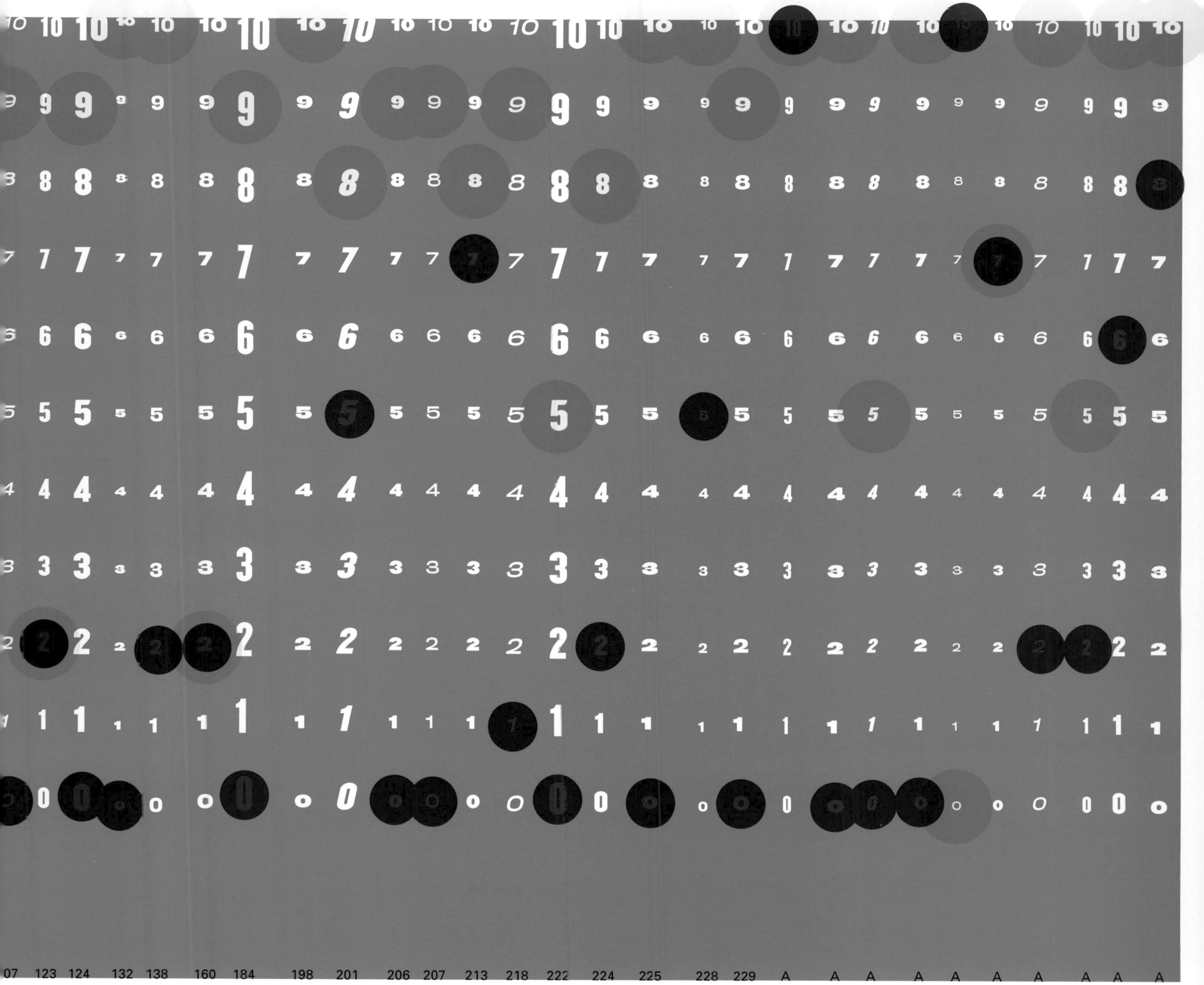
07 123 124 132 138 160 184 198 201 206 207 213 218 222 224 225 228 229 A A A A A A A A A A

# SOUNDBLAST

This category is dedicated to recognizing the power of design in packaging sound. A jury of indie and commercial insiders will pick the top music CDs in all market segments including:

alternative, rock, soul, R&B, gospel, E-Z listening, adult contemporary, jazz, oldies, soundtracks, New Age, techno, folk, country, Latin, reggae, crossover, pop and more. All kinds of music CD packaging are eligible, from regular CDs to special boxed sets.

**Chaired by Margo Chase** Margo Chase Design, Los Angeles **with Stefan Bucher** 344 Design, Los Angeles **Michael Hodgson** Ph.D, Los Angeles **Greg Ross** ORABOR, Pasadena **Tommy Steele** Capitol Records, Los Angeles

It's tough to have much clarity about what's happening in music design these days. There have been so many changes in the structure of the business over the last few years that most music designers' heads are still spinning just trying to figure out if any art directors they know still have the same jobs they had last month. And the changes aren't over yet.

Over the last 10 years, the big companies have gotten bigger and the mid-sized companies have either been acquired or disappeared, their staff designers scattering to form small design firms specializing in music. New indie labels have sprung up in niches where there wasn't even music before and numerous do-it-yourself musicians now publish their music online, starting a following without the help of a label at all. From a designer's point of view, all this change looks darn confusing.

The most visible and publicized change – and the one many music designers see as a descent into one of the nine circles of hell – is consolidation. What used to be many small-to-medium-sized labels, each with its own personality, has become the "Big Five." (These are: Warner Music Group, including Elektra, Sire, Atlantic, Maverick, and Warner Bros.; Universal Music Group, including MCA, Interscope, Geffen, A&M, and Verve; BMG Entertainment, including Arista, RCA, Bad Boy, J Records and Windham Hill; Sony Music Group, including Columbia, Epic, Work,

Question =
Briefly describe the
research methods
used for preliminary
design on this project.

For these huge companies, music means business, and business means making money. The Big Five focus their marketing and advertising dollars – and their most competent people – on celebrity artists, the few "good risks" that they know will make them rich. The Big Five's approach to design is usually formulaic, homogenized and rarely ground breaking. Where there used to be in-house art departments, each with its staff of talented designers, there are now marketing departments, often run by "creative directors" with no design background at all. At worst, designers have been reduced to wrists, simply putting type next to the photo of the artist.

There is a brighter side. Even from within the belly of the beast, good design still emerges that is true to the artistic vision of the music. Whether this comes from the corporate art departments themselves, or from outside firms, the thing that all good music design seems to require is someone inside the company willing to fight for it. Tommy Steele, one such creative director at Capitol Records, says, "We're struggling to compete with the great packaging from the indies now that the bean counters have taken over corporate. Radiohead's Kid A album went to number one its first week out last year due specifically to the special package that was available to fans on top of the regular jewel box."

Several strong designs from Big Five labels were entered in Soundblast this year. The Deftones and Olive packages (cat. 200 and 202) by Kim Biggs at Maverick are powerful examples of great design from inside a corporate art department. The beautiful K.D. Lang package designed for Warner Bros. by Jeri Heiden at Smog (cat. 225) and the elegant Phish special package for Elektra by Jager Di Paola Kemp (cat. 201) are notable examples of what good independent design firms can create when a big company gives them the chance.

There's more. Consolidations notwithstanding, the story doesn't end with corporate music. In a reaction against corporate homogenization, small and independent

# THINKING, LOOKING, THINKING, LOOKING

Response, cat. 207

music publishers have begun to proliferate. Both in the U.S. and throughout Europe, these indie labels are fresh, young and close to the roots of the artists they sign and promote. Only a few of these small labels have in-house design departments, but many are working with young independent designers, or designers who have fled large companies to form their own firms and do work they believe in again. Shoe-string budgets and short deadlines – not to mention the chaos that usually surrounds new companies managed by ex-musicians and producers – can hinder the best design, but the emphasis on creativity over marketing at these labels is making this brave new world into promising territory. The music business has always been international, and with the advent of the web – and the rise of online music sampling and sales – it has become a truly borderless media.

This is reflected in the large number of powerful designs from Germany this year. An outstanding group of 12-inch vinyl sleeves was submitted by Eikes Grafischer Hort in Frankfurt for the indie label Radikal (cat. 194, 198, 199, 209). The covers for Mouse on Mars, by Icon Kommunicationsdesign in Cologne (cat. 206, 207) were also excellent. Independent music designer Stefan Bucher observed, "All that German vinyl is a perfect example of the indie scene being the new frontier of music design. The whole show is really a testament to that, isn't it?" Margo Chase

The cover needed to honor the band's music and personality, a recent trip to Brazil and the interest in New York City street subcultures. The band liked the idea of a "grimy" presentation much like graffiti, ripped posters and sniper stickers. Rather than scan a photo of a street it was better to fabricate an environment unique to the project. The band chose a photo panorama for the cover. Different visual textures – like wood, ink, metal and varnish-filled in the space, and the rest of the package followed naturally. It's always the combination of well-placed details that make the package.

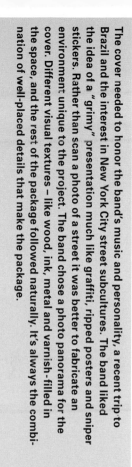

Medeski Martin & Wood: The Dropper CD packaging

Design firm
Chippy, New York

Art director/designer
Heung Heung Chin

Illustrator Heung Heung Chin

Photographer Danny Clinch

Client Medeski Martin & Wood/Blue Note Records (Capitol Records Jazz & Classics)

The design for (B)efore/(a)fter is a play on words translated visually. To express this, I used photos that look like snapshots and describe the connection between the "before and after" idea. The repetition of the imagery reinforces the feeling and emphasizes the idea of metamorphosis from one state to another. The production of the photos was quite difficult. We had to swim far from the beach to this little platform (with all our clothes and equipment wrapped in plastic), and every time someone jumped into the water the platform rocked so much that we thought we'd all fall into the water.

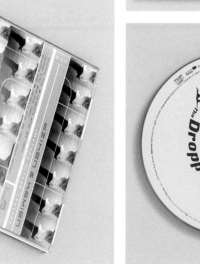

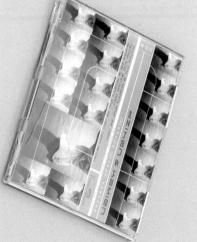

(B)efore/(a)fter CD packaging

Design firm Couch Visuals/Couch Records, Vienna, Austria

Art director/designer Mariana Brausewetter

Photographer Mariana Brausewetter

Publisher Couch Music

Client Couch Records

Spoiled & Zigo: More and More album cover

Design firm
Eikes Grafischer Hort, Frankfurt, Germany

Art directors/designers
Eike Koenig, Ralf Hiemisch

Illustrators Eike Koenig, Ralf Hiemisch

Client Polydor Zeitgeist/Universal

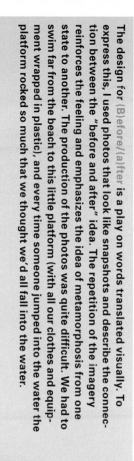

The concept came from the fact that SXSW is a music conference for A&R and music industry executives held in Texas where new and emerging acts are showcased. Capitol Records was hosting a party and wanted to incorporate a double-CD package with the party invitation. Because the event was being held in Texas – land of the BBQ – I chose that as the theme. My favorite part is the disc art: I scanned my husband's meat thermometer!

**190**

**Well Done**
CD packaging

Design firm Capitol
Records, Hollywood

Art directors
Wendy Dougan,
Tommy Steele

Designer
Wendy Dougan

Print production
Jennifer Peters

Illustrator
Tavis Coburn

**191**

**Jim White: No Such
Place** CD packaging

Design firm Doyle
Partners, New York

Creative directors
Paul Sahre, Jim White

Designers
Paul Sahre, Cara
Brower

Illustrations
Jim White, © Center
for UFO Studies

Photography
André Thijssen

Client Luaka Bop

Jim White's music defies categorization. It's been described as a fusion of southern folk and hip hop, thinking about God, Faulkner and maybe even Tom Waits and Beck. The main challenge with the design was figuring out a way of dealing with the large amount of visual material White offered for consideration, including artwork, photographs, writings, stories, observations, old textbooks, a collection of old newspaper clippings, amps and other oddities. Through editing, reworking and adding large amounts of UFO evidence and photography by André Thijssen, we developed a design that would accommodate this material.

We wanted the packaging of this CD to reflect its fluid and delicate but very real, hand-crafted music. We also wanted the packaging to have a visual hook – something that would create interest and bring the viewer closer. We decided to hand-cut letters and photos and create strong, simple, organic shapes while using a variety of backgrounds and textures, including the artist's own handwriting. This helped give the package a realness and tactility that enhanced the personal nature of the music. Music packaging needs to be adapted to a wide variety of formats, sizes and uses, while still remaining readable and interesting.

The initial concept of djmixed.com was to create a series that combined a website devoted to the DJ culture with the DJ mix market of electronic music. The combination of the html address and graphic elements of DJ culture were used to create the concept of the covers – images of turn-tables, headphones and needles. Metallic inks were also used to represent the electronic technology of the music and the Internet. In contrast from looking like a typical underground rave flyer, the design was kept simple, graphic and modern while still attracting the attention of electronic music enthusiasts.

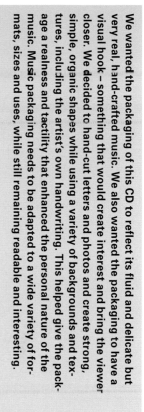

192

193

**Elliot Smith: Figure 8 CD packaging**

Design firm
Dreamworks Records, Beverly Hills

Art directors/illustrators
Autumn de Wilde, Dale Smith

Photographer
Autumn de Wilde

192

**djmixed.com: Keoki and Micro CD packaging**

Design firm
Moonshine Music, West Hollywood

Art director/designer
Jeff Aguila

Photographers
Raymond Lee, Paul Banks, Teri Jo

193

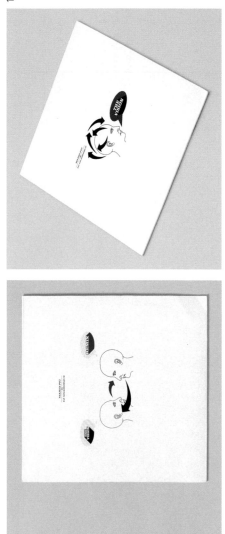

**194**

**Mario Piu: The Vision album cover**

Design firm Eikes Grafischer Hort, Frankfurt, Germany

Art director/designer Eike Koenig

Illustrator Eike Koenig

Client Polydor Zeitgeist/ Universal

**195**

**W.O.P.A.: Walking on Pennsylvania Avenue CD packaging**

Design firm Tim Kenney Design Partners, Bethesda, Maryland

Designer John Bowen

Project manager Julie Rasmussen

**This album was directed at the 20-plus electronica fan who has graduated from nightclubs to lounges. The final design is 100 percent true to the original concept.**

The goal of this project was to design a tiny version of a classic book with proportions similar to that of an illuminated manuscript. This would provide a system – a classically based grid – to work from, and this system would show the beauty and simplicity of the photographs and the poetry of the words in a simple and pure form. The calligraphy was incorporated to add another layer, a feeling of something handwritten, personal, feminine and elegant. The end product is almost exactly what was originally presented. I am most happy with the typographic details and the natural human feeling that comes across in the photographs.

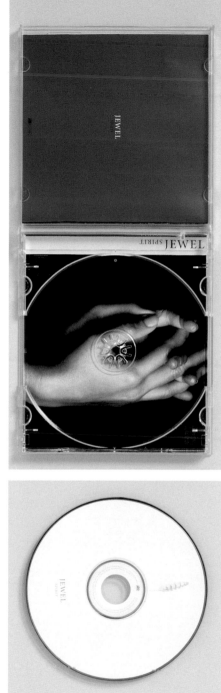

We set out to do something that related to the idea of how stories are passed along until they attain a certain sense of timelessness. E was cleaning out the basement at his parents' house and found this wonderful old children's book, and when we looked at it, everything kind of clicked. The trick was in packaging the album so that it looked like something that had been found in a basement as well. We wanted the package to have the tactile storybook feel that echoed the cardboard covers of the old Golden Books. We decided to use a digipak instead of the plastic jewel case. In the one-color booklet I added elements from the original storybook and combined them with newer elements such as the Eels logo and made them look as if they were there all along.

**196**

Jewel: Spirit
CD packaging

Design firm
Wink33, New York

Art director/designer
Brenda Rotheiser

Calligrapher
Jeanne Greco

Photographer
Matthew Rolston

Client Atlantic Records

**197**

The Eels: Daisies
of the Galaxy
CD packaging

Design firm
Dreamworks
Records,
Beverly Hills

Art director
Francesca Restrepo
(Design Palace), E

**198**

**Resistance D:
You Were There
album cover**

Design firm Eikes
Grafischer Hort,
Frankfurt, Germany

Art directors Eike
Koenig, Ralf Hiemisch

Designer/Illustrator
Eike Koenig

Photographers Gaby
Gerster, Eike Koenig

Writer Eike Koenig

Client
Polydor Zeitgeist/
Universal Planet Vision

Other Dog prototype
designed by Ralf
Hiemisch, built by
Susanne Walter

**199**

**Degeneration: Una
Musica Senza
Ritmo album cover**

Design firm
Eikes Grafischer Hort,
Frankfurt, Germany

Art director/designer
Eike Koenig

Illustrator
Eike Koenig

Client
Polydor Zeitgeist/
Universal

Phish fans are very dedicated to the band and revel in their live shows, to the extent that live recordings tend to be more cherished than studio recordings. This Hampton show in particular is a unique cross-section of Phish's music over the years, with some songs from early albums, some more recent and some very unusual covers. Our challenge was to create a unique, compact six-CD package containing CDs and a booklet that is reflective of the eclectic Phish character. The package opens from two directions – each compartment contains three CDs. The CDs are in individual sleeves, each containing a booklet listing the music for that CD. The concept was documentary – to divide the experience into a modular puzzle. The CD and case look and feel special and valuable. The graphics are progressive, contemporary, and in line with the current popularity of the band.

201

200

**201**

**Phish: Hampton Comes Alive CD box set packaging**

Design firm Jager Di Paola Kemp Design, Burlington, Vermont

Creative director Michael Jager

Art director Jared Eberhardt

Designer Todd Wender

Photographer C. Taylor Crothers

Client Dionysian Productions Design

**200**

**Deftones: White Pony album and album cover**

Design firm Maverick Recording Company, Beverly Hills

Creative director Kim Biggs

Art director/designer Frank Maddocks

Photographer James Minchin III

Printer Ivy Hill

Olive is an electronic-pop duo, so the graphic thread running through the campaign was man versus nature. To illustrate nature and technology melding together we had the barcode on every configuration grow into a different type of tree. Later, we took Olive to a strip club, but the only man versus nature at Crazy Girls was us trying to wrest a fistful of sweaty one-dollar bills from the ATM to feed to 'da ladies.

**Olive: Trickle**
**CD packaging**

Design firm Maverick Recording Company, Beverly Hills

Art directors/ designers Kim Biggs, David Harlan

Photographers Zoren Gold, David Harlan

Logo David Harlan

**Live: Run to the Water CD packaging**

Design firm Sagmeister Inc., New York

Art director Stefan Sagmeister

Designer/illustrator Motoko Hada

Photographer Danny Clinch

Client Radioactive Records

We had an original design dummy in a clear jewel case with cover, inside panel, CD disc, inlay and back cover. I was trying to create a visual story based on the music and a Mandala structure from front to back cover. This is the third in a series of CDs, and I tried to maintain a design continuity with the first two while at the same time creating a difference based on the music. The design is based on the lyrics which have a very Eastern influence.

The typical non-budget required us to keep all production "flourishes" to inexpensive ink tricks (in this case, reduced color palettes). It also meant no money for marketing, so we made the word "yes" in the title really big. Challenges included a lack of money, and a marketing and product management team of two people. Also, some of the poems were in Russian and had to be reproduced in the Cyrillic alphabet. Both the keystroking and proofreading were hard on the eyes. I'm happiest with the pink disc. I'm also glad to have had the experience of working for clients who initiated a project out of personal interest. In this particular case, the client went through all the hoops of starting up a record company (UPC codes, copyright lawyers, distribution arrangements, etc.) just for this recording. God bless 'em.

Yevgeny Yevtuschenko:
City of No, City of Yes
CD packaging

Design firm Greenberg
Kingsley, New York
Art director/creative
director/designer
D. Mark Kingsley

Client/publisher
The Van Winkle Clef

The challenge for the project was to design a CD and special-edition media kit for Void Where Prohibited's new release, Pete's Free Gig Summer. Based on the band's wit and sarcastic style, our design solution was an irreverent, humorous look at American pop culture. We referenced things that might be outlawed, or labeled "Void Where Prohibited." The CD cover presents a "dangerous" squirt gun and the inside of the CD shows the intended victim, a bikini-clad blonde. The special-edition kit references a dime-store bag of candy, containing goodies about the band's history and style, including baseball cards with each band member's vital stats. The strong colors and fun imagery create a high energy package that really gets noticed, which is half of the battle for a talented aspiring band.

Void Where
Prohibited: Pete's
Free Gig Summer
CD packaging

Design firm
IA Collaborative,
Chicago

Creative
director/designer
Dan Kraemer

Illustrator
Dan Kraemer

Writer Kevin Giglinto

Client Void Where
Prohibited

The CD cover, which is aimed at young listeners of electronic music, can be used as a small poster that has a mixture of painting and three-dimensional design.

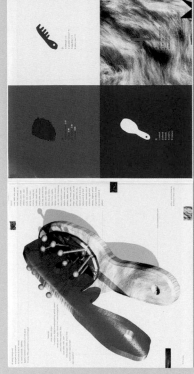

**Mouse on Mars: Niun Niggung CD packaging**

Design firm Icon Kommunicationsdesign, Cologne, Germany

Art director/designer Eva Rusch

Print production/ illustrator Eva Rusch

Publisher Warner/ Chappell, Thrill Jockey

Client Mouse on Mars

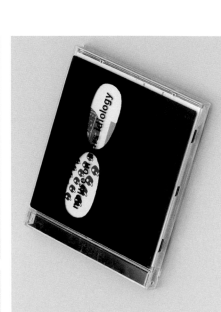

**Mouse on Mars: Idiology CD packaging**

Design firm Icon Kommunicationsdesign, Cologne, Germany

Art director/designer Friederike Luczak

Print production Volker Schwettmann

Writer Jan Werner

Publisher Zomba Records

Client Mouse on Mars

The goal with this design was to transmit the eclectic sense of the music; to show its ambiguity, politics and philosophy. As the designer, I had to act like a pamphleteer, using simple speech to associate the political atmosphere of the '60s. I especially like the individual variability between the outside sticker and the booklet.

The challenge was to visualize the music, which has a nice, warm, laid-back sound with a clubby bass. The design solution has been digipac packaging to create a natural atmosphere, and warm colors that draw the attention of people outside the stores. It's greatly in contrast to the technical design that's usually used for electronic music – a more atmospheric design that leads you to know what to expect when you're buying the CD. I'm really happy with the apartment inside "Coming Home." It shows the variety of the living experience, including the different materials used for the floor. The original intention of the record company was to create one room for each song. I've managed to create a symbiosis between sound and materials in the apartment.

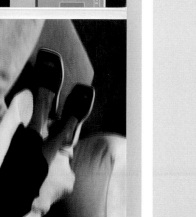

**Kay Cee: Escape
album cover**

Design firm
Eikes Grafischer Hort,
Frankfurt, Germany
Art director/designer
Eike Koenig
Illustrator/photographer
Eike Koenig
Client
Orbit Records/
Virgin Music

**209**

**Bassic Instinct II,
Bassic Instinct III,
Coming Home
CD packaging**

Design firm
Stereo Deluxe,
Nürnberg, Germany
Art director/designer
Elisabeth Rudner
Illustrator/photographer
Elisabeth Rudner
Publisher/client Stereo
Deluxe Rec. GmbH

**208**

The biggest challenge was starting something without having a clue how the whole thing might turn out. For two weeks, I did one little black-and-white illustration a day, then I just put them together in the CD package. Mood changes from hour to hour – and so did my daily illustration. The guys at Polydor did everything to make it work, but the placement of the sticker on the cover was a production nightmare. I'm happiest with the way that the production guys put a second barcode on the back, because somehow they weren't able to replace the FPO barcode with the real one.

**210**

**Hattler: No Eats Yes**
**CD packaging**

Design firm
Karlssonwilker Inc.,
New York

Art director/designer
Jan Wilker

Print production
Hjalti Karlsson

Illustrator/photographer
Jan Wilker

Writer Jan Wilker

Fabricator
Hjalti Karlsson

Client
Polydor/Universal

**211**

**Bang on a Can**
**mailer/CD packaging**

Design firm
Greenberg Kingsley,
New York

Art director/creative
director/designer
D. Mark Kingsley

Client/publisher
Bang on a Can/
Red Poppy Music

MICHAEL GORDON,
DAVID LANG +
JULIA WOLFE
FOUNDED
BANG ON A CAN

THIS IS
A CD SAMPLER
OF THEIR MUSIC

The clients needed the piece to be flexible so as many or as few elements could be mailed out. It needed to be visible in a sea of promotional mailings, so I decided to make it modular and red. The piece also needed to be expandable to accommodate continual updating. It took the better part of a year to complete. The piece is intended to solicit film score commissions, international music festival bookings and future tours. It is a way to improve my clients' image beyond their humble East Village origins and act as a brief introduction to anyone unfamiliar with their work.

The challenge was to communicate the idea of trust in a compelling graphic environment while staying true to the fairly rough-hewn style of the music. The design solution was to use the blank road sign as the centerpiece for not only the cover art, but the entire CD concept as well. The photographs of cars and roads – even the instructional drawing on how to use a car jack – all tie into the idea of the sign pointing toward the right way. The rustic, almost Western typography reflects the rootsy, guitar-based vibe of the music itself. The CD was to be an accurate musical representation of the life and struggles of being a Christian, and also an authentic slice of postmodern life that anyone could partake of.

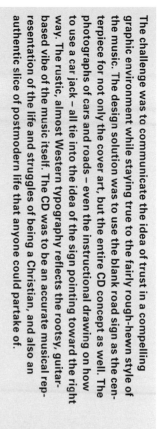

Since the budget limited the package structure, the visuals had to be very engaging. They also had to be arranged in a composition that would leave room for the lyrics to the songs, but maintain the look and flow of the package. The name "lab rat" came from experiments, as well as consumption and addictions in the music and in the world. I wanted to show the similarities between American culture and that of a lab rat – present the consumer world of addiction as a scientific experiment.

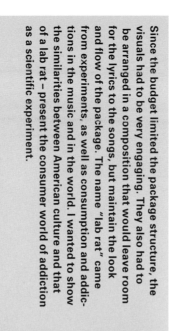

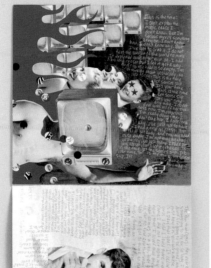

213

212

**Trust: Music from the Highway Community**
CD packaging

Design firm
Becky Brown,
Sunnyvale, California

Designer Becky Brown
Producer Kevin Marks
Client The Highway
Community, John
Riemenschnitter

**212**

**Big Umbrella:**
**Lab Rat**
CD packaging

Design firm
Torpedohead
Studio, Covina,
California

Art director/
illustrator
Keith Ewing

Client
Racer Records

**213**

**This band is a buncha super-cool Hispanic kids from Texas. We really tried to keep the Spanish flavah for them. Umlauts, Davida and a bullfighter on the cover…could you ask for anything more? Even the ultra-clever photo illustration of the splitting heads was inspired by common Mexican masks.**

Unloco: Unloco
CD packaging

Design firm
Maverick Recording
Company, Beverly Hills

Art directors/designers
Kim Biggs,
David Harlan

Photographer
Alison Dyer

Printer Ivy Hill

Photo illustrations
David Harlan

Logo Glen Nakasako
and Unloco

Tantric: Tantric
CD packaging

Design firm
Maverick Recording
Company, Beverly Hills

Art directors/designers
Kim Biggs, David Harlan

Photographers
Slow Hearth Studios/
Photonica,
Dennis Keeley

Logo Kim Biggs, David
Harlan, Glen Nakasako

**Tantric's logo was based on a modified script from the Thai alphabet (handsomely redrawn by young Glen Nakasako). At the desert photoshoot we discovered the band was going au naturel underneath their rented $5,000 leather pants, so we drove into town and found some boxers and giant ladies underwear for them to put on. They chose the ladies underwear (because we "forgot" to tell them about the boxers). That inspired the grunginess of the package.**

The special challenge in this project was to design from the point of view of a teenager. I chose to interpret the title *New Found Glory* through a 16-year-old's eyes.

The idea behind the design was to embody the energy of Blink 182's live show. I did this by using an illustration of their show, with a bonus photo book.

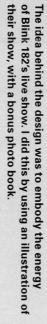

**New Found Glory CD packaging**

Design firm
MCA Records, Santa Monica

Creative director
Tim Stedman

Designers
Tim Stedman, T.J. River

Photographer
Justin Stephens

Client/publisher
New Found Glory/MCA Records

**216**

**Blink 182: The Mark, Tom and Travis Show CD packaging**

Design firm
MCA Records, Santa Monica

Creative director
Tim Stedman

Designers
Tim Stedman, T.J. River

Illustrator
Glen Hanson

Photographer
Justin Stephens

Client/publisher
Blink 182/MCA Records

**217**

**OHM: The Early
Gurus of Electronic
Music 1948–1980**
CD box set packaging

Design firm
Stoltze Design, Boston

Art director/
creative director
Clif Stoltze

Designers Clif Stoltze,
Tammy Dotson

Client/publisher
Ellipsis Arts

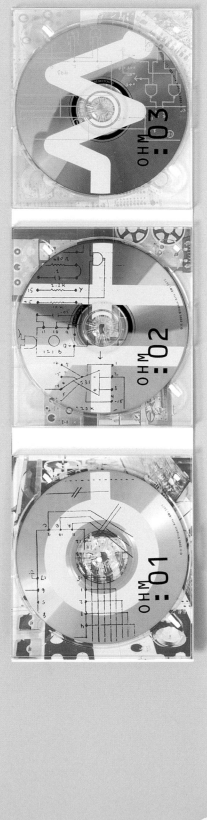

OHM is a large and eclectic mix of important contributions to electronic music spanning almost four decades. The challenge was to find a cohesive graphic and tactical device to package the three CDs with related stories, photographs and liner notes – all within a fairly modest budget. The three-CD digipak and 96-page book are housed in a transparent plastic slipcase, custom-designed for OHM; the outer packaging incorporates the electrical schematic line art of a theremin – one of the first electronic instruments ever created. The OHM logo mimics the visual language of the electronic diagrams. Additional schematics were combined with historical and documentary photography as well as stock photos manipulated with PhotoShop. The design reflects the retro-futuristic quality of this music, as well as the contrast between the high and the low technology used to create the music.

The special challenge of this design project was in the accuracy of its elements. The piece is intended to replicate the look and feel of an ancient alchemical journal. Historically correct typography, color palette and the use of extremely detailed illustrations had to be combined in a way that resembled a book from that era. To achieve the aged and well-handled feeling, we began by searching for dusty old volumes from used bookstores. Most of the interior pages of the book-let are re-photographed spreads from existing materials. The water-stained and aged yellowed pages were then retouched, erasing the existing type to allow us a clean surface for our copy and illustrations. From the washed-out look of the black type to the intentional misregistration of second color type, every detail was intended to duplicate the printing capabilities that would have existed during that time period.

220

219

**The Smashing Pumpkins: Machina/ The Machines of God CD packaging**

Design firm
Sylvester,
West Hollywood

Art directors
Gregory Sylvester,
Thomas Wolfe,
Billy Corgan,
Yelena Yemchuk

Designers
Gregory Sylvester,
Thomas Wolfe

Illustrator
Vasily Kafanov

**219**

**PALOALTO CD packaging**
**220**

Design firm
Sony Music,
Santa Monica, CA

Art director/designer
Aimée Macauley

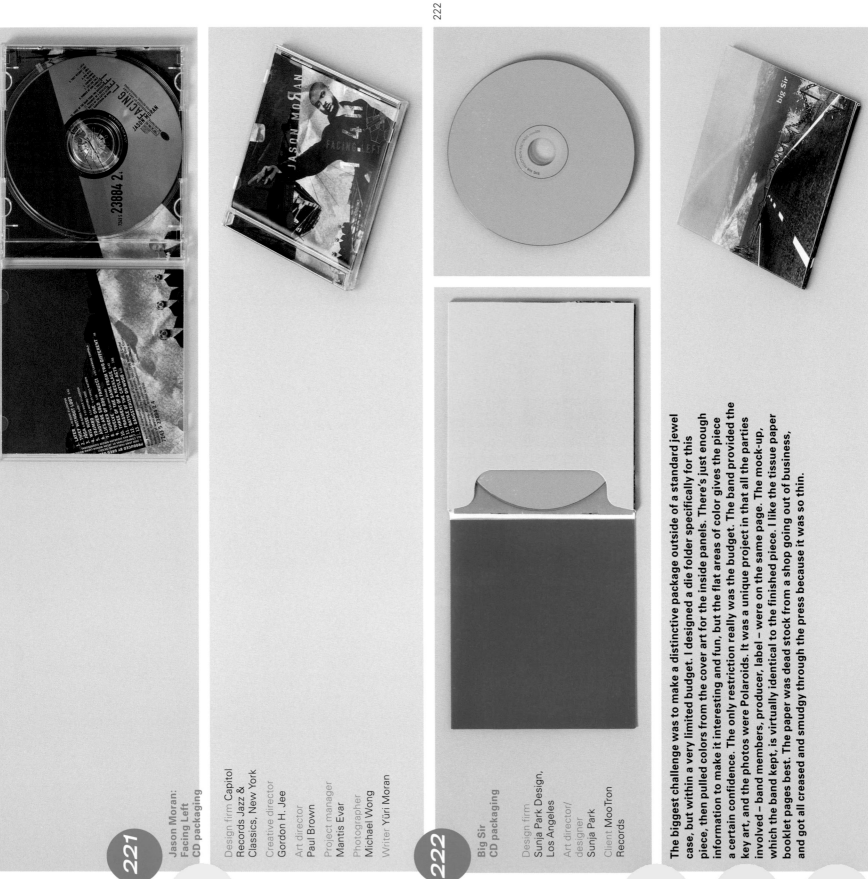

**221**

**Jason Moran:
Facing Left
CD packaging**

Design firm Capitol
Records Jazz &
Classics, New York

Creative director
Gordon H. Jee

Art director
Paul Brown

Project manager
Mantis Evar

Photographer
Michael Wong

Writer Yûri Moran

**222**

**Big Sir
CD packaging**

Design firm
Sunja Park Design,
Los Angeles

Art director/
designer
Sunja Park

Client MooTron
Records

The biggest challenge was to make a distinctive package outside of a standard jewel
case, but within a very limited budget. I designed a die folder specifically for this
piece, then pulled colors from the cover art for the inside panels. There's just enough
information to make it interesting and fun, but the flat areas of color gives the piece
a certain confidence. The only restriction really was the budget. The band provided the
key art, and the photos were Polaroids. It was a unique project in that all the parties
involved – band members, producer, label – were on the same page. The mock-up,
which the band kept, is virtually identical to the finished piece. I like the tissue paper
booklet pages best. The paper was dead stock from a shop going out of business,
and got all creased and smudgy through the press because it was so thin.

Visual resources from Federico Garcia Lorca's life were very scarce and difficult to acquire, especially given that his estate was located across the ocean in Spain. Through sheer happenstance, the creative team learned that a friend owned a book that had an extensive collection of Lorca drawings in it. Also a recent hire from Spain provided a host of beautiful, old Spanish books and the design of the CD package was inspired by the tactile, personal quality of these texts. The outcome is a booklike package that incorporates Euro-Spanish textures, Lorca's drawings, photography of Ben Sidran and Lorca and classic yet playful typography. Although artwork was limited and brought in from vastly different resources, as the package came together what elements were available seemed to fit perfectly into song concepts and spreads.

**223**

**Ben Sidran:
The Concert for
García Lorca
CD packaging**

Design firm
Planet Propaganda,
Madison, Wisconsin

Creative director
Kevin Wade

Designer Dan Ibarra

Print production
Ann Sweeney

Illustrator
Federico García Lorca

Photographer
The Community of
Heirs of Federico García
Lorca, Ben Sidran

Writers
Federico García Lorca,
Ben Sidran

Client
GoJazz Records,
Ben Sidran

The challenge was to use vellum paper and color in a way that is energetic, iridescent and lightly abstract. Bold colors were placed on the inside of the booklet, and white ink on the outside to subdue the color. Windows of images were then cut out from the white to reveal the color within. The resulting effect is a vibrant display of image, form, color and type. I am pleased with the sequence of the package and the progression of color – the way it begins with an opaque white cover, which slips off to reveal a creamy orange, then opens to a splash of solid blue and finally is unfolded to full saturation.

**Oasis Smooth Jazz
Awards Collection
CD packaging**

Design firm
Infinite Z, Los Angeles

Art director Joel Venti

Designer Jawsh Smyth

Photographer
Don Siedhoff/
Rock Island Studios

Producer
Joe Sherbanee

**K.D. Lang:
Invincible Summer
CD packaging**

Design firm Smog,
Los Angeles

Art directors/designers
Jeri and John Heiden

Photographer
Just Loomis

Client Warner Bros.
Records, Inc.

Our intention with the design was to capture New York at night, specifically 52nd Street circa 1940 – bop's breeding ground: the dimly lit, smoke-filled clubs that made up the nocturnal life of jazz. We did this by sticking with a monochromatic palette with duotones of black and red throughout. We were fortunate to use four-color blacks and reds on the inside of the booklet as well, enriching and deepening them. We decided on a metal box early on to differentiate this Miles box set from those Columbia had previously released. It also gives literal weight to the package, signifying – in my mind, anyway – the importance of these two musical titans. The photography is my favorite part of the design. Columbia's archives are replete with some of the most gorgeous and iconic jazz photographs you'll find anywhere.

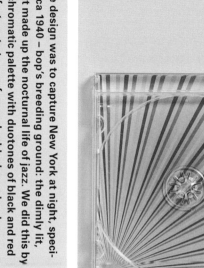

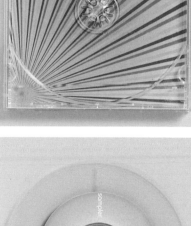

227

226

K.D. Lang:
Invincible sampler
CD packaging

Design firm
Smog, Los Angeles

Art directors/designers
Jeri and John Heiden

Photographer
Just Loomis

Client Warner Bros.
Records, Inc.

Miles Davis and John
Coltrane: Complete
Columbia Recordings
1955–61
CD box set packaging

Design firm
Sony Music, New York

Art directors
Frank Harkins, Arnold
Levine

Project manager
Michael Levine

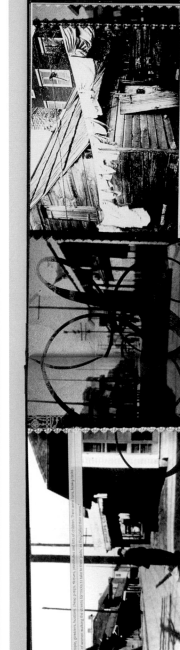

**THE MAIN PLAYERS**

LOUIS ARMSTRONG

228

Louis Armstrong:
The Complete
Hot Five
and Hot Seven
Recordings
CD box set
packaging

Design firm
Sony Music,
New York

Art director
Ian Cuttler

Designers
Ian Cuttler,
Christian Calabro

At the time I was working on very high-priority projects for the company, so it was a challenge to find the time that this project needed; many late nights were required. I wanted the final product to have a feel of an old photo album/scrapbook representing its historical time frame but produced with today's technology, mirroring the digital remastering of the music. The great images I had to work with, the historical timeline and liner notes were an important factor that helped determine the feel and flow of the design.

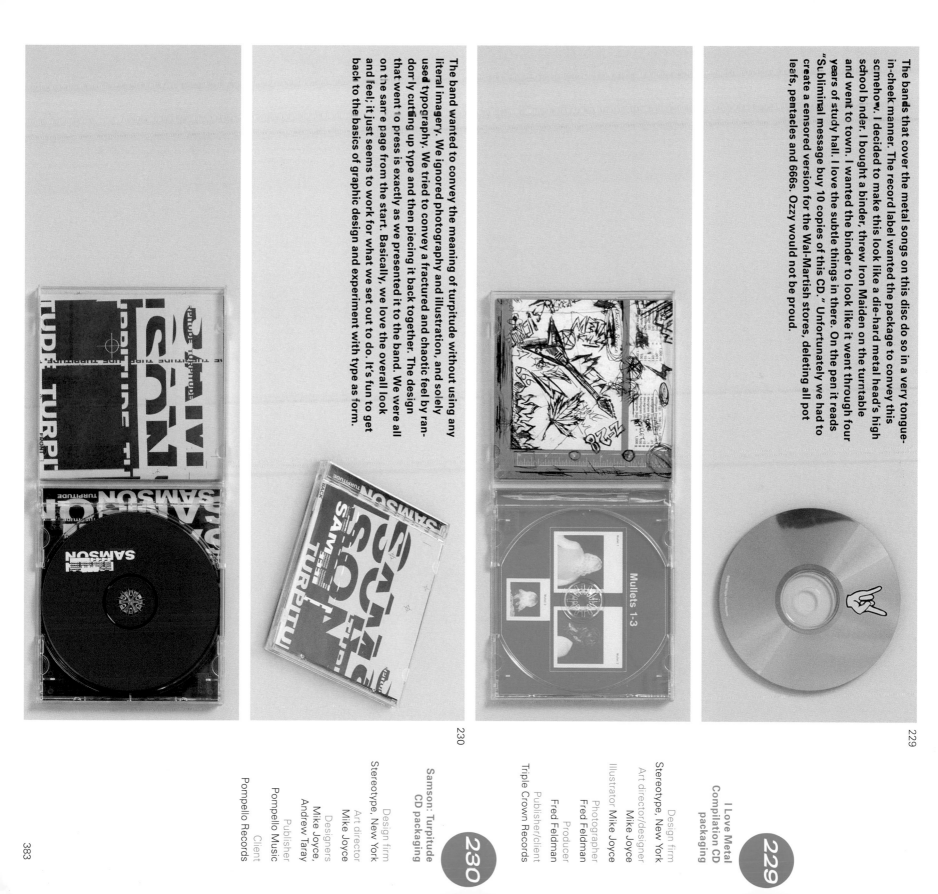

The bands that cover the metal songs on this disc do so in a very tongue-in-cheek manner. The record label wanted the package to convey this somehow. I decided to make this look like a die-hard metal head's high school binder. I bought a binder, threw Iron Maiden on the turntable and went to town. I wanted the binder to look like it went through four years of study hall. I love the subtle things in there. On the pen it reads "Subliminal message buy 10 copies of this CD." Unfortunately we had to create a censored version for the Wal-Martish stores, deleting all pot leafs, pentacles and 666s. Ozzy would not be proud.

The band wanted to convey the meaning of turpitude without using any literal imagery. We ignored photography and illustration, and solely used typography. We tried to convey a fractured and chaotic feel by randomly cutting up type and then piecing it back together. The design that went to press is exactly as we presented it to the band. We were all on the same page from the start. Basically, we love the overall look and feel; it just seems to work for what we set out to do. It's fun to get back to the basics of graphic design and experiment with type as form.

229

**I Love Metal Compilation CD packaging**

Design firm
Stereotype, New York

Art director/designer
Mike Joyce

Illustrator: Mike Joyce

Photographer
Fred Feldman

Producer
Fred Feldman

Publisher/client
Triple Crown Records

230

**Samson: Turpitude CD packaging**

Design firm
Stereotype, New York

Art director
Mike Joyce

Designers
Mike Joyce,
Andrew Taray

Publisher
Pompello Music

Client
Pompello Records

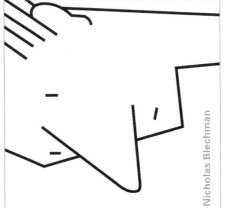

Michael Bierut

Stefan Bucher

Jack Anderson

Harlett Barton

Nicholas Blechman

Ayse Birsel

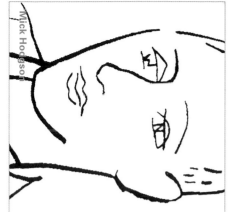

Mick Hodgson

Barbara Glauber

Karin Fong

Margo Chase

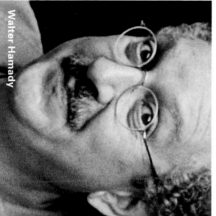

Walter Hamady

Janet Froelich

Barry Deck

Terry Irwin

Luke Hayman

Michael Donovan

Milton Glaser

Eric Madsen

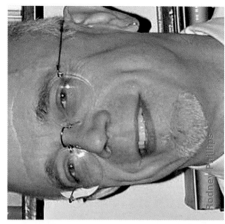

Rodney Phillips

Patrick Mitchell

Emily Oberman

Lana Rigsby

Michael Ian Kaye

Anita Meyer

Noreen Morioka

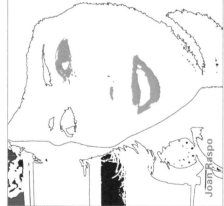

Joan Raspo

Clement Mok

Tommy Steele

Nathan Shedroff

Greg Ross

Gael Towey

Terry Swack

Jill Shimabukuro

1

2

**Jack Anderson Branding strategies and concepts, Branding applications and packaging** Jack Anderson is one of the founding partners of Hornall Anderson Design Works, whose roster of clients ranges from big guns like Microsoft, Starbucks, Pepsi and Kraft Foods to esoteric, obscurely named clients like Sun Dog, Rhino Chasers, Talking Rain and Cf2GS. Anderson is a graduate of Montana State University – the only school where students study logo design by creating cattle brands – and his background includes experience in virtually all areas of graphic design. He has been repeatedly recognized in such annual competitions as Communication Arts, New York Art Directors Club, AIGA and Print and has been featured in several publications including How, Graphis and Step-By-Step.
1 Twelve Horses stationery program, 2000 2 Twelve Horses website, 2000

**Harriet Barton 50 Books/50 Covers** Harriet Barton is creative director and staff manager of the hardcover children's book design group at HarperCollins Publishers, where she has worked for the last 25 years. She has also designed and illustrated 10 books of her own. Barton came to New York after graduating from the University of Kansas in 1964. She held design jobs at Dover Books, Chanticleer Press, the Viking Press, E.P. Dutton, Atheneum and Thomas Y. Crowell before joining Harper. On her arrival in the industry, she was inexperienced in the use of typography and book crafts, but soon learned the value of working attentively with artists, authors, editors and the many people required for book making. Barton's own work includes Sewing By Hand with Christine Hoffman, two books on geography and a title on libraries with Jack Knowlton. Another book with Knowlton, Great Deserts of the World, is forthcoming.
3 Sewing by Hand, HarperCollins Publishers, 1994 4 Great Deserts of the World, HarperCollins Publishers, 2001

**Michael Bierut (chair) Information graphics, Design and typography** Michael Bierut is a partner at Pentagram New York, where his clients include the Council of Fashion Designers of America, Walt Disney Company, Booz-Allen & Hamilton, the Minnesota Children's Museum, the Brooklyn Academy of Music, the Rock and Roll Hall of Fame and Museum and Alfred A. Knopf, Inc. Prior to joining Pentagram in 1990, Bierut was vice president of graphic design at Vignelli Associates. He has won many design awards and his work is represented in the permanent collections of museums in New York, Washington, D.C., and Montreal. He has served as president of both the New York chapter of AIGA and its national board of directors, and is a contributing editor to I.D. magazine and a senior critic at the Yale School of Art.
5 Next Wave Festival subscription brochure, Brooklyn Academy of Music, 1995
6 Light Years Beaux Arts Ball poster, Architectural League of New York, 1999

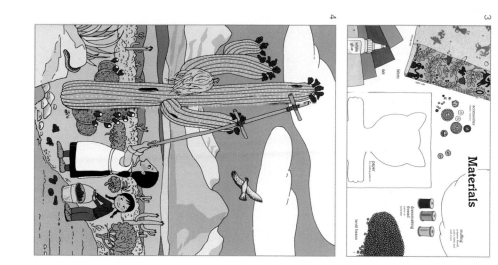

Materials

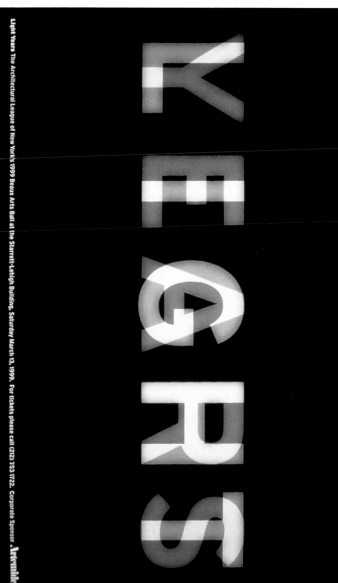

YEARS

1995 the Next Wave Festival

Brooklyn Academy of Music

BAM 1995 Next Wave
Festival is sponsored by
Philip Morris Companies Inc.

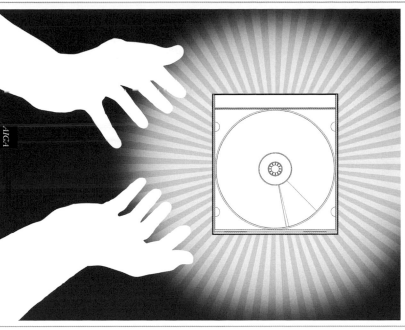

**Ayse Birsel Environmental graphics** Ayse Birsel is the founder of Olive Design, a New York–based design studio where a dedicated group of kindred spirits work together on the difficult and enlightening problems inherent in large projects for big corporations. Born and raised in Izmir, Turkey, Birsel studied industrial design at Middle Eastern Technical University in Ankara from 1981 to 1985 and then at Pratt Institute on a Fulbright fellowship. After two-and-a-half years at Pratt, she designed a collection of office accessories with her professor and mentor Bruce Hannah, and in 1995 designed a combination bidet and toilet for the Japanese company Toto. In June 1997, Birsel launched a relationship with Herman Miller, Inc., which has resulted in a series of award-winning furniture and office systems.
7 Oscar, Nuova Merati SRL, 2001 8 Red Rocket, Herman Miller, 2000

**Nicholas Blechman Editorial design** In January 2001, Nicholas Blechman launched Knickerbocker Design, an illustration and graphic design studio in New York with such clients as the New York Times, Suddeutsche Zeitung, Random House, the Nation, Parsons, Saturday Night, Shift, Audubon Society and Grand Street. Before becoming the art director for The New York Times Op-Ed page for four years, Blechman published, edited and designed eight issues of the award-winning political underground magazine NOZONE. He currently teaches design at the School of Visual Arts and copublishes a series of limited-edition illustration books and is the author of Fresh Dialogue One: New Voices in Graphic Design. Blechman has garnered numerous awards from such organizations as AIGA, Society of Publication Designers and the Art Directors Club.
9 "this is NOT sponsored by:" poster, Syracuse University, 2000

**Stefan Bucher Soundblast** Stefan Bucher is art director of the Pasadena-based studio 344 Design. After working as a freelance illustrator in his native Germany for several years, Bucher received a BFA in advertising from Art Center College of Design in 1996. This was followed by a tour of duty as an art director at Wieden & Kennedy's Portland office. Since 1998, Bucher has headed 344 Design, creating CD packages for Sting, The Matrix, Solar Twins, S Club 7 and bossa:nova. His work has been recognized by AIGA, the Art Directors Club, the Type Directors Club, Print and Communication Arts, and he has served as a vice president of AIGA's L.A. chapter since 1999.
10 Solar Twins CD cover, 1999 11 "Soundblast 2000" poster, AIGA/Los Angeles, 2000

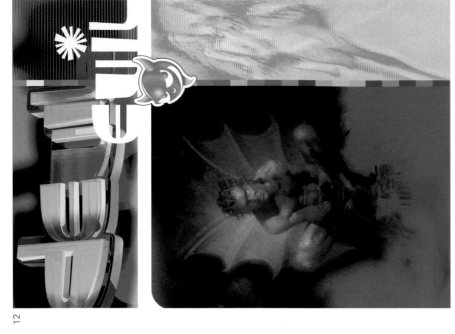

12

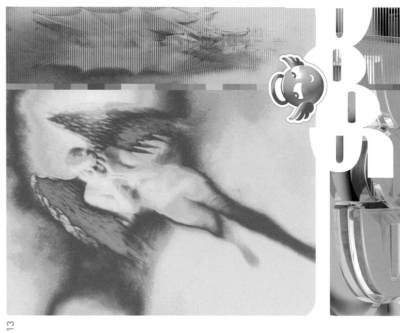

13

**Margo Chase Soundblast** Margo Chase is the founder of Chase Design Group, a Los Angeles–based design firm specializing in strategic brand design and image development for all media. Since its inception nearly 20 years ago, the studio has gained international recognition for its landmark work in corporate identity and brand extension for such innovative companies as Columbia Pictures, EStyle and Sony Music. The studio has been selected as one of I.D. magazine's "I.D. Forty" and its work has appeared in many design periodicals and books, including Communication Arts, How, Graphis, Radical Graphics/Graphic Radicals and New Design: Los Angeles, and includes award-winning movie identity campaigns for Francis Ford Coppola's Dracula, Candyman and Four Weddings and a Funeral, and logos for television shows such as the WB's "Buffy the Vampire Slayer," "Felicity," "Angel" and "Charmed."

12 "(d)EVIL" self-promotional poster, 2000, Merlyn Rosenberg, photographer
13 "G(o)OD" self-promotional poster, 2000, Merlyn Rosenberg, photographer

**Barry Deck Design and typography** Barry Deck grew up in an American suburb, where he spent long hours contemplating world domination while mowing the lawn. Upon graduation from Northern Illinois University in 1986, he was hired by a guy who wore suspenders and bifocals and set every client's name in centered Goudy Oldstyle. In 1987, he enrolled in the MFA program at California Institute of the Arts. By the time he graduated in 1989, he'd started to design seminal typefaces like Template Gothic, Cyberotica and Eunuverse that are distributed by Emigre and Thirstype. Deck currently works out of New York for such clients as Condé Nast, Sundance Channel, MCI Worldcom, TBWA/Chiat/Day, Reebok, Atlantic Records, MTV Networks, Raygun magazine and Attik. He has won numerous awards and been published in Emigre, Wired, Eye and I.D.

14 Eunuverse typeface, 1998 15 "Sundance Channel" poster, Sundance Channel, 1998

**Michael Donovan Branding applications and packaging, Environmental graphics** Michael Donovan is a founding partner of Donovan and Green, a 25-year-old branding, marketing communication and information design consultancy. He successfully sold his business to CKS in 1997, and continues as an active, creative entrepreneur. With his wife and partner Nancye Green, Donovan has engaged in the development of the next iteration of a strategy-based marketing and communication agency. He has served on the national boards of AIGA, SEGD and the National Design Center, and is currently on the board of governors of Parsons School of Design. Throughout his creative career, Donovan has received recognition and numerous awards for branding solutions, information design and environmental design. He is an NEA Fellow and received the Christian Petersen Award for Creativity from Iowa State University, where he serves as an advisor to the Design College. He has taught at Parsons School of Design and Pratt Institute.

16 Ronald Regan Presidential Library, 1991

sur dance channel

**Live webcast!**

**www.sundance channel.com**

OFFICIAL WEB SITE

sundance channel

WE **CHRONICLE,**

**COMMENT,**

AND **COLLUDE.**

All you have to do is read!

EUNIVERSE

ABCDEFGHIJKLMN
OPQRSTUVWXYZ
abcdefghijklmn
opqrstuvwxyz
[ 1 2 3 4 5 6 7 8 9 0 @ 8 ? ]

**Barry Deck 1999**
barrydeck.com

ABCDEFGHIJKLMNOPQRSTUVWXYZ
abcdefghijklmnopqrstuvwxyz
[1 2 3 4 5 6 7 8 9 0 ! @ № $ 8 % ? ]

ABCDEFGHIJKLMNOPQRSTUVWXYZ
abcdefghijklmnopqrstuvwxyz
[1 2 3 4 5 6 7 8 9 0 ! @ № $ 8 % ? ]

ABCDEFGHIJKLMNOPQRSTUVWXYZ
abcdefghijklmnopqrstuvwxyz
[1 2 3 4 5 6 7 8 9 0 ! @ № $ 8 % ? ]

Los Angeles, California (310) 395-3438

Developer is engaged in developing, manufacturing, marketing, licensing, publishing, manufacturing, publishing, marketing, licensing, and distributing digital typefaces for use in computerized imaging devices. Developer has designed and claims rights, title, and interest in and to certain fonts, including fonts which Developer has named as shown in exhibit a. in this Agreement. Distributor Agrees to the following: Developer hereby agrees...

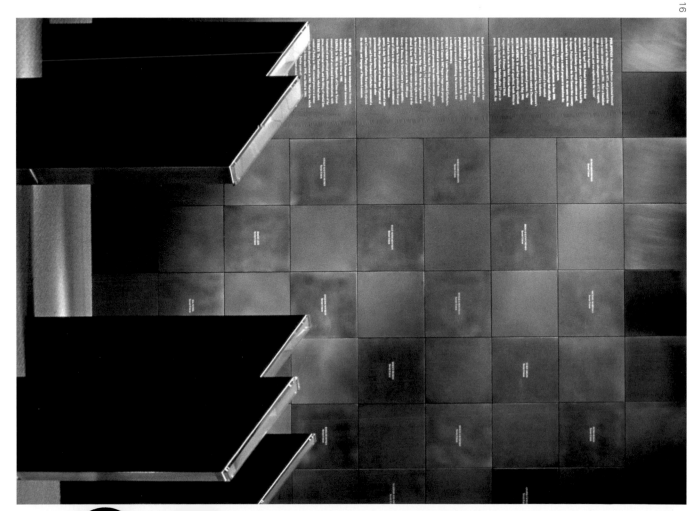

**Karin Fong Design for film and television** Karin Fong is a creative director and partner at Imaginary Forces, an internationally recognized design studio and production company. Before joining the Los Angeles studio in 1994, Fong received her BA in art from Yale, and worked at WGBH Boston as an animator on "Where in the World is Carmen Sandiego?" She currently directs and designs for a wide range of projects, including film titles, broadcast segments and commercials. Recent work includes the main title sequences for Bedazzled, which won the Saul Bass Award for title design; Dead Man on Campus, which won Best of Category in the I.D. Annual Design Review, The Avengers and Charlie's Angels. Broadcast client's have included MTV and WGBH, with whom she worked on the titles for Exxon-Mobil's "Masterpiece Theatre American Collection." She has directed the award-winning television campaign for Janus Mutual Funds for the past two years.

17 *Bedazzled* main title sequence, Twentieth Century Fox/Ocean Pictures, 2000 18 Janus Mutual Funds television campaign, Janus Mutual Funds, 2000

**Janet Froelich Design and illustration** Janet Froelich is art director of *The New York Times Magazine*. Under her direction, the magazine has produced a series of award-winning centennial and millennial issues, and has won numerous gold and silver awards from the Art Directors Club, the Society of Publication Designers and the Society of Newspaper Designers. In 1999 *The New York Times Magazine* won the Society of Publication Design's Magazine of the Year Award and was honored with a retrospective show at the Art Directors Club in New York City. Froelich is a member of the board of directors of the Society of Publication Designers, and is the current president of AIGA's New York chapter. Prior to her current tenure, Froelich was art director of the *Daily News Magazine*, a principal designer of the *Daily News Tonight Newspaper*, a teacher of drawing and painting and a painter. She received a BFA degree from Cooper Union and an MFA from Yale.

19 "Love in the Time of Castro" cover, *The New York Times Magazine*, 2001, Janet Froelich, art director

**Milton Glaser Design and illustration** Milton Glaser was educated at the Cooper Union in New York and later the Academy of Fine Arts in Bologna, Italy, via a Fulbright Scholarship. In 1954, he became cofounder and president of the venerable Pushpin Studios and went on to found *New York Magazine* with Clay Felker in 1968, his own Milton Glaser, Inc., in 1974, and later teamed with Walter Bernard in 1983 to form WBMG, a publication design firm located in New York. Glaser's graphic and architectural commissions include the "I ♥ NY" logo, the redesign of the Grand Union supermarket chain, the design of an International AIDS Symbol for the World Health Organization and the logo for Tony Kushner's Pulitzer Prize-winning play, *Angels in America*. Milton Glaser is at present design consultant to Stony Brook University, Screaming Media, Schlumberger Ltd. and a number of other businesses. His new book on design, *Art is Work*, was published in November 2000.

20 "Art is Whatever" poster, School of Visual Arts, 1996 21 "Experience Uncoated" poster, Fraser Papers, 1999

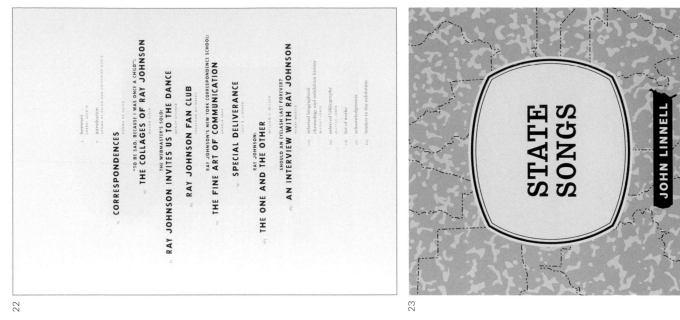

22

23

24

**Barbara Glauber Design and typography** Barbara Glauber is the principal of Heavy Meta, a graphic design studio that focuses on the design of publications, exhibition and information graphics, identities and other projects for clients in the arts and entertainment industries. In 1993, Glauber curated the exhibition "Lift and Separate: Graphic Design and the Quote Unquote Vernacular" at the Cooper Union and edited the accompanying publication. She served as the chair for the eighteenth annual American Center for Design 100 Show and from 1999 to 2001 was on the board of AIGA's New York Chapter. In 1984 Glauber received a BFA from SUNY Purchase and, in 1990, an MFA from California Institute of the Arts. She teaches at Yale University.

22 *Ray Johnson* catalogue, Wexner Center for the Arts, The Ohio State University/Flammarion, 1999 23 State Songs: John Linnell CD cover, Zoe Records/PGD, 1999 24 WMOB: The Wiretap Network website, The Smoking Gun/Court TV, 2001

**Walter Hamady 50 Books/50 Covers** Walter Hamady is proprietor of the Perishable Press Limited, established in 1964. To date, the press has published 126 adventurous handmade books of contemporary, original literature in limited edition. In addition to book collaborations, he spent 37 years teaching at the University of Wisconsin, Madison. Hamady himself makes collages, assemblage and objets-trouvés from diverse elements configuring "meaning" in their own voices. He claims that all his artwork is "text-driven," combining elements of absolute profundity with those of absolute absurdity and seems comfortable inhabiting that fine line between the two.

Hamady lives on a 160-acre farm next to nowhere, out of sight of the contemporary world, where he has collaborated on the raising of three wonderful children without television. He lives happily with his lovely wife, Anna, who is currently helping to transcribe the journals he has kept since 1963.

25 *Nullity, copy #58,* The Perishable Press Limited, 2000 26 *Travelling/Gabberjab No. 7, copy #89,* The Perishable Press Limited, 1991–1996

**Luke Hayman Editorial design** Luke Hayman is the creative director for all properties at Brill Media Holdings and Media Central, including the late *Brill's Content* magazine. Prior to joining *Brill's,* he was senior partner and associate creative director in the Brand Integration Group in the New York office of Ogilvy & Mather. Hayman also served as design director for *I.D.* magazine and was a senior designer at Design Writing Research, where he worked on print and exhibition projects including the redesign of *Architecture* and *Guggenheim* magazine. A graduate of Central Saint Martin's School of Art in London, Hayman has taught and lectured on graphic design at the Maryland Institute College of Art and judged competitions for the Society of Publication Designers. His own work has been recognized by such organizations as ASME, the Society of Publication Designers, AIGA, *Folio* magazine and the Art Directors Club.

27 *Brill's Content* cover, 2001 28 Folio Show promotional material, *Folio* magazine, 2001

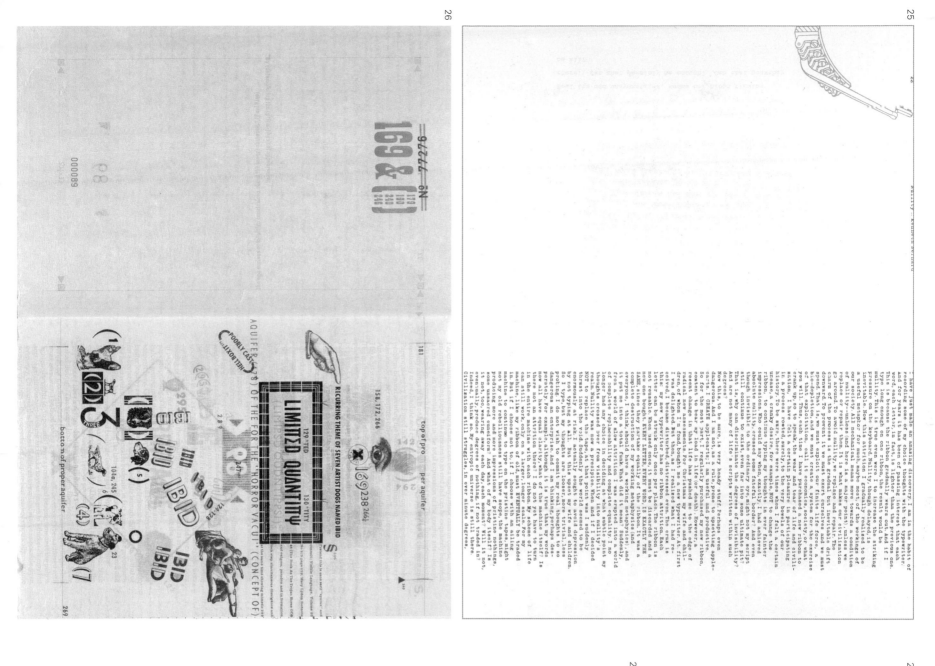

The Folio:Show Midwest

CHICAGO MARCH 18-20, 2002

BRILL'S CONTENT

IS THIS THE FACE OF WORLD DOMINATION?

Rupert Murdoch talks about his satellites, your TV, and taking on AOL Time Warner

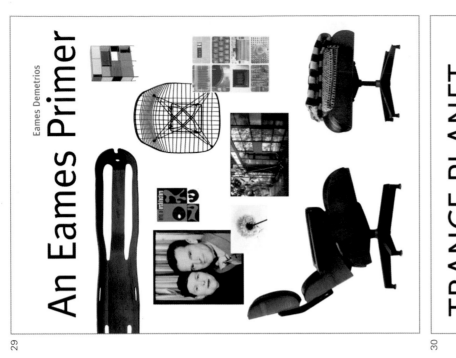

### An Eames Primer
Eames Demetrios

### TRANCE PLANET
volume 5    the essential compilation of eclectic, enchanting and soulful world music

**Mick Hodgson Soundblast** Mick Hodgson studied at St. Martin's School of Art in London and Brighton College of Art, England. He was art director of *Harpers & Queen* magazine until 1979, when he moved to Santa Monica. In 1988, after freelancing for several years in the music business, he established Ph.D, a design office with Clive Piercy that provides image development, identity systems, marketing materials and book design to innovative companies in consumer products, high technology services, publishing, music and advertising. The studio's work has won numerous awards, including three Grammy nominations. Hodgson taught at Art Center College of Design and Otis School of Art and Design and is on the advisory board of the L.A. chapter of AIGA. He is married with three beautiful daughters named Lily, Maudie Rae and Lucie.
29 *An Eames Primer* by Eames Demetrios, Universe/Rizzoli, 2001 30 Trance Planet, volume 5 CD cover, 2001

**Terry Irwin Information graphics, Experience design** Terry Irwin is a founding principal and creative director of the San Francisco office of MetaDesign, a multidisciplinary design firm working in both traditional and digital media where she has directed projects for Tandem Computers, the Getty Museum, Ernst and Young and a host of projects for dot-com start-ups. Prior to MetaDesign, Irwin was a project director with Landor Associates and Anspach Grossman Portugal, where she worked on projects for AT&T, Pacific Bell, Hilton Hotels, Intel, DuPont, Asiana Airlines and the Petroleum Authority of Thailand. Irwin completed four years of graduate studies at the Basel School of Design in Switzerland, where she studied with the renowned design educators Wolfgang Weingart and Armin Hofmann. She has taught at Otis College of Art and Design in Los Angeles, the University of Santa Cruz and the San Francisco Art Academy, and is currently an adjunct professor at California College of Arts and Crafts in San Francisco.
31 "The Landscape of Experience" conference announcement/poster, 2000, Neil Sadler, designer for MetaDesign

**Michael Ian Kaye Advertising and promotional** Michael Ian Kaye is an associate creative director in Ogilvy & Mather's Brand Integration Group. Formerly the creative director of Little, Brown and Company, art director at Farrar, Straus and Giroux and an associate art director at Penguin USA, Kaye is a designer of many books, and many more book jackets working with clients such as the Dial Press, Ecco Press, HarperCollins, Houghton Mifflin, Knopf, W.W. Norton, Random House, Simon and Schuster and Scribner. More recently Kaye has been working with handbag designer Kate Spade on developing a logo signature fabric and identity system for product and product packaging. His work has received numerous awards and has been featured in such publications as *Entertainment Weekly*, *Graphic Design New York 2*, *Less is more*, *Metropolis*, *Mixing Messages*, *Print*, *Type Play* and *U&lc*. Kaye teaches at the School of Visual Arts and currently serves as a board member of the New York chapter of AIGA.
32 Ad campaign, British Petroleum, 2000–2001

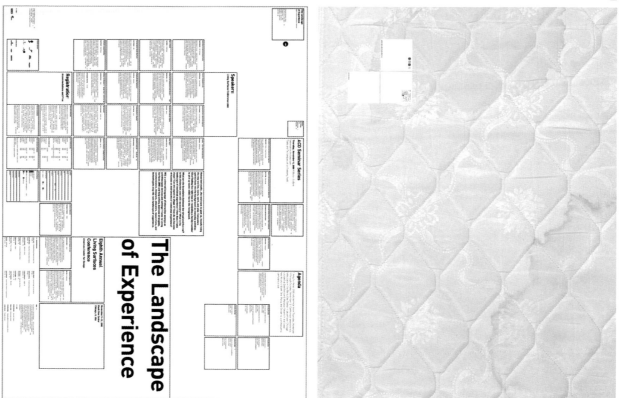

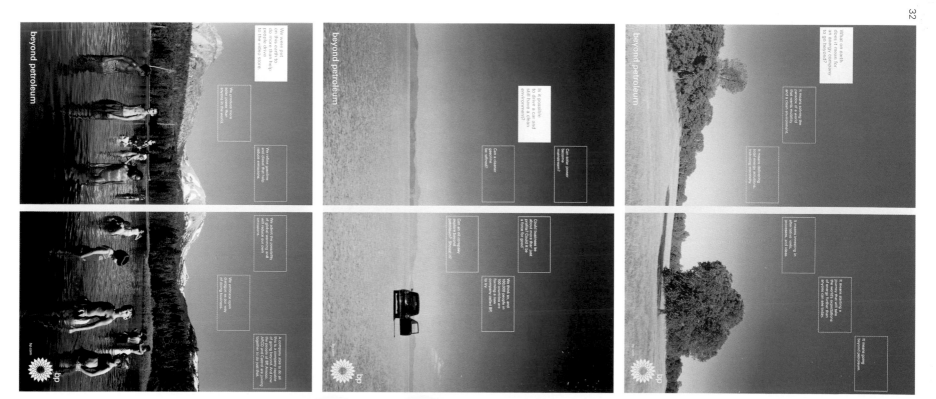

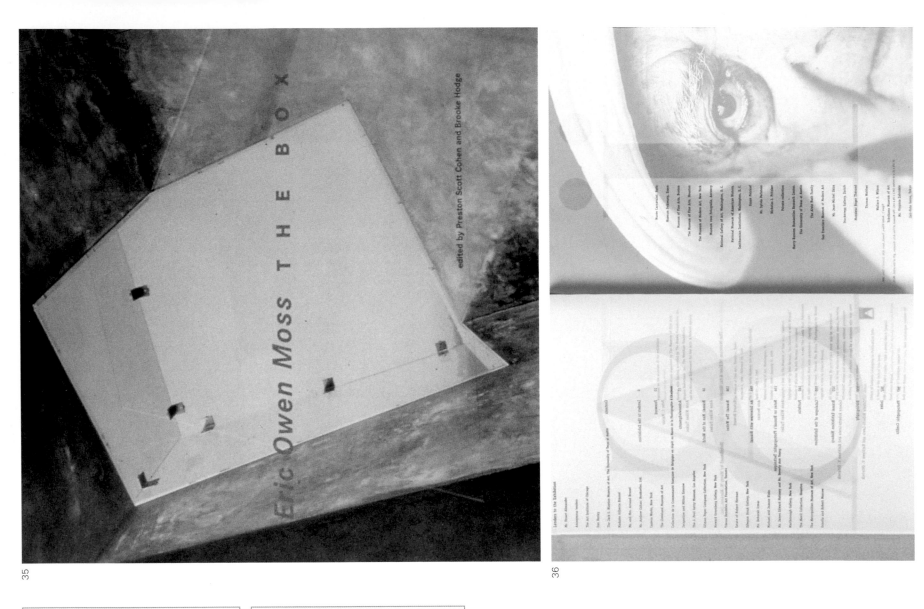

33

34

35

36

400

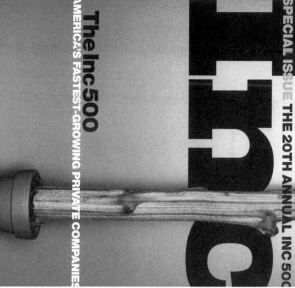

**Eric Madsen 50 Books/50 Covers** Eric Madsen is president of the Office of Eric Madsen, a full-service graphic design firm located in Minneapolis that specializes in all aspects of corporate identity and brand development, marketing and capability materials, magazines and book design for clients in the United States, Europe and Japan. His work has been recognized nationally and internationally by such organizations and publications as AIGA, the Society of Publication Designers, Communication Arts, Print, as well as the Art Directors Clubs of New York, Dallas, Houston, Los Angeles and Minneapolis. Madsen was a member of the National Board of Directors of AIGA until June 2001 and is currently a member of the Board of Trustees of the College of Visual Arts, St. Paul.
33 *With Two Voices: Selections of Western and American Indian Art from the Harmsen Collection* exhibition catalogue, University of St. Thomas, Minneapolis, 1998 34 Weyerhaeuser Lynx Opaque promotional brochure, Weyerhaeuser Company, 2000

**Anita Meyer 50 Books/50 Covers** Anita Meyer is a cofounder of plus design, inc., with partner Karin Fickett and practices collaborative design with architects, artists and fellow designers with the belief that the result of this process is a project that is informed by a broader perspective of vision, experience and thought. Meyer's design sensibility is informed by education, work and life experiences gained in Thailand, Japan, the Netherlands, Providence and Boston. She earned an MFA from RISD, was awarded a Henry Luce Fellowship, completed an Outward Bound program in the Okefenokee Swamp and learned the Rumba at Arthur Murray Dance Studios. She soon hopes to expand her passion for design into developing products and exploring architecture and three-dimensional space.
35 *Eric Owen Moss: The Box* by Preston Scott Cohen (Editor), Brooke Hodge (Editor), Harvard University Graduate School of Design, 1996 36 *Brassaï: The Eye of Paris* by Anne Wilkes Tucker, Peter C. Marzio, The Museum of Fine Arts, Houston, 1999

**Patrick Mitchell Editorial design, Design and illustration** Patrick Mitchell is the founding design director of Fast Company, where he is responsible for the look and feel of the brand across the entire enterprise. Mitchell has been the recipient of more than 120 awards, including the prestigious 2000 National Magazine Award for Excellence in Design, and was named one of *Folio* magazine's 40 most influential people in publishing. His responsibilities have grown to include the same duties at *Inc* magazine, including a recently launched major redesign and rebranding of the magazine and website. Before joining Fast Company, Mitchell was the corporate design director of Dovetale Publishers, whose titles included Old-House Interiors, Old-House Journal and the award-winning and critically acclaimed environmental journal Garbage. At the same time, he ran a design studio, p.m.design, whose clients included CD Review, Disney's Big Time, Design Times, Better Viewing, WebMaster, the Oxford American and Harvard Magazine.
37 *Fast Company* magazine, February/March 1999 38 *Inc* magazine special issue, October 30, 2001

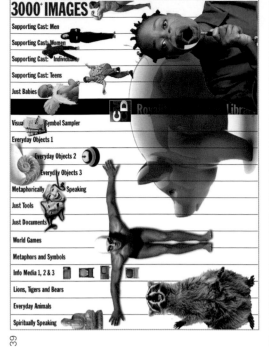

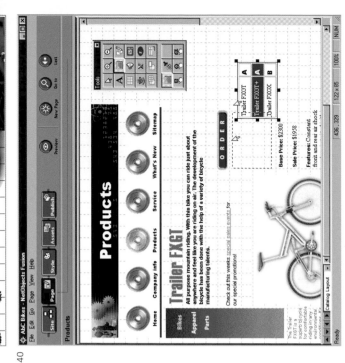

**Clement Mok Information graphics, Experience design** An award-winning designer, digital pioneer, software publisher/developer, international author and design patent holder, Clement Mok has founded multiple successful design-related businesses, including Studio Archetype, CMCD and NetObjects, one of *Fortune*'s 1996 Top 25 Coolest Technology Companies. Most recently he was the chief creative officer of Sapient, an S&P500 business and technology consulting firm, a role he's served since 1998 when his business was acquired. He is now an independent consultant. Over his 20-year career Mok has been involved with the launch of numerous new technologies and companies, including Apple's Macintosh, the Aeron chair, the Microsoft Network, interactive television, broadband applications, web cast events, expert publishing systems and major identity programs for clients like Apple, Adobe, E-Trade, Herman Miller, IBM, Mayo Clinic, Microsoft, Sony, UPS and Wells Fargo Bank. Mok is currently president of AIGA's board of director and is a trustee at the Art Center College of Design.

39 CMCD Royalty-Free Image Library, CMCD Inc., 1993–present
40 NetObjects Fusion software application, NetObjects, Inc., 1996

**Noreen Morioka Environmental graphics** Noreen Morioka cofounded AdamsMorioka, a strategy and communications firm, with Sean Adams in 1993. The firm's manifesto included an approach of "clarity, purity and resonance" as applied to content, form and business. In 1997, Morioka and Adams were named to I.D.'s "I.D. Forty," a list of the 40 most influential designers in the world. Recently AdamsMorioka was described in the *Los Angeles Times* as "major influencers of popular culture at the end of the century." Morioka has lectured extensively throughout the world and has been recognized in the I.D. Annual Design Review, and was named a Fellow of the International Design Conference at Aspen. Morioka currently serves as president of AIGA's Los Angeles Chapter. AdamsMorioka's clients include Nickelodeon, VH1 Music First, Gap, Old Navy, Sundance, Mohawk Paper Mills, Appleton Paper and the Walt Disney Company.

41 "AdamsMorioka Dallas" lecture poster, Appleton Papers, 2001 42 UCLA Extension catalogue cover, UCLA, 2001

**Emily Oberman Design for film and television** Emily Oberman is a copartner with Bonnie Siegler of Number Seventeen, a multidisciplinary design firm founded in 1993 that has created such work as the magazines Jane and Lucky, logos and title sequences for NBC's "Saturday Night Live," "The Late Late Show with Craig Kilborn," "Will & Grace" and Oxygen's "The Isaac Mizrahi Show." Other clients include HBO, MTV, Chiat/Day and André Belazs' Mercer Hotel in New York and Château Marmont in Los Angeles. Number Seventeen is currently designing a book about the television show "Sex and the City" for Melcher Media. Oberman has been on the National Board of AIGA and also teaches design for television at Cooper Union and at Yale University's graduate program. Before starting Number Seventeen, Oberman worked at Tibor Kalman's New York design studio, M&Co. Before that she graduated from Cooper Union.

43 "Saturday Night Live" titles, NBC, 2001

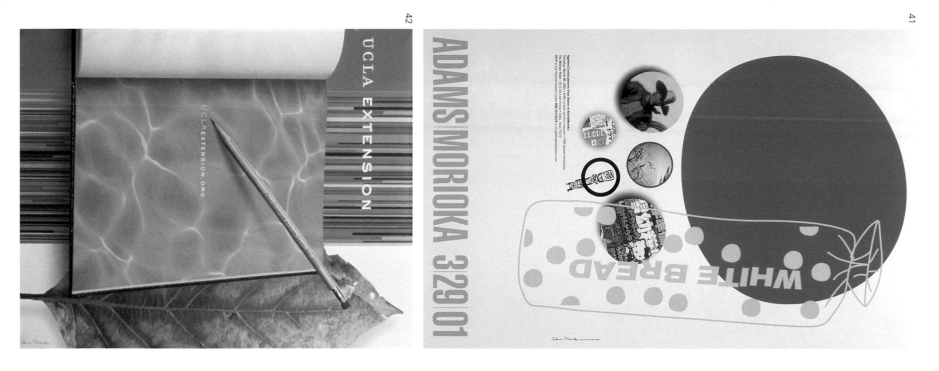

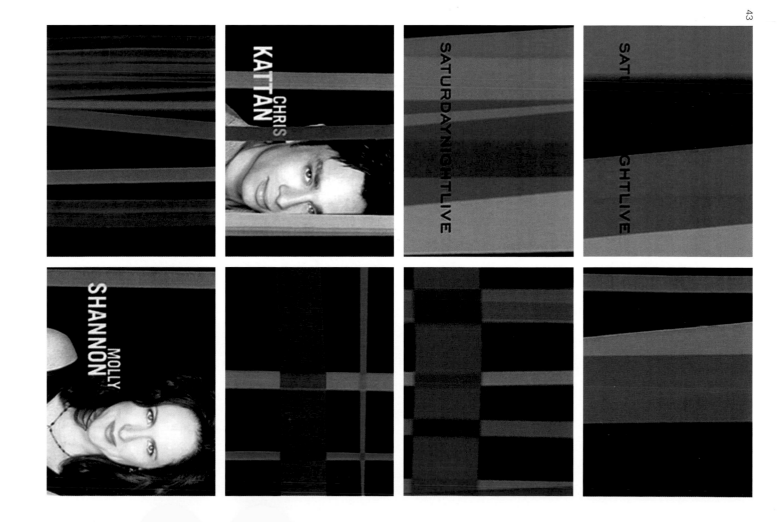

46

47

48
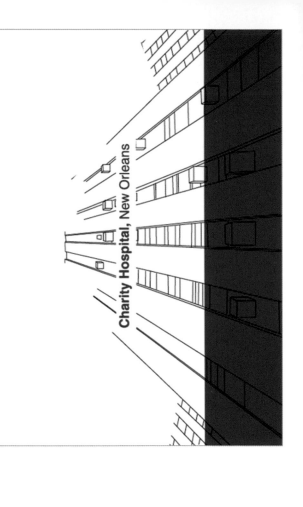
Charity Hospital, New Orleans

44
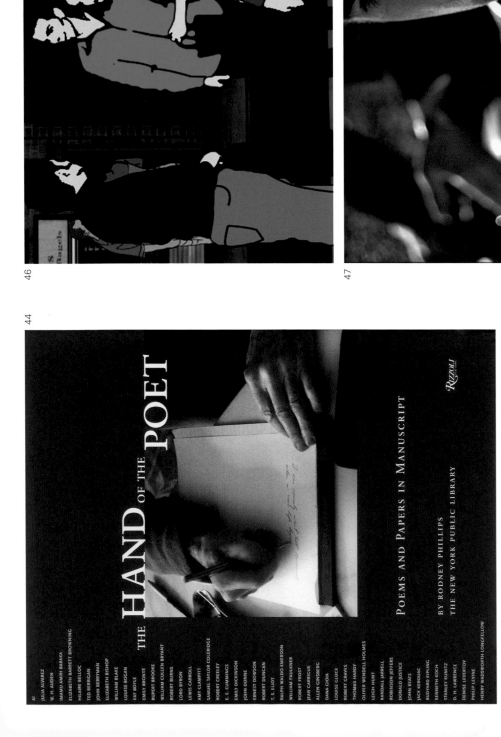

THE HAND OF THE POET

POEMS AND PAPERS IN MANUSCRIPT

BY RODNEY PHILLIPS
THE NEW YORK PUBLIC LIBRARY

RIZZOLI

AI
JULIA ALVAREZ
W. H. AUDEN
IMAMU AMIRI BARAKA
ELIZABETH BARRETT BROWNING
HILAIRE BELLOC
TED BERRIGAN
JOHN BERRYMAN
ELIZABETH BISHOP
WILLIAM BLAKE
LOUISE BOGAN
KAY BOYLE
EMILY BRONTE
RUPERT BROOKE
WILLIAM CULLEN BRYANT
ROBERT BURNS
LORD BYRON
LEWIS CARROLL
AMY CLAMPITT
SAMUEL TAYLOR COLERIDGE
ROBERT CREELEY
E. E. CUMMINGS
EMILY DICKINSON
JOHN DONNE
ERNEST DOWSON
ROBERT DUNCAN
T. S. ELIOT
RALPH WALDO EMERSON
WILLIAM FAULKNER
ROBERT FROST
JEAN GARRIGUE
ALLEN GINSBERG
DANA GIOIA
LOUISE GLUCK
ROBERT GRAVES
THOMAS HARDY
OLIVER WENDELL HOLMES
LEIGH HUNT
RANDALL JARRELL
ROBINSON JEFFERS
DONALD JUSTICE
JOHN KEATS
JACK KEROUAC
RUDYARD KIPLING
KENNETH KOCH
STANLEY KUNITZ
D. H. LAWRENCE
DENISE LEVERTOV
PHILIP LEVINE
HENRY WADSWORTH LONGFELLOW

45

A Chronological Timeline of the Literary Underground, 1950–1980

**Rodney Phillips 50 Books/50 Covers** Rodney Phillips is the director of the Humanities and Social Sciences Library of the New York Public Library's Research Libraries. He was previously curator of the renowned Henry W. and Albert A. Berg Collection of English and American Literature, where he curated six exhibitions on literary subjects, including "Nabokov," "Yeats," "First Books," and "Mimeograph Publishing in the 1960s." With others he has produced two books, The Hand of the Poet: Poems and Papers in Manuscript (Rizzoli, 1997) and A Secret Location on the Lower East Side: Adventures in Writing, 1960–1980 (NYPL/Granary Books, 1998). 44 *The Hand of the Poet* by Rodney Phillips et al, Rizzoli, 1997 45 *A Secret Location on the Lower East Side* by Steven Clay and Rodney Phillips, NYPL/Granary Books, 1998

**Joan Raspo Design for film and television** Joan Raspo is a filmmaker and designer based in New York City. Her most recent project was cocreating and directing "Avenue Amy," an animated comedy series based on the love life of writer Amy Sohn that is currently in its second season on the Oxygen Network. Life before "Avenue Amy" included a stint as art director at VH-1 and commercial directing at Curious Pictures. Raspo is currently one of three partners in the design collective Stiletto. Stiletto was included in the 2001 Young Gun Art Directors Show and invited to be one of two firms in AIGA's "Fresh Dialogue: Emerging Voices in Graphic Design" presentation, which was held in May 2001. Raspo graduated from the California College of Arts & Crafts in San Francisco with a BFA in Graphic Design and earned a BA in English Literature from Santa Clara University. 46 *Avenue Amy*, Oxygen Network, 2001 47 Showtime Extreme branding, Showtime Networks, 2000 48 TLC promotional spot, TLC (The Learning Channel), 2000

**Lana Rigsby Branding applications and packaging. Advertising and promotional** Lana Rigsby is principal and design director for Rigsby Design, a Texas-based firm known for creating engaging, intelligent communications for a diversity of organizations. Her work includes brand identity development, corporate communications and website applications for such companies as Dell Computer Corporation, Weyerhaeuser, American Oncology Resources, Mohawk Paper Mills, Mead, Ashford.com, the Earth Technology Corporation, Contemporary Arts Museum/Houston and International Papers. Rigsby is a founding member of AIGA's Texas chapter, and has served as a national director for AIGA. 49 Sternhill Partners website, Sternhill Partners, 2000 50 "A Periodic Table of Cultural Elements" poster, Strathmore Papers, 2001

51

52

**Greg Ross Soundblast** Greg Ross is coprincipal of ORABOR, a multidisciplinary design firm based in Pasadena whose projects range from corporate identity systems and retail packaging to website development and custom publishing. Prior to the inception of the firm, Ross was senior art director at both Warner Brothers Records and A&M Records in Los Angeles. He has taught at both Art Center College of Design and Otis College of Art and Design, and his work has been selected for numerous competitions including "AIGA SoundBlast" and the American Center for Design's "100 Show," as well as for publication in such leading publications as I.D and Print.
51 Ms. Toi: That Girl CD packaging, Universal Records, 2001 52 Metro Rapid Bus brochure, Surface Transit Project, Los Angeles, 2001

**Nathan Shedroff Branding strategies and concepts, Experience design** Nathan Shedroff has been an information and interface designer for more than 12 years, focusing on developing online experiences, building online brand strategies and business models, and developing online communities. Shedroff cofounded vivid studios, a decade-old pioneering company in interactive media. Prior to that, he worked with Richard Saul Wurman as a senior designer at Understanding Business. He earned a BS in Industrial Design with an emphasis on Automobile Design from Art Center College of Design. Shedroff was nominated for a Chrysler Innovation in Design Award in 1994 and 1999 and, while a student, received an Honorable Mention in the 1987 Unisys Industrial Design Competition. Shedroff's latest book, Experience Design 1, explores common characteristics in all media that make experiences successful.
53 Herman Miller RED website, Herman Miller, 2001 54 Nathan Shedroff's World website, Nathan Shedroff, 2001–present

**Jill Shimabukuro 50 Books/50 Covers** Jill Shimabukuro is the design manager at the University of Chicago Press, where she has worked since 1996. Educated at Grinnell College and Northwestern University, she has also taught book production and design at the University of Chicago's Graham School of General Studies. More than 20 of her book and jacket designs have been recognized with awards from both the Association of American University Presses and the Chicago Book Clinic. In addition to serving on numerous committees and panels for the AAUP, Shimabukuro freelances for clients throughout the country, and also bears the distinction of being an artist for Chicago's immensely popular "Cows on Parade" civic art program of 1999.
55 Process: A Novel by Kay Boyle, University of Illinois Press, 2001 56 A River Runs through It and Other Stories by Norman Maclean, Twenty-fifth Anniversary Edition, Chicago University Press, 2001

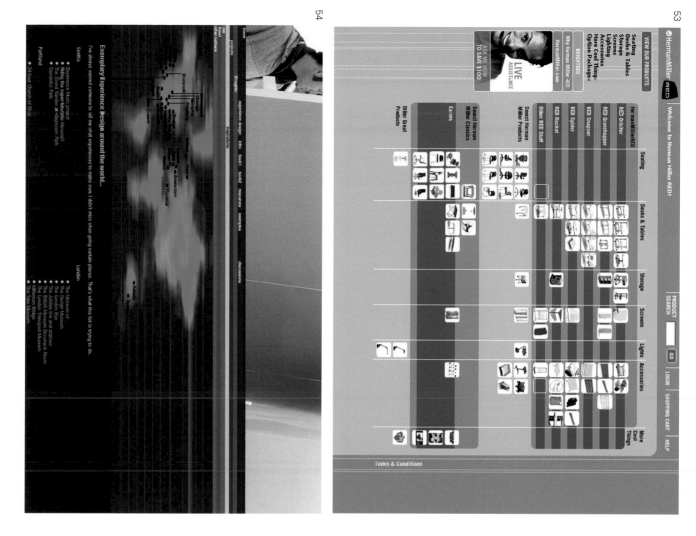

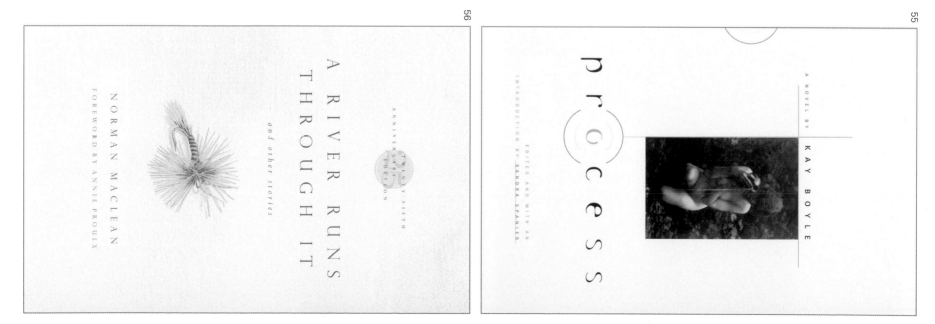

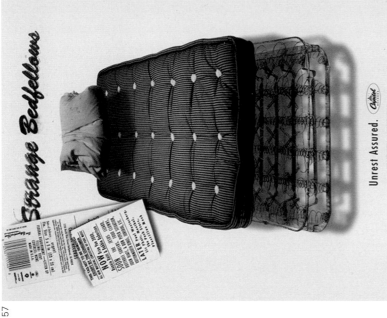

**Tommy Steele Soundblast** Tommy Steele is vice president of Creative Services at Capitol Records, where he manages the company's worldwide entertainment packaging, including compact discs, record sleeves and box sets, television commercials and short film projects. A six-time Grammy nominee, Steele also supervises all merchandising, advertising, media and print operations for the label. As head of Capitol's in-house team for the past 14 years, he has spearheaded creative campaigns for such renowned artists as Radiohead, Tina Turner, Frank Sinatra, The Beastie Boys and The Beatles. From 1984 to 1988, Steele owned his own Los Angeles–based studio that created top-selling covers for Tom Petty, Neil Young, Steve Miller and Sheena Easton. He is the author/designer/photographer of four best-selling graphics books for Abbeville Press: The Hawaiian Shirt, Bowl-O-Rama, Close Cover Before Striking and Lick'em, Stick'em.

57 Strange Bedfellows: Unrest Assured CD packaging, Capitol Records, 1997
58 Blind Melon: Soup CD packaging, Capitol Records, 1995

**Terry Swack Experience design** Terry Swack is a leading digital strategist and designer. She founded TSDesign as a graphic design firm in 1985, and redefined it as an Internet strategy and product design firm in 1995. In 1999, TSDesign was acquired by Razorfish, and Swack became vice president/Experience Design, strategizing the redesign of the company's service delivery organization and practices. In 1998 Swack and Clement Mok organized the Advance for Design Forum, which has since become the AIGA Experience Design Community of Interest, with groups in major U.S. cities and London. Swack now consults independently on experience auditing, brand experience and product strategy, and organizational planning for digital service delivery. She is a contributing reviewer to Internetworld's "Deconstructing" column and is working on a book about digital experience strategy and design.

59 3M Worldwide website, 3M, 1999

**Gael Towey Branding strategies and concepts** Gael Towey is creative director of Martha Stewart Living Omnimedia (MSLO), where she oversees three magazines, the mail order catalogue, the merchandising businesses, the website, the television graphics and all advertising and marketing efforts associated with each business. In 1990, Towey helped found the Martha Stewart Living magazine with Martha Stewart and Isolde Motley. Under her creative direction, Martha Stewart Living has won numerous awards from the Society of Publication Designers, the Art Directors Club and ASME awards for design and photography. In 1999, Towey was awarded the Daimler Chrysler Design Award, which celebrates designers (or design teams) who innovate within a broad range of disciplines. Prior to her career with MSLO, Towey was an associate art director at Viking Press. She then went on to become the first art director at Clarkson N. Potter, where she designed award-winning books, including English Country and Martha Stewart's Gardening. After Potter, she began working as a magazine art director with a one-year stint at HG prior to the start-up of Martha Stewart Living.

60 Martha Stewart Baby special issue magazine cover, Martha Stewart Omnimedia, Spring 2001 issue 61 Martha Stewart Living magazine spread, Martha Stewart Omnimedia, March 2001 issue

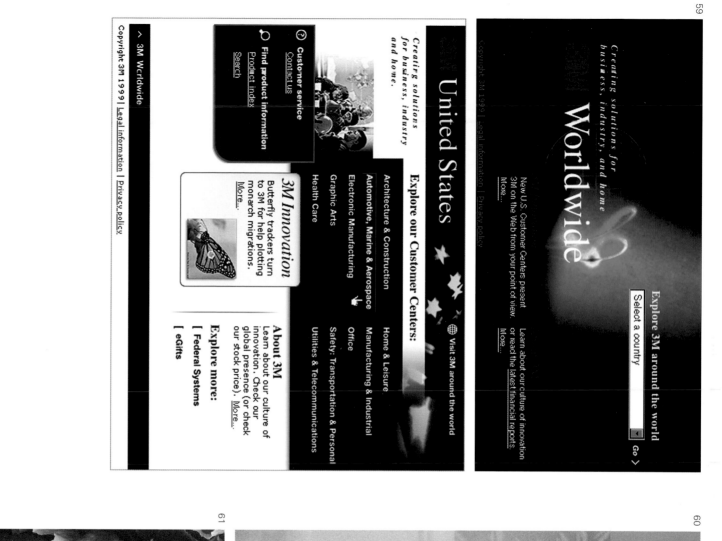

*Creating solutions for business, industry, and home*

Copyright 3M 1999 | Legal information | Privacy policy

3M

## Worldwide

New U.S. Customer Centers present 3M on the Web from your point of view. More...

Learn about our culture of innovation or read the latest financial reports. More...

**Explore 3M around the world**

Select a country ▾  Go >

---

*Creating solutions for business, industry and home.*

3M

## United States

Visit 3M around the world

**Explore our Customer Centers:**

Architecture & Construction
Automotive, Marine & Aerospace 👉
Electronic Manufacturing
Graphic Arts
Health Care

Home & Leisure
Manufacturing & Industrial
Office
Safety: Transportation & Personal
Utilities & Telecommunications

**Explore more:**
[ **Federal Systems**
[ **eGifts**

**3M Innovation**
Butterfly trackers turn to 3M for help plotting monarch migrations. More...

**About 3M**
Learn about our culture of innovation. Check our global presence (or check our stock price). More...

**Customer service**
Contact us

**Find product information**
Product index
Search

> **3M Worldwide**

Copyright 3M 1999 | Legal information | Privacy policy

---

## 60

MARTHA
STEWART

*baby*

SPECIAL ISSUE

SPRING NURSERY
ALL ABOUT MILK
CHANGING TABLE
COOKING WITH CARROTS
SWADDLING
EMBROIDERY

DISPLAY UNTIL 5/14/01
$4.75 USA (CAN. $7.75)
www.marthastewart.com

---

## tree peonies

Although their ethereal beauty has made them the darlings of emperors and plant connoisseurs, these surprisingly hardy shrubs need not be pampered to put on a majestic show.

## Branding strategies

**1 The Armed Forces' Exchange Credit Program identity** Design firm BrandEquity International, Newton, Massachusetts Creative director Joe Selame Designer BrandEquity Design Team Credit card embosser First Data Resources

**2 Nickelodeon identity reface** Design firm Adams Morioka, Beverly Hills Creative directors Sean Adams, Noreen Morioka Designers Sean Adams, Noreen Morioka, Volker Dürre, David Van Riper, Matthew Dunteman, George Guzman Print production Terry Stone, Michelle Gray, Karen Dragotto Illustrators Chip Wass, Michael Mabry Writer Eric McPaul Typeface Venus, Berthold Akzidenz Grotesk, Courier, Rockwell On-air producer Lu Olkowski Software Illustrator, Photoshop, After Effects Audio Andy Caploe Client Nickelodeon

**3 Xootr Scooter brand development** Design firm Lunar Design, San Francisco Art director Kristen Bailey Designers Becky Brown, Florence Bautista Client Nova Cruz Products LLC

**4 H&R Block identity revitalization** Design firm Landor Associates, San Francisco Creative director Margaret Youngblood Senior design director Eric Scott Designers Kistina Wong, Cameron Imani, Tina Schoepflin, Irena Blok, David Rockwell, Mary Hayano Writers Daniel Meyerowitz, Susan Manning Account directors Russ Meyer, Liz Magnusson Project management Bill Larsen, Stephen Lapaz Realization Tom Venegas Client H&R Block

**5 BP Amoco merger identity** Design firm Landor Associates, San Francisco Creative directors Margaret Youngblood, Nancy Hoefig, Courtney Reeser Senior brand strategist Peter Harleman Design director, environments David Zapata Design director, interactive Brad Scott Designers Cynthia Murnane, Todd True, Frank Mueller, Michele Berry, Cameron Imani, Ivan Thelin, Ladd Woodland, Maria Wenzel Writers Jane Bailey, Susan Manning Account director, Interactive Wendy Gold Project management Greg Barnell, Stephen Lapaz, Bryan Vincent Realization Russell DeHaven Client BP Amoco

**6 HP Invent identity system** Design firm Landor Associates, San Francisco Creative director Margaret Youngblood Senior design director Patrick Cox Designers Frank Mueller, Paul Chock, Christian Guler, Jean Loo Writers Mark Welte, Daniel Meyerovich, Susan Manning Account directors Hunter Marshall, Peter Mack, Brett Mangels, Liz Magnusson Project management Scott Briefer Realization Wayne DeJager, Brian Green, Monica Lee, Rose Robinson, Russell DeHaven, Judy Wurstler, Emma Rybakova Client Hewlett-Packard Company

**7 Audrey branding** Design firm Turner Duckworth, San Francisco Creative directors David Turner, Bruce Duckworth Designers David Turner, Mark Waters, Sara Geroulis, Mary Foyder, Allen Raulet, Jonathan Warner, Lian Ng Photographers Stan Musilek, Lloyd Hyrciw Illustrator Brian Cronin Typeface Trade Gothic Printers ExpedEx/Advanced Litho, Glenbard Printing, Paper N Inc Client 3Com Corporation

## Branding applications and packaging

**8 Thomas E. Wilson Foods cooked meat packaging** Design firm Duffy Minneapolis Creative director Alan Colvin Design director Kobe Suvongse Designers Kobe Suvongse, Joe Monnens, Craig Duffney Production artist Mike White Print production Bridget Schumacher, Anne Hughes Photographer Deborah Jones Art buyer Katie Cook Writers Mark Wirt, Scott Barger Printer Rock Tenn, Cryovac Client IBP, Inc.

**9 NapaStyle packaging** Design firm Pentagram Design, San Francisco Art director Kit Hinrichs Designer Erik Schmitt Project manager Jon Scheuning Typeface Modified News Gothic Printers Santa Rosa Label Company, Phoenix Glass Client NapaStyle

**10 Orthopaedic Surgery and Sports Medicine Specialists corporate identity** Design firm Renée Rech Design, Norfolk, Virginia Art director/designer Renée Rech Printer Teagle & Little Paper Neenah Classic Crest Super Smooth Solar White Client Orthopaedic Surgery and Sports Medicine Specialists

**11 Red Canoe identity system** Design firm Red Canoe, Deer Lodge, Tennessee Creative director Deb Koch Designer Caroline Kavanagh Writer Deb Koch Typefaces Clarendon, Officina Printer Lithographics, Inc. Papers Fox River Starwhite Tiara smooth and Evergreen Kraft Software Adobe Photoshop, Adobe Illustrator, QuarkXPress, Microtek ScanMaker, Agfa 1640 Digital Camera Client Red Canoe

**12 Merge Inc. identity system** Design firm Merge, Atlanta Art director Ash Arnett Creative director Michael Taylor Designers Ali Harper, Rebecca Klein Illustrator Rebecca Klein Typeface Univers Printer Claxton Software QuarkXPress

**13 Duffy identity system** Design firm Duffy Minneapolis Creative director Alan Colvin Designers Alan Leusink, Tom Riddle Print production Bridget Schumacher, Becky Amell Production artist Tracy Hogenson Typefaces Alphaheadline, Conduit ITC Trim size A4, 8 x 11 inches Printer Reflections, Kea Inc. Paper #51 Yupo translucent envelope, 70 lb. Mohawk Superfine Text Software Adobe Illustrator Client Duffy

**14** **AM PM Design identity system** Design firm AM PM Design, Centreville, Virginia Designer/writer Tamera Lawrence Typeface Meta Printer L.J. Cowie Company, C + R Printing, Paper Crane's Cover Fluorescent White, Crane's Writing Unwatermarked Fluorescent White, Crane's #10 Square Flap Fluorescent White

**15** **de Young Museum brochure** Design firm Cahan and Associates, San Francisco Creative director Bill Cahan Designer Michael Braley Project manager Katie Kniestedt Illustrator's Nanette Biers, Walter Hood Photographer Jock McDonald Writers Peterson Skolnick, Dodge Typeface Sabon Printer George Rice and Sons Paper 50 lb. Weyerhaeuser Opaque Vellum Text Software QuarkXPress, Adobe Photoshop Client de Young Museum

**16** **Martha Stewart Everyday case study** Design firm Doyle Partners, New York Creative director Stephen Doyle Designers Tom Kluepfel, Rosemarie Turk, Lisa Yee, Ariel Apte, Viv an Ghazarian, John Clifford, Liz Ahrens, Gratia Gast, Michelle Cosentino, Jia Hwang, Craig Clark, Naomi Mizusaki, Lizzy Lee, Vanessa Eckstein Project managers Cameron Mannin, Goizalde Mintegia Client Kmart, Martha Stewart Living Ommimedia

**17** **Takashimaya Volume 8 catalogue** Design firm Design: MW., New York Creative directors Allison Williams, J.P. Williams Art director Allison Williams Designers Allison Williams, Yael Eisele Photographer Gentl and Hyers Writer Laura Silverman Trim 8 1/2 by 8 1/2 inches Printer Lithographix Paper Curious Papers Client Takashimaya New York

**18** **3Com 2C00 annual report** Design firm Howry Design Associates, San Francisco Art director Jill Howry Designer Calvin Jung Print production Shellie Cohen Photographer Tom Feiler Writer Ethan Place Typeface DIN Trim size 7 x 9 1/2 inches Printer Anderson Lithograph Paper Mohawk Options Client 3Com Corporation

**19** **San Francisco International Airport 2000 annual report** Design firm Morla Design, San Francisco Art director Jennifer Morla Designers Jennifer Morla, Hizam Haron Photographers Richard Barnes, Fred Cramer, Thomas Heinser, Daniel Stachurski et al. Writer San Francisco International Airport Typefaces Bell Gothic, Clarendon Trim size 5 x 6 1/2 inches Printer Fong & Fong Paper 100 lb. McCoy Silk White Cover and Text, 100 lb. Carnival Smooth White Text Software QuarkXPress, Adobe Illustrator, Adobe PhotoShop Client San Francisco International Airport

**20** **The George Gund Foundation 1999 annual report** Design firm Nesnadny + Schwartz, Cleveland Creative director Mark Schwartz Designer Michelle Moehler Photographer

Douglas Lucak Writers David Bergholz, Deena Epstein Trim size 8 x 8 inches with 6 1/2-inch gate on inside front cover Printer Fortran Printing, Inc. Paper 80 lb. French Parchtone White Cover, 100 lb. Sappi Lustro Dull Text Uncoated, 60 lb. French Parchtone White Text Client The George Gund Foundation

**21** **Swiss Army Brands Inc. 1999 annual report** Design firm SamataMason, Inc., Dundee, Illinois Art director Dave Mason Designers Pamela Lee, Dave Mason Print production Pamela Lee Photographer Victor John Penner Writer Steve Zousmer Typeface Folio Trim size 5 1/2 x 8 inches Printer H. MacDonald Paper 110 lb. Fox River Sundance Smooth Bright White Cover and 70 lb. text, 100 lb. Appleton Coated Utopia Two Dull Blue White text, 36 lb. Appleton Coated Canson Satin Client Swiss Army Brands, Inc.

**22** **Fisher 1999 annual report** Design firm The Leonhardt Group, Seattle Art director Steve Watson Designers Steve Watson, Ben Graham Project manager Lori Kent Photographer Don Mason, stock Writers Steve Watson, Chris Wheeler Typeface Interstate, Screen Metrix Trim size 12 3/8 x 8 1/2 inches Printer GAC/Allied Paper Zanders Vellum, NeeKosa Solution Gray Software Quark Client Fisher Companies, Inc.

**23** **IBM 2000 annual report** Design firm VSA Partners, Inc., Chicago Creative directors Curt Schreiber, Jeff Walker Designers Scott Hickman, Michelle Platts Photographer Christian Witkin Typeface Jansen Printer Anderson Lithograph Trim size 8 x 11 1/4 inches Paper Mohawk Superfine, Mohawk Opaque Animators Mattie Langenburg, Theo Fels Programmers Theo Fels, Mattie Langenburg, Chester Schendel Interface Chester Schendel Software Adobe PhotoShop, QuarkXPress, Adobe Illustrator, Flash Client/publisher IBM

**Advertising and promotional**

**24** **CAE Spring Show 2000 announcement** Design firm Cosmic Art Enterprises, Inc., Brooklyn Illustrator/designer Veit Schuetz Software Adobe Illustrator

**25** **Parsons Spring 2001 poster** Design firm Felixsockwell.com, New York Art director Evelyn Kim Designer/illustrator Felix Sockwell Printer Rosepoint Typeface Azkidenz Grotesk Trim size 30 x 40 inches Paper Rives bfk Software Adobe Illustrator Client Parsons School of Design

**26** **Moët & Chandon par James Victore poster** Design firm James Victore, Inc., Beacon, New York Art director Alan Weill Designer James Victore Trim size 27 1/2 x 40 inches Printer Stipa Imprimerie Paper Job Publisher/client Moët & Chandon

**27** **Spoon poster** Design firm Planet Propaganda, Madison, Wisconsin Designer Michael Byzewski Typeface Helvetica Trim size 19 x 25 inches Printer Aesthetic Apparatus Paper French Construction Steel Blue Software Adobe Illustrator, Adobe PhotoShop Client University of Wisconsin

**28** *Jack's Destiny poster* Design firm Edward Tamez, San Antonio Art director/designer Edward Tamez Illustrator Edward Tamez Writer Gloria Prieto Typefaces Trade Gothic Light, Trade Gothic Bold no. 2 Client Nicole Kobs

**29** *Falling For Her poster* Design firm Edward Tamez, San Antonio Art director/designer Edward Tamez Illustrator Edward Tamez Writer Gloria Prieto Typefaces Trade Gothic Light, Trade Gothic Bold no. 2 Client Nicole Kobs

**30** **Lupton Lecture invite** Design firm Visual Dialogue, Boston Art director Fritz Klaetke Designers Fritz Klaetke, Ian Varrassi Typefaces News Gothic, Hand lettering Trim size 4 3/4 x 6 1/2 inches (envelope), 3 x 3 inches (Post-it) Printer Alpha Press (envelopes) Fabrication Emily's Specialty Products (Post-its) Paper White-woven envelopes, 3M Post-its Software QuarkXPress, Adobe PhotoShop Client AIGA/Boston

**31** *Where The Better Half Live poster* Design firm Vanka, Montreal Creative director/designer Matthew Vanka Print production Matthew Vanka, Danielle Belanger Printer Imprimerie Tom Desmarais Client Feathered Publisher Forgery

**32** **Art Real postcards** Design firm Templin Brink Design, San Francisco Creative directors Joel Templin, Gaby Brink Designer/illustrator Brian Gunderson Typeface Akzidenz Grotesk Trim size 7 3/4 x 4 3/4 inches Printer Art Real Paper Industrial board Client Art Real

**33** *Burton "Snow Monkey" animated advertisement* Design firm Jager Di Paola Kemp Design, Burlington, Vermont Creative director/designer Michael Jager Art director/designer Jared Eberhardt Project manager Leslie E. Dowe Illustrator/animator Geoff McFetridge Producer Leslie E. Dowe Client Burton Snowboards

**34** **Motion Theory website** Design firm Motion Theory, Venice, California Creative director Mathew Cullen Designers Mathew Cullen, Ryan Alexander Photographer Javier Jimenez Writer Carm Goode Programmer Ryan Alexander Software Macromedia Flash, Adobe Illustrator Client Motion Theory

**35** **Target "Fashion/Housewares" print ads** Design firm Kirshenbaum Bond & Partners, New York Art director Minda Gralnek Designers Scott McDonald, Mike Hahn, Kirshenbaum Bond & Partners Project manager Karen Preston, Bill Barrett, Kirshenbaum Bond & Partners Photographer Karina Taira Writer Ryan Blank, Kirshenbaum Bond & Partners Client Target Stores

**36** **Target "Sign of the Times" Spring print ads** Design firm PMH Art directors Minda Gralnek (Target), Dave Peterson (PMH) Print production Gary Tassone (PMH) Photographer Meyers Robertson Associate creative director/copywriter Amie Valentine Client Target Stores

**37** **Portfolio Center Change catalogue** Design firm James Victore, Inc., Beacon, New York Art director Gemma Gatti Designer James Victore Project manager Hank Richardson Writer Dan Monroe Typefaces Caslon, Helvetica Trim size 23 x 16 inches Printer Graphic Press Fabricator Graham Thorpe Paper French Butcher Publisher/client Portfolio Center

**38** **Nike ACG Pro Purchase catalogue** Design firm Nike, Inc., Beaverton, Oregon Creative director Michael Verdine Art director/designer Angelo Colletti Print production Ann Riedl Project manager Susan Roy Photography Marcus Swanson, Sean Reynolds (product); Trevor Graves, Mark Gallup, Tammy Kennedy (athlete) Copy Naomi Gollogly Typefaces Akzidenz Grotesk, Orator Trim size 9 1/2 x 6 1/2 inches Printer Irwin Hodson Color house Colourscan Inc. Paper 80 and 60 lb. French Dur-o-tone Butcher White Software Adobe Illustrator, QuarkXPress Client Nike, ACG

**39** **Anni Kuan, Spring/Summer 2001 fashion brochure** Design firm Sagmeister, Inc., New York Art director/designer Stefan Sagmeister Illustrator/photographer Stefan Sagmeister Writer Stefan Sagmeister Typeface Hand type Trim size 11 1/2 x 10 inches Printer Jae Kim Printing Co. Fabricator O.K. Kayo Corp. Paper Newsprint Client Anni Kuan Design

**40** *Simple Truths 1999 annual report/fundraiser* Design firm Slaughter Hanson, Birmingham Art director Marion English Powers Project manager Stacy Pope Illustrator David Webb Photographer Don Harbor Writer Kathy Oldham Typefaces Helvetica, News Gothic, Bell Centennial, Century Schoolbook Trim size 5 x 6 1/4 inches Printer Ad Shop Paper Crowne Vantage Blotter Cover, 80 lb. Blue Basis Graphika Vellum White Software QuarkXPress, Adobe PhotoShop, Adobe Illustrator Client Greater Alabama Council/Boy Scouts

**Illustration**

**41** *Richard III poster* Design firm Sommese Design, State College, Pennsylvania Art director/creative director Lanny Sommese Designer/illustrator Lanny Sommese Digital production Mat Flick Typeface Gill Sans Software Adobe Illustrator, Adobe Streamline Trim size 24 x 34 inches Printer Penn State Center for Academic Computing Client Penn State University

James Victore Print production Christopher Chu Writer Henry David Thoreau Typeface Left hand Trim size 8 1/2 x 11 inches Printer Hemlock Printers Ltd. Paper Fox River Publisher/client *Critique*

**60** *The New York Times Magazine* "Love in the Time of Castro" cover Design firm *The New York Times Magazine*, New York Art director Janet Froelich Photo editor Kathy Ryan Designer Joele Cuyler Photographers Virginia Beahan, Laura McPhee

**61** *The New York Times Magazine* "Spending" cover Design firm *The New York Times Magazine*, New York Art director Janet Froelich Designers Joele Cuyler, John Fulbrook

**62** *Rolling Stone* "Crosby, Stills, Nash & Young" story Design firm *Rolling Stone* magazine, New York Art director Fred Woodward Designers Fred Woodward, Siung Tjia Photographer Mark Seliger Photography editor Rachel Knepher

**63** *Rolling Stone* "The Hot Issue" special issue Design firm *Rolling Stone* magazine, New York Art director Fred Woodward Designers Fred Woodward, Siung Tjia Photographer Mark Seliger Photo editor Rachel Knepher

**64** *2wice* "Rites of Spring" issue Design firm Pentagram Design, New York Creative director J. Abbott Miller Designers J. Abbott Miller, Roy Brooks Project manager John Porter Typefaces FK Eureka, AT Sackers Trim size 8 1/4 x 11 1/2 inches Printer Strine Printing Co. Paper 120 lb. Donside Gleneagle dull cover, 80 lb. dull text, 100 lb. Cromática Publisher Patsy Tarr Client 2wice Arts Foundation

**65** *2wice* "Ice" issue Design firm Pentagram Design, New York Creative director J. Abbott Miller Designers J. Abbott Miller, Jeremy Hoffman Project manager John Porter Typefaces FK Eureka Sans, Burin Sans Trim size 8 1/4 x 11 1/2 Printer Strine Printing Co. Paper 120 lb. Donside Gleneagle Dull Cover, 100 lb. Dull Text Publisher Patsy Tarr Client 2wice Arts Foundation

**66** *Insurance magazine* Design firm goodesign, New York Art director/designer Diane Shaw Typefaces Akzidenz Grotesk, Linotype Didot Trim size 6 1/2 x 8 3/4 Printer Intel Printing Software QuarkXPress Publisher Each Press Editors Kostas Anagnopoulos, Chris Tokar Client *Insurance magazine*

**50 books**

**67** *Artists Books* book Design firm Brooklyn Museum of Art, Brooklyn Creative director Deirdre Lawrence Designer Stacey Wakefield, Evil Twin Publications Photographer Pak Fung Wong Production coordinator Stacey Wakefield Trim size 4 1/2 x 4 3/4 inches Pages 64 Quantity printed 1,000 Compositor Stacey Wakefield Typeface New Gothic Printer/binder Karr Graphics Paper 65 lb. Mohawk Superfine cover weight Method of binding Spiral-bound with wrap-around cover, stepped sheets Binding materials Curtis Corduroy corrugated paper with gold foil on front (cover), spiral-bound. Author Deirdre Lawrence Editor James Leggio Publisher Brooklyn Museum of Art

**68** *Maakies* book Art director/designer Chip Kidd Illustrator Tony Millionaire Production coordinator Eric Reynolds Trim size 10 5/8 x 8 3/8 inches Pages 130 Quantity printed 15,000 Typefaces Splimpy bold, Farggy italic Printer Quebecor Paper 50 lb. Crinklecote Binder Sta-Prest, Inc. Method of binding Squeezing and waiting Binding materials Glue, cardboard Author Tony Millionaire Publisher Fantagraphics

**69** *Jimmy Corrigan: The Smartest Kid on Earth* book Design firm Alfred A. Knopf, Inc., New York Art director Chip Kidd Designers Chip Kidd, Chris Ware Illustrator Chris Ware Production coordinator Andy Hughes Trim size 8 x 6 1/2 Pages 380 Quantity printed 25,000 Compositor Chris Ware Printer/binder Toppan Paper 70 lb. OK Bright Method of binding Sewn Binding materials 86 lb. TopKote gloss/matte with foil stamp Endpapers Printed 4/4 on 70 lb. Jacket designer Chris Ware Author Chris Ware Publisher Pantheon Books

**70** *Listening to Cement* book Design firm Arena Editions, Santa Fe Creative director Elsa Kendall Designer/compositor David Skolkin Photographer Robert Stivers Production coordinator Lara Colombaroli Trim size 9 1/2 x 12 inches Pages 108 Typefaces Centaur, Futura Printer/binder EBS (Editoriale Bortolazzi Stei) Paper Gardapatt Method of binding Sewn Binding materials Reggent limon Endpapers Nettunio Author John Stauffer Publisher Arena Editions

**71** *A Contemporary Cabinet of Curiosities* book Design firm Aufuldish & Warinner, San Anselmo, California Designer Bob Aufuldish Production coordinator Celeste McMullin Trim size 7 1/4 x 9 1/4 inches Pages 52 Quantity printed 75 Typefaces New Clear Era Mix Two, New Clear Era Mix Three, Engravers Gothic Printer Hemlock Printers, Ltd. Paper 100 lb. Mohawk Superfine Eggshell text sticker sheets, 60 lb. Mactac Starliner White Cinema Binder Lincoln & Allen Method of binding Perfect-bound Binding materials Skivertex Silver Firenze Endpapers 100 lb. Mohawk Superfine Eggshell Text printed with one match color Author Ralph Rugoff Publication manager Genoa Shepley Editor Nancy Crowley Publisher California College of Arts and Crafts

**72** *Babylon 1.7* book Design firm Babylon AG c/o Eclat NY, Ithaca, New York Creative director Robert Kruegel-Durband Designers Gion-Men Kruegel-Hanna, Elke Schultz Production

60/81

**73** **American Contemporary Furniture book** Design firm Cabra Diseño, San Francisco Art director Raul Cabra Designers Santiago Giraldo, Jeremy Stout, Raul Cabra Photographers Richard Barnes, Diro Dinco, James Chian, Debra Seidman Production coordinator Dung Ngo Trim size 8 1/2 x 8 1/2 Pages 208 Quantity printed 7,500 Typeface Bell Gothic Printer/binder Sfera International, Italy Paper 150 gsm Matte Method of binding Hardcover imitation cloth over 3 mm gray board, sewn h/t bands, paperback-sewn cover-scored 14 pt. c1s Endpapers140 gsm Wood-free 1/1 Editors Raul Cabra, Dung Ngo Publisher Universe Publishing

**74** **TM: Trademarks Designed by Chermayeff & Geismar book** Design firm Chermayeff & Geismar, New York Art directors Ivan Chermayeff, Tom Geismar, Steff Geissbuhler Photographers Various Trim size 8 1/2 x 8 5/8 inches Pages 288 Quantity printed 9,000 Printer Phoenix Offset Paper 157 gsm Top-Kcte Dull Matte Art Binder Kolbus Method of binding Smythe sewn, case-bound, square-backed with head and tail bards Binding materials Brillanta cloth with blocking over 3 mm boards, 4072 purple (front), 4031 yellow (spine), 4070 red (back), Lustrofoil B5G/Silver and W417H/ red (front block ng), B56/silver (spine blocking) Endpapers 140 gsm Woodfree front paper printed 1/1 solid PMS 355, back paper printed 1/1 solid PMS 286 Publisher Princeton Architectural Press (U.S.), Lars Müller Publishers (Europe)

**75** **Krijn de Koning: Inside Outside book** Design firm Coma, Brooklyn Designers Cornelia Blatter, Marcel Hermans Illustrator Krijn de Koning Photographers Krijn de Koning et. al. Productio coordinator Barbera van Kooij Trim size 8 3/11 x 6 11/16 inches Pages 160 Quantity printed 1,500 Typeface Scala Sans Printer Die Keure, Belgium Paper 135 gsm Perigord Matte White Binder De Haan, The Netherlands Method of binding Cold glue Authors Rutger Wolfson, Valentijn Byvanck, Daniel Buren, Michel Gauthier Publisher NAI Publishers

**76** **Progressive Design in the Midwest book** Design firm Deb Miner, Designer, Minneapolis Art director/designer Deb Miner Production coordinator Donald Leurquin Trim size 9 1/2 x 9 1/2 inches Pages 200 Quantity printed 7,500

coordinator Arbeitsgruppe Babylon 1.7 Trim size 9 x 11 4/5 Pages 40 Quantity printed 2,500 Compositor Typolitho AG Typefaces Filosofie, Transit, Pravda, Quanta Printer Vontobel Druck AG Pape Gmund Havanna Structuros and Reaction (cover), Gmund Valentinoise Method of binding Combination of hard and paper cover, Asiatic and perfect-bound Jacket designer Robert Kruegel-Durband Authors Roland Müller, Robert Foos, Rolf Todesco, Emil Zopfi

Compositor Deb Miner Typefaces Bembo, Futura, Copperplate Printer/binder Snoek-Ducaju & Zoon, Belgium Paper Japanese, 300 gsm Invercote Creatto cover, 170 gsm Japanese machine-coated matte text Method of binding Smythe-sewn Author Jennifer Komar Olivarez Publisher Minneapolis Institute of Arts

**77** **Exhibiting Experimental Art in China book** Design firm Froeter Design, Inc., Chicago Creative director Chris Froeter Designer Tom Zurawski Production manager Rachel Perez-Stable Publication manager Stephanie Smith Trim size 7 1/4 x 11 inches Pages 224 Quantity 2,000 Typefaces Univers, Sabon Printer H. MacDonald Printing Method of binding Perfect-bound Author Wu Hung Editor Margaret Farr Publisher Smart Museum of Art Distributor University of Chicago Press

**78** **Faces book** Design firm Gittings Design, Tucson Art director Dane Arnett Designer Jane Gittings Authors/photographers François and Jean Robert Production coordinator Tera Killup, Chronicle Books Trim size 5 1/2 x 6 1/2 inches Pages 272 Quantity 15,000 Compositor Bright Arts Graphics Pte., Ltd. Singapore Typeface Akzidenz Grotesk Printer/binder Tien Wah Press, Singapore Paper 150 gsm Nymolla Matte Method of binding Smythe-sewn cover drawn on Binding materials 310 gsm C2S Art card Publisher Chronicle Books

**79** **Achille Castiglioni book** Art directors Marzia and Maurizio Corraini Designer Maurizio Corraini Illustrator Steven Guarnaccia Trim size 5 1/4 x 8 inches Pages 165 Quantity printed 6,000 Compositor/printer Tipographia Commerciale, Italy Typeface Memphis Paper 150 gsm Garda Pat, Cartiera Del Garda Binder Legatoria Moderna, Italy Method of binding Sewn Author Paola Antonelli Publisher Corraini Editore

**80** **The Fine Art of Letters book** Design firm Jerry Kelly LLC, New York Art director/illustrator Hermann Zapf Designer/production coordinator Jerry Kelly Trim size 8 x 11 11/16 inches Quantity printed 1,000 Compositor Jerry Kelly Typefaces Linotype Zapfino, Zapf Renaissance Printer Finlay Printing Paper 80 lb. Mohawk Superfine Softwhite Smooth Binder Acme Bookbinding Method of binding Smythe-sewn, case-bound Binding materials Brillanta Endpapers Fabriano Ingres Author Hermann Zapf Publisher The Grolier Club

**81** **Made in California book** Design firm LACMA, Los Angeles Designer Scott Taylor Supervising photographer Peter Brenner Production coordinators Rachel Ware Zooi, Chris Coniglio Compositor Scott Taylor Typefaces CA40 (drawn for the exhibition), Minion, Tarzana, Emperor, Chicago

Germany Paper 150 gsm Phoenix Motion Xantur Binder Dollinger GmbH, Germany Method of binding Smythe-sewn Binding materials Schneidersöhne Gemini 1 (soft cover) Editor Julie Warnement Curator Alan Shestack Publisher National Gallery of Art

**87** ***The Patricia G. England Collection of Fine Press and Artists' Books book*** Design firm National Gallery of Art, Washington, D.C. Art director/designer Margaret Bauer Photographer Lyle Peterzell Production coordinator Margaret Bauer Trim size 7 1/4 x 11 inches Pages 88 Quantity printed 1,500 Compositor National Gallery of Art Typeface Mrs. Eaves Printer Grafisches Zentrum Drucktechnik, Germany Paper 135 gsm Gardapat, 120 gsm Musterzettel/ Papago Binder Dollinger GmbH, Germany Method of binding Smythe-sewn Binding materials Arches Expression Natur Editor Ulrike Mills Curator Ruth E. Fine Publisher National Gallery of Art

**88** ***Ezekiel's Horse book*** Design firm Pentagram Design, Austin Art director DJ Stout Designers/compositors DJ Stout, Nancy McMillen Photographer Keith Carter Production coordinator David S. Cavazos Trim size 11 x 11 inches Pages 168 Quantity printed 7,500 Typefaces Helvetica, Helvetica Bold, Helvetica Bold Condensed Printer/binder C & C Offset Printing Co. Ltd., Hong Kong Paper 157 gsm Japanese SSS Matte Art Method of binding Smythe-sewn, hardcover Authors Keith Carter, John Wood Publisher University of Texas Press, in cooperation with the Wittliff Gallery of Southwestern & Mexican Photography at Southwest Texas State University

**89** ***Whitney 2000 Biennial Exhibition book*** Design firm Pentagram Design, New York Creative director J. Abbott Miller Designers J. Abbott Miller, Roy Brooks, Scott Devendorf Trim size 8 x 10 inches Pages 272 Typefaces Cachet, Swit Printer Cantz GmbH, Germany Paper Phoenix Xantur Publisher Whitney Museum of American Art

**90** ***Wonderland book*** Design firm Pentagram Design, New York Creative director J. Abbott Miller Designers J. Abbott Miller, Roy Brooks, Scott Devendorf Photographer Peter Mauss/Esto Production coordinator John Porter Trim size 9 x 10 inches Pages 176, plus 10 inserts Typeface Corporate Printer Strine Printing Co. Paper Phoenix Xenon, Cougar Opaque Editor Rochelle Steiner Publisher The St. Louis Art Museum

**91** ***Parallax book*** Design firm 2x4, New York Art director Michael Rock Designers Conny Purtill, Michael Rock Production coordinator Clare Jacobson Trim size 5 1/2 x 7 5/8 inches Pages 384 Quantity printed 12,000 Typefaces Monotype Grotesque 1 Bold, Berthold Baskerville Regular

---

Trim size 9 x 12 inches Pages 352 Quantity printed 30,765 Printer Gardner Lithograph Paper Appleton Utopia Two matte text Binder Roswell Bookbinding Binding materials Offset on Appleton Utopia Two with matte lamination (cover), offset and silkscreen on Canson Satin with matte lamination (jacket) Method of binding Smythe-sewn, case-bound, square spine Endpapers Papan ESP Authors Stephanie Barron, Sheri Bernstein, Ilene Susan Fort, Michael Dear, Howard N. Fox, Richard Rodriguez Editors Nola Butler, Thomas Frick Publisher LACMA and University of California Press

**82** ***Maeda @ Media book*** Design firm Maeda, Cambridge, Massachusetts Art director/designer John Maeda Production coordinator Kris Maeda Trim size 8 1/2 x 8 inches Pages 480 Quantity printed 40,000 Compositor John Maeda Typeface Berthold Univers Printer/binder Dai Nippon Hong Kong Paper Art matte, craft, textured Method of binding Perfect-bound Author John Maeda Publishers Thames & Hudson, Rizzoli, Bangert Verlag, Digitalogue

**83** ***Glen Ligon and Gary Simmons book*** Design firm Matsumoto Incorporated, New York Creative director/art director Takaaki Matsumoto Designers Takaaki Matsumoto, Thanh X. Tran Author Thelma Golden Printer Studley Press Paper 100 lb. Mohawk Superfine text, ultrawhite eggshell Typeface Franklin Gothic Trim size 17 x 21 inches Publisher The Fabric Workshop and Museum

**84** ***Sugimoto: Theaters book*** Design firm Matsumoto Incorporated, New York Creative director Takaaki Matsumoto Art director Hiroshi Sugimoto Designers Takaaki Matsumoto, Hiroshi Sugimoto Photographer Hiroshi Sugimoto Printer Larissa Nowicki Photographer Hiroshi Sugimoto Printer Meridian Printing Paper 100 lb. Mohawk Superfine Eggshell text Typeface Univers family Trim size 12 1/2 x 11 1/4 Author Hans Belting Publisher Sonnabend Sundell Editions and Eyestorm.com

**85** ***Each Wild Idea book*** Design firm MIT Press Design Department, Cambridge, Massachusetts Designer Ori Kometani Production coordinator Terry Lamoureux Trim size 7 1/2 x 9 inches Pages 249 Quantity printed 2,500 Typefaces Adobe Garamond, Engravers Gothic Printer/ binder Quebecor Kingsport Paper 70 lb. Utopia Book Binding materials Kennett Black Jacket printer Phoenix Color Author Geoffrey Batchen Publisher MIT Press

**86** ***Art for the Nation: Collecting for a New Century book*** Design firm National Gallery of Art, Washington, D.C. Art director/designer Margaret Bauer Production coordinator Margaret Bauer Trim size 8 1/2 x 12 inches Pages 320 Quantity printed 1,925 Compositor Duke + Design Typefaces Van Dijck, Cronos Printer Grafisches Zentrum Drucktechnik,

Printer Artegraf ca Paper 150 gsm Gardamatt Cartiera Del Garda Binder Legatoria Camisana Method of binding Paperback sewn in 14/16-inch plus 1/8-inch folded Binding materials Real Cloth Cialux Coverpapers Two pieces gray cardboard 275 gsm on front and back with blue real cloth on spine only Author Steven Holl Publisher Princeton Architectural Press

**92 Celebrating Modern Art: The Anderson Collection book** Design firm San Francisco Museum of Modern Art, San Francisco Art director/designer Tracey Shiffman Photographer Ian Reeves, et al. Illustrator Tracey Shiffman Production coordinator Kara Kirk Trim size 11 3/4 x 13 inches Pages 398 Quantity printed 7,200 Compositor Tracey Shiffman Typefaces Sabon, Sabon Expert, Futura Medium Printer/binder Mondadori, Italy Paper 200 gsm Phoenix Imperial White Semi-matte, 118 gsm Classic Crest Saw Grass Smooth Text Uncoated Method of binding Smythe-sewn Binding materials Van Heek Scholco, Dubletta cloth Endpapers Zanders Efalin, Neuleinin Finish Editor Gary Garrels, et al. Publisher San Francisco Museum of Modern Art, University of California Press

**93 Writing on Hands: Memory and Knowledge in Early Modern Europe book** Design firm Studio A, Alexandria, Virginia Art director Antonio Alcalá Designers Antonio Alcalá, Mary Dunnington, Helen McNeill Trim size 9 x 12 inches Pages 280 Quantity printed 2,000 Typeface Minion Printer/binder Hagerstown Bookbinding and Printing Paper 80 lb. Finch Vanilla Opaque Text, 100 lb. Vintage Velvet cover Method of binding Perfect-bound Author Claire Richter Sherman Publisher The Trout Gallery, Dickinson College

**94 Spirit Stones of China book** Design firm studio blue, Chicago Art directors Kathy Fredrickson, Cheryl Towler Weese Designers Cheryl Towler Weese, Radhika Gupta Illustrator studio blue Photographer Michael Tropea Typographer Matt Simpson Production coordinators Matt Simpson, Sarah Guernsey Trim size 10 1/4 x 7 1/2 inches Pages 112 Typefaces Balance, hand-drawn numbers Printer Asia Pacific Offset, Inc. Binding Chinese fan-fold binding Author Stephen Little Editor Kate Steinmann Publisher The Art Institute of Chicago, in association with University of California Press

**95 Marcel Duchamp: The Art of Making Art in the Age of Mechanical Reproduction book** Design firm studio blue, Chicago Art directors Kathy Fredrickson, Cheryl Towler Weese Designers Cheryl Towler Weese, Heather Corcoran, Garrett N ksch Illustrator studio blue Production coordinator Matt Simpson Trim size 11 3/4 x 9 inches Pages 332

Typefaces Handmade type from a Cyrillic eye chart owned by Duchamp, Metro, Agency, Ariston, Kaufmann, Becka Script, Clarendon, Cooper Black, Nobel, Memphis, Bodoni 72, Truesdell Paper Mewdon uncoated cover Binding Smythe-sewn Author Francis Naumann Publisher Ludion (Belgium), Abrams (U.S.)

**96 Campbell Collection of Soup Tureens at Winterthur book** Design firm studio blue, Chicago Art directors Kathy Fredrickson, Cheryl Towler Weese Designers Heather Corcoran, Garrett Niksch, Cheryl Towler Weese Production coordinator Matt Simpson Trim size 12 x 9 inches Pages 260 Typefaces Bell Gothic, Bodoni 72, Bodoni 12 Printer Balding & Mansell Paper Job Parilux Dull Binding Smythe-sewn Authors Donald Fennimore, Patricia Halfpenny Editors Onie Rollins, Teresa Vivolo Publisher Winterthur Museum

**97 Christina Ramberg Drawings book** Design firm Studio/Lab, Chicago Designer Marcia Lausen Illustrator Christina Ramberg Photographers Christina Ramberg; Tom van Eynde, Jeff Crisman (copy photographers) Trim size 8 1/2 x 10 inches Pages 128 Quantity printed 1,400 Typeface Myriad Printer/binder Active Graphics Paper Esleeck Translucent Sulfite Bond Binding materials Heavy-duty staples, foam, glue Author Judith Russi Kirshner Publisher University of Illinois at Chicago

**98 The Fairest Fowl: Portraits of Championship Chickens book** Design firm The Grillo Group, Inc., Chicago Art director Maria Grillo Designers Julie Klugman, Gabrielle Schubart, Winifred Gundeck Photographer Tamara Staples Trim size 8 3/4 x 8 inches Pages 108 Author Christa Velbel, Ira Glass Publisher Chronicle Books

**99 Lennon: His Life and Work book** Design firm Pentagram Design, New York Creative director/designer J. Abbott Miller Trim size 7 x 10 inches Pages 176 Typefaces Burin Sans, FF Avance Printer Strine Printing Co. Paper Mohawk Options Editor James Henke Publisher Rock and Roll Hall of Fame and Museum

**100 Other Pictures book** Design firm Twin Palms Publishers, Santa Fe Art director Jack Woody Designers Jack Woody, Arlyn Nathan Production coordinator Jack Woody Trim size 10 x 7 1/2 inches Pages 184 Quantity printed 5,000 Typeface Gill Sans Author Thomas Walther Publisher Twin Palms Publishers

**101 Contents book** Design firm Michael Ian Kaye, New York Creative directors Kate and Andy Spade Art director Michael Ian Kaye Photographer Dan Bibb Stylist Jerry Schwartz Producer Julia Leach Assistant producer Jennifer Ruske Production coordinator Barbara Greenberg Assistant designer

Dean Nicastro Trim size 9 3/4 x 9 3/4 Pages 124 Quantity printed 10,000 Typeface New Baskerville Printer/binder Meridian Printing Paper 100 lb. Glen Eagle text, 100 lb. Plainfield Opaque Smooth text Method of binding Smythe-sewn Binding materials Black Brillianta over Primer Gold Durotone (spine), mounted to .98 board, flush trim with raw edge, foil stamped spine in gold, hand stamp red ink sequence number in red ink Publisher Kate Spade

**102** *Without Sanctuary: Lynching Photography in America* **book** Design firm Twin Palms Publishers, Santa Fe Art director Jack Woody Designers Jack Woody, Arlyn Nathan Trim size 10 x 7 1/2 inches Pages 212 Quantity printed 4,000 copies Typeface Centaur Author James Allen Publisher Twin Palms Publishers

**103** *The Boomer* **book** Design firm Alfred A. Knopf, Inc., New York Art director Chip Kidd Production coordinator Roméo Enriquez Trim size 5 1/8 x 6 5/8 inches Pages 364 Quantity printed 30,000 Compositor North Market Street Graphics Typeface Mrs. Eaves Printer R. R. Donelley Crawfordsville Method of binding Burst hardcover flatback Binding materials Preprinted cover Endpapers printed one color on 80 lb. uncoated Jacket printer Coral Graphics Author Marty Asher Publisher Alfred A. Knopf, Inc.

**104** *The Accidental Indies* **book** Design firm David Drummond Design, Athelstan, Quebec, Canada Designer David Drummond Trim size 5 1/2 x 8 3/4 inches Pages 102 Typeface Baskerville Author Robert Finley Publisher McGill-Queen's University Press

**105** *The Rumi Card Book* **book** Design firm doubleu-gee, Petaluma, California Creative director/designer Michele Wetherbee Illustrator Stefan Gutermuth Production coordinator P.J. Tierney Trim size 4 7/8 x 8 1/2 inches Pages 112 Print quantity 15,000 Compositor Stefan Gutermuth Typefaces Bradlo Slab, Futura, Sabon, Trajan Printer/binder Palace Press International Paper 120 gsm uncoated stock Binding method Case-bound, smythe-sewn, square back Binding materials 128 gsm gloss artpaper over 2.5 mm boards Endpapers 115 gsm uncoated artpaper, 1/1 Author Eryk Hanut Publisher Journey Editions

**106** *Genuine Value: The John Deere Journey* **book** Design firm McMillan Associates, West Dundee, Illinois Art director Michael McMillan Designer/compositor Megan Kearney Production coordinators Anne McMillan, Janice Sewell, Jeanne Thomson Trim size 11 x 11 inches Pages 286 Quantity printed 75,000 Typefaces Adobe Garamond, Helvetica Neue Printer White Renewal Binder Lincoln and Allen Bindery Method of binding Case-bound Binding materials Black Cialux cloth

Endpapers Strathmore Renewal Chic Author John Gerstner Publisher John Deere

**107** *Lou Reed: Pass Thru Fire* **book** Design firm Sagmeister, Inc., New York Creative director Stefan Sagmeister Designers Hjalti Karlsson, Jan Wilker, Stefan Sagmeister Photographer Lou Reed Production coordinator Lisa Stokes Trim size 6 x 8 1/2 inches Pages 468 Quantity printed 10,000 Typeface Caslon Author Lou Reed Editor Leigh Haber Publisher Hyperion Press

**108** *On the Ceiling* **book** Design firm University of Nebraska Press, Lincoln, Nebraska Art director/designer Richard Eckersley Illustrator Richard Eckersley Production coordinator Alison Rold Trim size 5 1/2 x 8 1/2 inches Pages 152 Quantity printed 1,400 Compositor Richard Eckersley Typefaces Adobe Minion, Bodoni Printer/binder Data Reproductions Corporation Paper 50 lb. white offset Method of binding Notch-bound Binding materials Paperback Jacket printer Printing Services, University of Nebraska Author Eric Chevillard Publisher University of Nebraska Press

**109** *Animal Triste* **book** Design firm University of Nebraska Press, Lincoln, Nebraska Art director/designer Richard Eckersley Illustrator Sandra Brandeis Crawford Production coordinator Alison Rold Trim size 5 1/2 x 9 inches Pages 144 Quantity printed 2,400 Compositor Tseng Information Systems Typeface Adobe Minion Printer/binder Data Reproductions Corporation Method of binding Notch-bound Binding materials Paperback Jacket printer Printing Services, University of Nebraska Author Monika Maron Publisher University of Nebraska Press

**110** *Nabokov's Butterflies* **book** Design firm Beacon Press, Boston Creative director Sara Eisenman Designer Lucinda Hitchcock Photographer Anonymous, courtesy the estate of Vladimir Nabokov Production coordinator Dan Ochsner Trim size 7 x 9 inches Pages 800 Quantity printed 13,000 Compositor Wildstead + Taylor Type-face Adobe Sabon Printer/binder R. R. Donnelley Paper 60 lb. Finch Fine Vanilla Method of binding Notch three-piece case-bound Binding materials Pearl linen and rainbow antique black Endpapers Rainbow antique felt Jacket printer Coral Graphics Author Vladimir Nabokov

**111** *El Capitán* **book** Art director Sara Schneider Designer Meryl Pollen Photographers Ed Cooper, Tom Frost, Greg Epperson, Corey Rich, Eric Perlman Production coordinator Steve Kim Trim size 7 1/2 x 9 3/4 Pages 144 Quantity printed 10,000 Compositor Meryl Pollen Typefaces Franklin Gothic, Bembo Printer/binder Dai Nippon Printing Paper 157 gsm matte-coated paper Method of binding Smythe-sewn, case-bound, square back Author Daniel Duane Publisher Chronicle Books

112 **After the Fall: Srebrenica Survivors in St. Louis book** Design firm Design Kitchen, Chicago Designer Sam Landers Photographer Tom Maday Production coordinator Katie Heit Trim size 7 3/4 x 9 3/4 Pages 156 Quantity 5,000 Typefaces Minion, Lucida Sans, Trebuchet Printer CS Graphics Paper Leykam Magnomatt Method of binding Sewn Binding materials Cloth Endpapers Nordland Woodfree Author Patrick McCarthy Publisher Missouri Historical Society Press

113 **Tigersprung book** Design firm MIT Press Design Department, Cambridge, Massachusetts Designer Ori Kometani Production coordinator Terry Lamoureux Trim size 7 x 9 inches Pages 560 Quantity printed 3,000 Typeface Frutiger Printer/binder Cuebecor Kingsport Paper 70 lb. Utopia Book Method of binding Notch bound Binding materials Odyssey black Jacket printer Phoenix Color Author Ulrich Lehmann Publisher MIT Press

114 **Packaging White Book book** Design firm Morillas & Associates, Barcelona Creative director Lluis Morillas Art director Francesc Ribot Designer Ingrid Toran Photographer Joan Angeles Trim size 6 3/10 x 9 5/11 inches Pages 300 Quantity printed 4,000 Typefaces Futura, Franklin Gothic Bembo Editor Hispack Publisher Fira de Barcelona

115 **Design Writing book** Design firm University of Michigan School of Art + Design, Ann Arbour, Michigan Art director/designer/compositor Dennis Miller Trim size 6 3/8 x 9 3/8 inches Pages 168 Quantity printed 5,000 Typeface Mrs. Eaves Paper 80 lb. Champion Carnival cover, 80 lb. Champion Carnival text Binder University of Michigan Printing Services Method of binding Perfect-bound Editor Jack Williamson

## 50 covers

116 **Fackel Wörterbuch: Redensarten book** Creative director/designer Anne Burdick Typographic consultant Jens Gelhaar Pages 1,056 Quantity printed 2,000 Typefaces Cree Serif, Akzidenz Grotesk, Century Oldstyle Editor Dr. Werner Welzig Publisher Austrian Academy of Sciences

117 **Hatch Show Print: The History of the Great American Poster Shop cover** Design firm Hatch Show Print, Nashville Art director Jim Sherraden Designers The staff at Hatch Typeface Sans Serif Gothic Printer Jim Sherraden Paper French Speckletone Authors Jim Sherraden, Elek Horvath, Paul Kingsbury Publisher Chronicle Press

118 **The Poetry of Our World cover** Design firm HarperCollins, New York Art director Joseph Montebello Designer John

119 Fullbrook III Trim size 5 5/16 x 8 Pages 544 Quantity printed 4,000 Typeface Trade Gothic Printer Phoenix Color Editor Jeffery Paine Publisher HarperCollins

**Je Me Souviens du Lait cover** Design firm Nolin Branding & Design, Montreal Art director/designer René Clément Production coordinator Marie Noël-de-Tilly Trim size 6 1/2 x 9 1/2 inches Pages 224 pages Quantity printed 3,000 Printer Quebecor World Graphique Couleur Paper 100 lb. Mead Prima cover dull, 28 lb. Gilclear white jacket paper Method of binding Perfect-bound

120 **Learning to Look cover** Design firm David Drummond Design, Athelstan, Quebec, Canada Designer David Drummond Trim size 6 x 9 inches Pages 293 Typefaces Bembo, Futura Author Lesley D. Clement Publisher McGill-Queen's University Press

121 **Fresh Cream cover** Design firm Phaidon Press, New York Art director Julia Hasting Production coordinator Veronica Price Trim size 11 7/10 x 5 9/10 inches Pages 656 Typeface Akzidenz Grotesk Method of binding Hardcover Editor Gilda Williams Publisher Phaidon Press Inc.

122 **Demonology cover** Design firm Office of Paul Sahre, New York Creative director/designer Paul Sahre Photographer Michael Northrup Trim size 6 x 8 1/2 inches Typeface Garamond 3 Author Rick Moody Publisher Little Brown & Co.

123 **Oh cover** Design firm Apogee Press, Berkeley Designer Philip Krayna, Philip Krayna Design Photographer Eustachy Kossowski Trim size 6 x 7 inches Pages 72 Quantity printed 1,000 Typeface The Sans Printer Thompson-Shore Paper 70 lb. Glassfelter book, recycled Method of binding Perfect-bound Author Cole Swensen Publisher Apogee Press

124 **Genealogies, Miscegenations, Missed Generations cover** Designer Jeff Bellantoni Trim size 5 x 9 inches Pages 24, including center fold-out Quantity printed 1,500 Typeface Trade Gothic family Printer/binder Hull Printing Method of binding Perfect-bound Editor Erin Valentino Publisher The William Benton Museum of Art, University of Connecticut

125 **Yes: Yoko Ono cover** Publishers Harry N. Abrams, Inc., and Japan Society, New York Art director Michael J. Walsh Designer/compositor Miko McGinty Photographer Iain Macmillan, courtesy LENONO Photo Archive, New York Production coordinator Hope Koturo Trim size 9 3/4 x 11 3/4 inches Pages 352 Quantity printed 13,000 Typefaces Frutiger, Franklin Gothic Jacket printer Mondadori, Italy Authors/editors Alexandra Munroe, Jon Hendricks

126 **Public Health Law: Power, Duty, Restraint cover** Designer/photographer Lee Friedman Production coordinator Sam Rosenthal Typeface Requiem Printer Friesens Trim size 6 x 9 Author Lawrence O. Gostin Publisher University of California Press

127 **Leonardo da Vinci cover** Art director Michael Walsh Designers Judith Michael, Ergonarte Production coordinator Keri Mordue Smith Trim size 11 x 13 inches Pages 384 Quantity printed 10,000 Compositor Tina Thompson Typeface Simoncini Garamond Jacket printer Motta Author Pietro Marani Publishers Harry N. Abrams, Inc., and Federico Motta Editore S.p.A

128 **Econometrics cover** Design firm Helfand/Drenttel Inc., Falls Village, Connecticut Art director/jacket designer Jessica Helfand Production coordinator Betsey Litz Trim size 7 x 10 inches Pages 712 Quantity printed 16,500 Compositor Type Weight Typefaces Marten Grotesque, Bembo Printer/binder Maple Vail Method of binding Sewn Binding materials Pre-printed case Jacket printer Lehigh Press Editor Fumio Hayashi Publisher Princeton University Press

129 **Hillbilly Hollywood cover** Design firm Werner Design Werks, Inc., Minneapolis Art director Sharon Werner Designers Sharon Werner, Sarah Nelson Photographers Kyle Ericksen et al. Production coordinator Signe Bergstrom Trim size 10 1/2 x 11 1/4 inches Pages 122 Typefaces Wendy, Trade Gothic, Rockwell, Hillbilly Hollywood, Fournier Author Debby Bull Publisher Rizzoli International Publications, Inc.

130 **Farrar, Straus and Giroux catalog cover** Design firm Farrar, Straus and Giroux, New York Art director Susan Mitchell Designer Lynn Buckley Typeface Sackers Gothic Printer Rasco Graphics Publisher Farrar, Straus and Giroux

131 **10 x 10 cover** Design firm Phaidon Press, New York Art director/designer Julia Hasting Production coordinator Paul Hammond Trim size 11 7/10 x 11 7/10 inches Pages 468 Typeface Din Mittelschrift Method of binding Hardcover Editor Vivian Constantinopoulos Publisher Phaidon Press Inc.

132 **The Power Book cover** Design firm Pantheon Books, New York Art director Carol Carson Photographer Archie Ferguson Production coordinator Claire Bradley Ong Trim size 5 3/16 x 7 3/4 Pages 289 Jacket printer Coral Graphics Author Jeanette Winterson Publisher Alfred A. Knopf

133 **Mall cover** Design firm Spot Design, New York Art directors Drew Hodges, Jackie Seow Designer Kevin Brainard Photographer Andres Serrano Trim size 6 1/4 x 9 1/8 inches

Quantity printed 12,000 Typeface Interstate Printer Coral Graphics Author Eric Bogosian Publisher Simon and Schuster

134 **Sidetracks: Explorations of a Romantic Biographer cover** Design firm Pantheon Books, New York Art director/designer Archie Ferguson Project coordinator Kathy Grasso Trim size 6 3/16 x 9 7/16 inches Pages 420 Typeface Bodoni Bold Condensed Jacket printer Coral Graphics Author Richard Holmes Publisher Pantheon Books

135 **What She Saw cover** Design firm Random House, Inc., New York Art director Robbin Schiff Designer Kapo Ng Trim size 5 5/8 x 8 1/2 inches Typefaces Garamond 3, Rotis San Serif Author Lucinda Rosenfeld Publisher Random House, Inc.

136 **Waterloo Sunset cover** Creative director/designer David Zachary Cohen Photographer Marc Yankus Production coordinator John Marius Trim size 5 1/2 x 8 1/4 Typefaces Rotis Semi-Serif, Trade Gothic Author Ray Davies Publisher Hyperion

137 **The Book of Revelation cover** Design firm Pantheon Books, New York Art director Carol Carson Designer Archie Ferguson Photographer Radek Grosman Production coordinator Claire Bradley Ong Trim size 5 3/4 x 8 9/16 inches Pages 260 Typeface OCR Paper 80 lb. Mohawk White Irish Linen Jacket printer Coral Graphics Author Rupert Thomson Publisher Alfred A. Knopf

138 **A Thousand Moons on a Thousand Rivers cover** Design firm Columbia University Press, New York Creative director/designer/compositor Linda Secondari Production coordinator Jennifer Jerome Trim size 6 x 8 inches Pages 320 Quantity printed 3,500 Typefaces Bembo, Gill Sans Regular Printer Sheridan Books Method of binding Notch-bound, hard back Binding materials One-piece multicolor black antique Jacket printer Coral Graphics Author Hsiao Li-Hung Publisher Columbia University Press

139 **Panicking Ralph cover** Design firm Doubleday, New York Art director Ellen Chung Designer Rodrigo Corral Photographer Stephen H. Sheffield Trim size 5 1/2 x 8 1/4 Pages 282 Quantity printed 15,000 Author Bill James Publisher W.W. Norton

140 **The Verificationist cover** Design firm Vintage Books, New York Art director/designer John Gall Trim size 5 3/16 x 8 inches Quantity printed 15,000–20,000 Typeface Helvetica Neue Printer Coral Graphics Author Donald Antrim Publisher Vintage Books

141 **Faster cover** Art director John Gall Designer Jamie Keenan Trim size 5 3/16 x 8 inches Quantity printed 50,000 Typeface

126/154

Trade Gothic Bold Condensed Printer Coral Graphics Author James Gleick Publisher Vintage Books

**142** *The Bridegroom cover* Design firm Pantheon Books, New York Art director Archie Ferguson Photographer Jane Yeoman's Production coordinator Kathy Grasso Trim size 5 9/16 x 8 7/16 Pages 225 Typefaces Confidential, Baskerville Jacket printer Martinsberg Author Ha Jin Publisher Pantheon Books

**143** *The Weather of Words cover* Design firm Alfred A. Knopf, Inc., New York Art director Carol Devine Carson Designers Abby Weintraub; collage by Sharon Horvath Trim size 5 x 7 1/2 inches Typefaces Alternate Gothic, Democratica Printer Coral Graphics Paper 80 lb. Cougar Coated one side Author Mark Strand Publisher Alfred A. Knopf, Inc.

**144** *Inside Out cover* Design firm Pylon Design Inc., Toronto Art director/designer Kevin Hoch Production coordinator Doubleday Canada Author Evelyn Lau Publisher Doubleday Canada

**145** *False Papers cover* Design firm Anne Fink Design, New York Art director Susan Mitchell Designer Anne Fink Trim size 6 1/4 x 9 7/16 inches Typeface Univers Author André Aciman Publisher Farrar Straus and Giroux

**146** *Observatory Mansions cover* Design firm Pylon Design Inc., Toronto Art director/designer Scott Christie Illustrator Gary Clement Production coordinator Random House Author Edward Carey Publisher Random House of Canada

**147** *Wings cover* Design firm Scholastic, Inc., New York Art director/designer David Saylor Illustrator Christopher Myers Production coordinator Alison Forner Trim size 7 1/2 x 11 inches Pages 32 Quantity printed 15,000 Compositor David Saylor Typefaces Devinne, Bauer Bodoni Printer/binder Tien Wah Paper 150 gsm Nymclla matte (text) Method of binding Smythe-sewn Binding materials 2.4 mm Smythe board, added reinforcing concealed cambric Endpapers 150 gsm Wood-free, 2–3 and 6–7 marbled PMS 292U, 4–5 solid PMA 292U stock Author Christopher Myers Publisher Scholastic Press

**148** *The Brave Little Tailor cover* Design firm Harry N. Abrams, Inc., New York Director Howard Reeves Typographic designer Barbara Sturman Illustrators Olga Dugina, Andrej Dugin Product on coordinators Keri Smith, Diane Sahadeo Trim size 11 x 13 3/11 inches Pages 32 Quantity printed 15,000 Compositor Barbara Sturman Typefaces Poetica, Galliard Printer/binder Proost Binding materials Paper over board with reinforced binding Author Retold by Olga Dugina and Andrej Dugin Publisher Harry N. Abrams, Inc.

## Information graphics

**149** *I REFLECT poster* Design firm The Cultural Construction Co., Boston; Rick Rawlings/Work, Boston Art directors/designers Thomas Starr, Rick Rawlins Writer Thomas Starr Typeface Trade Gothic Trim size 72 x 48 inches Printer/fabricator AFM Inc. Paper Heatsheets, metalized mylar Software QuarkX-Press Publisher Industrial Designers Society of America Client (ELEVEN)

**150** *AmphetaZINE zine* Design firm Modern Dog, Seattle Art director Michael Strassburger Designers Michael Strassburger, Rosynne Raye Print production Michael Strassburger Illustrators Michael Strassburger, various Writers James Fisher, Michael Hanrahan, Susan Kingston, D.L. Scott Z Trim size 7 x 8 1/2 inches Printer The Copy Company Paper 20 lb. bond plus cover Software Adobe Photoshop, Adobe Illustrator, QuarkXPress Client Stonewall Recovery Services

**151** *SamataMason website* Design firm SamataMason, Dundee, Illinois Art directors Dave Mason, Kevin Krueger Designers Kevin Krueger, Steve Kull Print production Kevin Krueger Photographers Kevin Krueger, Rob Schroeder Writer Dave Mason Typeface Arial Digital video producer Mike Holmes/Performance Networks Client Samata-Mason

**152** *United Airlines EasyInfo Gate Display information display system* Design firm Pentagram Design, San Francisco Art directors Duane Bray, Brian Jacobs Designers Matt Rogers Typeface Helvetica Neue Programmer Allen Interactions Interface designer Duane Bray Photographer Un ted Airlines Creative Services Software Macromedia Flash Client United Airlines

**153** *Prada store kiosk* Design firm R/GA, New York Producer Anje Ludewig Associate creative director Vincent Lacava Art director Vander Ray McClain Senior designer Lesli Karavil Junior designers Jesse McGowan, Dieter Weichman Production artist Kohsuke Yamada Account director Matt Howell Account manager Andrew Rodbell Senior interaction designer Ted Metcalfe Programmer John Jones Production coordinator Sheila Dos Santos Senior test engineer Diane Lichtman

**154** *Understanding USA online book* Design firm R/GA, New York Producer David Frankfurt Art director Vincent Lacava Interaction designer Ted Metcalfe Senior designer Winston Thomas Designers Helen Kim, Jean Knapp, Jeff Vock Programmer Raymond Vasquez Managers/quality assurance Daniel Harvey, Yamelin Castillo Testers Diane Lichtman, Ben Oderwald Executive producer Reven T.C. Wurman Principal Ricard Saul Wurman

**155** **IBM ThinkPad TransNote: Getting Started Guide guidebook** Design firm IBM, Durham Art directors/creative directors Amy Dupavillon, Rebecca Welles Designers Amy Dupavillon, Mary Johnson, Susan Jasinski Print production Amy Dupavillon, Ron Smith, Masaru Masuda Illustrators Luis Elizalde, Amy Dupavillon Writers Michelle Marple Thomas, Kristine Olka Typefaces Helvetica, Paul Ultra Trim size 8 1/2 x 11 1/2 inches Printer HarperPrints Paper 60 lb. Warren Lustro Dull Cover, 40 lb. Cougar Opaque Smooth Text Software Corel Draw Client IBM PCD Mobile Solutions

**156** **"Under the Weather" map** Design firm mgmt, Brooklyn Designer Alicia Yin Cheng Project manager Angela Riechers Writer Charis Conn Typefaces Scala Sans, Goudy, Opticaslon 3 Printer Quad Graphics Trim size 8 x 10 1/2 inches Client Harper's magazine

## Environmental graphics

**157** **Amtrak's Acela specialty station signage** Design firm Calori & Vanden-Eynden, New York Creative director David Vanden-Eynden Project manager Jordan Marcus Designers David Vanden-Eynden, Chris Calori, Jordan Marcus, Denise Funaro Photographer Elliott Kaufman Typefaces Frutiger, Frutiger Bold Fabricator Andco Industries Software Adobe Illustrator Client Amtrak/National Railroad Passenger Corporation

**158** **National Basketball Association New York office interior** Design firm Gensler, New York Project director Patric O'Malley Creative director John Bricker Design director Peter Wang Designers Dicie Carlson, Susan Merrell, Daniel Park Project managers Julie Applebaum, Unjoo Noh Project architects/managers Kent Hikida, Lawrence Taormina Architectural designer Mary Sz Photographer NBA Photos Fabricator Modern Age, Signature Industries, Paulette Giguerre Software Illustrator, Photoshop Client National Basketball Association

**159** **IMAX Theatre interior** Design firm Gensler, New York Creative director John Bricker Design director Peter Wang Senior graphic designer Lisa Van Zandt Designers Jamie Brizzolara, Susan Merrell Project managers William Staempfli, Lisa Van Zandt Fabricator Gordon Signs Digital video producer IMAX Client IMAX

**160** **New 42nd Street Studios/The Duke Theater interior** Design firm Pentagram Design, New York Art director Paula Scher Graphic designers Paula Scher, Dok Chon, Rion Byrd, Bob Stern, Tina Chang Print production Tina Chang Environmental production Rion Byrd, Bob Stern Architects Platt Byard Dovell Photographer Peter Mauss/Esto Typefaces Bank Gothic, Agency, Renner Bold Architype, Bill Architype, Tschichold Architype Fabricator VGS (interior), Lettera Sign & Electric Co. (exterior), Dale Travis Associates (donor walls) Client Cora Cahan, New 42nd Street

**161** **"Made in California" exhibition** Design firm Los Angeles County Museum of Art Exhibition designers/information architects Durfee Regn Sandhaus (Tim Durfee, Iris Regn, Louise Sandhaus) Designer, graphics Scott Taylor Designer, lifestyle environments Bernard Kester Design assistance Agnes Anderson, Katherine Go, Jeff Haber, Petra Michel, Frederick Nilsson, Rebecca Rudolph, Tricia Sanedrin, Giorgos Sinas, Paul Wehby Design coordination Jim Drobka, Daniel Young, Rachel Ware Zooi Typefaces CA40 (designed for the exhibition), Tarzana, Minion Software Form Z, Adobe Illustrator, QuarkXPress, Adobe PhotoShop, Fontographer Fabricators LACMA in-house staff, AAA Flag and Banner, PPI Exhibit Design and Fabrication, Gary Murphy, Warner Center Signs, Olson Color Expansions, Skye Graphics Curators Stephanie Barron, Sheri Bernstein, Ilene Susan Fort Client LACMA

**162** **"Cold War Modern: The Domesticated Avant-Garde" exhibition** Design firm Pentagram Design, New York Art director J. Abbott Miller Designers J. Abbott Miller, Jeremy Hoffman Photographer Peter Mauss/Esto Curator Judith Hoos Fox Typeface Grotesque MT Fabricator In-house, Wilson Art (laminates) Sound consultant Joel Gordon, Art of the States Client Davis Museum & Cultural Center, Wellesley College

**163** **AIGA Snow Shovels donor recognition artifact** Design firm The Office of Eric Madsen, Minneapolis Art director/designer Eric Madsen Project manager/fabrication consultant Steve Beaudry Photographer Ripsaw, Inc. Fabricator Rainville Carlson/Panto-Gravers Client AIGA

## Experience design

**164** **Workspheres website and kiosk** Design firm Method, Inc., New York Creative director/lead designer Olivier Chêtelat Designers Alicia Cheng, Thomas Noller Interaction designers April Starr, Ted Booth Content strategist Chris Torrens Site engineering Jonathan Synder Producer Natalia Maric Account manager Monte Bartlett Typeface Verdana Software Adobe Illustrator, Adobe PhotoShop, Flash Client Museum of Modern Art

**165** **Driveway product demo** Design firm Factor Design, Inc., San Francisco Creative director Jeff Zwerner Designer Gabriel Campodonico Illustrators Gabriel Campodonico, Eva Ralle Writer Peter Chase Typeface Font Bureau Interstate Flash programmers FORCEQUIT Client Driveway

**166 Shutterfly website** Design firm Eleven Inc., San Francisco Creative director/art director Michael Borosky Designer Matt Magana Photographer Katharyn Ledner Copywriter Jay Rendon Technical directors Crystal Trexel, Karen Quek Account executives Michele Jacobs, Betsy Woudenberg Information architects Jordan Warren, John Skidgel Programmers Chris Brown, Joseph Oster, Sue Quek Client Shutterfly

**167 010101 Art in Technological Times website** Design firm Perimetre-Flux, San Francisco Project directors Anthony Amidei, Steve Barretto, Stephen Jaycox Project team James Ken Buter, Curtis Christophersen, Willow Cook, Vanessa Dina-Barlow, Judith Hardy, Sharon Holgado, Henry Liu, Alex Lord, Srilla Menarshani, Tim Mohn, Dina Tooley Writer SFMOMA Pixel parameter 1024 x 768 pixels Typeface Trade Gothic OCRA Software Adobe Illustrator, Flash Client San Francisco Museum of Modern Art

**168 Art as Experiment/Art as Experience website** Design firm Perimetre-Flux, San Francisco Project directors Anthony Amidei, Steve Barretto, Stephen Jaycox Project team Vanessa Dina-Barlow, Sharon Holgado, Alex Lord Writer SFMOMA Pixel parameter 1,024 x 768 pixels Typefaces Avenir, Sabon Software Adobe Illustrator, Flash Client San Francisco Museum of Modern Art

**169 Continental Harmony website** Design firm Popular Front, Minneapolis Creative director Laurence Bricker Design director Eric Kassel Project manager Marny Stebbins Writer Bill Snycer Programmer Nate Clark Producer Mike Keefe Interface design Eric Kassel, TJ Shaffer Flash programming David Holmdah, Rebecca Smith, Nate Clark Client Twin Cities Public Television (TPT), PBS.org TPT producer Erika Herrmarn TPT programming Chuck Olson TPT executive produce Catherine Allan

**170 Katherine Dunn, Illustrator website** Design firm Red Canoe, Deer Lodge, Tennessee Art director/creative director Deb Koch Designer Caroline Kavanagh Developers Deb Koch, Benjamin Kaubisch Flash animator Benjamin Kaubisch Sound editor Benjamin Kaubisch Illustrator Katherine Dunn Writers Katherine Dunn Deb Koch Sound Katherine Dunn Typefaces Platelet, Courier Software Adobe PhotoShop, Adobe Go Live, Adobe Illustrator, Macromedia Flash, Macromedia Sound Editor Client Katherine Dunn

**171 The 1009 Journal Project interactive art form** Design firm Brian Singer, San Francisco Project creator Brian Singer Contributing cover designers Brian Singer, Joshua Swanbeck, Anders Hornstr Jp, Jemma Gura, Chris Robbins, Tim Sauder, Vanessa Enriquez, Greg Durrell, Simon Powell, Judith Zissman ChristDpHer Pacetti, Rick Valicenti, Brian McMullen,

Jon Sauder, Geoff Ahmann, Amy Franceschini, Mike Cina, Shirin Kouladjie Programmer Nate Koechley/Vicksburg Collective

**172 Bthere.TV website** Design firm Tangram Design, Charlestown, Massachusetts Creative director Justin Crawford Art directors Brian Oakes, Chris Franzese Designers Paul Szypula, Jenny Woo Typefaces Akzidenz Grotesk, Kipp No.3, custom Animator Justin Crawford Programmers Drew Millechia, David Chang Technical director Damien Morton Producer Doug Hoffman Account supervisor David Cherry Software Macromedia Flash, Flash Generator Client/publisher Bthere.TV

**173 Gettysburg Expedition Guide interactive experience** Design firm TravelBrains, Lake Forest, California Creative director/writer Paul C. Davis Designer Catherine R. Davis Multimedia developer Victor J. Davis Historian Wayne E. Motts Producer Paul C. Davis Software Macromedia Director Sound design Scorpio Sound Voice actor Reg Green

**174 MoodLogic browser** Design firm Triplecode, Beverly Hills Designers Lindi Emoungu, Pascal Wever, David Young Client MoodLogic, Inc.

**175 ExxonMobil Masterpiece Theatre Online website** Design firm WGBH Interactive, Boston Art director John Tyler Howe Designer John Tyler Howe Producer Louise Weber Programmer Molly Frey Writer Caitlin O'Neil Editorial review Julie Wolf Research assistant Jessica Cavano Software Adobe Photoshop, Adobe Imageready, Adobe Illustrator, Macromedia Flash, BBEdit Client ExxonMobil Masterpiece Theatre

**Motion graphics**

**176 Centers for IBM e-business Innovation interactive environment** Design firm Imaginary Forces, Hollywood Creative director/designer Mikon van Gastel Art director/designer Matt Checkowski Animators Matt Checkowski, Peter Cho, Chun-Chien Lien Head of production Saffron Kenny Executive producers Peter Frankfurt, Chip Houghton Producer Holly Kempner Technologist Jamie Houghton Editors Carsten Becker, Jason Kool, Jason Webb Inferno artists Kirk Balden, Rob Trent Coordinator Seri Bryant Writer Jed Alger Music Musikvergnuegen Creative director/composer/mixer Walter Werzowa Additional composers John Luker, Justin Burnett Sound designer Larry Jones Executive producer Pat Weaver Engineers Damien Chock, Jason Ford Technical assistant Benjamin Wynn Design office credits: Principal architects George Yu, Jason King Project designers Sandra Levesque, Davis Marques,

**181** **MTV's "SoCal Summer" TV ad** Design firm MTV Networks, New York Creative director Jeffrey Keyton Design director Romy Mann Director/art director/senior producer Jennifer Roddie Designer Assaf Cohen SGI Animation Emily Wilson Director of photography Mike Piscitelli Editor Todd Antonio Somodovilla Sound designer Malcolm Francis/Popular Beat Combo Software Avid, After Effects, Soft Image

**182** **MTV's "Spring Break Chicks" TV ad** Design firm MTV Networks, New York Creative director Jeffrey Keyton Design director Romy Mann Director/designer/producer Keira Alexandra SGI animation Emily Wilson Director of photography Peter Agliata Editor Holle Singer/Consulate Composer Shay Lynch

**183** **MTV's "Fashionably Loud" identity** Design firm Brand New School, Santa Monica Designers/illustrators Sean Dougherty, Jens Gehlhaar, Jonathan Notaro Editors/animators Brumbly Boylston, Sean Dougherty, Jens Gehlhaar, Jonathan Notaro Copywriter/type designer Jens Gehlhaar Photographers Jonathan Notaro, Pat Notaro Producer Angela de Oliveira Typefaces Akzidenz Grotesk, BNS Chevron Software Adobe Macromedia Sound design Machinehead Client MTV Networks

**184** **TV Land Network redesign** Design firms TV Land, New York; Trollbäck and Company, New York Sr. VP/creative director Kim Rosenblum Creative director Kenna Kay Executive producer Gwen Powell Producer Catherine Mulcahy Art director Marie Hyon Creative director (Trollbäck) Jakob Trollbäck Art director/designer (Trollbäck) Nathalie De la Gorce Producer (Trollbäck) Meghan O'Brien

**185** **Novell "Line of Information" TV ad** Design firm Motion Theory, Venice, California Creative director/designer Mathew Cullen Typeface Akzidenz Grotesk Animators Mathew Cullen, Kaan Atilla Producer Javier Jimenez Sound Designer Pete Kneser/Wimbo Writer Carm Goode Software Adobe After Effects, Adobe Illustrator

**186** **Corning "Future" TV ad** Design firm Imaginary Forces, Hollywood Creative director Peter Frankfurt Director/art director Adam Bluming Designers Adam Bluming, Philip Shtoll, Joel Lava Executive producer Saffron Kenny Producer Candy Renick Editors Philip Shtoll, Jeff Consiglio Inferno artists Kirk Balden, Clyde Beamer 2-D animator Josh Graham Coordinator Brian Kludas Advertising agency Doremus Agency producer Kate Ayrton Agency creative director Danny Gregory Agency art director Guy Marino Music Tomandandy

**Soundblast**

**187** **Medeski Martin & Wood: The Dropper CD packaging** Design firm Chippy, New York Art director/designer Heung

---

Kai RiedesserDesign Team Jonathan Garnett, Samson Chua, Toshi Nagura, Kevin Wronski, Kaho Chan, Basil Mahjoub, Hisako Ichiki, Tom Raymont, Jamie Norden, Israel Kanderian, Ben Hidalgo, Arlene Lee

**177** **Comedy Central Network redesign** Design firm Imaginary Forces, Hollywood Creative director Peter Frankfurt Art director Adam Bluming Designers Philip Shtoll, Chris Lopez, Jason Doherty, Joel Lava, Adam Bluming, Calvin Lo Executive producer Saffron Kenny Producer Candy Renick Editors Philip Shtoll, Danielle White Inferno artists Kirk Balden, Clyde Beamer, Don Pascoe, Sam Edwards, Carie Chadwick 2-D animators Joel Lava, Jason Doherty, Philip Shtoll, Chris Lopez, Jennifer Lee, Calvin Lo Coordinator Brian Kludas Sr. VP, marketing (Comedy Central) Cathy Tankosic Sr. VP, on-air promotion and off-air creative (Comedy Central) Peter Risafi Music Musikvergnuegen Composer Bernie Locker Software/hardware Adobe After Effects, Flame

**178** **Target "Sign of the Times" Spring TV ad** Design firm PMH Art directors Minda Gralnek (Target), Dave Peterson (PMH) Director Anouk Besson Associate creative director/copywriter Amie Valentine (PMH) Producer Gary Tassone (PMH) Sound design Hest & Kramer Editor Brett Astor/Fischer Edit Effects Mark Youngren/Fischer Edit Client Target

**179** **Lifetime Network redesign** Design firm Imaginary Forces, Hollywood Creative director Peter Frankfurt Directors Michelle Dougherty, Eric Smith, Michael Riley, Kurt Mattila Codirectors Eric Smith, Sara Marandi, Lynne Gelman, Dana Yee Art director Michelle Dougherty Co-art director Eric Smith Designers Elaine Alderette, Sara Marandi, Dana Yee, Lynne Gelman, Eric Smith, Michelle Dougherty, Peter Cho, Peggy Oei, David Clayton Branding strategist Anita Olan Head of production Saffron Kenny Producer Maureen Timpa Hendricks Live-action producers Caroline Pham, Brad English, Denise Pouchet Director of photography Giles Dunning 2-D animators Lynne Gelman, Elaine Alderette, Jennifer Lee, Marcus Garcia Editors Tony Fulgham, Mark Hoffman, Jason Kool, Philip Shtoll, Carsten Becker, Rich Marchewka Inferno artists Clyde Beamer, Rob Trent, Rod Basham, Don Pascoe, Kirk Balden Writers Anita Olan, Kelly Sopp, Nick Frankfurt, Maureen Timpa Hendricks Editorial assistant Justine Gerenstein Coordinators Rosalie Concepcion, Eva Prelle, Seri Bryant, Keith Bryant Music Musikvergnuegen Composer Walter Werzowa

**180** **Lost Souls movie titles** Design firm YU+co., Los Angeles Creative director/designer Garson Yu Designer/animator Steve Kusuma Producer Jennifer Fong

**188** Heung Chin n Illustrator Heung Heung Chin Photographer Dan ny Clinch Typefaces Koten, Army, Chuzpah, Besonio, rubber-stamps Trim size 5 19/32 x 4 15/16 inches Fabricator Shore-wood Packaging Client Medeski Martin & Wood/Blue Note Records (Capitol Records Jazz & Classics)

**(B)efore/(a)fter CD packaging** Design firm Couch Visuals/ Couch Records, Vienna, Austria Art director/designer Mariana Erausewetter Photographer Mariana Brausewette-Printer/fabricator SNA Compact Disk GmbH Paper Standart Software Adobe PhotoShop, QuarkXPress Client Couch Records

**189** **Spoiled & Zigo: More and More album cover** Design firm Eikes Grafischer Hort, Frankfurt, Germany Art directors/ designers Eike Koenig, Ralf Hiemisch Illustrators Eike Koenig, Ralf Hiemisch Typefaces Block, Machine Trim size 12 3/8 x 12 7/16 inches Software Softimage, Adobe PhotoShop, Adobe Freehand, QuarkXPress Client Polydor Zeitgeist/ Universal

**190** **Well Done CD packaging** Design firm Capitol Records, Hollywood Art directors Wendy Dougan, Tommy Steele Designer Wendy Dougan Print production Jennifer Peters Illustrator Tavis Coburn Typefaces Brothers, Council, Textile Trim size 4 3/4 x 9 1/2 inches (open), 4 3/4 inch square cover Color separator Color Service Printer/fabricator AGI Paper WestVaco 16-point board

**191** **Jim White: No Such Place CD packaging** Design firm Doyle Partners, New York Creative directors Paul Sahre, Jim White Designers Paul Sahre, Cara Brower Illustrations Jim White, © Center for UFO Studies Photo-graphy André Thijssen Typefaces Futura, Clarendon Clien-Luaka Bo3

**192** **Elliot Smith: Figure 8 CD packaging** Design firm Dreamwcrks Records, Beverly Hills Art directors/illustrators Autumn ce Wilde, Dale Smith Photographer Autumn de Wilde

**193** **DJ Mixed.com: Keoki and Micro CD packaging** Design firm Moonshine Music, West Hollywood Art director/designer Jeff Aguila Photographers Raymond Lee, Paul Banks, Teri Jo Typeface Helvetica Trim size 4 8/11 x 9 1/2 Printer Color Image Printing Software QuarkXPress, Adobe PhotoShop, Adobe Illustrator

**194** **Mario Piu: The Vision album cover** Design firm Eikes Grafischer Hort, Frankfurt, Germany Art director/designer Eike Koenig Illustrator Eike Koenig Typefaces Clarendon, Avant Garde Condensed Trim size 12 3/8 x 12 7/16 inches Software Adobe Freehand, QuarkXPress Client Polydor Zeitgeist/Universal

**195** **W.O.P.A.: Walking on Pennsylvania Avenue CD packaging** Design firm Tim Kenney Design Partners, Bethesda, Maryland Designer John Bowen Project manager Julie Rasmussen

**196** **Jewel: Spirit CD packaging** Design firm Wink33, New York Art director/designer Brenda Rotheiser Calligrapher Jeanne Greco Photographer Matthew Rolston Typeface Minion Trim size 4 3/4 x 4 11/16 inches Printer/Fabricator Ivy Hill Client Atlantic Records

**197** **The Eels: Daisies of the Galaxy CD packaging** Design firm Dreamworks Records, Beverly Hills Art director Francesca Restrepo (Design Palace), E

**198** **Resistance D: You Were There album cover** Design firm Eikes Grafischer Hort, Frankfurt, Germany Art directors Eike Koenig, Ralf Hiemisch Designer/illustrator Eike Koenig Photographers Gaby Gerster, Eike Koenig Writer Eike Koenig Typefaces Lineto, Alpha Headline Trim size 12 3/8 x 12 7/16 inches Software Softimage, Adobe PhotoShop, Adobe Freehand, QuarkXPress Client Polydor Zeitgeist/Universal

**199** **Degeneration: Una Musica Senza Ritmo album cover** Design firm Eikes Grafischer Hort, Frankfurt, Germany Art director/designer Eike Koenig Illustrator Eike Koenig Typeface Block Trim size 12 3/8 x 12 7/16 inches Software Adobe PhotoShop, Adobe Freehand, QuarkXPress Client Polydor Zeitgeist/Universal

**200** **Deftones: White Pony album and album cover** Design firm Maverick Recording Company, Beverly Hills Creative director Kim Biggs Art director/designer Frank Maddocks Photographer James Minchin III Typefaces Avante Garde, Helvetica Printer Ivy Hill Fabricator Specialty Paper 80 lb. Ivy Hill offset Software Adobe PhotoShop, Adobe Illustrator, QuarkXPress

**201** **Phish: Hampton Comes Alive CD box set packaging** Design firm Jager Di Paola Kemp Design, Burlington, Vermont Creative director Michael Jager Art director Jared Eberhardt Designer Todd Wender Photographer C. Taylor Crothers Client Dionysian Productions Design

**202** **Olive: Trickle CD packaging** Design firm Maverick Re-cording Company, Beverly Hills Art directors/designers Kim Biggs, David Harlan Photographers Zoren Gold, David Harlan Barcode farming Popglory Typefaces City, Helvetica Printer Ivy Hill Fabricator Specialty Paper 80 lb. Ivy Hill gloss Soft ware Adobe PhotoShop, Adobe Illustrator, QuarkXPress, Infini-D, Vector Effects Logo David Harlan

**203** **Live: Run to the Water CD packaging** Design firm Sagmeister Inc., New York Art director Stefan Sagmeister

**211 Bang on a Can mailer/CD packaging** Design firm Greenberg Kingsley, New York Art director/creative director/designer D. Mark Kingsley Typeface PIXymbols, Mrs. Eaves Printer Outer shell and individual composers' inserts, final fulfillment (Hudson Printing); CD and wallet (A to Z Music Services) Trim size 5 1/2 x 8 1/8 inches Software QuarkXPress, Adobe Illustrator, Adobe PhotoShop Client/publisher Bang on a Can/Red Poppy Music

**212 Trust: Music from the Highway Community CD packaging** Design firm Becky Brown, Sunnyvale, California Designer Becky Brown Producer Kevin Marks Client The Highway Community, John Riemenschnitter

**213 Big Umbrella: Lab Rat CD packaging** Design firm Torpedohead Studio, Covina, California Art director/illustrator Keith Ewing Typefaces Chicago, handlettering Fabricator Old West Client Racer Records

**214 Unloco: Unloco CD packaging** Design firm Maverick Recording Company, Beverly Hills Art directors/designers Kim Biggs, David Harlan Photographer Alison Dyer Typefaces Davida, Helvetica Printer Ivy Hill Fabricator Specialty Paper 80 lb. Ivy Hill offset Software Adobe PhotoShop, Adobe Illustrator, QuarkXPress Photo illustrations David Harlan Logo Glen Nakasako and Unloco

**215 Tantric: Tantric CD packaging** Design firm Maverick Recording Company, Beverly Hills Art directors/designers Kim Biggs, David Harlan Photographers Slow Hearth Studios/Photonica, Dennis Keeley Typefaces Garamond, Helvetica Printer Ivy Hill Fabricator Specialty Paper 80 lb. Ivy Hill offset Software Adobe PhotoShop, Adobe Illustrator, QuarkXPress Logo Kim Biggs, David Harlan, Glen Nakasako

**216 New Found Glory CD packaging** Design firm MCA Records, Santa Monica Creative director Tim Stedman Designers Tim Stedman, T.J. River Photographer Justin Stephens Typefaces Vitrina, Orator, old-school Dyno label maker Printer AGI Media Trim size 28 x 4 3/4 inches Client/publisher New Found Glory/MCA Records

**217 Blink 182: The Mark, Tom And Travis Show CD packaging** Design firm MCA Records, Santa Monica Creative director Tim Stedman Designers Tim Stedman, T.J. River Illustrator Glen Hanson Photographer Justin Stephens Typeface Universe 57 Condensed Printer AGI Media Client/publisher Blink 182/MCA Records

**218 Ohm: The Early Gurus of Electronic Music: 1948–1980 CD box set packaging** Design firm Stoltze Design, Boston

Wilker Writer Jan Wilker Typeface Hattler Trim size Regular CD size Fabricator Hjalti Karlsson Client Polydor/Universal

Designer/Illustrator Motoko Hada Photographer Danny Clinch Trim size 4 7/8 x 4 7/8 inches Software Adobe Photoshop, Adobe Illustrator, QuarkXPress Client Radioactive Records

**204 Yevgeny Yevtuschenko: City of No, City of Yes CD packaging** Design firm Greenberg Kingsley, New York Art director/creative director/designer D. Mark Kingsley Typeface Univers, Univers Cyrillic, custom Printer A to Z Music Services Trim size 4 13/16 inches square Software QuarkXPress, Adobe Illustrator, Adobe PhotoShop Client/publisher The Van Winkle Clef

**205 Void Where Prohibited: Pete's Free Gig CD packaging** Design firm IA Collaborative, Chicago Creative director/designer Dan Kraemer Illustrator Dan Kraemer Writer Kevin Giglinto Typeface Eunuverse Trim size Various Printer Unique Printers and Lithographers Software QuarkXPress, Adobe Illustrator, Adobe PhotoShop Client Void Where Prohibited

**206 Mouse on Mars: Niun Niggung CD packaging** Design firm Icon Kommunicationsdesign, Cologne, Germany Art director/designer Eva Rusch Print production/illustrator Eva Rusch Typeface Akzidenz Grotesk Software Cinema 4D, QuarkXPress Publisher Warner/Chappell, Thrill Jockey Client Mouse on Mars

**207 Mouse on Mars: Idiology CD packaging** Design firm Icon Kommunicationsdesign, Cologne, Germany Art director/designer Friederike Luczak Print production Volker Schwettmann Writer Jan Werner Printer/fabricator Verwohlt Paper Lenza Top Recycliing Publisher Zomba Records Client Mouse on Mars

**208 Bassic Instinct II, Bassic Instinct III, Coming Home CD packaging** Design firm Stereo Deluxe, Nürnberg, Germany Art director/designer Elisabeth Rudner Illustrator/photographer Elisabeth Rudner Typefaces Neue Helvetica, Info Text Trim size 12.1 x 12 cm (Bassic Instinct II), 13.9 x 12.5 cm (Bassic Instinct III), 42.9 x 12.5 cm (Coming Home) Printer Topac Fabricator Optimal Production Software Adobe PhotoShop, Adobe Freehand, QuarkXPress Publisher/client Stereo Deluxe Rec. GmbH

**209 Kay Cee: Escape album cover** Design firm Eikes Grafischer Hort, Frankfurt, Germany Art director/designer Eike Koenig Illustrator/photographer Eike Koenig Typeface Eurostile Trim size Trim size 12 3/8 x 12 7/16 inches Software Adobe PhotoShop, Adobe Freehand, QuarkXPress Client Orbit Records/Virgin Music

**210 Hattler: No Eats Yes CD packaging** Design firm Karlssonwilker Inc., New York Art director/designer Jan Wilker Print production Hjalti Karlsson Illustrator/photographer Jan

**219** Art director/creative director Clif Stoltze Designers Clif Stoltze, Tammy Dotson Photographer Various Typefaces Helvetica, Trade Gothic Condensed Printer Triplex, NYC Trim size 5 x 5 1/2 inches Software QuarkXPress, Adobe Illustrator, Adobe PhotoShop Client/publisher Ellipsis Arts

**The Smashing Pumpkins: Machina/The Machines of God CD packaging** Design firm Sylvester, West Hollywood Art directors Gregory Sylvester, Thomas Wolfe, Billy Corgan, Yelena Yemchuk Designers Gregory Sylvester, Thomas Wolfe Illustrator Vasily Kafanov Typefaces Historical Allsorts, Volgare Trim size 4 3/4 x 4 3/4 inches Printer EMI Music Group Press

**220 PALOALTO CD packaging** Design firm Sony Music, Santa Monica, CA Art director/designer Aimée Macauley Typeface Futura

**221 Jason Moran: Facing Left CD packaging** Design firm Capitol Records Jazz & Classics, New York Creative director Gordon H. Jee Art director Paul Brown Project manager Mantis Evar Photographer Michael Wong Writer Yüri Moran

**222 Big Sir CD packaging** Design firm Sunja Park Design, Los Angeles Art director/designer Sunja Park Typeface Gill Sans Printer/fabricator Digitek Paper Carolina Cover, Gilbert Superase Typewriter Paper Software Adobe PhotoShop, QuarkXPress Client MooTron Records

**223 Ben Sidran: The Concert for García Lorca CD packaging** Design firm Planet Propaganda, Madison, Wisconsin Creative director Kevin Wade Designer Dan Ibarra Print production Ann Sweeney Illustrator Federico García Lorca Photographer The Community of Heirs of Federico García Lorca, Ben Sidran Writers Federico García Lorca, Ben Sidran Typeface Mrs. Eaves Trim size 5 1/2 x 5 1/2 inches Software Adobe PhotoShop, QuarkXPress Client GoJazz Records.

**224 Oasis Smooth Jazz Awards Collection CD packaging** Design firm Infinite Z, Los Angeles Art director Joel Venti Designer Jawsh Smyth Photographer Don Siedhoff/ Rock Island Studios Typeface Template Gothic Paper Curious Paper Collection, Canson Satin Producer Joe Sherbaree

**225 K.D. Lang: Invincible Summer CD packaging** Design firm Smog, Los Angeles Art directors/designers Jeri and John Heiden Photographer Just Loomis Typeface Bauhaus Printer Ivy Hill Graphics Client Warner Bros. Records, Inc.

**226 K.D. Lang: Invincible sampler CD packaging** Design firm Smog, Los Angeles Art directors/designers Jeri and John Heiden Photographer Just Loomis Typeface Bauhaus Printer Ivy Hill Graphics Client Warner Bros. Records, Inc.

**227 Miles Davis and John Coltrane: Complete Columbia Recordings 1955–61 CD box set packaging** Design firm Sony Music, New York Art directors Frank Harkins, Arnold Levine Project manager Michael Levine Printer Shorewood

**228 Louis Armstrong: The Complete Hot Five and Hot Seven Recordings CD box set packaging** Design firm Sony Music, New York Art director Ian Cuttler Designers Ian Cuttler, Christian Calabro Paper 100 lb. SD Warren Sappi Lustro Dull Cream Text

**229 I Love Metal Compilation CD packaging** Design firm Stereotype, New York Art director/designer Mike Joyce Illustrator Mike Joyce Photographer Fred Feldman Typeface Hand Drawn Printer/fabricator EMI Printing Paper Potlatch Northwest Dull Coated Producer Fred Feldman Software QuarkXPress, Adobe Photoshop Publisher/client Triple Crown Records

**230 Samson: Turpitude CD packaging** Design firm Stereotype, New York Art director Mike Joyce Designers Mike Joyce, Andrew Taray Typeface Akzidenz Grotesk modified Printer/ fabricator Imprint Paper Finch Fine uncoated white Software QuarkXPress, Adobe Photoshop, Xerox copier Publisher Pompello Music Client Pompello Records

Margo Chase is the founder of Chase Design Group, a Los Angeles–based design firm specializing in strategic brand design and image development for all media. Since its inception nearly 20 years ago, the studio has gained international recognition for its landmark work in corporate identity and brand extension for such innovative companies as Columbia Pictures, EStyle and Sony Music. The studio has been selected as one of *I.D.* magazine's "I.D. Forty" and its work has appeared in many design periodicals and books including *Communication Arts, How, Graphis, Radical Graphics/Graphic Radicals* and *New Design: Los Angeles* and includes award-winning movie identity campaigns for Francis Ford Coppola's *Dracula, Candyman* and *Four Weddings and a Funeral,* and logos for television shows such as the WB's "Buffy the Vampire Slayer", "Felicity," "Angel" and "Charmed."

Andrea Codrington was editorial director of AIGA from December 1999 to November 2001, and is a critic specializing in contemporary design and visual culture. Before coming to AIGA, she was a columnist for *The New York Times* and contributed to such publications as *I.D.* magazine, the *Washington Post* and *Harper's Bazaar.* She is author of a forthcoming monograph about the motion-graphics designer and director Kyle Cooper (Laurence King, 2002) and is currently developing a television series about design and architecture for public broadcast with the award-winning television journalist John Hockenberry and Washington Square Films.

Darcy Cosper writes about design and visual culture, and some other things. She has been an editor at *Interiors* magazine, a copywriter for *iDeutsch* and is currently a columnist for *Artforum's* literary supplement *Bookforum.* Cosper lives in Brooklyn with her pug Bruno.

Melissa Milgrom is an independent journalist who writes about popular culture, subcultures, and people with eccentric areas of expertise. Her work has appeared in *The New York Times, The Wall Street Journal, Metropolis, Travel & Leisure,* and many other publications. Milgrom has a master's degree in American studies from University of Pennsylvania, and a bachelor's degree in philosophy from Miami University in Ohio. She lives in Brooklyn.

Margo
Chase

Andrea
Codrington

Darcy
Cosper

Melissa
Milgrom

428

Gabriela
Mirensky

Andrea
Moed

Nathan
Shedroff

studio
blue

Alice
Twemlow

**Gabriela Mirensky is** director of competitions and exhibitions at AIGA, where she has worked since 1996. Mirensky coordinates AIGA's graphic design competitions, traveling shows, exhibitions and events at the National Design Center. She earned a master's degree in fine arts from the City College of New York and brings 10 years of arts-related production and administrative experience to the organization.

**Andrea Moed is a writer,** editor and content developer who specializes in working out new editorial formats and strategies for emerging media. She began her career at Edwin Schlossberg Inc., where she developed interactive exhibits for clients such as NASA, Sony, Ben & Jerry's and the Chicago Symphony Orchestra. From 2000 to 2001, Moed served as the first web editor of AIGA, and is now completing her master's thesis at New York University's Interactive Telecommunications Program. She is a contributing editor at *eDesign* magazine.

**Nathan Shedroff has been** an information and interface designer for more than 12 years, focusing on developing online experiences, building online brand strategies and business models, and developing online communities. Shedroff cofounded vivid studios, a decade-old pioneering company in interactive media. Prior to that, he worked with Richard Saul Wurman as a senior designer at the Understanding Business. He earned a BS in Industrial Design with an emphasis on Automobile Design from Art Center College of Design. Shedroff was nominated for a Chrysler Innovation in Design Award in 1994 and 1999 and, while a student, received an Honorable Mention in the 1987 Unisys Industrial Design Competition. Shedroff's latest book, *Experience Design 1*, explores common characteristics in all media that make experiences successful.

**Studio blue** – with partners Kathy Fredrickson and Cheryl Towler Weese, and studio members Tammy Baird, Garrett Niksch, Denise Rynkar, Matt Simpson, and Gail Wiener – is a Chicago-based design firm that creates publications, identities, collateral systems, web sites, and environmental graphics. The firm works with professional and financial service organizations, and educational and cultural institutions, focussing on projects that involve close collaboration, rewarding client relationships, and the opportunity to develop and shape content. Studio blue has received the Carl Hertzog Award for Excellence in Book Design, and their work has been recognized by the American Center for Design, AIGA, the Society of Publication Designers, and the Stiftung Buchkunst among others.

**Alice Twemlow is the** director of programming at AIGA. She is program director for Voice: AIGA 2001 National Design Conference. Alice earned a master's degree in design history from a joint program of the Royal College of Art and the Victoria & Albert Museum in London. She has worked previously as a freelance curator, lecturer and has written about design for *AIGA Journal, Eye, Graphics International, I.D.* magazine, *Metropolis, Print* and *Typographic*.

# AQUENT

Aquent is the Official AIGA Career Development Sponsor, providing an array of support services and professional training opportunities for AIGA members nationwide. Through this multiyear partnership, Aquent sponsors numerous AIGA national conferences, exhibitions and events, and offers customized packages of financial services – including insurance, retirement and cash-flow management bene-fits – for AIGA members. We live and work in extraordi-nary times. The old rules of how companies work, how work gets done and who does the work are out the window. Talented people by the millions have gone out on their own. In fact, one in four American workers today is a freelancer.

Aquent is a new and very different kind of company for this new world of work. It is a worldwide talent agency for designers, assisting them in locating freelance and permanent job opportunities. Aquent's 37 domestic local offices are committed to working with AIGA's 43 local chapters to support activities that educate and inform designers about professional advancement and career-planning issues. This partnership, like all that AIGA pursues, is geared toward expanding and enhan-cing member benefits as well as increasing the value of the profession to the public. To that end, Aquent, as underwriter of the Salary Survey, helps AIGA expand the scope of the survey and make it more readily available not only to AIGA members, but also to companies that hire design professionals across the country. www.aquent.com

Recognizing that students are the future of the industry, MeadWestvaco has long offered both students and educators inspirational tools and programs like Lingo and the MeadWestvaco Annual Report Student Competition. MeadWestvaco's partnership with AIGA as the Official Education Sponsor is a natural extension of its position in this community, and will enhance the programs that are already in place, as well as provide new services, support, inspiration and guidance for over 4,000 AIGA student members, educators and all AIGA members who are committed to the future of graphic design.

MeadWestvaco's commitment as the Official Education Sponsor supports AIGA's enhanced student activities at both the national design conference in Washington, D.C., and the business & design conference, which will take place in 2002. The company's support will also help maintain and grow AIGA online outreach to students, and increase activities with design educators and schools across the country.

MeadWestvaco provides high-quality products and services that help customers communicate efficiently and effectively. MeadWestvaco manufactures coated printing papers in a wide variety of grades, finishes and weights suitable for virtually every printing need.
www.meadwestvaco.com

**MeadWestvaco**

Potlatch Corporation, the leading manufacturer of premium papers, understands your unique paper needs and puts the right tools in your hands to help you succeed. Potlatch's broad line of high-performance printing papers – including Potlatch McCoy™, new McCoy Uncoated, Vintage®, Northwest®, Mountie®, and Potlatch Scout™ – are available in a choice of versatile finishes and shades.
For Potlatch, paper is just the beginning of the partnership.
www.potlatchpaper.com

**Potlatch**

**G / P**

studio blue
Pamela Aviles

Production coordinators:

Cover separations:
Andrea Codrington

Professional Graphics,
Rockford, Illinois

studio blue, Chicago

Design services:
Alice Twemlow
Nathan Shedroff and
Mirensky, Andrea Moed,
Milgrom, Gabriela
Darcy Cosper, Melissa
Andrea Codrington,
Margo Chase,

Printing:
Professional Graphics,
Rockford, Illinois

GZD, Germany

Typefaces:
HTF Champion Gothic,
Rhode, and Univers